Palgrave Studies in the History of Finance

Series Editors: **Martin Allen, D'Maris Coffman, Tony K. Moore,** and **Sophus Reinert**

The study of the history of financial institutions, markets, instruments and concepts is vital if we are to understand the role played by finance today. At the same time, the methodologies developed by finance academics can provide a new perspective for historical studies. Palgrave Studies in the History of Finance is a multi-disciplinary effort to emphasize the role played by finance in the past, and what lessons historical experiences have for us. It presents original research, in both authored monographs and edited collections, from historians, finance academics and economists, as well as financial practitioners.

Titles include:

Wadan Narsey
BRITISH IMPERIALISM AND THE MAKING OF COLONIAL CURRENCY SYSTEMS

Adrian Leonard
MARINE INSURANCE: Origins and Institutuions, 1300–1850

Alisdair Dobie
ACCOUNTING AT DURHAM CATHEDRAL PRIORY

Roman Zaoral
MONEY AND FINANCE IN CENTRAL EUROPE DURING THE LATER MIDDLE AGES

Ali Coskun Tunçer
SOVEREIGN DEBT AND INTERNATIONAL FINANCIAL CONTROL: The Middle East and the Balkans, 1868–1914

Kiyoshi Hirowatari
BRITAIN AND EUROPEAN MONETARY COOPERATION, 1964–1979

Adrian Williamson
CONSERVATIVE ECONOMIC POLICYMAKING AND THE BIRTH OF THATCHERISM, 1964–1979

Rafael Torres Sanchez
CONSTRUCTING A FISCAL MILITARY STATE IN EIGHTEENTH CENTURY SPAIN

Stuart J. Barton
POLICY SIGNALS AND MARKET RESPONSES

Ali Kabiri
THE GREAT CRASH OF 1929

Martin Allen, D'Maris Coffman
MONEY, PRICES AND WAGES

Guy Rowlands
DANGEROUS AND DISHONEST MEN: The International Bankers of Louis XIV's France

Duncan Needham
UK MONETARY POLICY FROM DEVALUATION TO THATCHER, 1967–1982

D'Maris Coffman
EXCISE TAXATION AND THE ORIGINS OF PUBLIC DEBT

BREVE TRATTATO DELLE CAVSE,

CHE POSSONO FAR ABBONDARE

Li Regni d'oro, & argento.

DOVE NON SONO MINIERE

Con applicatione al Regno di Napoli.

DEL DOTTOR ANTONIO SERRA.

della Città di Coſenza.

DIVISO IN TRE PARTI.

IN NAPOLI,

Appreſſo Lazzaro Scorriggio. M.DC.XIII.

CON LICENZA DE' SVPERIORI.

The cover of the original edition of Serra's Breve Trattato, reproduced with permission of the Reinert Family Collection.

Antonio Serra and the Economics of Good Government

Edited by

Rosario Patalano
Professor of the History of Economic Thought,
University of Naples "Federico II", Italy

and

Sophus A. Reinert
Assistant Professor of Business Administration,
Harvard Business School, USA

palgrave
macmillan

First published 2016 by
PALGRAVE MACMILLAN

Palgrave Macmillan in the UK is an imprint of Macmillan Publishers Limited, registered in England, company number 785998, of Houndmills, Basingstoke, Hampshire RG21 6XS.

Palgrave Macmillan in the US is a division of St Martin's Press LLC, 175 Fifth Avenue, New York, NY 10010.

Palgrave Macmillan is the global academic imprint of the above companies and has companies and representatives throughout the world.

Palgrave® and Macmillan® are registered trademarks in the United States, the United Kingdom, Europe and other countries.

ISBN: 978–1–137–53995–3

This book is printed on paper suitable for recycling and made from fully managed and sustained forest sources. Logging, pulping and manufacturing processes are expected to conform to the environmental regulations of the country of origin.

A catalogue record for this book is available from the British Library.

Library of Congress Cataloging-in-Publication Data

Names: Patalano, Rosario, editor. | Reinert, Sophus A., editor.

Title: Antonio Serra and the economics of good government / edited by Rosario Patalano, Professor of the History of Economic Thought, University of Naples, Federico II, Italy and Sophus Reinert, Assistant Professor of Business Administration, Harvard Business School, USA.

Description: New York : Palgrave Macmillan, 2016. | Series: Palgrave studies in the history of finance | Includes index.

Identifiers: LCCN 2015040557 | ISBN 9781137539953 (hardback)

Subjects: LCSH: Serra, Antonio, active 1613 – Political and social views. | Economics – Italy – History. | Finance – History. | BISAC: BUSINESS & ECONOMICS / Economic History. | BUSINESS & ECONOMICS / Finance. | HISTORY / Europe / Italy.

Classification: LCC HB109.A2 .A58 2016 | DDC 330.945—dc23

LC record available at http://lccn.loc.gov/2015040557

Contents

Acknowledgements

The project to celebrate the 400th anniversary of the publication of Serra's Breve trattato had many supporters, and we are pleased to express our gratitude here. An initial meeting in Oslo, Norway was funded and organized by Erik S. Reinert and The Other Canon Foundation, and a conference organized by Rosario Patalano in Naples, Italy was made possible by the Istituto Italiano per gli Studi filosofici, the Istituto Banco di Napoli-Fondazione, where we are particuarly grateful to Honorary President Adriano Giannola, and by Carlo Panico, Dean of Economists in the Department of Jurisprudence at the Università di Napoli Federico II. For fruitful contributions to these meetings, we would also like to thank Pasquale Commendatore, Xavier Duran, Robert Fredona, Bruno Jossa, Rainer Kattel, Patrick O'Brien, Annalisa Rosselli, Francesca Viano, Paolo Savona, Jomo Kwame Sundaram, and Eugenio Zagari. We are furthermore indebted to Graham Sells, who translated chapters 2, 4, 7, 10, 12, 13, and 14, and edited several others, and to Robert Fredona, who translated chapter 5. And, finally, at Palgrave we would also like to thank Aimee Dibbens, Alexandra Morton, the editors of the series "Palgrave Studies in the History of Finance", and, for excellent editorial assistance, Anja Goethals, Rena Hanlon, Fernanda Reinert, and particularly Vidhya Jayaprakash.

List of Contributors

Luca Addante is Assistant Professor of History at the University of Turin, Italy.

Lilia Costabile is Professor of Political Economy at the University of Naples "Federico II", Italy.

Francesca De Rosa is Assistant Professor of the History of Medieval and Modern Law at the University of Naples "Federico II", Italy.

Francesco Di Battista is Emeritus Professor of the History of Economic Thought at the University of Bari, Italy.

Jan Kregel is Director of Research at the Levy Economics Institute of Bard College, Unites States and Professor of Finance and Development at the Ragnar Nurkse School of Innovation and Governance at the Tallinn University of Technology, Estonia.

Gabriel Paquette is Professor of History and the Director of the Program in Latin American Studies at The Johns Hopkins University, USA.

Rosario Patalano is Professor of the History of Economic Thought at the University of Naples "Federico II", Italy.

Cosimo Perrotta is Professor of the History of Economic Thought at the University of Lecce, Italy.

Erik S. Reinert is the President of the Other Canon Foundation, Norway and Professor of Technology Governance and Development Strategies at the Ragnar Nurkse School of Innovation and Governance at the Tallinn University of Technology, Estonia.

Sophus A. Reinert is Assistant Professor of Business Administration in the Business, Government, and the International Economy Unit at Harvard Business School, USA.

Alessandro Roncaglia is Professor of Economics at the University of Rome "La Sapienza", Italy.

Gaetano Sabatini is Professor of Economic History in the Department of Philosophy, Communication, and Visual Arts at the Roma Tre University of Rome, Italy.

Koen Stapelbroek is Associate Professor in the Department of Public Administration at Erasmus University Rotterdam, Netherlands and an Academy of Finland Senior Research Fellow at the University of Helsinki, Finland.

André Tiran is Professor of Economics at the University of Lyon 2, France.

Antonio Trampus is Professor of Modern History at the Ca' Foscari University of Venice, Italy.

Giovanni Zanalda is Associate Research Professor at Duke University, USA in the Social Science Research Institute and in the Departments of Economics and of History. He is the Director of the Duke University Center for International Studies and International Area Studies.

Introduction: Antonio Serra and the Economics of Good Government

Rosario Patalano and Sophus A. Reinert

In the great Harvard economist Joseph A. Schumpeter's posthumously published masterwork *History of Economic Analysis*, he "credited" the Southern Italian lawyer and economic writer Antonio Serra (f. 1613) with being "the first to compose a scientific treatise ... on Economic Principles and Policy".[1] What follows is the first ever anthology of essays dedicated to Serra, who, though long having been eulogized in the historiography of economics as a thinker of precocious sophistication, has seldom received sustained attention from scholars, especially outside of Italy. In fact, no monograph-length study has ever been dedicated to him in any language, and he remains a dark horse in the historiography of political economy – often quoted, but seldom understood or appreciated in his historical context. Partly, this might be because of the many mysteries surrounding the man and his work.

Little is known of Serra, except that he wrote his extraordinary 1613 *Breve trattato delle cause che possono far abbondare li regni d'oro e d'argento dove non sono miniere*, or *Short Treatise on the Causes that Make Kingdoms Abound in Gold and Silver Even in the Absence of Mines*, in the Neapolitan jail of the Vicaria, and that he died there soon afterwards.[2] We have few details beyond these, but the *Breve trattato* reveals that he was a doctor (probably in law) and that he intended to write a book on the *Forza dell'ignoranza*, or *The Power of Ignorance*. The text of the book itself makes it clear that he furthermore both had a humanist education and was well versed in legal arguments and, strikingly, the languages and methods of contemporary trade and international finance.[3] A contemporary Neapolitan chronicler furthermore mentions a meeting between Serra, "incarcerated in the Vicaria for a long time", and the Duke of Osuna, Viceroy of Naples from 1616 to 1620, which occurred on Wednesday 6 September 1617, when the former wished to present a plan for reforms "of great use to the court" but, ultimately, was thrown back in his cell.[4] Two royal dispatches discovered in the late-19th century by the Neapolitan historian and politician Luigi Amabile during his work on the mystic friar Tommaso Campanella, dated 11 November 1612 and 27 May 1614, describe the arrest of one "doctor Antonio Serra" on a charge of counterfeiting, but nothing proves that this was the same Serra.[5] Around the mid-20th century, the economic historian Luigi De Rosa in turn discovered a notarial contract, dating from 1591 and plausibly relating to the author of the *Breve trattato*, that mentions one "doctor Serra" as the owner of a sizeable estate.[6] Finally, in recent work in the Neapolitan State Archives, Rosario Patalano has discovered two further Viceregal dispatches that mention the name of Antonio Serra. The first, dated 18 June 1613, is particularly interesting because it reveals a connection between Serra and Miguel Vaaz, Count of Mola, a converted Jewish Portuguese merchant very close to the Count of Lemos, Viceroy of Naples in the period from 1610 to 1616. The dispatch says "Antonio Serra…see the Viceroy; bring him this afternoon when the Count of Mola arrives". The second one, dated 28 June 1613, mentions a Serra facing legal charges for debt.[7]

Plausibly, then, and though we may never be certain, Serra was a well-educated doctor of law, formerly of some means and with practical experience in trade and finance, perhaps in connection to Portuguese merchant circles, who might have been jailed either for counterfeiting or for the lesser crime of indebtedness. Whatever his life story and the reasons for his incarceration, however, the *Breve trattato* was, much like the plan for reforms that he presented the viceroy, an attempt at ingratiating himself with the authorities to be let out of jail.[8] Yet, the wider context of his work's publication, and indeed the focus of his writings, was a deep financial crisis in the Kingdom of Naples and an ensuing debate over its nature, causes, and possible remedy.

The *Breve trattato* itself is so rare that only a handful of copies are extant, and for a long time it was believed that only a single volume had survived the ravages of time, passing, in the words of the great philosopher Benedetto Croce, like a "lamp of life" through the hands of Italy's greatest economists, from the Neapolitan Ferdinando Galiani in the 18th century to the Piedmontese Luigi Einaudi in the 20th.[9] The "legendary rarity" of the *Breve trattato*, not to mention its unique content, in effect made it something of a Holy Grail among bibliophiles over the course of the four centuries since its first publication.[10] A veritable mythology has come to surround Serra – about whom popular accounts have been penned, poems have been recited, and imaginary portraits have been painted – the intensity of which can only be compared to the likes of Adam Smith, Karl Marx, and Thorstein Veblen in the history of economics.[11]

With recent translations of Serra's *Breve trattato* into Portuguese and English, Serra's text has finally been made available to a wider scholarly and lay audience, and the time is therefore right to present a definitive volume on the state of scholarship regarding Serra's context, life, work, and foundational role in the history of economics.[12] After all, his *Breve trattato* truly represents a watershed not only in the discipline of economics and in the longer history of financial crises and debates but in the history of social science and intellectual history more generally, explicitly and self-consciously formalizing a distinct sphere of economic knowledge in early modern Europe. The ancients, he argued in a humanist vein, were unsurpassable in all areas that had interested them, and there was little value in adding to the vast corpus of classical commentary. Yet, the dynamics of the modern world and the rise to prominence of economic forces had unveiled new areas of political life that the authorities of antiquity had not addressed. Hence, Serra did not want to discuss politics or the "art of government in general", because whether one preferred monarchies or republics, one could not deal with such issues better than "Plato and Aristotle" had, nor would he struggle with jurisprudence and how to "distinguish just from unjust", because in that one could not supersede the Emperor Justinian's corpus of Roman Law. What Serra *did* want to turn the attention of the reader towards was a third, hitherto neglected, aspect of statecraft – an aspect, however, which was of painful relevance for contemporary Naples:

> My aim is to discover the causes that can make a kingdom abound in money even if it possesses no gold or silver mines, a subject on which not a single word has been written by any of the ancient or modern writers on the ideal disposition of the political state.[13]

Where later "codifications" of economic knowledge as a "science" in early modern Europe, especially in England, tended to emerge from an explicit refutation of more erudite currents of contemporary humanism and a concomitant embrace of technical expertise and merchant custom, Serra approached the nascent discipline very differently. Though clearly well versed in the minutiae of contemporary banking and the practice of international trade – to the extent that he formulated one of the very earliest analyses of a balance of payments – he resolutely quoted his Petrarch and preceded with "scholarly rigour" to uncover the true sources of the comparative, significantly competitive, wealth and poverty of nations in the real economy.[14]

Serra's key insight, studying the economies of Venice and Naples, was that wealth was not the result of climate or providence but of policy. While Venice, built on rotting poles in a malarial swamp, through sound policy had risen to the very pinnacle of the world economy, Naples, gifted by nature in every way, languished in poverty, destitution, and dependence. Through a very systematic taxonomy of economic life, Serra then went on from this insight to theorize about the causes of the wealth of nations and the measures through which a weak, dependent economy could achieve worldly melioration. Most importantly, Serra realized, was that where a polity was located in the architecture of the international economy, and which economic activities it pursued, was of genuinely existential importance. Where Venice imported raw materials from all over the world to produce and export some of the most technologically sophisticated finished goods in Europe, Naples did the opposite, exporting its raw materials in exchange for foreign manufactures. Structures of international trade, which Serra theorized, in a revolutionary manner in light of the difference between increasing and diminishing returns to scale, could have deeply debilitating consequences for a nation's economic, cultural, and social life that could only be reversed through policy.

The following essays situate Serra and his work in their historical contexts – economic, cultural, and intellectual – and explore the enduring appeal of his *Breve trattato* across a number of fields. Not only does the present volume uncover new, hitherto unknown and unpublished materials relating to Serra's life and succinctly present the state of the art of Serra scholarship, whether exploring the finer details of his theory regarding international financial interactions or his indebtedness to Renaissance legal traditions, but it further highlights its continuing relevance for facing some of the cardinal problems of the present. We again find ourselves at a turning point not only for the international economy but also for its ostensible "science". Past certainties are dissolving in light of the ongoing crisis and the return – both good and bad – of state capitalism to international political economy. In the wake of the Asian Tigers and China's spectacular reappearance on the world stage, scholars and laymen alike are being forced to rethink some of the fundamentals of economics as it has developed since World War II. And historians have an important role to play in this process, grounding theoretical debates and providing venerable yet crucial perspectives on current events.

The importance of studying Serra and rediscovering the origins of economic knowledge is testified to by the fact that the very issues with which his contemporaries were concerned are currently at the forefront of our political and scholarly consciousness, from the role of policy in economic development to the challenges and possibilities of international competition, the balance between finance and the real economy, and the vexing nature of economic dependence and interdependence. Though history may not supply immediate answers to our most pertinent questions, a deeper, more nuanced, and less triumphalist understanding of the history of economics – in short a more historical understanding of political economy – can certainly inform our thoughts and policies. And in few cases is this resonance deeper than with Serra and his *Breve trattato*.

The first chapter, by Gabriel Paquette, sets the stage for appreciating Serra's context through an analysis of "The Spanish Empire and their Viceroyalties: Structures, Policies, and Historiography". It situates Serra's Neapolitan milieu in the global context of the Spanish Empire, its contemporary policies for political and economic reform in Viceroyalties such as Naples, and how the ongoing re-appreciation of Serra must be understood in light of recent historiographical developments in the study of the reforms, political economy, and intellectual and cultural history of the Spanish Empire.

This is followed by Francesca De Rosa's short essay "The Vicaria Prison of Naples in the time of Antonio Serra", which contextualizes the origins of the *Breve trattato* through an exploration of the little-known conditions of incarceration in early 17th-century Naples. This facilitates De Rosa's historiographical discussion of the various theories that have been proposed for Serra's incarceration and helps set the stage to better analyse the physical and legal world that Serra inhabited at the time of his writing and how someone jailed at the time was able to write a work like the *Breve trattato* to begin with.

Building on this background, Giovanni Zanalda's chapter on "The Cost of Empires: Antonio Serra and the Debate on the Causes and Solutions of Economic Crises in the Kingdom of Naples in the Early 17th Century" connects the structural problems that Serra's Naples faced to the intellectual life of the time and adumbrates the larger echoes of both in the history of economic development. Tripartite in nature, it opens by exploring a number of macroeconomic factors to shed light on the crisis facing Neapolitans of Serra's generation, including demographic changes, the balance of payments, and institutional structures. It then charts Serra's reaction to these problems in terms of his emphasis on the "real" rather than "financial" economy, before concluding with an analysis of the extent to which Serra can be seen to have foreshadowed subsequent views about wealth and the role of institutions which emerged in later debates about the political economy of the Dutch and English commercial empires, not to mention in recent and contemporary discussions regarding economic growth and development.

The fourth chapter, by Rosario Patalano, entitled "Serra's *Breve trattato* in a World-System Perspective: The Dutch Miracle and Italian Decline in the Early 17th Century", considers the dynamics of Serra's larger European economic context at the time. It employs a framework of world-systems analysis to revisit Serra's *Breve trattato*, and the contemporary debate in which he partook regarding economic reforms triggered by the so-called "twelve years' truce" between the great powers of the period, in light of contemporary developments in the European economy at large. Largely retrograde and agricultural, Southern Italy's integration into a larger European and increasingly global economic architecture offered new possibilities as well as challenges, and Serra's "industrial" model, which looked back to the experiences of the Italian city-states of earlier centuries, was from this perspective in the process of being overcome by the rise of territorial powers such as England and the Low Countries.

Following these different macroeconomic contexts for Serra's work, Gaetano Sabatini turns in Chapter 5 to the local milieu with which Serra might have engaged in "The Influences of Portuguese Economic Thought on the *Breve trattato*: Antonio Serra and Miguel Vaaz in Spanish Naples". Exploring the *Breve trattato*'s indebtedness to the Portuguese tradition of political economy known as *arbitrismo*, this chapter breaks new ground in Serra scholarship by charting the existence of newly converted Portuguese Jews in Naples known as *cristãos novos*, or "new Christians", who soon occupied positions of privilege and served as a conduit for Portuguese political and economic thought to the Spanish Viceroyalty of Naples. On the basis of suggestive evidence, not only from Lisbon and Naples but also from Serra's hometown of Cosenza – and corroborated also by Patalano's recent archival discoveries – it further suggests that Serra might have been close to this circle of Portuguese thinkers and politicians and that his mysterious imprisonment can be explained by virtue of his theoretical opposition to many of the main tenets of the Neapolitan *arbitristas*.

Setting aside the question of Serra's contexts, the sixth chapter, Sophus A. Reinert's "Authority and Expertise at the Origins of Macroeconomics", revisits the epistemological origins of thinking about macroeconomic phenomena in early modern Europe. Examining the longer history of "economic expertise", it focuses on key debates over the relationship between theory and practice and the appropriate sources of trust in arguments about economic matters in two "founding" moments of the discipline: the Naples of Serra and the Williamite Settlement in England. In both cases, the question of what sort of expertise could confer "authority" to economic ideas was brought to the forefront, and, though through very different channels in vastly different cultures of learning, both cases ultimately saw influential theories emerge from the codification and generalization of successful historical practices, both micro and macro.

Linking the debate surrounding the *Breve trattato* more explicitly to questions of political philosophy, Luca Addante's "Wealth and Freedom in the Republic: The Politics of Antonio Serra" turns to Serra's faith in the primacy of politics over the economy. Drawing on a current of political realism that emerged from Niccolò Machiavelli and a Southern Italian tradition of naturalism represented by Scipione Capece, Bernardino Telesio, and Tommaso Campanella, Addante unveils Serra's argument for the importance of republican institutions in explaining Venice's rise to economic greatness. Though forced to embrace a certain discursive opacity by the censorial context in which he wrote, the *Breve trattato* nonetheless made powerful claims regarding the stability of republics and their unique ability to direct elite behaviour towards the patriotic aim of the common good. The rise to prominence of economic forces in international affairs had profound political consequences for Serra, and he considered the Italian republican paradigm uniquely able to harness the commercial revolution.

A similar comparison informs Lilia Costabile's "External Imbalances and the Money Supply: Two Controversies in the English 'Realme' and in the Kingdom of Naples". Turning more strictly to the *Breve trattato*'s economic theories, she returns to Serra's debate with his contemporaries to shed new light on the theoretical origins of balance of payments analysis. Comparing and contrasting the debate between Serra, Marc'Antonio de Santis, and later the Neapolitan economic writer Giovanni Donato Turbolo to a contemporary debate in London between Gerard de Malynes and Edward Misselden, Costabile considers how they created sophisticated frameworks for analysing the relationship between financial markets, the real economy, and the international system. On the foundation of this deeper understanding of the origins of balance of payments analysis, she reassesses the school of economic thinking known as "mercantilism".

The ninth chapter, André Tiran's "Real and Monetary Factors in the de Santis–Serra Controversy", similarly argues for Serra's extraordinary role in the history of economic analysis by virtue of his pathbreaking attempt to formulate a comprehensive theory of economic development. Not only did the *Breve trattato* analyse the problems of a country's trade balance and balance of payments in a precocious manner, but in it Serra more generally theorized the relationship between economic development, the real economy, and physical space. Serra highlighted the fact that the balance of trade is a result of economic conditions in the country in relations to others and that monetary phenomena are consequences rather than causes of changes in the real economy. Economic growth thus resulted from a plurality of economic and non-economic factors in the real economy for Serra, who refused to allow money as such to have a decisive role in the story.

Cosimo Perrotta then turns to "Serra and Underdevelopment", considering the *Breve trattato* in the context of mercantilism and exploring its similarities to, and divergences from, iconic works published elsewhere in Europe. In this larger debate, Serra's position was unique in that he wrote in a context of political and economic dependence (to Spain as well as to Northern merchants). Naples was unable to adopt an effective development policy of its own, because it was a colony in terms of its international politics, dominated by foreign merchants and domestically oppressed by feudal landlords. So though Serra's analysis of the causes of economic development was extraordinary in a European context, the focus of his work was on backwardness and dependence. In examining the Kingdom of Naples, in short, Serra insightfully revealed the other face of the coin of comparative growth in an international system: underdevelopment, the mirror image of development.

Turning to Serra's rich reception, Koen Stapelbroek's "'To Console and Alleviate the Human Mind': Ferdinando Galiani's Attempted Republication of Serra in the 1750s" opens the long history of Serra's historical influence, beginning with Ferdinando Galiani's rediscovery – and attempted republication – of the *Breve trattato* in the 1750s and his public praise of it in 1780. Serra's work became an inspirational text for the first great generation of political economists in Enlightenment Italy, including not only Galiani, a thinker whom Friedrich Nietzsche considered among the greatest of his century, but also Antonio Genovesi, Italy's first professor of political economy. On the basis of unpublished manuscript evidence as well as in-depth analysis of Galiani's work, Stapelbroek shows how the *Breve trattato* served as a model for economic reforms in a Naples that, though formally a sovereign polity in the 18th century, continued to struggle with different yet similar problems of decline and dependence as it had during the time of Serra.

The twelfth chapter, Antonio Trampus's "Francesco Saverio Salfi and the Eulogy of Antonio Serra: Politics, Freemasonry, and the Consumption of Culture in Early Nineteenth-Century Italy" subsequently maps the real beginning of Serra's rise to Italian and international fame in the context of the Neapolitan Revolution of 1799 and the political programs of Masonic networks throughout the peninsula. In particular, he focuses on Francesco Saverio Salfi's 1802 *Elogio di Antonio Serra*, or *Eulogy of Antonio Serra*, and Serra's subsequent 1803 inclusion in Baron Pietro Custodi's 50-volume collection of Italian economics, the vehicle for the *Breve trattato*'s eventual fame in 19th-century Europe.

Salfi's importance for the historiography on Antonio Serra is also highlighted in Francesco Di Battista's essay on "Serra's Discovery and Ill Fate in the Liberal Nineteenth Century", which places the *Breve trattato* in a longer tradition of Italian "civil" political economy rendered famous by Antonio Genovesi, the peninsula's first professor of the subject. Considering the text's mixed fortunes in the 19th century, Di Battista focuses particularly on the debate that raged across Europe over the "primacy" in economics and Serra's eventual fall from grace as a mere "mercantilist" and later more "social" writer in light of the rising influence of economic liberalism.

Building on this, Alessandro Roncaglia's "The Heritage of Antonio Serra" adopts a bird's-eye view of Serra's *Breve trattato* and its legacy. Partly theoretical, partly historiographical, Roncaglia analyses the main themes of Serra's work and engages critically with many of the main currents of interpretation that dominated scholarship on the *Breve trattato* over the past four centuries, from libertarians to fascists, even including those that suggest that Serra was a nationalist, a chrysohedonist who confused specie with the wealth of a nation, and a proto-Meridionalist – that is, a champion of Southern Italian interests in opposition to an abusive North. Roncaglia, in short, highlights both some of Serra's main contributions to economics and their polyvalent reception in the history of the discipline.

Adopting an explicitly presentist stance, Jan Kregel then turns to "Serra's *Breve trattato* and the Theory of Economic Development". Considering the debate between Serra and his opponent de Santis in light of the longer history of financial crises, he asks what one still might learn from the treatise after four centuries, how the "political economy" of the *Breve trattato* differs from more recent traditions of economics, and what the consequences are, for large parts of the world, of his warnings not having been heeded. Focusing on Serra's early analysis of a balance of payments, Kregel particularly emphasizes the continuing dangers of precocious liberalizations of capital accounts for developing countries, one of several pressing contemporary problems on which Serra can still shed light.

The *Breve trattato*'s continuing relevance for economics and economic policy is also the topic of Erik S. Reinert's "Antonio Serra and the Problems of Today". His chapter focuses on two dichotomous aspects of Serra's theories: first, the relationship between the financial and the real economy; second, the role of increasing and diminishing returns in economic development. Strikingly, both of Serra's dichotomies have frequently gone in and out of fashion in the economics profession. They were strong in the period immediately following WWII, but, because of the chosen tools of economics since then, they were neglected with disastrous results. Engaging in wilful yet informative anachronism, he asks what Serra still might teach us regarding the problems of the EU, green growth, and the importance of a large division of labour in a multitude of increasing return activities for economic development.

Apart from the continuing use of Antonio Serra's *Breve trattato* by modern economists and the historical curiosity that no similarly sophisticated work of political economy would appear in Europe for well over a century if not more, Serra's treatise remains an invaluable source for understanding a crucial period in Neapolitan, Italian, and European history. It testifies to the changing nature of political liberty as the pressures of international economic competition first became paramount; it uniquely affected the cultural and political histories of economics and nationalism in Italy for centuries; and it is a powerful, still fertile argument for the economics of good government – for political economy as such. Taken together, the essays in this volume provide a wholly new perspective on one of the most mysterious and striking figures in the history of finance and of economics. But, drawing inspiration from their subject, they also strikingly address the importance of history for economics. The image that emerges of Serra and his book ultimately reminds us that the kinds of ideas and policies that were actually successful in history for promoting development may be more important than the ideologies that emerged to explain that development. In other words, Serra's work can provide pertinent answers to some of the most difficult questions of political economy, but it can also reveal to us the questions we have for so long forgotten to ask.

Notes

1. Schumpeter, J.A., *History of Economic Analysis*, ed. Schumpeter, E.B., Oxford: Oxford University Press, 1954, p. 195.
2. For what little we do know, and think we know, see Reinert, S.A. "Introduction" to Antonio Serra, *A Short Treatise on the Wealth and Poverty of Nations*, translated by J. Hunt, ed. Reinert, S.A., London: Anthem, 2011, pp. 9–17.
3. Serra, 1613, pp. 225–226.
4. Zazzera, F., *Giornali di Francesco Zazzera napolitano nel felice governo dell'Eccmo. D. Pietro Girone, Duca d'Ossuna, Viceré del Regno di Napoli, dalli 7 di luglio 1616, con il modo tenuto nel dare il possesso al Signore Cardinale Borgia suo successore, dalli signori eletti di questa fidelissima cittá, con intervento del Conseglio Collaterale*, 1667, p. 78.
5. Amabile, L., *Fra Tommaso Campanella: la sua congiura, i suoi processi e la sua pazzia*, 3 vols, Naples: Morano, 1882, vol. III, pp. 646–648.
6. De Rosa, L., "Antonio Serra e i suoi critici", *Clio*, vol. I, no. I, 1965, pp. 115–137.
7. The readable text of the first dispatch states "Antonio Serra [...] acuda al V.rey; traerlo esta tarde cuando venga el conde de Mola", both in *Viglietti originali, Segreterie del Viceré, N. 6 1613–1614*, Archivio di Stato di Napoli, Naples, Italy.
8. Reinert, "Introduction", p. 11; Serra, 1613, p. 133.
9. Croce, B., *Storia del regno di Napoli*, Bari-Rome: Laterza, 1925, p. 160.
10. Famous Bologna bookdealer Gino Brighenti, pencil annotation on inside front board of Antonio Serra, *Breve trattato delle cause che possono far abbondare li regni d'oro e d'argento dove non sono miniere*, Naples: Lazzaro Scorrigio, 1613, Reinert Collection, Hvasser, Norway.
11. Reinert, "Introduction", p. 6 and *passim*.
12. Antonio Serra, *Breve Tratado das causas que podem fazer os reinos desprovidos de minas ter abundância de ouro e prata* (1613), translated by M.T. Vicentini, Curitiba, Brazil: Segesta Editora, 2002; Antonio Serra, *A Short Treatise on the Wealth and Poverty of Nations (1613)*, translated by J. Hunt, edited and with an introduction by S.A. Reinert, London: Anthem, 2011.
13. Serra, 1613, p. 115.
14. Serra, 1613, p. 115.

1
The Place of Naples in the 17th-Century Spanish Empire

Gabriel Paquette

Karl Marx contended that the Spanish monarchy should be grouped "in a class with Asiatic forms of government", considering it nothing more than the "agglomeration of mismanaged republics with nominal sovereignty at their head". But while denouncing it as "despotic", he noted that Spanish sovereignty "did not prevent the provinces from subsisting with different laws and customs, military banners of different colors, and with their respective systems of taxation".[1] Marx partly subscribed to a "black legend" concerning Spanish rapacity and incompetence, an image whose origins date from the Dutch revolt against Spanish rule in the waning decades of the 16th century and which subsequently gathered force in England and other Protestant countries threatened by Spain's purported aspirations to universal monarchy.[2] This disparaging image would be disseminated across Europe in the seventeenth and eighteenth centuries, finding special resonance in Naples, the efforts of the Spanish crown to contest it notwithstanding.[3] Yet Marx, as a careful historian, could not help but recognize the legal and customary pluralism that flourished in the lands under Spain's dominion. Marx explained this phenomenon away as a strategy typical of "oriental despotism", which is more than satisfied "to allow these institutions to continue so long as they take off its shoulders the duty of doing something and spare it the trouble of regular administration".[4] Marx thus reproduced two opposing and recurrent images of the Spanish empire: on the one hand, an entity whose weakness and sprawl necessitated its decentralization; on the other hand, a robust state with incorrigible centralizing tendencies.

In 1613, the year in which Antonio Serra published his *Breve trattato*, the Spanish monarchy stretched from Naples to the Philippines. Its boundaries encompassed an astonishingly vast amount of noncontiguous territory, separated by oceans, seas, and mountain ranges.

The monarchy's heterogeneity was striking, embracing a panoply of languages and ethnicities. It absorbed numerous formerly independent kingdoms, each of which boasted its own long-established customs, economies, and, crucially, juridical traditions. The Spanish monarchy was far from a static entity. Its borders were in constant flux. Military triumphs and defeats routinely necessitated their reconfiguration, whether geographic, fiscal, or legal. Bringing this morass of distinctive cultures, economies, and polities under the sway of a single sovereign and making these disparate, far-flung pieces function in relative harmony posed, therefore, a challenge on a scale with few parallels in early modern European history.

Where did Naples fit in this broader political panorama? Naples was but one of several constituent kingdoms of the Spanish Atlantic monarchy. While not a federation, it was a composite polity that sheltered many smaller entities under a single sovereign. Portugal, the Basque provinces, Catalonia, the Netherlands, Navarre, Sicily, Aragon, Valencia, and Naples had been attached to the Spanish monarchy's Castilian nucleus in varying contexts. The circumstances of entry were important. Each kingdom retained a hotchpotch of fiscal exemptions, spheres of autonomy, and unique privileges – all negotiated, formally and informally, upon integration. Even after their union, they continued to be treated as distinct entities, each maintaining its unique identity and status.[5] The Spanish monarchy, as a result of this situation, was a legal mosaic, though ultimately under the sovereignty of the Spanish king. Such heterogeneity complicated the formulation of a common policy applicable to all of its component states. As in other composite monarchies, there was an inherent tension between "centripetal impulses toward centralization and centrifugal tendencies toward localism".[6] In Spain, the severity of this tension was exposed starkly in the 17th century, especially during its middle decades, which were marked by incessant war on multiple fronts.

The problem of linking the centre of the Spanish monarchy with its peripheral kingdoms, whether in Europe or in America, produced several potential solutions. Ultimately, a new administrative structure was developed in the 16th century, though it borrowed heavily on practices and techniques of the late medieval Aragonese-Catalan Mediterranean Empire.[7] Councils were formed, composed of spokesmen for each kingdom. These met at court and consulted with the king, both directly and through his advisers. The importance of the Councils should not be discounted. As a Polish visitor to Spain noted in 1611, "what is surprising about Spain is that, though their government is absolute, their kings do nothing without the Councils".[8] The Councils received information from, and sent orders to, a viceroy who had been assigned to one of the peripheral kingdoms.[9]

In each peripheral kingdom, whether Naples or New Spain, the most powerful figure was the viceroy, the highest magistrate sent from Spain and, in most cases, a Castilian by birth. In *Política Indiana* (1647), Juan de Solórzano Pereira rationalized the institution of the viceroy. He explained that it was created "so that vassals who live and reside in remote provinces need not go seek their king, who is so far away, having his vicar nearby to ask for and get all those things they could expect and get from their king".[10] The viceroy was considered to "be the monarch's image and *alter ego* and held to be in possession of all the majesty, power and authority of the king".[11]

But the viceroy was not all powerful. He was compelled to work in conjunction with the aforementioned Councils in the Iberian Peninsula. These councillors were usually natives of the respective territory who responded vigorously to any perceived threat to their homeland (and, it must be said, their interests and those of their allies and retainers). The Councils, as John H. Elliott argued in his *Imperial Spain* (1963), were

> much more than mere administrative organs in that they also fulfilled some of the functions of representative bodies (...) a body of representative native councilors attendant on the person of the king could at least help to restrict the deleterious consequences of royal absenteeism.[12]

Though outfitted with all of the pomp of royalty, empowered to issue decrees and execute justice, the viceroy in Naples was forbidden to infringe on local laws.[13] Elsewhere viceregal autonomy was further circumscribed by leaving local privileges unmolested. In Milan, for example, the municipal council's authority remained robust. Furthermore, a local senate was installed there after the advent of Spanish rule to deter viceregal ambition.[14]

These interlocking local constraints were matched by massive impediments to viceregal volition at the apex of the imperial system. The Spanish monarch remained the sole arbiter of most facets of government in each kingdom. Just as importantly, the vast complex of local states were linked in a personal union with the king alone.[15] In this way, there were few horizontal links among the kingdoms but a great number of separate vertical ties between each kingdom and the Spanish monarchy. In each component state, the king's capacity for patronage was formidable. The grant of ecclesiastical benefices, the sale of offices, the appointment of officials, and the approval over the sale and transfer of feudal properties emanated directly from the crown.[16] The strategic distribution of these much-coveted plums guaranteed direct communication between the crown and the beneficiaries of its largesse, not to mention unmediated loyalty and service obligations.

Within well-defined limits, however, the viceroy maintained a degree of autonomy in setting the direction of the kingdom to which he was assigned. His military authority was undivided.[17] He was not compelled to enforce passively the laws emanating from the Councils at Court. On the contrary, it was a firmly established and fully recognized principle that viceroys (and other crown officials) judged whether local conditions were propitious for the imposition of any given law. Castro de Bobadilla noted in his widely read manual *Política para Corregidores* (1616) that royal provisions and decrees that were "contrary to justice and in prejudice" to the crown's ultimate interests could be "obeyed but not executed".[18]

By invoking this curious formula, "obdezco pero no cumplo" (in Spanish), the viceroy reaffirmed his loyalty and subordination to the monarch while simultaneously indicating that the best expression of his obedience was the non-enforcement of a particular act until circumstances, which were unknowable except by those "men-on-the-spot", favoured its execution. In this way, the overlapping administrative structures of the Spanish monarchy were neither a byzantine aggregation caused by the meshing of disparate, not entirely compatible systems of governance nor the enablers of a lusty, arbitrary leviathan. Instead, blurring lines of authority and the creation of a dazzling mosaic of checks and balances mitigated the obstacles intrinsic to rule at a great distance. It betrayed the crown's deep-seated distrust of its agents posted beyond Castile's borders. It also reflected a keen appreciation of the hazards latent in imposing laws that failed to account for, in Philip II's words, "the diversity and difference of lands and peoples". Spanish administration in its non-peninsular kingdoms, to borrow the historian John Phelan's memorable phrase, was a "dynamic balance between the principles of authority and flexibility".[19]

Many of the same institutions existed, in one form or another, across the monarchy. There were viceroys both in Spain's European provinces and its ultramarine territories. But the prevalence of the same office did not necessarily mean that it worked in the identical fashion in each constituent kingdom. In European kingdoms, many of the signature institutions of the Spanish monarchy were modified to fit the existing institutional framework. The Americas, or the Indies (*Indias*), as they were known, were considered part of the crown of Castile. The laws and institutions of the New World were modelled on those of Castile. Philip II summarized the relationship in an address to the Council of the Indies in 1571: "because the kingdoms of Castile and the Indies belong to one crown, their laws and manner of government ought to be as alike as possible".[20]

This legal status influenced the scope of the viceroy's authority in the New World. The vast wealth, great distance from Europe, and the distasteful memory of disruptive recalcitrance of several conquistadors in the 16th century impelled the Spanish crown to devise institutions to carefully monitor and check the viceroy's activities. Various legal restrictions and overlapping authority conspired to limit his authority. Of course, as the Spanish monarchs and their ministers fully realized, America could not be micro-managed from Madrid. The difficulties of transatlantic communication forced some patronage to be left under the viceroy's control, particularly the authority to dispense minor governmental appointments and judicial offices. Although subject to a greater degree of oversight, the colonial treasury remained under the viceroy's purview. He could issue proclamations [*bandos*] and measures [*ordenanzas*], but not laws in the strict sense. Although American viceroys shared some of the responsibilities of their European counterparts (e.g. defence of the realm from external attack and the maintenance of domestic tranquillity), others were peculiar to the New World. These included the expansion of Catholicism through the promotion of evangelization and conversion, the negotiation of treaties with Amerindians, and responsibility for rewarding the descendants of the conquistadores and first settlers.

In the New World, the greatest limitation on viceregal authority was posed by the *Audiencia*, the highest court of Spanish America, of which thirteen had been established by 1661. The judges [*oidores*], appointed directly by the king, were empowered to correspond directly with the sovereign. The *Audiencias* also retained attorneys [*fiscales*] responsible to the king for everything that pertained to the treasury. Viceregal autonomy was further checked by the *Residencia*. At the expiration of their term of service, all officials underwent this remarkably thorough evaluation of their conduct. Perhaps the greatest brake on viceregal power in Spanish America was a relatively short tenure in office. If in the 16th century, the viceroy was appointed for an undetermined number of years, with the average length of service hovering around six years, then after 1629 viceroys were appointed for three years with the possibility of a three-year renewal.[21] Such a short stint ensured not only that various men of aspirations got a turn but also that each viceroy remained an "outsider", whose roots in the economy and society he administered were shallow and easily extirpated.

In contrast to the situation in Spanish America, the passage of Naples from Aragonese to Castilian rule in 1504 heralded neither major changes in the fiscal system nor significant modification to its fundamental political structure. Only under the viceregal tenure of Pedro de Toledo (1532–1553) would its comprehensive integration into the Spanish monarchy be contemplated.[22] Some historians have viewed Toledo's period in Naples as less than salubrious. Giuseppe Galasso, for example, argued that Toledo's initiatives inaugurated "a process of fiscal expansion and corruption ... financial and fiscal problems [which was] to emerge as the greatest bane and the most odious aspect of the [Spanish] regime".[23]

But this result did not necessarily happen against the wishes of important sectors of Neapolitan society. Spanish government in Naples, as elsewhere, would have been unthinkable without collaborators. Provincial aristocracies recognized, and scampered toward, the benefits offered by Spanish rule. As Elliott has observed, "paradoxically, the greatest strength of the Spanish monarchy lay in its very weakness.... [H]owever many orders might issue from Madrid, viceregal administrators were incapable of carrying them out without the assistance of the local governing class".[24] And local elites were remarkably adept at harnessing the institutions of the state to serve their own economic and political ends.[25] In Naples, a delicate balance calibrated the autonomy of Neapolitans with the monarchy's goals.[26]

But geopolitical pressure from without, at least as much as discontent from within the incorporated kingdoms, changed the terms of the relationship. Between 1618 and 1621, Spanish involvement in Germany led, ultimately, to its effort to control the military corridors which linked Vienna, Milan, and Brussels. These decisions also resulted in the resumption of hostilities with the Dutch. The expenditure necessitated by these excursions coincided with the sharp decline in remittances of American silver. Fiscal crisis was nothing new in the Spanish empire: under Philip II in the late 16th century, revenues had tripled, but public debt had quadrupled.[27] But the acuteness of the early 17th-century shortfall compelled the crown to identify new sources of revenue and resulted in the levying of additional taxes. Crown bureaucrats first surveyed Castile for possible sources and, subsequently, extended their reach to other parts of the monarchy, including Naples. The problem, as Elliott has noted, was that each province "retained [its] own customary laws and representative assemblies, so that any attempt to extract larger financial and military contributions could well lead to disruptive constitutional conflict".[28]

Nevertheless, such a conflict proved exceedingly difficult to avoid. The Spanish economic reformer and royal secretary Pedro Fernández Navarrete (1564–1632) complained that new kingdoms brought into Spanish monarchy must neither "appear to be separate nations nor [the subjects] be considered to be foreigners".[29] Building on these ideas, the Count-Duke of Olivares, Philip IV's chief minister, recognized that the Spanish empire's diversity must be replaced by uniformity, or at least with closer relationships between kingdoms befitting of a supranational polity. In Count-Duke Olivares's far-reaching plan for a "Union of Arms" (1625), a shift towards homogeneity entailed the expansion of royal power and the curtailment of provincial customary rights, privileges, and constitutions. Their existence hampered the Spanish monarchy's capacity to respond punctually and decisively to geopolitical threats.[30] The problem was dire. As Calabria has noted, the administration and collection of taxes in Naples was "chaotic, marred by overlapping and competing jurisdictions, and plagued by a bewildering variety of exemptions and loopholes".[31] Crown and viceregal aspirations for centralization and administrative efficiency were hindered by "concessions and compromises and essential respect for the norm of autonomy".[32]

The Spanish crown, then, was forced to tighten the reins. In spite of the ubiquity of symbols – architectural, ceremonial, and artistic – of Spanish power, these reins had been kept extraordinarily slack. The fiscal requirements of a state engaged in war on multiple fronts necessitated a policy shift. As one contemporary historian has contended, these "heavy fiscal demands drained the productive structures of the Southern Italian economy, heightened inflation, and led to urban and rural revolt".[33] These revenue-generating efforts provoked a range of responses and analyses, not least from commentators like Antonio Serra.[34] They also undoubtedly played a role in the revolts and riots that broke out across the Spanish empire: Mexico City (1624), Catalonia (1640), Portugal (1640), Naples (1647), Palermo (1647), and Andalusia (1651), not to mention the disturbances in Castile itself.[35] The pacification of these revolts burdened Spain's already strained resources. Yet it is by no means easy to conclude that Madrid's centralizing efforts caused the revolts. After all, unrest was rife across Europe, with revolutions more widespread than they were at any other period except 1848.

England, France, and the Netherlands were convulsed by revolution and civil war. As one eminent historian argued, "the various countries of Europe seemed merely the separate theatres upon which the same great tragedy was being simultaneously, though in different languages and with local variations, played out".[36]

With the notable exception of the independence of Portugal (and its colony Brazil), however, the Spanish monarchy surmounted the "General Crisis" of the 1640s and 1650s with its territorial integrity largely intact.[37] This outcome may be attributed to the fact that elites in the different constituent states of the empire realized that "they could do better for themselves within the framework of the monarchy than if they struck out on their own".[38] Dissatisfaction with Spanish rule did not dissipate entirely. The assassination of the Viceroy of Sardinia in 1668 is ample testament to discontent that simmered just beneath the surface. The Spanish response to such discontent was mixed. While it is true that the parliament of Naples was abolished in 1642, the parliaments of Sicily and Sardinia continued to be summoned through the period of Spanish rule, right into the 18th century.[39] The end of Spanish rule in Naples (and Milan, Sicily, and Flanders), it must be stressed, ultimately was achieved not through domestic rebellion, riot, or revolt but rather by the terms stipulated in the Treaty of Utrecht (1713), which ended the War of Spanish Succession. Clearly, the strategies of accommodation, negotiation, and compromise, which had served the Spanish monarchy so well for so long, were not easily cast aside.

The cobbled-together Spanish monarchy did more than merely hobble along. In fact, far from being a steadily declining power, it remained surprisingly resilient until at least the first decade of the 18th century.[40] Historians need not become apologists for the Spanish empire (or defenders of its economic record in Naples in particular) to recognize, as Marx reluctantly did, the formidable administrative achievements of that great "composite monarchy". Its elaborate and relatively flexible institutional mechanisms enabled it to hold, however loosely and ineffectually, a breathtaking diversity of polities, on multiple continents, under a single crown, for two centuries.

Notes

1. Marx, K., "Revolution in Spain [I]", *New York Daily Tribune*, 9 September 1854, in Marx and F. Engels, eds, *Revolution in Spain*, London: Lawrence and Wishart, 1939, p. 26.

2. For an excellent survey of the origins and impact of this "Black Legend", see García Cárcel, R., *La Leyenda Negra: Historia y Opinión*, Madrid: Alianza, 1992.
3. On Neapolitan political writers' analyses of Spanish rule, see Pagden, A., "*Fede Pubblica* and *Fede Privata*: Trust and Honour in Spanish Naples", in Pagden, ed., *Spanish Imperialism and the Political Imagination: Studies in European and Spanish-American Social and Political Theory 1513–1830*, New Haven, CT and London: Yale University Press, 1990, pp. 65–90; on long-standing efforts to contest disparaging depictions of the Spanish monarchy, see Kagan, R.L., *Clio and the Crown: The Politics of History in Medieval and Early Modern Spain*, Baltimore, MD: Johns Hopkins University Press, 2009.
4. Marx, 1854, in Spain, p. 26.
5. For a discussion of composite monarchies in the sixteenth and seventeenth centuries, see Elliott, J.H., "A Europe of Composite Monarchies", *Past and Present* 137, 1992, pp. 48–71.
6. Greene, J.P., "State Formation, Resistance, and the Creation of Revolutionary Traditions in the Early Modern Era", in Mornson, M.A. and M.S. Zook, eds, *Revolutionary Currents: Nation-Building in the Transatlantic World*, Lanham, MD: Rowman and Littlefield, 2004, p. 4.
7. For these late medieval Mediterranean (and Eastern Atlantic) institutional precedents, see Fernández-Armesto, F., *Before Columbus: Exploration and Colonization from the Mediterranean to the Atlantic, 1229–1492*, Philadelphia, PA: University of Pennsylvania Press, 1987, esp. part I.
8. Quoted in Thompson, I.A.A., "Castile", in Miller, J., ed., *Absolutism in Seventeenth-century Europe*, Basingstoke: Macmillan, 1990, p. 87.
9. Elliott, J.H., "Spain and Its Empire in the Sixteenth and Seventeenth Centuries", in Elliott, ed., *Spain and its World 1500–1700*, New Haven, CT and London: Yale University Press, 1989, p. 15.
10. Quoted in Cañeque, A., *The King's Living Image: The Culture and Politics of Viceregal Power in Colonial Mexico*, New York, NY and London: Routledge, 2004, p. 17.
11. Cañeque, 2004, p. 25.
12. Elliott, J.H., *Imperial Spain, 1469–1716*, London: Penguin, 1963, p. 176; one historian has argued that the Council of Italy held less authority than other Councils. She argues that the confluence of its late founding (1558), limited prerogatives, mixed composition and the heterogeneity of the Italian dominions diminished its authority. See Peytavin, M., "Government/Administration: The Italian Kingdoms within the Spanish Monarchy", in Dandelet, T. and J. Marino, eds, "Introduction" to their *Spain in Italy: Politics, Society and Religion, 1500–1700*, Boston, MA and Leiden: Brill, 2007, p. 366.
13. Sánchez, C.J.H., *Castilla y Nápoles en el Siglo XVI: El Virrey Pedro de Toledo. Linaje, Estado y Cultura (1532–1553)*, Salamanca: Junta de Castilla y León, 1994, p. 197.
14. Guarino, G., "The Politics of Appearances: State Representations and Images of Power in Spanish Naples during the Seventeenth Century", PhD Dissertation, Cambridge University, 2004, p. 5.
15. An idea developed in Musi, A., "The Kingdom of Naples in the Spanish Imperial System", in Dandelet and Marino, eds, 2007, p. 83.

16. Villari, R., *The Revolt of Naples*, Cambridge: Polity Press, 1993, p. 10.
17. Phelan, J.L., *The Kingdom of Quito in the Seventeenth Century: Bureaucratic Politics in the Spanish Empire*, Madison, WI and London: University of Wisconsin Press, 1967, p. 124.
18. Haring, C.H., *The Spanish Empire in America*, New York, NY: Oxford University Press, 1947, pp. 114–115.
19. Phelan, J.L., "Authority and Flexibility in Spanish Imperial Bureaucracy", *Administrative Science Quarterly* 5, 1960, pp. 47–65.
20. Quoted in Haring, 1947, pp. 5–6.
21. Figures taken based on New Spain. See Cañeque, 2004, p. 17.
22. Calabria, A., *The Cost of Empire: The Finances of the Kingdom of Naples in the Time of Spanish Rule*, Cambridge: Cambridge University Press, 2001, p. 37.
23. Galasso, G., "Trends and Problems in Neapolitan History in the Age of Charles V", in Calabria, A. and J.A. Marino, eds, *Good Government in Spanish Naples*, New York, NY: Lang, 1990, pp. 43–44. See also his *Alla periferia dell'impero. Il Regno di Napoli nel periodo Spagnolo (secoli xvi–xvii)*, Turin: Einaudi, 1994.
24. Elliott, J.H., "A Provincial Aristocracy: The Catalan Ruling Class in the Sixteenth and Seventeenth Century", in Elliott, ed., 1989, p. 90; as Elliott has observed elsewhere, Neapolitan elites enjoyed "substantial leverage, which could be used on the one hand to exert pressure on the crown, and on the other to extend their social and economic dominance over their own communities". See Elliott, 1992, p. 56.
25. See Yun Casalilla, B., "The Castilian Aristocracy in the Seventeenth Century: Crisis, Refeudalisation or Political Offensive?", in Yun Casalilla and I.A.A. Thompson, eds, *The Castilian Crisis of the Seventeenth Century: New Perspectives on the Economic and Social History of Seventeenth Century Spain*, Cambridge: Cambridge University Press, 1994; the similarities to the Portuguese case are striking. See Bouza Álvarez, F., *Portugal no Tempo dos Filipes: Politica, Cultura, Representações (1580–1668)*, Lisbon: Cosmos, 2000.
26. Guarino, 2004, p. 21. Dandelet and Marino have recently made a similar point: "the *pax hispanica* in Italy was not only the result of military pacification, but also in large measure a product of this reciprocal exchange under Spanish imperial rule". See Dandelet and Marino, "Introduction", 2007, p. 7.
27. Parker, G., *Philip II*, 4th ed., Chicago, IL: Open Court, 2002, pp. 178–179.
28. Elliott, J.H., *Richelieu and Olivares*, Cambridge, Cambridge University Press, 1984, pp. 63–64.
29. Quoted in Pujol, X.G., "Un Rey, una Fe, Muchas Naciones: Patria y Nación en la España de los Siglos XVI y XVII", in Álvarez-Ossorio, A. et al., eds, *La Monarquía de las Naciones*, Madrid: Fundaciòn Carlos de Amberes, 2004, p. 64.
30. Elliott, J.H., *The Count-Duke of Olivares: The Statesman in an Age of Decline*, New Haven, CT and London: Yale University Press, 1986, pp. 193–197 *passim*; see also Stradling, R.A., *Philip IV and the Government of Spain 1621–1665*, Cambridge: Cambridge University Press, 1988.
31. Calabria, 2001, p. 45.
32. Villari, 1993, *Naples*, p. 4.
33. Marino, J., "The Rural World in Italy under Spanish Rule", in Dandelet and Marino, eds, 2007, p. 429.

34. Interestingly, efforts to augment revenues in the short-term did not necessarily require raising taxes and other heavy-handed measures. In Castile in the 1620s and 1630s, "activities still administered directly by the state were turned over the private enterprise". See Thompson, I.A.A., "The Government of Spain in the Reign of Philip IV", in Thompson, ed., *Crown and Cortes: Government, Institutions and Representation in Early Modern Castile*, Aldershot: Variorum, 1993, p. 80.
35. Among other works on various aspects of these revolts and riots, see Elliott, J.H., *The Revolt of the Catalans: A Study in the Decline of Spain, 1598–1640*, Cambridge: Cambridge University Press, 1963; Gelabert, J.E., *Castilla Convulsa (1631–1652)*, Madrid Marcial Pons, 2001; and McFarlane, A., "Challenges from the Periphery: Rebellion in Colonial Spanish America", in Thomas, W., ed., *Rebelión y Resistencia en el Mundo Hispánico del Siglo XVII*, Leuven: Leuven University Press, 1992.
36. Trevor-Roper, H.R., "The General Crisis of the Seventeenth Century", in Trevor-Roper, *The Crisis of the Seventeenth Century: Religion, the Reformation and Social Change*, New York: Harper & Row, 1968, p. 46. The "General Crisis" is the subject of an enormous scholarly literature and debate. For the most important assessments, see Koenigsberger, H.G., "The Crisis of the Seventeenth Century: A Farewell?", in Koenigsberger, ed., *Politicians and Virtuosi: Essays in Early Modern History*, London: Hambledon Press, 1986; Parker, G., "Crisis and Catastrophe: The Global Crisis of the Seventeenth Century Reconsidered", *American Historical Review* 113, 2008, pp. 1053–1079; and Elliott, J.H., "The General Crisis in Retrospect: A Debate without End", in Elliott, ed., *Spain, Europe, and the Wider World 1500–1800*, New Haven, CT and London: Yale University Press, 2009.
37. Elliott, J.H., "Foreign Policy and Domestic Crisis: Spain, 1598–1659", in Elliott, ed., 1989, p. 132. There were notable losses, of course: the northern Netherlands (1648), Jamaica (1655), and the western half of Hispaniola (1664).
38. Kagan, R. and G. Parker, "Introduction: The Centre and the Periphery", in Kagan and Parker, eds, *Spain, Europe, and the Atlantic World: Essays in Honour of J.H. Elliott*, Cambridge: Cambridge University Press, 1995, p. 24.
39. Koenigsberger, H.G., "*Dominium Regale* or *Dominium Politicum et Regale*: Monarchies and Parliaments in Early Modern Europe", in Koenigsberger, ed., 1986, p. 13.
40. Storrs, C., *The Resilience of the Spanish Monarchy, 1665–1700*, Oxford: Oxford University Press, 2006.

2

The Vicaria Prison of Naples in the Time of Antonio Serra

Francesca De Rosa

1 Corruption and crimes in the cellars of Castel Capuano

The Vicaria Prison of Naples, the largest of the Kingdom, was housed in the cellars of Castel Capuano from 1537, when the Viceroy Pedro de Toledo determined that the various law courts scattered throughout the Capital should be concentrated in one place.[1] However, the Viceroy's aim of centralizing the administration of justice was fully implemented only in 1540, when the four *wheels* of the Vicaria (two criminal and two civil) – the Collaterale, the Sommaria, the Zecca, and the Bagliva – were brought together and began functioning in the new premises.[2] Meanwhile the prison, serving as a drain to collect "all the woes of the Kingdom", had – as we have seen – already been functioning for some years. In 1692 Carlo Celano wrote:

> Under these Courts of Law are the prisons; and there have at times been as many as two thousand prisoners or more, for incarcerated here are not only the prisoners of the City, but also of the entire Kingdom.[3]

The area serving for imprisonment was occupied by vast rooms and broad corridors where the prisoners were separated according to the type of crime they had committed; these rooms also housed the poor and the homeless. A description of these places was provided in a long *Report*, dated 1674, on the *State of the prisons of the G.C. of the Vicaria of Naples before the year 1609 and the changes brought about and maintained to the present year of 1674 by the permanent commission instituted by the Fathers of the Society of Jesus and the constant protection accorded to the mission by the ministers of the Kingdom*. This report, conserved by the Società Napoletana di Storia Patria (Neapolitan History Society), describes a grim and overcrowded environment where the Kingdom's prisoners lived under foul conditions.[4]

An outer courtyard was used by the prisoners for recreation or simply walking, above all in the summer months; it was, however, also reserved for disposal of the rubbish of the entire prison, which piled up there and "fermented, causing a great many infections".

Nevertheless, the prisoners needed somewhere to take

> a little air, unhealthy as it may be, to escape from the smoke in the passageways where almost everyone cooked over wood fires, and the foul-smelling atmosphere of the rooms, much like dark and dreadful caves, black and full of cobwebs.[5]

In this insalubrious environment,

> there vegetated, teeming and making trouble, a mass of over a thousand prisoners, the dregs of every sort of nation, more or less hardened to crime and far from God-fearing.

The prison gathered in convicts from all the Kingdom's provinces,

> held together by chains tight round their necks like animals, they were dragged there on foot and looked more dead than alive.[6]

It was the established custom for the newcomers to be subjected to mistreatment by the "old-timers" who, having stripped them of clothes and money, tormented them with all sorts of abuse. In particular, by night

> they put out the light and some of the newcomers had their feet burnt with paper soaked in oil, others were beaten, and none were able to rest.[7]

The food, distributed daily, consisted of seven pieces of bread and some water for each prisoner, although, on payment, there was also the option of a hot meal in a tavern on the premises, enjoying cooked food by day and going hungry only by night.[8]

No beds were provided in the sleeping quarters – a circumstance that raised the prisoners' mortality rate, with particularly high peaks in the winter months[9]. A few privileged prisoners could have a bed of their own, brought there, on payment, from their homes; others could rent a bed, but few could take advantage of this option, the rate for a single night being very high. The system was controlled by

> unscrupulous people who enjoyed the protection of the jailers, who in turn had an interest in the bed renting business, which they could profit from.[10]

Gambling, rigged card games and dice were generally tolerated, and veritable gambling dens were created, brawls continually breaking out, possibly ending in murder.[11]

In order to play a part in this "criminal society", the prisoners needed money, which was readily obtained by stealing from the newcomers:

> thefts were so frequent that no sooner was some poor wretch imprisoned than he was immediately stripped of his clothes to be sold to the bystanders; they were so skilfully stripped that the hapless victims had no time to realise what was being done to them, and even if they had realised they would not have been able to report the theft for fear of retaliation, fearing even that they might be killed in the ambushes that were customary in those places. Very often the prisoners themselves went on committing their crimes within the prison, having by then formed a very profitable internal criminal society; life outside the prison would not have afforded them such convenient conditions as they found in their confinement, where everything was allowed with the connivance of the jailers.[12]

Money was needed not only for the pleasures of hot meals or gambling but also to enjoy the services of the "free women", who haunted the prison unimpeded; a practically licit form of liberty.[13]

Subsequent to the intervention of the Jesuits, who sought to provide assistance to the Vicaria prison, a spiritual transformation came under way, but change was also coming about in material terms. One of the first steps taken by the Jesuits was to divide the prisoners into *Congregations*; a prison chapel was then created with capacity for about three hundred people, and a library was set up. The division of the prisoners into congregations resulted, among other things, in the poor prisoners being separated from the nobles.[14]

In 1618 a congregation was created in the name of the Holy Trinity to bring succour to

> the women under sentence and the young prisoners and the poor prisoners lying sick in the Royal Infirmary.[15]

The principal aim of the Jesuits was to eliminate all the "promiscuity" that was so customary in the prison; the nobles were separated from the "commoners", the young from the elderly and, finally, the men from the women. With the aim of stemming the prison's staggering mortality rate, measures were taken to improve the hygienic and health conditions on the premises: in the case of prisoners' suffering from pneumonia, hospitalization was authorized in the Royal Infirmary in order to contain contagion. The Jesuits chose to organize the system, introducing a special rule for alms for the maintenance of the facility and the prisoners. To ensure fair distribution of the offerings the prisoners would be summoned, assembling for a "rolecall" to receive their share of the money raised thanks to the various confraternities and religious institutions at work in the Kingdom's capital.[16] The procedure for trials also came from an initiative on the part of the Jesuits; we read in the *Report* that greater incentives were introduced for the provision of free legal aid to the more impoverished prisoners by the counsel for the poor.[17]

2 Antonio Serra's prison

In these circumstances, amid neglect and abuse, prostitution and gambling, Antonio Serra wrote his *Short treatise on the causes that can make kingdoms abound in gold and silver even in the absence of mines, with particular reference to the Kingdom of Naples* (*Breve trattato delle cause che possono far abbondare li regni d'oro e d'argento, dove non sono miniere, con applicazione al Regno di Napoli*) in 1613.[18] In the text, the author stated that he had completed his work while confined in the Vicaria Prison where, as he went on to point out, he had been confined for over a year. He dedicated his treatise to the Count of Lemos, but with no plea for improvement in his condition as a prisoner.

The reasons for his imprisonment have been much debated: Ferdinando Galiani,[19] the first author to cite Serra's treatise in print, made no reference to the conditions that the economist from Cosenza found himself in, apart from the fact that Serra was confined in the Vicaria Prison and that his text was printed by Lazzaro Scoriggio,[20] as Serra himself had noted. Based on the evidence of the descriptions we have of the Vicaria Prison in those times, it appears quite likely that a prisoner may have been able to enjoy some "liberties" – granted only on payment, of course – and we may even suspect that Serra had to pay a price to be able to work on his treatise. However, we have no sufficient evidence to determine with any certainty the reasons for Serra's internment or how long it lasted. On the basis of certain 19th-century sources, we can go no further than a few tentative suppositions. In 1802, in his *In praise of Antonio Serra. First writer on Civil Economy*,[21] Salfi not only sang fulsome praise of the author of the *Brief Treatise*, who hailed from his own city, but also provided a description of the political situation in the Kingdom in those years. Together with his references to Serra's evident merits, expressed with a touch of provincial pride, Salfi also discussed the reasons that had led to Serra's incarceration, associating them with the plot hatched by Campanella with the aim of proclaiming Calabria a republic, with the help of the Ottomans. Salfi's assumption was subsequently taken up in drafting various biographical entries on Serra. In particular, in the *Biography of the Illustrious Men of the Kingdom of Naples*, Giuseppe Boccanera da Macerata, author of the entry on Serra, coming to the reasons why the author of the *Brief Treatise* was imprisoned, observed that it was indeed highly likely that Antonio Serra had taken part in the plot planned by Campanella, offering as evidence not only the simultaneous occurrence of events – both Serra and Campanella being imprisoned in those years – but also the fact that the plot had its origins in Calabria, Serra's homeland.[22] Up until the end of the 19th century, a series of biographers gave this version of the events, while Luigi Amabile, having pieced together a picture of the events connected with the plot on the archival evidence, writing on Campanella in 1882[23] published a number of documents in which the name of Antonio Serra appeared. In particular, one of these contained reference to a certain prisoner named Antonio Serra, but without the title of doctor, accused of producing counterfeit money.

In the Kingdom, counterfeiting was a very common crime, and indeed the *Prammatica* (i.e. Sanction) VIII *De Monetis*, issued in 1609, was conceived with the precise intention of putting a stop to the innumerable disorders breaking out over the counterfeiting of money. There had already been a great many Prammatiche to address the practice of counterfeiting or clipping coins, thereby reducing their real value, but despite the severe sentences passed on counterfeiters and clippers, there was no effective fall in the incidence of the crime. Prammatica VIII determined the punishment for this crime, establishing, in the first place, the sentence of three years of *galea* (i.e. in the galleys) for commoners guilty of passing counterfeit money and three years of confinement for the nobles, on top of which came a fine which was divided between the Treasury and the Royal Ministry.[24]

The same *Prammatica* VIII established that, in the process of judgment, the judges could interrogate the culprits, who to begin with had to provide evidence as to how and from whom they had received the money, and, should these same persons have already been convicted for the same crime, they could be subjected to torture for the acquisition of further evidence. The *Prammatica* went on to decree that anyone who had shown connivance with the counterfeiters or clippers would be considered guilty and, moreover, added to these measures was the aggravating circumstance of repetition of the offence, even if there was no evidence. Indeed, the sole possession of one of the objects or pieces of equipment normally used to commit these crimes constituted sufficient ground to impute the crime to the owners, and the *Prammatica* also ruled that the judges could at their own discretion even pass the death sentence. Life sentence was passed on those who worked coins without official authorization; moreover, for anyone acquiring coin clippings, the *Prammatica* established a punishment of five years of *galea* for commoners and five years of confinement for nobles. The same sentence also applied to persons who distilled "alchemic mixtures" without a licence. Anyone who came to learn of places where such crimes could be committed or was acquainted with persons who clipped, incised, or otherwise reduced the value of coins was obliged to report them; should they fail to do so, they would be liable to a sentence of ten years of *galea* if commoners, while again the same term applied to the nobles, but in more tolerable conditions of confinement. Obviously, such a severe sentence for people failing to report crimes known to them served above all to favour delation; in fact, informers were allowed to remain anonymous, and, as a reward, they would receive half the value of whatever was confiscated.[25]

In his *History of the Kingdom of Naples*, Benedetto Croce wrote that Antonio Serra was imprisoned for counterfeiting money, a piece of gold or alloy having been found in his dwelling, and that four years after his imprisonment he succeeded in gaining the ear of the Count of Lemos, but to no avail; after the consultation he was taken back to prison.[26] In the light of this scant evidence and of a few archival references provided by Amabile, and above all in consideration of the provisions set out in the *Prammatica* VIII, it appears quite likely that Serra had been accused of counterfeiting money by somebody, probably an enemy of his, and that in consequence he was incarcerated in the Vicaria Prison. To this tentative reconstruction of events, it remains to be added that the Calabrian economist was evidently sentenced to a term of more than five years, probably life.[27]

3 Orders and instructions for government of the prison

Returning to our reconstruction of the conditions in the Vicaria Prison, conserved in the National Library of Naples are a number of decrees issued between 1621 and 1629, affording evidence of the various needs and consequent actions regarding the prison. These documents show just how determined the government authorities were to intervene in the management of the prison, and above all they offer some details on how the organization functioned and on the previous conditions.[28] The first document, dated 21 May 1621, concerned the alms and in particular the supply of bread:

> the Congregation created with the Title of the Holy Trinity entered the Vicaria premises not only for spiritual succour for all the Tribunal, but also to take care of the sick lying in the Royal Infirmary, of the children of the prisoners and of the convicted women present there. The charity that was collected in the city and its districts in aid of the poor prisoners, the distribution of bread, and all the alms came under the responsibility of this Congregation who were in charge of distribution in aid of the said poor prisoners.[29]

The document also refers to breaches of the agreements regarding payment of fee for the service of taking in alms, which had been made to the prison porter up until 1619, when the sums of money involved were confiscated by the governor of the Vicaria. From that time, it was determined in accordance with the specific instructions on the congregation that the money was to be entrusted to some party other than the porter in order to limit the thefts committed at the expense of the prisoners.

Further evidence of the interest which the Grand Court of the Vicaria took in the activities performed by the Jesuit fathers is offered by the order of 24 February 1623 with which the Grand Court sent *Instructions* to the infirmary chaplains that they should duly observe the provisions of the fathers of the Society of Jesus and follow their guidance. The instructions placed great emphasis on the assistance – both spiritual and material – to be given to the sick.

This series of documents, all of considerable significance, is of great help in filling out the picture of the conditions that reigned in the Prison of Vicaria. Particularly interesting are the various *orders* sent to the *head jailer* by the Grand Court, requiring that for the

> sound governance and safekeeping of the Prison, in particular preventing the escapes which the prisoners are continually accomplishing in various ways

Closer control must be kept over the premises:

> the nightly procedure was to close the courtyard of the said prison, where by day the Prisoners would linger, and so to inspect all the suspicious places, and, having safely locked up the courtyard, all the Heads of the Dormitories, both of the Nobles and of the Common People, and of the passageways, as well as the renters of beds were obliged to report if anyone was missing from their places or rooms; in such a case action was to be taken with due diligence and the procedure was to be straightforward. It was thus ordered that when a certain hour of the night struck all had to return to their rooms or the places where they habitually spent the night, after which the rooms and halls were locked from the outside, admitting no exception to the rule. All persons in the habit of frequenting those places for gambling or any other reasons were to be accompanied outside, and after completing inspection of the places, if there were any absences, the disappearance was to be reported immediately in order to be able to inform the Regent residing on the premises of the Grand Court and the prison.[30]

The "safekeeping" of the prison was the object of a great many *orders* issued by the Grand Court of the Vicaria. After the first years of large-scale intervention by the Jesuit fathers, a gradual rift came about between the spiritual side of the assistance, which they remained in charge of, and the formal control of the Prison, which came within the competence of the Vicaria Tribunal. The Grand Court was in charge of the control activities, ensuring order and respect for the rules; surveillance of the premises was also extended to the surrounding areas, and in 1628 a squad was organized to keep watch over the outer limits of the prison, their duty being "to patrol around the Tribunal all night long".[31]

Another document offering significant evidence is, again, conserved in the BNN, under the title *Instructions for the sound governance of the prison, infirmary and penitentiary*, and again, it was Zapata who called for them in 1621.[32] The *Instructions* reiterated the prohibitions already officialized on various occasions – forbidding, for example, blaspheming, causing scandal, bearing arms, or gambling; it was ordered to keep clerics and laymen separate, to grant no one access to the rooms of the nobles on payment, to prevent free circulation in the passageways, to inform the governor or judge of any brawls breaking out in the dormitories, and, finally, to keep constant watch to ensure that prisoners sentenced to death or to the galleys remained "handcuffed in the cells".[33] Together with these instructions of a general nature regarding prison surveillance, there were also *Instructions* for running the infirmary: the doctor was ordered to visit the prison twice a day to respond to any immediate need to hospitalize the sick; the "spezieria", or apothecary's store, was to be kept under constant watch to ensure that all the necessary medicines were there, while convalescents were to be kept in the infirmary until completely cured to prevent relapse or further contagion. Then there were the instructions for the penitentiary annexed to the Vicaria Prison and reserved for convicted women. The provisions concerned the "necessary mortifications" to be applied to reform the women: haircut, woollen clothes, silence, and obedience.

Observance of these provisions, as in the case of the others mentioned above, came under the control of the Grand Court of the Vicaria. Particularly interesting, too, are the *Instructions* regarding selection of the jailers, who were to be chosen among the "respectable" persons approved of by the *Fiscale* (Treasury) and not under investigation by the Grand Court; the selection was to entail no charge, but obviously there was a gulf between rule and actual practice, abuse and corruption still characterizing the procedure. Within a short period, the Grand Court sent out two orders, the first on 7 June 1626, calling for daily inspections of all the rooms and the prisoners to curb the use of arms made by the latter and to prevent outsiders from loitering or spending the night on the premises. Soon after, on 29 March 1627, a new order was issued to put a stop to prison escapes, determining that, should the order be disregarded, the conniving prison staff themselves would immediately be imprisoned. Evidently, the Grand Court resolved that conniving jailers would not only be removed from office but also be subjected to further actions at the Court's own discretion.[34]

A great many *Prammatiche* were brought in during this period, and notably four were issued between 1645 and 1687, while *Prammatica* XIX brought together all the previous *Prammatiche* from 1577 onward in a general overview – provisions that had never actually worked in effectively addressing the challenging situation in the Kingdom's prison.[35] There is yet another interesting source to draw upon for the purpose of reconstructing conditions in Naples' Vicaria Prison, namely a report – now conserved in the State Archive of Naples – dated 23 October 1737, which was sent by the King from the Royal Chamber of Santa Chiara. Although it is of a rather later date, the text contains information of considerable relevance to our period, actually covering a span of about two hundred years.[36] While dealing mainly with the functioning of the tribunal and, in particular, of the Vicaria Grand Court, the report also tells us something about the origin of the inspections of the prisoners and the reasons why they were introduced, which were mainly to do with the abuses perpetrated in the prisons, not only the Vicaria, and more or less "tolerated" by the government. The report spelt out the various expedients that could be adopted to put an end to this state of affairs. The aim of the inspections, started in 1540 by Charles V, was to ascertain the conditions of the convicts and ensure that punishment was meted out with the utmost seriousness, but without, as the author of the report wrote, the prisoners being "unduly mistreated".

For this function a *Prammatica* was proclaimed, namely *De visitatione, seu recentione captivorum*, assigning a Regent of the Chancellery and a Counsellor of Santa Chiara to carry out the prison inspections. These orders were reiterated by Philip II in 1567 with a Royal Order (Real Cedola) inserted in the *Prammatica De Officio Magistri Iustitiarii*, establishing additionally that thrice yearly a general inspection was to be made of all the prisoners to ascertain the reasons for their incarceration and verify whether the sentences were just. In 1624 Philip III, having been informed of the conditions of the prisoners by the inspector Don Francesco Antonio Alarcon, determined that the inspections should be carried out by only one of the regents and empowered them to pass sentence to the galleys[37] and send the prisoners there; they were also empowered to proceed to a settlement, should the conditions exist, even before the court had concluded deliberation. These measures should have reduced expenditure for the treasury,[38] but, although the provisions for prison inspection were clearly of great utility, the writer reported that in the course of time observance fell off while the regents would, against payment, commute the sentences, releasing prisoners or lifting the death sentence, thereby playing their part in the abuse that was so rife in prison.[39]

What emerges from this picture is not only a thoroughly corrupt prison system but also the fact that it fitted in perfectly with an equally corrupt judiciary system. The post of jailer was much sought after because it was seen as particularly profitable. Despite a steady stream of legislation on the functioning of the Kingdom's prisons, there was no remission in the abuses perpetrated at the expense of the prisoners, who not only had to pay for their sojourn in prison but were also obliged to hand over sums of money to the "old-timers", as we have seen; a special *Prammatica* had been issued to address this problem, but it was regularly disregarded.

Ample evidence of the abuse that prisoners endured emerged from the prisoners' accounts and appeals, but the government, aware as it was of the circumstances, failed to arrive at the appropriate measures to curb these criminal practices.

The series of *Prammatiche* issued between the mid 16th century and the end of the 17th century served only to harshen the sentences, without tackling the problem of the prison as a whole – without any analysis of the circumstances and factors that led to such corruption – thus having no real effect on the existing criminal system.

Actually, scant importance was attached to the prison issue because it constituted a sort of self-enclosed system where a rationale based on corruption created a circuit to the advantage of a fortunate few who were by no means inclined to relinquish the power that they had gained.[40]

Notes

1. On Castel Capuano and its history, cfr. Petroni, G., *Del Gran Palazzo di Giustizia a Castel Capuano in Napoli,* Naples: Stamperia e Cartiere del Fibreno, 1861; Garrucci, G., *Il Castel Capuano e le sue storiche vicende invertito poi dal 1540 a sede de' Tribunali,* Naples: Stamperia della R. Università, 1871; Capasso, B., *La Vicaria vecchia, pagine di storia napolitana, studiata nelle sue vie e nei suoi monumenti,* in Archivio Storico per le Provincie Napoletane, XV (1890), pp. 632–635; Lernia, L. and V. Barrella, *Castel Capuano. Memoria storica di un monumento da fortilizio a Tribunale,* Naples: Edizioni Scientifiche Italiane, 1993; Mangone, F., ed., *Castel Capuano da Reggia a Tribunale. Architettura e arte nei luoghi della giustizia,* Naples: Massa Editore, 2011.
2. On the Court of the Vicaria, cfr. Pescione, R., *Le Corti di giustizia nell'Italia meridionale,* Milan-Rome-Naples: Società editrice Dante Alighieri, 1924, in particular, pp. 77 ff. A number of provisions entitled *De Carceris* were issued between 1540 and 1577 with the aim of curbing the abuses, violence and bullying perpetrated in the Kingdom's prisons; cfr. Giustiniani, L., *Nuova collezione delle Prammatiche del Regno di Napoli,* Naples: nella Stamperia Simoniana, 1804, pp. 141–143.
3. Celano, C., *Notizie del bello dell'antico e del curioso della città di Napoli,* ed. Chiarini, G.B., Naples: Stamperia Floriana, 1856, vol. II, tome I, p. 376; Giannone, P., *Istoria civile del Regno di Napoli,* V, Naples: Lombardi, repr. 1865, p. 496: "He also had a prison built in the cellars under the castle and had all the prisoners that had been in the old Vicaria brought there in their hundreds, and all those that were incarcerated in the various prisons. He ordered that in this palace should be accommodated the president of the Supreme Court (Sacro Consiglio), and the officer in charge of the Sommaria, and the Regent of the Vicaria with a judge of criminal cases. This amalgamation proved

immensely convenient for the tradesmen, who had formerly had to go all over the city for the various offices but now, with all of them concentrated in that castle, were able to expedite their business with great facility. And this was not the only advantage, since the neighbourhood had hitherto been virtually uninhabited but now became much frequented and populated". On the prison of the Vicaria in the 17th century, cfr. Scaduto, M., *Le carceri della Vicaria di Napoli agli inizi del Seicento*, in *Redenzione umana*, VI, n. 4, October 1968, p. 393 ff.

4. The printed *Report* is conserved in the Library of the Società Napoletana di Storia Patria (henceforth SNSP), Banco Nap. 01. D. 29, p. 3. The writer of this text evidently emphasized certain aspects, mixing description of the actual facts and functioning of the places with the Jesuits' pastoral mission to change them. Indeed, Aurelio Lepre argues that the *Report* is not entirely credible, permeated as it is with religious sentiments. At the same time, however, our knowledge of these places is, in fact, very limited, and the report contains useful evidence to piece together the picture. It was also extensively quoted by Scaduto in his text on the Vicaria prison, although he drew on the manuscript source, thanks to which we can identify the dedicatee, namely the Jesuit General Muzio Vitelleschi: cfr. Scaduto, M., 1968, *passim*. Reference to the *Report* can also be found in Lepre, A., *Storia del Mezzogiorno d'Italia. vol 1. La lunga durata e la crisi (1500–1656)*, Naples: Liguori editore, 1986, p. 135. On the Society of Jesus, cfr. Santagata, S., *Istoria della Compagnia di Gesù appartenente al Regno di Napoli*, Naples: nella Stamperia di Vincenzo Mazzola, MDCCLVII, parts III and IV.
5. SNSP, *Relazione sullo stato delle carceri*, cit. p. 4.
6. *Ibid.*, p. 3.
7. *Ibid.*, p. 8.
8. *Ibid.*, p. 8.
9. M. Scaduto, M., 1968, p. 394.
10. *Relazione sullo stato delle carceri*, cit. p. 7. In relation to the bed renting procedures, the *Report* mentions various *Notices for the prisoners who can rent beds*, in which the terms were set for payment. In charge of payment in 1611 was the preceptor of the Vicaria, while the rate per bed could not exceed three grana (pp. 143–144); with the *Proclamation* of 27 March 1619, payments were to be made to the *Company of bed renters*; on this point, cf p. 194. A *Proclamation* of October 1629 made provision that the price of a bed could not exceed three grana and that the credit accorded a prisoner could not extend beyond three nights; for anyone who favoured prisoners by extending credit beyond that period, the punishment was to be fifteen days in prison; cfr. p. 196 of the *Report*.
11. *Ibid.*, p. 8. The *Report* cites the Order of the Grand Court of the Vicaria, dated 12 July 1613, prohibiting dice games and indeed any other game on the prison premises. This prohibition applied to the area in front of the chapel in the prison courtyard. *Ibid.*, p. 60.
12. *Ibid.*, p. 14
13. *Ibid.*, p. 5.
14. The first congregation of the poor was named after the Madonna del Carmine, while that of the nobles bore the name of Congrega dell'Annunziata. Cfr. Vitale, G., *Ricerche sulla vita religiosa e caritativa a Napoli tra Medio Evo e Età Moderna*, in the Historical Archive for the provinces of Naples, V. VII–VIII, (1968–1969) p. 210 ff.

15. *Relazione sullo stato delle carceri*, cit. p. 23.
16. In particular, money was collected by the Knights of the Monte di Pietà, and the Congregations of Santa Maria degli Angeli and of the Santissima Annunziata, as well as the monks of San Martino and the nuns of San Marcellino. The *Relazione sullo stato delle carceri* cites an order of the Ministers of the Court requiring the jailers to distribute the alms amongst the prisoners fairly, proceeding with a rollcall in accordance with the wishes of the benefactors themselves.
17. In July 1621 the Counsellor Caravita and Judge Urries sent Cardinal Zapata a *Report* on the conditions in the Vicaria Prison subsequent to intervention by the Fathers of the Society of Jesus. The document, ordered by Zapata, reports that the presence of the Fathers had led to a number of improvements and that their good works proved of great importance for the control, both spiritual and material, of these places; cfr. *Relazione fatta al Cardinal Zapata dal Consigliere Caravita e dal Giudice Urries delle opere introdotte nelle carceri dai Padri della Compagni di Gesù*, in *Relazione sullo stato delle carceri*, cit. pp. 33–34.
18. On this point, cfr. Musi, A., *Mezzogiorno spagnolo. La via napoletana allo Stato modern*, Naples: Guida Editori, 1991, pp. 174–175 and the bibliography therein contained.
19. Galiani, F., *Della Moneta*, Lib. V, pp. 409–410, Naples: Raimondi, MDCCL. "Doctor Antonio Serra, from Cosenza, in 1613, had Lazzaro Scoriggio publish a *Brief Treatise*... divided into three parts. Whoever reads this treatise will observe with surprise and admiration how clear and correct, in a century of total ignorance of economic science, were the ideas of the author on the subject, upon which he wrote, and how seriously evaluated the causes of our ills and the only effective remedies".
20. Lazzaro Scoriggio was one of the most important printers working in the Kingdom of Naples; some years after the publication of Serra's text, Scoriggio was accused of having published in 1615 the *Letter by the Reverend Carmelite Father Maestro Paolo Antonio Foscarino on the opinion of the Pythagoreans and of Copernicus on the mobility of the Earth and the fixedness of the Sun, and the new Pythagorean System of the World*, without having obtained the approval of the Archiepiscopal Court. After a brief period on the run, the printer was imprisoned. In his defence, he stated that he had been deceived by the author of the *Letter*, declaring that the manuscript had the approval of the Archiepiscopal Court. The matter was settled with the printer being fined the sum of one hundred ducats in favour of the Archiepiscopal Court, but he was able to avoid the actual payment thanks to the intervention of some religious authorities whose protection he sought. About a year later, the text by the Carmelite Father was banned by the Sacred Congregation of the Roman Inquisition; on this point, cfr. *Relazione delle stamperie e stampatori e proibizione de'libri per causa di giurisdizione. Con nota di Scipione Volpicella*, in the Historical Archive for the Provinces of Naples, Third Year, Fascicle I, Naples: 1878, pp. 202–205.
21. Salfi, F.S., *Elogio di Antonio Serra. Primo scrittore di Economia civile*, Milan: Presso Nobile e Tosi libraio-stampatore, 1802.
22. Boccanera da Macerata, G., *Antonio Serra*, in *Biografia degli uomini illustri del Regno di Napoli. Ornata dei loro rispettivi ritratti. Compilata da diversi letterati*

nazionali. Dedicata a S. E. il Marchese Donato Tommasi, Segretario di Stato Ministro della Giustizia del Culto e dell'Interno, vol. III, Naples: Nicola Gervasi, 1816, pp. 187–190.

23. Amabile, L., *Fra Tommaso Campanella. La sua congiura, i suoi processi e la sua pazzia*, Naples: Antonio Morano, 1882. In particolare vol. III, pp. 648–649.
24. On the *galea* sentence, cfr., Alessi Palazzolo, G., Pene e "remieri" a Napoli tra Cinque e Seicento. Un aspetto singolare dell'illegalismo d'ancien regime, in the *Historical Archive for the Provinces of Naples*, 1977.
25. Giustiniani, L., *Nuova collezione delle Prammatiche del Regno di Napoli*, Naples: nella Stamperia Simoniana, 1804, Tome VII, pp. 258–263.
26. Cfr. Croce, B., *Storia del Regno di Napoli*, Bari: Laterza, 1931, pp. 155–159.
27. Researches on Serra are still in progress, and we can as yet go no further than tentative hypotheses.
28. *Per il buon governo delle carceri, infermeria e casa della Penitenza e Congregazione della Santissima Trinità*, Biblioteca Nazionale di Napoli (National Library of Naples), (henceforth BNN) ms. XV. C. 41.: *"Istruzioni per il buon governo delle Carceri Infermeria e casa di Penitenza fatte dal Card. Zappata consigliere del Duca d'Aula; Biglietto del cardinal Zapata al Giudice Urries per promuovere la Congregazione degli Scrivani della Vicaria; 1621 Decreto della Vicaria per eseguire le ordinanze di S. E. perché nell'infermeria si diano due Cappellani; Biglietto del Card Zapata per l' Infermeria, la Congregazione degli scrivani, e per la Cappella del Cortile del Carcere; 1623 Istruzioni fatte dalla Vicaria per i due Cappellani dell' Infermeria; 1623 Decreto della Vicaria per l' elezione dei Cappellani dell' Infermeria e loro salario; Biglietto del Duca d'Aula al Marchese de Manzera per l' applicazione delle pene alle donne libere che vanno in carrozza o in sedia all'Infermeria; Biglietto del Duca d'Aula al Marchese de Manzera perché li Ministri del Tributo e gli scrivani visitino l'Infermeria; 1627 Ordine della Vicaria per quello hanno d'osservare li mastri d'atti e scrivani fiscali per la visita dell'Infermeria; 1627 Istruzioni per detta visita; 1626 Ordine della Vicaria per la visita delle Carceri al Carceriere Maggiore; 1627 Ordine della Vicaria per le donne inferme della Casa de la Penitenza; 1627 Ordine della Vicaria Circa il Serrare le Camere de Carcerati; 1627 Ordine de la Vicaria per l' ingresso delle donne libere nelle Carceri e che no vengano inviati figli, ne vi pernotti chi non è Carcerato; Inventario delle Robe della Infermeria; Opere pie le quali s'esercitano dentro la Vicaria; 1629 Decreto per l'elezione di I portinaio de la Casa de la Penitenza"*.
29. BNN, ms. XV. C. 41., *Applicazione dell'alaggio del pane, e altre elemosine per sussidio dei carcerati*, f. 11.
30. This text describes the situation in the prison during the night, and it contains the order of the Grand Court of the Vicaria to proceed with nightly surveillance of the premises in order to curb the disorders arising over gambling and prostitution; the document is dated 29 May 1627; a similar order had been issued about a month before, requiring the head jailer to ascertain whether any persons other than the prisoners spent the night there.
31. BNN, ms. XV. C. 41., *Ordine del Carceriere Maggiore presente e futuro da parte de la Gran Corte della Vicaria circa quello che s'ha d'osservare per la buona custodia della carcere. Dato ne. N.R.O. Palazzo della Vicaria die 7 Dmbr. (dicembre) 1628.*
32. BNN, ms. XV. C. 41., *Istruzioni per il buon governo delle Carceri Infermeria e casa della Penitenzia fatte dal Card. Zapata controfirmate dal Duca d'Aula.*
33. *Ibid.*

34. BNN, ms. XV. C. 41., *Ordine della Vic. A per la Visita delle Carceri al Car.ro Magg.re.*
35. Cfr. Giustiniani, L., *Nuova collezione delle Prammatiche del Regno di Napoli*, Naples: nella Stamperia Simoniana, 1804, Tome III, pp. 148, 150, 156, 157, in particular Sanctions XV of 1645, XVI of 1657, XVIII of 1680 and XIX of 1687.
36. Archivio di Stato di Napoli (State Archive of Naples; henceforth ASN), *Camera di Santa Chiara, Bozze di Consulta*, V.17, inv. 55. As from 1738 intervention by the Bourbon Crown led to prohibition of the practice of torture and of the underground pits for isolation of the prisoners; there followed a succession of measures in accordance with the changes introduced in the judiciary facilities following the trend to modernize the juridical systems. The pursuit of modernization in the Kingdom entailed a sharp reduction in the ecclesiastical privileges which had burgeoned there. The expulsion of the Society of Jesus in 1767, so dearly sought after by Bernardo Tanucci, and consequent confiscation of the order's property, constituted a great leap forward in the secularization of the Kingdom, in line with the ideas proclaimed by the exponents of Southern Italian and European illuminism; in this connection, see the important studies by Ajello, R., *Il problema della riforma giudiziaria e legislativa nel Regno di Napoli durante la prima metà del secolo XVIII*, Naples: Jovene, 1961, *passim*, ID. *La vita politica napoletana sotto Carlo di Borbone: la fondazione e il 'tempo eroico'*, in Storia di Napoli vol. 7, Naples: Cava de Tirreni 1972, pp. 461–717.
37. Alessi Palazzolo, 1977, *passim*.
38. Bianchini, L., *Della Storia delle finanze del Regno di Napoli*, vol. I, Palermo: Lao, 1839, p. 240; "the conditions reigning in the Kingdom's prisons were always bleak. In the city of Naples the prisons were located mainly in places belonging to private estates, and the jailers paid rent to the private owners; to bear this cost they demanded payment of a certain sum by the prisoners… [I]t is to be noted that the food supplied to the prisoners in 1601 was calculated at the rate of about four *grana* a day".
39. Coniglio, G., *Visitatori del Viceregno di Napoli*, Bari, Tipografia del Sud, 1974, *passim*.
40. On this point, cfr. Volpicella, F., 'Delle prigioni', in *Annali civili del Regno delle due Sicilie*, marzo-aprile 1833, pp. 114–121.

3

The Cost of Empires: Antonio Serra and the Debate on the Causes and Solutions of Economic Crises in the Viceroyalty of Naples in the 17th Century

Giovanni Zanalda

1 Introduction

Between the 1580s and the middle of the 17th century, the Kingdom of Naples – then a Viceroyalty part of the so-called Spanish Habsburg empire – went through a series of economic crises whose causes and management became the subject of lively debates among Neapolitan and Spanish administrators, merchants, foreign bankers, and observers of political and economic events. This Italian kingdom had a central role in the organization of the Spanish economic and political power having contributed with capital and in kind to the consolidation of the Habsburgs' hold on large part of Europe and expansion in the New World.

The management of the crises brought to the forefront some of the existing tensions between domestic – that is, Neapolitan – and Spanish interests, a reflection of contemporary and future problems experienced by Spanish rulers and administrators of such a vast and "composite" empire. On the basis of Antonio Serra's *Breve trattato* (ca. 1613), contemporary treatises, and policy memos, this paper discusses some of the most salient aspects of this debate, in particular those related to the discussion about the "monetary" and "real" origin of crises and their influence on the policymaking process. The policy implications of this dichotomy were evident then, as now, contributing to the emergence of analyses that, by focusing on a country's economic structure and position in the international economy, seek to reduce the exposure to crises and promote long-term growth.

After a brief overview of the state of the Kingdom's economy at the beginning of the 17th century, the first section presents the main terms of the debate on *cambi*, foreign exchange, with a particular focus on the work of Marc'Antonio de Santis and his opponents. This debate reveals what contemporary experts understood about linkages between domestic and international economy and reveals how in turn they influenced the adoption by the Spanish representatives of specific measures aimed to tackle economic crises – from monetary reforms to the establishment of new credit institutions. The second section discusses Antonio Serra's contribution which in contrast to the mainstream "monetarist" interpretation of the time identified "real" factors – from an absence of manufacturing and entrepreneurial spirit to a lack of good governance – as the primary causes of the Kingdom's economic problems. The analysis of Serra's contribution, as I shall suggest at the end of this section, might offer some insights to questions about determinants of economic growth and development which were relevant in early modern Europe as much as in modern debates about development policy.

* * *

Over the course of the 16th century, the population of the Kingdom of Naples had grown to the extent that at the beginning of the 17th century the capital, Naples, with a population of 300,000, had become, along with Paris and London, one of the largest cities in Europe.[1] Population expansion meant an increase in the consumption of commodities such as wheat, wine, and oil that traditionally had constituted, with silk, the largest share of Neapolitan exports. Increased consumption combined with a decline in manufacturing activities during the same period translated into a decrease in exports, an increase in imports, a worsening of the balance of payment position, and therefore a net outflow of specie. The primary role that agriculture played in the Kingdom also meant that bad harvests, such as those occurring in 1593, 1595, 1598, and 1607, tended to weigh heavily on Neapolitan finances given the reduction in export revenues and increase in payments for the import of wheat and other commodities. The existence of a large public debt exacerbated the already precarious financial situation of the Kingdom, in particular since the largest share of debt service was paid to Genoese bankers. All the attempts to reduce the outflow of precious metals for debt service and to inject liquidity in a kingdom constantly plagued by shortages of money failed. The most famous of these occurred in 1594 when the Neapolitan banker Antonio Belmosto, under the auspices of the Spanish viceroy, managed to import large quantities of silver from Spain in exchange for the concession of exclusive banking rights. The large injection of liquidity, more than a million silver *ècu* over a two-year period, failed to achieve its original goal and only contributed to a rapid increase in both prices and exchange rate.[2]

Decrees and treatises from the first decades of the 17th century reflect the precariousness of the Neapolitan economic position. The level of debt and monetary issues relating to the shortage of money and the level of the exchange rate in particular occupied a central role in these analyses, and influenced the Spanish viceroys The Counts of Benavente (1603–1610) and Lemos (1610–1616) in their efforts to rein in the Kingdom's financial disarray and secure sufficient revenues to be transferred to Spain. Ambitious reforms like the 1609's call for a complete overhaul of the monetary system did not succeed. Furthermore, a series of debasements contributed to a drastic decline in the quality and quantity of the Neapolitan coinage, which resulted in a devaluation of 30% over the course of the 1610s.[3] This state of affairs was well summarized by an officer of the mint, Giovanni Donato Turbolo, who reported that of the thirteen million ducats minted in Naples during the period 1599–1629, only three million were still in circulation in the late 1620s.

Another important feature of the Neapolitan economy at the turn of the century, which had far-reaching implications for the financial world, was the demise of foreign banks and the simultaneous rise of domestic public banks – a reversal of fortune that raised a great deal of interest among administrators, bankers, and chroniclers of the time. Between 1584 and 1600, seven Neapolitan *Monti di Pietà* obtained the official patent of "public bank". The ascendancy of these local banks signalled the rise of a local bourgeoisie that had finally obtained the tools to sever the Genoese bankers' almost complete control of the Kingdom's finances. In the course of the first two decades of the 16th century, the *Monti di Pietà*, through the use of fiduciary money, discounting, and supporting the circulation of low quality coins clipped or lightened of their metal contents, contributed to a *de facto* injection of liquidity and credit expansion.[4]

However, these new "public banks" had not the same success in dealing with transactions that involved *cambi*, an area in which Genoese bankers held an international monopoly. Debates about the causes and consequences of the *cambio alto*, high exchange, reflected the different position and influence of local and foreign bankers. The Neapolitan Antonio de Santis, for instance, held foreign merchant bankers responsible for the chronic *cambio alto* – in particular the Genoese, who – by controlling the international fairs of Piacenza, where the largest share of international operations involving exchange rates were settled – exercised an almost complete control over the European market of these credit instruments. On the other hand, there were those like a Genoese merchant banker who argued that it was the shrewd management of Neapolitan "public banks" that determined a high exchange, high interest rates, and capital (silver and gold) flight. On the basis of a thorough analysis of exchange rate movements in the Kingdom of Naples in the 17th century, Luigi De Rosa has demonstrated that a high level of exchange – that is, a decline in the value of the Neapolitan currency – operated as an incentive to Neapolitan exports and in turn contributed to an improvement in the balance of trade. According to De Rosa, a cyclical pattern emerged: periods of a high exchange corresponding to economic expansion alternated with periods of a low exchange characterized by a contraction of economic activity.[5] The degree of the exchange-rate increase determined the extent of the increase in trading activity and therefore the extent of economic expansion. Likewise, a decline in the exchange rate brought economic depression. However, seasonal fluctuations in agriculture output and monetary speculation could quickly reverse a cycle. For instance, in the first two decades of the 17th century, a high level of exchange seemed to correspond to a worsening in the balance of payments.[6]

In Italy, *cambio* had been at the centre of a vast literature of how-to books published in the most famous Italian city-states – Genoa, Venice, and Florence – as well as a subject widely debated among theologians for more than a century before the Neapolitan debate. In general, the how-to books focused on technical aspects of the profession of *cambista* and made no attempt to explain the role of exchange in relation to trade and economic conditions. The Florentine merchant and translator of Tacitus, Bernardo Davanzati, who in the short tract *Notizia de' Cambj* (1588) provided a historical overview of the instrument of foreign exchange, *cambio*, as well as an analysis of its different roles, represented an exception. *Cambio*, according to Davanzati, should be considered one of the most revolutionary credit instruments of the early-modern period, a crucial tool for supporting commerce but also a financial instrument in its own right.[7] It was precisely this dual nature that explained how foreign exchange became the subject of lively debate in Naples in the first decade of the 17th century, the subject of the next section.[8]

* * *

Marc'Antonio de Santis was a well-known merchant banker from Naples who specialized in the brokerage of oil and wheat and the import of goods from Venice as well as an expert in exchange arbitrage with an extended network of correspondents in other Italian cities. De Santis was also an adviser of the Collaterale, the institution in charge of the economic administration of the Kingdom of Naples under Spanish supervision. In 1605 he published a treatise titled *Discorso di Marc'Antonio de Santis intorno all'effetto che fa in regni il cambio* in response to a question raised by the president of the Royal Sacred Committee about how it was possible that the Kingdom of Naples, "perhaps the wealthiest in the world", could experience a shortage of money. In the same year, de Santis published a second treatise, *Secondo Discorso di Marc'Antonio de Santis intorno all'effetto che fa in regni il cambio, sopra una risposta, che è stata fatta adverso del primo*, to respond to criticism stirred by the first one.[9]

For de Santis, the level of exchange in Naples, in relation to other Italian states, explained the contemporary "lack of cash inflow and excessive cash outflow". The high level of the exchange rate (i.e. an undervaluation of Naples currency vis-à-vis foreign coins) caused, according to de Santis, foreigners to pay with bills of exchange rather than with cash for commodities from Naples. On the other hand, exporters to Naples wanted to be paid in cash. Furthermore, the high level of profit derived from conducting arbitrage operations with Neapolitan money in *piazza*, markets, outside the Kingdom contributed to an increase in the outflow of coins, "because of the high profit that can be made by carrying cash from the kingdom to Rome or other places in Italy and sending it back via bills of exchange".[10]

In the *Prammatica* of 1607 (a decree), the Spanish viceroy, Count of Benavente, followed some of de Santis's advice that all transactions involving foreign exchange should be settled at a lower exchange rate. De Santis believed that an aggressive reduction of the exchange rate, a *de facto* revaluation of Neapolitan currency, would solve the monetary problems of the Kingdom. He resolutely dismissed objections that a revaluation of Neapolitan currency would hurt trade. For de Santis, the Kingdom's export commodities – essentially "silk, oil, many wines, saffron, wheat, wool, livestock and many other items" – were so vital to the "life and well being" of people in "all other Italian cities", that increases in their prices would not deter foreign demand. He believed that all other nations would "conform to the orders of this Kingdom" since the "whole World needs the Kingdom, and the Kingdom needs no one".[11] According to balance of payment figures included in the *Discorsi*, the Kingdom enjoyed a trade surplus of almost five million *écu*, calculated as follows: the income transferred to foreigners amounted to "600,000 ducats per year", and the "total cost of imports [amounted] to about the same" for a total of 1,200,000. Since the total amount of exports amounted to 6,000,000 ducats, the Kingdom enjoyed a surplus of almost 5,000,000, enough to demonstrate, according to de Santis, that "shortage of money was not caused" by a trade deficit but rather by "the high price of the exchange".[12]

But what was a "high price of exchange" for de Santis? The silver *carlino* was the unit of account of the Neapolitan monetary system. The official rate was the exchange rate between the silver *carlino* and the golden *écu* of Piacenza, called *scudo di marco*, the international benchmark. A high exchange rate meant that more silver *carlini* were needed to buy one golden *écu* of Piacenza. Since the *écu* of Piacenza was worth thirteen carlini, or 130 grains of silver, at the beginning of the 17th century, an exchange above the official rate was considered a high exchange. Therefore, a low exchange was an incentive to export cash to the Kingdom, given the difference between the official rate (130 grains) and the market rate (anything below 130). A high exchange had the opposite effect: Neapolitan exports would be paid for with bills of exchange rather than with cash.

De Santis identified two "true causes" of the high level of exchange rate in Naples. The first was "Antonio Belmosto's injection of one and one-half million ducats, cash,...and this was a direct cause because a large amount of cash tends to increase the exchange". The other was the Spanish decree of suspension of debt repayment, and this "was an indirect cause because it helped, indirectly, to maintain a high exchange rate".[13] The second explanation is of particular interest; it points to the international transmission of financial crises, in this case the impact of the King of Spain's default on the rest of Europe, an example of what is now called contagion. De Santis explained that the 1597 Spanish decree, a *de facto* default on Spanish debt, had two contrasting effects on the Neapolitan exchange rate. It directly lowered exchange rates all over Europe, since Spain's main creditors, the Genoese bankers, in turn suspended all payments at the first Piacenza Fair after the 1597 decree. This created a shortage of coins throughout Europe and thereby lowered the exchange rate. As a result, Genoese businessmen in a desperate need of cash at the incoming international Piacenza Fair rushed to transfer "at any price" money from Naples to the fair. The combination of these two forces determined instability in the exchange rate that lasted until "the readjustment of Spanish affairs".[14]

However, the normalization of Spanish affairs did not take place, so, as de Santis expected, the lowering of the Neapolitan exchange rate never occurred. De Santis had no difficulty in finding the culprit for this missed realignment in a coalition of two powerful groups, namely Genoese businessmen and Neapolitan exporters. The businessmen, de Santis pointed out, "stopped reinvesting their profits in new activities in the Kingdom, not, as they say, because the government had stopped offering opportunities [to invest in securities or estates] but because they had no interest in investing in the Kingdom". The exporters of commodities from the Kingdom continued to support, "for their own benefits, a high exchange rate" and did so "with *violentia*", since "where there is a shortage of money, as in the Kingdom, the exchange should be naturally low".[15] *Violentia*, in the Latin sense of action against nature, meant the coercive power exercised by traders in fixing exchange rates at their convenience. With these remarks, de Santis intended to cast a sinister light on the practices of traders who by manipulating exchange rates could determine shortages of silver, gold, and coins in any state.

De Santis argued that both the public and the government would benefit from the implementation of the decree containing his suggestions: the public at large would benefit from a reduction in the price of imports (mainly apparel), while the King "would greatly benefit from an increase in the activity of the customs, since more commodities would flow to the Kingdom". In addition, a low exchange rate would attract cash from abroad, solving the shortage of money problem, because foreigners would perceive the Neapolitan securities as less risky and more trustworthy, "schiveranno il rischio della fede".[16] Even though the 1607's *Prammatica* plan failed in few months, de Santis maintained his relationship to the Spanish viceroy, as signalled by his official appointment in 1610 to represent Naples in an international committee on finance, a task force encompassing deputies from other states under Spanish rule or influence. In addition to de Santis, there were two from Genoa, one from Florence, one from Milan, and one from Flanders.[17]

An anonymous Genoese author, most likely a banker, attacked de Santis's 1605 *Discorso* in a short pamphlet published in the same year.[18] First, the author rejected the idea that a group of bankers could manipulate with *violentia* the level of the exchange of an entire nation. He considered the exchange to be the result of "voluntary action" between two persons who by necessity reach an agreement. If as supported by de Santis the government would fix the value of the exchange by decree and place a ban on the export of coins, a "decline of exchange trade activities" would follow.[19] The author used the failure of a *Prammatica* issued in 1597 by the previous viceroy, the Count of Olivares, to support his argument. In it Olivares had fixed the exchange between Naples and the *écu* of Piacenza (the international fair benchmark) at 126 and prescribed severe penalties for transgressors. The measure failed because traders considered the official exchange rate at 126 completely out of line with the real market rate (which was 130) and, fearing punishment, decided to stop dealing with *cambi* in Naples. The market rate subsequently shot up to 145. For the anonymous Genoese, this episode signalled the clear failure of "an action against freedom", while, for de Santis, it revealed the existence of a powerful lobby of international traders who tried to maintain tight control over international operations by curtailing all attempts to reign in their business.[20]

The anonymous author also disagreed with de Santis's proposed ban on the export of coins, stating that a ban would never work since the geographical configuration of the Kingdom, with "long borders surrounded by sea", made smuggling very easy. Moreover, he explained, forced actions on monetary matters never work and actually would increase the outflow of gold and silver. He noted that when the viceroy obliged some traders to introduce coins in the Kingdom, these "same coins immediately were exported" or hoarded, a clear reference to Antonio Belmosto's failed attempt to increase the supply of coins. Instead, the author supported a complete overhaul of the monetary system through the withdrawal of all coins and the minting of a new coinage. His rationale was that nobody likes to hold poor quality coinage (*moneta trista*) as the one circulating in the Kingdom of Naples. New coins would restore credibility in the Neapolitan currency, and this together with the liberalization of monetary movements would give the Kingdom plenty of gold and silver.[21] In 1609 the viceroy, Count of Benavente, embraced the anonymous Genoese author's suggestion in a new *Prammatica*, in practice reversing his *Prammatica* of 1607 (the one containing de Santis's suggestion) and ruling in favour of a general overhaul of the monetary system. The paramount cost of this entire operation, which included the withdrawal of all coins, the minting of new ones, and the circulation of good coins at their nominal value and of bad coins according to their weight, determined its failure. Indeed, both *Prammatiche* were recalled by the new viceroy, Count of Lemos, in

1610.[22] And it was this viceroy whom Antonio Serra addressed from the prison of Vicaria, opening a new front in the by then "old" debate on foreign exchange and shortage of money.

* * *

In a note to the second edition of *Della Moneta*, the 18th-century political economist Ferdinando Galiani extolled Antonio Serra as

> the first and oldest author in the science of political economy...This man, whom I dare to compare to Melun for the French and to Locke for the English, is superior to them both for having lived so long before them in a century of darkness and ignorance about the science of economics; this man, of such shrewd intellect, such wise judgment, was disgraced when alive and has remained, together with his treatise, completely forgotten after his death... Worse than that: Serra dedicated his treatise to the Count of Lemos (the Viceroy), and he wrote it from the prison of Vicaria. It is no wonder that monetary affairs were in complete disarray, as one Antonio Serra languished in prison and one Marcantonio de Santis was loaded with riches and was the oracle of the Collaterale!... Certain it is that none of Serra's suggestions was followed, and this confirms the truth of one of our popular proverbs, which affirms that there are three things not esteemed in this world: "the strength of a coarse man, the beauty of a prostitute, and the advice of an ignoble man."[23]

In a few sentences and with characteristic sarcasm, Ferdinando Galiani saved Serra and his treatise from obscurity. Little is known about Antonio Serra (fl. 1613) except that he was a "dottore" from Cosenza in Calabria, a region in the Kingdom of Naples,[24] confined to the prison of Vicaria in Naples in 1613 at the time of the publication of his only surviving written work, the *Breve trattato delle cause che possono far abbondare li regni d'oro e d'argento dove non sono miniere con applicazione al Regno di Napoli*.[25] According to 19th-century historiography, Serra was in jail either under an accusation of conspiracy, with Tommaso Campanella, against the Spanish government in the failed revolt of Calabria during the last decade of the 16th century, or under indictment for counterfeiting.[26] Serra was still in prison in 1617 when, according to a contemporary document, he begged the new viceroy, Duke of Ossuma, for a meeting so that he could present his ideas about how to improve the finances of the Kingdom of Naples. The author of this document, perhaps an officer of the viceroy's Chamber, tersely reported that on "Wednesday 6th of May

1617, a doctor, Antonio Serra, jailed in Vicaria for a long time, pleaded to be received by His Excellency for the good of the court". At the palace before the Chamber, having impressed the duke minimally, "with talk and nothing more than talk, he was sent back to prison".[27]

Galiani's comparison of the different fortunes of Serra and de Santis was not casual. Serra wrote his *Breve trattato* in response to de Santis's treatises on money shortages and the exchange rate, attacking not only the remedies contained in those two works but, more importantly, de Santis's assumptions about the origin of the economic malaise in the Kingdom of Naples. With his treatise, Serra also wanted to influence the debate on economic and institutional reforms ignited by the implementation of the new *Prammatica* in 1612. The latter, prepared and introduced by the new viceroy, Count of Lemos (1610–1616), represented the first attempt to sustain a complete overhaul of the cumbersome fiscal and administrative system of the Kingdom under Spanish rule. Starting with a change in obsolete accounting practices, the viceroy was determined to streamline the government budget and reduce expenses. Once he determined that the current revenues of the Kingdom amounted to almost two million ducats, Lemos established a military treasury, *Cassa Militare*, with oversight of the army, the police, public works, and the salaries of the viceroy and the viceroy's dependents; it existed next to the traditional treasury that oversaw public servants. The Military Treasury became the more important body, in terms of both number of officers and number of resources. The viceroy's reforms also aimed to use the current surplus in order to reduce the outstanding debt (ten million ducats in 1610), and the service on this debt, which amounted to 800,000 ducats per year. Lemos planned to reduce current expenses by curtailing the number of tax inspectors, introducing simpler methods of bookkeeping and rationalizing the funding of expenses to avoid misallocation. On the revenue side, Lemos tried to reverse the trend of increasing taxes by withdrawing those on silk, salt, and public registry.[28]

In addressing the viceroy, Count of Lemos, to whom the *Breve trattato* was dedicated, Serra stated his main goal: to identify the sources of plenty and decrease the shortage of money in kingdoms where there were no silver and gold mines. He also took the opportunity to explain in the introduction, the difference between his and de Santis's approach to the *arte di governare*, which according to Serra was the most difficult of all arts.[29] People, Serra wrote, consider "ruling kingdoms as well as determining what justice is" a very simple task, while in reality the difficulties "can be compared to the difficulty and uncertainty of medicine". Thus, Serra continued, "not surprisingly Marco Antonio de Santis, a very experienced businessman", using simplistic reasoning, identified in the level of the exchange the main cause for the scarcity of money in the Kingdom of Naples, and on the basis of this faulty analysis, he supported a lowering of the exchange rate [*Prammatica* of 1607], "causing the final ruin of the Kingdom".[30]

For Serra, de Santis's major fault was having considered the level of *cambio* the cause rather than the symptom of the recurrent crises of the Kingdom. Serra believed, instead, that monetary shortages were the result of economic, political, and institutional problems that only a thorough analysis of the economic and institutional structure of a country could reveal. He identified a series of determinants of prosperity and assessed whether their presence or absence could explain the economic problems of the Kingdom. He then analysed the composition of the balance of payments to determine whether anything could be done to improve trade as well as to stabilize the foreign exchange. However, he also made clear from the beginning that his work was not confined to the analysis of money, production, and commerce but also included factors such as the "quality" of people and the capability of governments to implement the right policies.

Though Serra's systematic approach to the analysis of a nation's economic problems and his insistence on the role of manufacturing and agriculture in determining the wealth of a nation was a novelty in Naples, it echoed similar previous attempts in Spain as well as contemporary (and later) proposals in France, England, and Holland. The work of Luis Ortiz is one of the most famous examples of this approach in 16th-century Spain. In a document for Philip II, Ortiz tried to convince the Spanish king of the need to implement a programme of industrial and agricultural development for Spain. This plan would, in Ortiz's view, have helped to develop a national manufacturing sector and in this way decrease Spain's excessive reliance on American silver and gold.[31] However, according to Schumpeter, Serra should be credited "with having been the first to compose a scientific treatise, though an unsystematic one, on Economic Principles and Policy". He praised Serra for having demonstrated the role played by factors such as "natural resources, quality of people…industry and trade, the efficiency of government", and for pointing out that these factors, more than money, determined the success of production and commerce. Serra, according to Schumpeter, clearly indicated that "if the economic process as a whole functions properly, the monetary element will take care of itself and not require any specific therapy". For several decades, Schumpeter noted, "there was nothing like this [analysis] anywhere".[32]

Serra's remarks at the beginning of the *Breve trattato* indicate that he was conscious of the particular nature, or uniqueness, of his contribution:

> My aim is not to analyze *governo politico*... the ancients having written exhaustively and with great knowledge about it; nor to discern between justice and injustice, Justinian having already provided enough explanations;... but only to show the determinants of plenty of money in a kingdom with no gold and silver mines, an issue which neither ancient nor modern authors of works of politics have dealt with. And this is not to suggest the irrelevance or simplicity of the topic, since everybody knows that the question of plenty and scarcity of gold and silver in the State is relevant for both the public and private benefit of the government.[33]

Serra's insistence on labelling his work as "non-political" was understandable if one considers the climate of the time, the strict policing of political activities in the Kingdom of Naples under Spanish rule, and Serra's particular status as an inmate of the Vicaria prison. Once he made clear the nature of his work, Serra pointed out what distinguished it from other works dealing with the origin of the wealth of nations. Other authors, he remarked, like "de Santis in his *Discorso sopra la riforma del cambio* [had] dealt with this matter without using a clear methodology, *metodo di dottrina*, or seeking a general explanation but rather by adopting a narrow and practical approach... considering a low level of exchange rate or a high price of money as the only thing that can make gold and silver plentiful in the Kingdom".[34] Serra, instead, characterized his own work as more scientific, a work of general principles for the proper economic and institutional functioning of a state. Seeking general principles was not merely a theoretical exercise, though; it was in fact a necessary step for the formulation of practical remedies to halt and reverse Naples' economic decline. Knowledge of "general principles" could help other kingdoms to improve their accumulation of wealth and prevent wars.

Serra compared the debates about accumulation of wealth to those surrounding the concept of justice – where he refers to the Greek concept of *dikaiosyne*, the sense of justice. The debates in Plato's *Republic* and Aristotle's *Politics* about ideal forms of government and justice in different cities and regions contained lessons, according to Serra, about the difficulty of agreeing on a common set of rules "to profess universally a common practice of justice". This failure to agree on "what is just and unjust", Serra remarked while quoting Plato, had been "responsible for the majority of wars and fights since the beginning of the world".[35] As we shall see, the economic success of a kingdom, for Serra, depends on growth in manufacturing and agriculture, an internal process in which a series of factors, including quality of people and good government, play a crucial role. In his view, if kingdoms would have adopted remedies on the basis of his "check-up" and principles they would have specialized in productions not necessarily in conflict with other states. The growth of a nation could be achieved in agreement with other nations, and this common understanding among nations like in the case of "universal justice" would have prevented "wars and fights". In this interpretation, Serra's message differed from the traditional mercantilist idea that "my neighbor's loss is my gain".[36]

Serra divided the *Breve trattato* in three sections. In the first, he identified the general determinants of shortage and abundance of silver and gold; in the second, he critiqued proposals that considered the quantity of money and the level of the exchange as the key variables for promoting the wealth of a state; and in the third, he advanced his own proposal on how to increase the wealth of the Kingdom of Naples.

Serra believed that two groups of *accidenti* (in English they could be defined as causes, factors, or determinants), "natural and collateral", determine the economic success of a state – in the language of the time, make for states "plenty of silver and gold". The presence of gold and silver mines in a country corresponded to the "natural" causes, a special case that Serra dismissed immediately since it was not relevant for the Kingdom of Naples. He focused, instead, on the "collateral causes" and grouped them into two broad categories, "*propri,* particular" factors and "*comuni,* common" factors. The former depend on the specific endowment (mainly agricultural endowment, given the structure of the early-modern economies) and geographical position of a state. Agriculture could create "a surplus of products grown in a kingdom" and, through exports, generate an inflow of silver and gold. The Kingdom of Naples, with its large exports of agriculture commodities, represented a good example of this "particular factor". It should be noted that, for Serra, exports were the result of a natural and, for this reason, specific endowment of the Kingdom and not the result of an increase in productivity in agriculture, as would be the case with very different implications for the French physiocrats in the 18th century. On the other hand, the Kingdom of Naples was not endowed with the other particular factor, a valuable geographical position "with respect to other kingdoms and other parts of the world". Location played an important role in increasing the volume of trade and had positive benefits for the balance of payments. Venice, in this sense, represented Naples' nemesis, as it held "the first place", in terms of commerce, "not only in Italy but in Europe and Asia" in part because of its location, while Naples, the "most deprived of this factor than any other country", had very little trade.[37]

However, it was with the analysis of the four "common" causes (*accidenti comuni*), "quantity of industry, quality of population, extensive trading operations, and regulations of the sovereign", that Serra differed from previous and contemporary attempts to explain how economic growth could occur in "any kingdom" regardless of its natural endowment. Giovanni Botero, in both his *Ragione di stato* and its appendix *Delle cause delle grandezze delle città* anticipated some of Serra's *accidenti* in emphasizing location (one of Serra's "particular" factors), productivity of the soil, entrepreneurship in manufacturing, and trade ("*facilità della condotta*", in Botero's definition). Population was a crucial factor for Botero in terms of size, while Serra focused on "quality of people", which in this sense seems closer to Botero's entrepreneurship factor. The two authors also saw Venice as a model because it encompassed most of the determinants of wealth, including good governance and institutions. For instance, while describing the wonders of Rome and Venice, Botero remarked that in Venice "visitors admire", among other things, "the order of the government and the beauty of both sexes".[38] Then, he continued, while Rome certainly could offer visitors unparalleled remains of the past, Venice represented the best example of a successful state where good government played a crucial role in supporting the accumulation of wealth, military might, technical advances, and cultural achievements. Hence, in contrast to past models of power and a state's success based on the use of force, violence, and plunder, Botero considered Venice a virtuous example of success based on new and more lasting premises. Violence as an act against nature would not guarantee lasting development of the state, while business, trade, and manufacturing would certainly put the state on solid ground.

For Serra, manufacturing, "quantity of industry", held a central role in the development of an economy. On this point, he expanded previous analyses about the prominence of manufacturing over agriculture by explaining the reasons for this prominence. First, in contrast to agriculture, manufacturing is less dependent on external factors like weather and availability of labour. Second, it has more potential for growth since artisans and merchants can multiply their production "two hundredfold…with proportionately less expense" than agriculture, which has a potential "two-fold" expansion.[39] Furthermore, considering the advances in transportation and the market expansion that had been taking place for more than a century, Serra viewed the return on investments in manufacturing as several times higher and less uncertain than the return in agriculture. He made this point clearly when he wrote:

> In the case of industry...the products are easily preserved, not only for a short but also for a long time; and for the same reason, they may readily be exported to any distant country. And the art of navigation being in our time so improved that in this alone the moderns have surpassed the ancients, having developed trade not only between the east and the west and between the south and the north, but even between one hemisphere and the other, so that commodities are readily transported from one place to another, who will not admit that the market for the trades is surer than that for produce, and the profit therefore more certain?[40]

Serra also explained how manufactures enjoyed a greater value-added than agriculture products. As he pointed out, value-added was particularly high in "the manufacture of wool (especially fine cloth), linen, silks, arms, pictures, sculptures, printing, and in all branches of *drogherie*".[41] Overall, Serra had no doubt that a well-diversified industry together with a commercial network represented the best option for increasing the overall income and future revenues of a country, and Venice and its burgeoning industry and commercial activities was the best model – and Naples the worst.

"Quality of people" represented the second major determinant of a country's success. For Serra, this factor had numerous positive effects, since the presence of industrious and innovative people determined not only the success of a particular sector at home but also its success abroad because these people "not only will extract money from industries which they establish in their own country, but also from those they develop in foreign states".[42] The ability and will to emerge in any market, a characteristic of people from Genoa, Florence, and Venice, explained the commercial success of these cities. Inhabitants of the Kingdom of Naples, Serra commented, instead "lack entrepreneurial spirit"; they "do not traffic outside their own country, either in the other provinces of Europe, such as Spain, France, Germany, and others, or even in Italy itself; nor do they manage the industries of their own state, so that inhabitants of other places...such as the Genoese, Florentines, Lombards, Venetians, and others come in for this purpose".[43] Serra believed that the Neapolitans could have readily taken advantage of the pervasive presence of Genoese businessmen in the Kingdom and acquired from them the necessary skills to become successful entrepreneurs and merchants, not only in Italy and Europe "but in other parts of the world, and even in the new Indies". The quality of people in Genoa thus explained the paradox of why Genoa, a country "so very barren", could have "such an abundance of money" while "the citizens of this Kingdom" (Naples) even though they live in a "country so rich" were "so poor".[44]

With the discussion of this factor, Serra expanded the analyses of Botero and Bodin, for whom the quality of education greatly contributed to the success of a population and in turn of their country. Serra defined a determinant of growth that economists today call "human capital" and with his factual account of how Neapolitans could acquire skills by collaborating with foreign businessmen in Naples, he pointed towards another important factor of development: the transfer of skills. This concept was of crucial relevance in Serra's general discourse because it showed that underachievers – that is, the Neapolitans – had an opportunity to reverse the declining trend of their economy by learning from direct contact with successful businessmen – that is, the Genoese merchants in Naples. Showing how locals could benefit from the presence of foreign merchants represented an important step in changing the negative attitude towards foreign investors that permeated contemporary debates about the origin of the Kingdom's decline as in the case of de Santis.

The third common cause of "great trade" was a combination of other factors such as a country's geographical position (that is, one of the two "particular" causes), its manufacturing, and quality of its people. Given the traditional connection between trade and credit – two factors that support one another at the core of the success of Italian merchant bankers in the late Middle Ages and throughout the 16th century – and the reference to credit techniques in the second part of the treatise, it is conceivable that Serra included the knowledge and presence of financial and credit techniques in the "great trade" factor. In this sense, one could interpret Serra's statement that "commerce cannot be carried on without money" to mean "where there is great commerce, there must necessarily be much money".[45] The Venetian Republic represented the best model of a country with "great trade" since it held location advantage, had developed manufacturing, and had the best trading (commercial and credit) capabilities of any city "not only in Italy itself, but in Europe".[46] Serra pointed out that the combination of all these factors ignited a self-reinforcing process of growth, a virtuous cycle with manufacturing at its centre. This process is well exemplified in the following passage with two factors, namely manufacturing and quality of people, reinforcing each other:

> Extensive manufactures bring a great many people there, not only by reason of the trade itself (in which case the effect would be attributed to trade), but also as a result of the combination of these two factors; for one furnishes strength to the other, the great concourse due to commerce and to the situation being increased by the manufactures, and the manufactures being increased by the great concourse due to commerce, while commerce is made greater by this same assembling of people.[47]

By contrast, trade in the Kingdom of Naples was limited to local commodities, mainly agricultural goods. Serra conceded the unfavourable geographical position of the Kingdom, "so bad that nobody ever has to go through there to go to other countries, whatever part of the world he comes from or desires to go to".[48] Serra's claim seems exaggerated given that the location of Naples at a convenient midway point in the Mediterranean was often given as reason for its success as a port in Roman times. Also, in the 18th century, Galiani claimed that the location of the Kingdom of Naples was the best in the Mediterranean. This "particular" factor combined with the absence of "common" factors such as quality of people (Naples had a "population without enterprise") and industry (it had a "scarcity of manufactures") represented in Serra's view formidable impediments to the development of the third "common factor" of extensive trade in the Kingdom.

After this gloomy description of the Kingdom of Naples, Serra introduced the last of the common factors, the "regulations of the sovereign", the most important and yet the most difficult to obtain of all the factors. A sovereign, according to Serra, faces a formidable task in finding the right mix of measures to achieve his desired outcome since he needs to know the situation of the "various factors" in his own state together with those of "neighboring and distant States with which his kingdom has or may have commerce, and, considering the causes and opportunities which could increase and decrease the quantity of money in his domain, adopt various regulations according to the desired outcome, removing the impediments which might prevent the achievement of that outcome". In this description, Serra showed how a wise sovereign, given the presence of several factors outside his control, should try to minimize errors by considering "more than one cause, since the same cause generally produces different effects with respect to different subjects" before deliberating. Using "force upon his subjects", for instance, was not advisable, because the subjects "could obstruct" the sovereign's action "in various indirect ways, of which there are many". Likewise, a wise sovereign should make regulations "attractive to foreigners and even change them if necessary, so that they may come readily".[49] Serra's choice of Pope Sixtus V as a model of a prudent and virtuous policymaker, rather than a Venetian or Genoese doge, might be explained by his desire to show how this "common" factor could improve the economic situation of the Papal States, a kingdom like that of Naples with neither "particular" nor "common" factors. Perhaps, the fact that the papacy was also, like Naples, a monarchy may explain the inclusion of such a model. It was this capacity to change the fate of a country endowed with unfavourable conditions that made good government the most powerful of all factors and yet the most difficult and "unpredictable of all", where unpredictable, Serra poignantly remarked, referring to the quality of the "operator", the sovereign.[50]

With his analysis of the *accidenti propri* and *accidenti comuni*, Serra clarified his vision of development. He then used this matrix of "particular" and "common" factors to explain wealth differentials among the Kingdom of Naples and other states such as Venice and Genoa. This exercise became instrumental for demonstrating not only why the Kingdom fared so poorly in comparison to these other states and identifying possible remedies but also for showing how contemporary claims about the richness of the Kingdom of Naples had no foundation whatsoever. To strengthen his argument, Serra supplemented his qualitative analysis with a quantitative one based on a thorough assessment of the balance of payments. This quantitative analysis revealed that, contrary to contemporary claims based only on the analysis of the balance of trade, the Kingdom of Naples had a chronic balance of payments deficit. In fact, the inclusion of items from the capital account component of the balance of payments revealed that the six-million ducats trade surplus boasted by de Santis was completely wiped out, not only by a correct estimation of commodities imports (which de Santis had underestimated) but also by a large deficit in the account balance.[51] Not only was de Santis's statement that the "Kingdom was the wealthiest in the world" preposterous but, more relevant for Serra, all exchange rate and monetary manipulations implemented by Viceroy Benavente following the advice of de Santis and other experts were doomed to fail because they were based on wrong assumptions.

On the basis of Serra's quantitative and qualitative analysis of Venice and Genoa, the former emerged as the most strikingly different from

Naples. It had no agricultural surplus; the value of silver and gold money was lower in Venice than in Naples; there were no limits to the export of money in Venice (except that of foreign money) while a total ban existed in Naples; and there were lower returns on public debt in Venice (between 4% and 5% per year) than in Naples (between 7.5% and 10%).[52] The latter caused not only a constant drainage of gold and silver from Naples but also, given the deficit in the balance of trade, a constant increase in the consolidated debt.[53]

The main reason for Venice's success was to be found in its good government. The Venetian government facilitated positive interaction among the other "common" factors by removing the "impediments" to the regular work of trading and manufacturing activities and by creating "occasions" for merchants and artisans to develop their own businesses – by providing the right incentives and a good environment in modern economic terms. Serra identified in Venice's *medesimo governo*, in institutional continuity, the most powerful explanation of Venetian good government. Monarchs change, and with them objectives and policies, while in the Venetian Republic the objective of common good had been consistently pursued over time through a constant improvement in the working of various institutions, such as the senate, and in the selection and management of magistrates, administrators, and various offices. The interaction among institutions and across generations, as for example in the senate where old and young senators learned how to cooperate, and the development of institutional mechanisms, as for instance the passing of laws in the senate which required the majority of votes, guaranteed the necessary institutional stability and yet allowed for the frequent and necessary renewal of the governing bodies. For all these reasons, Serra wrote, "as history has shown, there has never in the world been a monarchy or a republic which has lasted and still lasts more than Venice, she is still virgin, even though one thousand and two hundred years have passed since her foundation after Attila's wrath".[54]

Serra's analysis of the balance of trade revealed that the value of imports, which included primary commodities and manufactures, exceeded that of exports, mainly agriculture commodities. Fabrics, spices, metals, books, glass, paper, weapons, and other artefacts, most of which had a high value-added, were not produced in the Kingdom and were generally imported from Venice. Even a commodity in high demand, such as sugar, was shipped from Naples to Venice and then, after being refined in the latter, re-imported to Naples, constituting a double loss for Naples: Neapolitans paid twice as much, and the profit went to Venetian traders, only because Neapolitans "could not bother to learn how to refine it".[55] Since Serra was not sure for how long the Kingdom had been running a current account deficit, he wanted to show that even in the case of a current account surplus, a large share was controlled by foreigners. Contrary to de Santis, Serra used this argument not to attack foreign businessmen, in particular the Genoese, but to praise them and condemn Neapolitan lack of entrepreneurial initiative. In fact, the presence of foreign businessmen and their involvement in the economy of the Kingdom represented, for him, the main impediment to a complete collapse of economic activity and a total shortage of money. "After having paid for exports, foreigners are still left with some income which they invest in activities and bonds in the Kingdom. And this explained why there was some money left in the Kingdom".[56]

In terms of policy remedies, all the measures suggested by de Santis – a low exchange, a ban on the export of money, and high taxes on foreigners – were all doomed to fail. For instance, the impact of a low exchange rate could readily be neutralized by foreign governments. Likewise, a ban on the export of money from the Kingdom ought to be avoided since "freedom of monetary movements generates more trade".[57] He observed that any outflow of money finds correspondence either in an import of commodities for the same value or in a future inflow of capital. Free movement of money had beneficial effects on the economic activity of the state, even when foreigners used bills of exchange to pay for Neapolitan exports – a practice condemned by de Santis – since even in this case "sooner or later cash will flow to the Kingdom".[58] Serra praised Venice's ban on the export of foreign coins because merchants, foreign and local, had to bring foreign coins to the Venetian mint, and this had two key advantages: local mint authorities could control the quality and quantity of money in circulation, and merchants could reduce the exchange risk by using Venetian coins – renowned for their quality and stability in value – in their business activities.

In terms of monetary measures, Serra aligned himself with the prevailing views of authors of treatises on money about the evil of debasement and other forms of monetary alterations. Serra, however, conceded that, contrary to general opinion, the "circulation of large amounts of small coins", often the result of frequent debasements, did not affect trade in "cities and states", and therefore, there was "no reason for withdrawing them".[59] On the other hand, Serra warned of the risks of excessive debasement – a rise in counterfeiting, an increase in prices, and the damage to the reputation of the sovereign.[60]

In terms of large coins, gold and silver coins, Serra concentrated on the value of the gold-to-silver ratio, a constant problem in the bimetallic systems of ancient and early-modern times.[61] Even on this issue, Serra maintained a heterodox approach, considering the gold-to-silver ratio a price, which therefore varied according to the use of these metals, rather than a fixed ratio, as traditionally sustained by previous authors from Plato to Bodin.[62] Serra wrote, "neither justice nor truth can be contained in such a ratio, and this search is fruitless; ... and all have been mistaken in this endeavour".[63] In policy terms, a sovereign could fix the price of these metals, but only after assessing the value of gold and silver in adjacent countries and trading partners and after gathering information about the amount of these metals circulating within his domain. An unrealistic gold-to-silver ratio would have opened the way to speculation, as has been the case in more recent history with misaligned exchange rates in countries with a fixed exchange-rate regime.

The *Breve trattato* ends with a list of proposals to help sovereigns in their "difficult task" of steering the economy of their states. With the Kingdom of Naples in mind and the Spanish viceroy, Count of Lemos, as a potentially interested reader, Serra invited the Spanish administration to avoid measures that could seriously damage the economy, such as seizing the income realized by foreigners in the Kingdom or lowering the exchange rate. Rather, Serra argued for the overtaking of foreign-controlled production by local entrepreneurs, in a slow manner to avoid any trade disruption. But to achieve this goal – through what today would be called an import substitution strategy – it was necessary to invest, "to introduce in the Kingdom" those "common" factors that would support the development of manufacturing. It was the duty of the sovereign – that is, it was "good government" – to create conditions that would generate the development of domestic activities in countries with no gold or silver mines and, as in the case of the Kingdom of Naples, compensate for the "poor quality of the site".[64] The Kingdom would decrease the value of imports, have new commodities to export, and in this way reduce its dependence on an agriculture surplus. All this would guarantee plenty of money and prosperity throughout the Kingdom and in turn benefit the Spanish crown. Thus, good government, as remarked several times, played a central role in the *Breve trattato*, a role, I shall stress, that did not necessarily imply direct involvement of the government in the production of commodities. It seems that Serra came very close to Botero, who in the seventh book of the *Reason of State* acknowledged that people and money, "*tesoro*", constitute the forces on which to construct a more powerful state; thus a "prudent prince" should know how to make a correct assessment of these forces and rule on the basis of them.[65] However, while Botero believed that trade and manufacturing, like all human activities, were determined by God's will, Serra believed there was room to change the course of events, the economic position of a country, through the establishment of good institutions and good governance.

The crucial role played by good governance and institutions to explain how states – with or without similar endowments – might experience different levels of growth and development trajectories has emerged over the course of the last two decades as one of the most debated topics in development circles. The main terms of this debate can be found in the recent work of Acemoglu and Robinson, for whom the presence of inclusive institutions (positive) in contrast to extractive institutions (negative) explain differences in wealth between nations. Inclusive institutions allow wider participation in economic activities that make the best use of people's talents and skills. These institutions in turn arise from political institutions that tend to distribute power in society. In contrast, extractive institutions are defined as practices and policies designed to extract incomes and wealth to benefit a small subset of society, and they arise from absolutist political institutions.[66] In Serra's analysis, Venice would represent the best model of a state whose success relied on the existence of inclusive institutions. The Kingdom of Naples instead would be an example of a failed state, one dominated by extractive institutions under the control of a local feudal aristocracy and representatives of the Spanish empire.[67] Serra's analysis could have been extended to other regions under Spanish rule – as well as to other European absolutist powers – in stark contrast to republics like Venice and the rising commercial empires of northern Europe, including the Netherlands which indeed had revolted against Spain. As the Spanish empire steadily declined during the late 16th century and the 17th century, the power of extractive institutions became more pervasive and detrimental to the development of those regions. This trend had a profound negative impact on the future of both the centre, Spain, and the periphery, Naples, a legacy that came to represent the real cost of empire.

Notes

1. Chiappini, S., "Il dibattito monetario a Napoli e il *Breve Trattato* di Antonio Serra", *Il Pensiero economico moderno* 3, 1986, p. 46.
2. De Rosa, L., ed., *Il Mezzogiorno agli inizi del Seicento*, Bari: Laterza, 1994, p. xxvii.
3. Calabria, A., *The Cost of Empire: The Finance of the Kingdom of Naples in the Time of Spanish Rule*, Cambridge: Cambridge University Press, 1991, p. xiv.

4. Galasso, G., "Contributo alla storia delle finanze del Regno di Napoli nella prima metà del Seicento", *Annuario dell'Istituto Storico Italiano per l'Età Moderna e Contemporanea* 11, 1961, p. 205.
5. De Rosa, L., *I cambi esteri del Regno di Napoli dal 1591 al 1707*, Naples: Biblioteca dell'Archivio Storico del Banco di Napoli, 1955.
6. Chiappini, 1986, p. 51.
7. Davanzati, B., *Lezione Delle Monete E Notizia De' Cambj [1588]*, ed. Ricossa, S., Turin: Fogola, 1988.
8. On the debate in Naples, see A. Rosselli's outstanding contribution: "Early Views on Monetary Policy: The Neapolitan Debate on the Theory of Exchange", *History of Political Economy* 32 (1), 2000, pp. 61–82.
9. De Rosa, L., "Antonio Serra e i suoi critici", *Clio* 1 (1), 1965, pp. 115–136.
10. de Santis, M.A., *Discorso di Marc'Antonio de Santis intorno all'effetto che fa in regni il cambio* [1605a] in *Il Mezzogiorno agli inizi del Seicento*, De Rosa, L., ed., Bari: Laterza, 1994, p. 9.
11. de Santis, 1605, p. 14.
12. de Santis, 1605a, pp. 15–16.
13. de Santis, 1605a, p. 33. As noted above, Antonio Belmosto was a Neapolitan merchant who in the 1590s, in collusion with the Spanish Viceroy, managed through a complex monetary scheme to inject some liquidity into Naples' economy. De Rosa, 1994, p. xxxiii.
14. de Santis, 1605a, p. 40.
15. de Santis, 1605a, p. 62.
16. de Santis, 1605a, p. 25.
17. Colapietra, R., ed., *Problemi monetari negli scrittori napoletani del Seicento*, Rome: Accademia Nazionale dei Lincei, 1973, p. 16.
18. The content of this pamphlet is included in de Santis's second short treatise. References are to the following reprinted version: de Santis, M.A., *Secondo Discorso di Marc'Antonio de Santis intorno a gli effetti che fa il cambio in regno, sopra una risposta che è stata fatta adverso del primo* [1605b] in De Rosa, L., ed., 1994, pp. 51–74.
19. de Santis, 1605b, p. 52.
20. de Santis, 1605b, p. 53.
21. de Santis, 1605b, pp. 61–63.
22. Colapietra, ed., 1973, p. 25.
23. Galiani, *Della Moneta* [1780], in *Opere di Ferdinando Galiani*, (eds) Diaz, F. and L. Guerci, Milan-Naples: Ricciardi, 1975, pp. 308–309.
24. On Calabria at the time of Serra, see Galasso, G., *Economia e società nella Calabria del Cinquecento*, Milan: Feltrinelli, 1975, pp. 215–224.
25. The treatise was published in Naples by Lazzaro Scoriggio in 1613. After the inclusion of the treatise in the first volume of the multivolume collection of Italian economists edited by Pietro Custodi at the beginning of the 19th century, the *Breve trattato* has been reprinted in Italian several times. A few sections of the treatise translated into English appeared under the title "A brief Treatise on the Causes which can make Gold and Silver plentiful in Kingdoms where there are no Mines", in Monroe, A.E., ed., *Early Economic Thought. Selections from economic literature prior to Adam Smith*, Cambridge, MA: Harvard University Press, 1951, pp. 145–167. A complete translation into English edited by S.A. Reinert with an updated historiography and

critical bibliography appeared in 2011; see Serra, A., *A Short Treatise on the Wealth and Poverty of Nations (1613)*, ed. S.A. Reinert, London and New York, NY: Anthem Press, 2011. References to Serra's treatises are from the reprinted edition in De Rosa, ed., 1994, pp. 75–170. Translations are my own unless otherwise noted.

26. De Rosa, 1965, pp. 115–116. Campanella, too, spent several years in Neapolitan prisons for his involvement in a failed coup. On Serra in relation to Campanella, see Colapietra, ed., 1973, pp. 85–100; and Amabile, L., *Fra Tommaso Campanella, la sua congiura, i suoi processi e la sua pazzia*, Naples: Morano, 1882, 3, pp. 646–650. For similarities with Condorcet, who spent time in isolation following Jacobins' accusation that he was a traitor to the French Revolution, during which time he composed one of the most famous treatises of the Enlightenment, *Esquisse d'un tableau historique des progrès de l'esprit humain*, published a year after his death in 1794, see Grilli, E., *Antonio Serra*, Rome: Luiss University Press, 2006, p. 24.
27. Zazzera, F., "Narrazioni tratte dai giornali del governo di Don Pietro Giron Duca d'Ossuma (1616–1620)", *Archivio Storico Italiano* 9, 1846, p. 520.
28. Galasso, 1961, pp. 5–8.
29. Serra, A., *Breve trattato delle cause che possono far abbondare li regni dove non sono miniere con applicazione al Regno di Napoli [1613]*, in De Rosa, ed., 1994, pp. 77–80.
30. Serra, 1613, pp. 81–85.
31. Ortiz, L., *Memorial Del Contador Luis Ortiz a Felipe II [1558]*, Madrid: Instituto de España, 1970. J.A. Schumpeter includes another Spanish work in this genre, *Memoriales. De la politica necessaria á la republica de España* (1600) by G. de Cellorigo. Schumpeter cites Barthelemy de Laffemas, who was active during the reign of Henry IV, and Josiah Child (1630–1699) as representatives of this approach for France and England, respectively. Schumpeter, J.A., *History of Economic Analysis*, New York, NY: Oxford University Press, 1954, pp. 194–195.
32. Schumpeter, 1954, p. 195
33. Serra, 1613, p. 84.
34. Serra, 1613, p. 84.
35. Serra, 1613, pp. 82–83.
36. On Serra's position in the history of economic thought, see among others De Rosa, 1965, pp. 115–136; and Roncaglia, A., *La ricchezza delle idee. Storia del pensiero economico*, Bari: Laterza, 2001, pp. 48–60.
37. Serra, 1613, pp. 88.
38. Botero, G., *Ragion di stato e Delle cause della grandezza della città [1598]*, Firpo, L., ed., Turin: UTET, 1948, pp. 316–318.
39. Serra, 1613, pp. 89–90.
40. Serra, 1613, p. 90.
41. Serra, 1613, p. 90.
42. Serra, 1613, p. 91.
43. Serra, 1613, p. 93–94.
44. Serra, 1613, p. 92.
45. Serra, 1613, p. 93.
46. Serra, 1613, p. 93.
47. Serra, 1613, p. 93.

48. Serra, 1613, p. 94.
49. Serra, 1613, pp. 94–95.
50. Serra, 1613, p. 97.
51. De Rosa, 1994, p. xlii; in Grilli, 2006, pp. 56–57.
52. Serra, 1613, p. 100.
53. Calabria, 1991, p. 110.
54. Serra, 1613, pp. 102–104.
55. Serra, 1613, pp. 106–108.
56. Serra, 1613, pp. 164–165.
57. Serra, 1613, p. 168.
58. Serra, 1613, p. 168.
59. Serra, 1613, p. 153.
60. On the positive impact of debasement on markets in the late Middle Ages and early-modern period, see Cipolla, C., *Le avventure della lira*, Milan: Edizioni di Comunità, 1958; and Sargent, T.J. and F.R. Velde, *The Big Problem of Small Change*, Princeton, NJ: Princeton University Press, 2002.
61. Serra, 1613, pp. 152–159.
62. On the relationship between price and use, Serra referred to the juridical tradition of the *Praetia rerum*, law of the Digest. According to this tradition, the value of a commodity depends on its use, and use varies according to time, place, circumstances, and quantity. This definition had been widely discussed among canonists, theologians, and jurists from the 14th century onwards.
63. Serra, 1613, p. 160.
64. Serra, 1613, pp. 168–170.
65. Botero, 1948, p. 320.
66. Acemoglu, D. and J.A. Robinson, *Why Nations Fail: The Origins of Power, Prosperity and Poverty*, New York, NY: Crown Publishers, 2012.
67. Villari, R., *Un sogno di libertà. Napoli nel declino di un impero*, Milano: Mondadori, 2012.

4

Serra's *Brief Treatise* in a *World-System* Perspective: The Dutch Miracle and Italian Decline in the Early 17th Century

Rosario Patalano

1 Introduction

The intense debate on the economic conditions of the Kingdom of Naples in the first three decades of the 17th century marked an important advance in Neapolitan culture: for the first time, economic problems were separated from ethical thinking and approached in an autonomous way.[1] In Naples, as in other dominions of the Spanish Empire, a copious literature in the form of *arbitrios* (advice) appeared, proposing measures to reverse the decline of the economy.

This literature was facilitated by the truce with France, England, and the Dutch Republic (Twelve Years' Truce), which led to suspension of the "war economy" of the Spanish Empire, with time for some hard thinking on possible solutions to the economic problems. The interval of peace allowed King Philip III and his favourite minister, the Duke of Lerma, to disengage from the conflict in the Low Countries and devote their energies to the internal problems of the Spanish Monarchy. In Naples, various reforms approved and promoted by several Viceroys, in particular Pedro Fernández de Castro, count of Lemos (1610–1616), constituted a major overhaul for Neapolitan public finance. The institution of viceroy was not a simple bureaucratic office totally subordinate to the Court of Madrid but an instrument of mediation between the imperial strategic necessities and local interests.[2] From this perspective, the debate on the economic conditions of the Kingdom of Naples in the early 17th century can be seen in terms of the contrasts among different models of development in the context of the *world-system*. These different models were understood, though only partially, constraints and opportunities resulting from the integration of the Southern Italy economy into the wider structure of exchanges and international division of labour represented by the *world-system*.

The debate between an anonymous Genoese writer, Marc'Antonio de Santis, and Antonio Serra focused on the contrast of different models of development. De Santis proposed a process of development focused on the mobilization of local forces against the Kingdom's subjection to foreign investors and rentiers, based on the myth that Southern Italy's natural fertility would confer upon Naples an advantage in terms of trade. Antonio Serra defended the role of the foreign investors, proposing as model the commercial and manufacturing development of the Northern Italian city-states (Genoa, Florence, and, above all, Venice).

Both these proposals were based on the opinion that the fertility of the Kingdom was a major advantage, but in the early 17th century, Southern Italy's agriculture was in severe crisis, not imputable to normal fluctuations of the cycle. This crisis, which turned out to be a generalized crisis of subsistence, became the main object of analysis for other Neapolitans authors – such as Francesco Imperato, Fabio Frezza, Tommaso Campanella, and Carlo Tapia; they indicated a different model of development, based on solving the agrarian problem. Not only did Serra's "industrialist" proposal, based on the experience of Northern Italian city-states, contrast with the conditions of backwardness and dependence of the Kingdom of Naples, but the "Italian" model itself was outdated, lagging behind Dutch and English development.[3] Indeed, Serra's analysis, unlike the analyses of other coeval authors (like the French author Antoine de Montchrétien), neglected the Dutch Miracle in the world economy, the aggressive English presence in the Mediterranean Sea and the decline of Venice in exchanges with the Levant.

2 Opposing models of development for the Kingdom of Naples in the early 17th century

With the conclusion of peace with the United Provinces in 1609 and, as from 1610, the achievement of stable hegemony in the Italian dominions, the Court of Spain was able to concentrate on tackling some of the many serious problems that it faced. In Naples the opportunity came with the Viceroy Pedro Fernández de Castro, better known as the second Count of Lemos (1610–1616), whom Spain had to thank for the most thorough endeavour made by the Spanish government in the entire

17th century, reorganizing the administrative and accounting apparatus of the Neapolitan Kingdom, reconstructing the state finances, and developing the local economy.[4]

In particular, Lemos lowered interest on the public debt with the aim of favouring productive rather than speculative investment, reduced the tax on exports with the aim of boosting their growth and, finally, embarked upon the necessary reclamation works in Terra di Lavoro. All these efforts went into raising the Kingdom's productive capacity. On the monetary front, too, the action undertaken by the Count of Lemos in the face of steadily deteriorating conditions for exchange was equally incisive. In 1611 he arranged an ingenious ploy, a sort of devaluation craftily concealed with the minting of a new coin, the *Tre Cinquine* (or *Tre mezzi carlini*), coined not on the foot of the old *carlino* but on that of the *zannette*; in practice, the *carlino* was devalued by 8.40%, with particularly detrimental effect not only on the domestic price level but also on the exchange rate since the carlino constituted the base of the Neapolitan unit of account.[5] This strategy, too, pursued the same goal of productiveness, offering an incentive to increase exportation with effects on the domestic price level.[6]

It is not clear whether this type of policy found support in a Neapolitan viceroy's party, but it obviously enjoyed the support of Madrid and clashed with local vested interests. Lemos was certainly set on mobilizing local productive forces, also to the direct advantage of Madrid, given that after the United Provinces operation, its Neapolitan dominion constituted the only external resource of the Spanish monarchy in Europe. In July 1613, as this reformist policy came to its apogee, Antonio Serra published from prison his *Brief Treatise*, dedicated to the Count of Lemos himself. This happy period of peace that characterized the rule of Lemos opened up scope for comparison of the various solutions to the economic and social crisis afflicting the Kingdom of Naples. Both the strategic needs of Madrid and the heterogeneous local interests gravitated around the viceroy's line of policy.[7] The debate on economic issues which saw different analyses and remedies contrasted and compared in the early years of the 17th century proved an absolute novelty for Neapolitan culture.[8] In fact, diverse models of development came into play that were to some extent able to identify the constraints and opportunities created by the, by then, definitive inclusion of the *Mezzogiorno* (Southern Italy) in the international division of labour and the *world-system* exchange structure.

The first line that we can identify lay in the position that found a spokesman in Marc'Antonio de Santis, an exponent of the local class of merchants with important duties as an adviser in the administration.[9]

De Santis focused his attention on the "bizarre" phenomenon[10] of a country that was, in his opinion, "the richest in the world",[11] engaged in trade at a very high level,[12] but characterized by a rarefied circulation of money of singularly low quality. As de Santis saw it, the one cause of this particular condition was the high exchange rate that resulted from speculative activities backed by foreign finance, which controlled the bill of exchange market. The solution proposed by de Santis was consistent with this analysis: determination of the exchange rate should come within the prerogatives of the sovereign state and withdrawn from the foreign merchants who controlled it through the system of fairs and their commercial networks. The idea was, then, to lay down by law a maximum exchange rate for every market which no market rate could exceed.[13] In this way, according to de Santis, anyone importing goods from the Kingdom would be obliged to pay in cash while those exporting would make use of bills of exchange; this stratagem would, finally, put an end to the speculative activity in the foreign exchange market.[14]

In practice, reducing the exchange rate corresponded to revaluation of the Neapolitan currency, which – according to de Santis – would in no way have compromised exports from the Kingdom, accounted for by necessities that no one could do without. Revaluation of the currency would improve the terms of trade in favour of the Kingdom with the effect of generating an abundance of money subsequent to the agricultural surplus ("abbondanza di robba"). Fixing the exchange rate by law was no novelty: in 1596 the viceroy, the Count of Olivares, had done so, but with no success. De Santis's proposal and his attack on foreign merchantry and finance had become possible as a result of the weakening of the latter resulting from the financial crisis of 1598, which swept the private bank out of the Kingdom (as de Santis himself remarked, credit activity was by then restricted to Mounts of Piety and other religious pawnbrokers, called lochi pii)[15]. Thus an opening was created which the businessmen, the *hombres de negocios* of the Kingdom, wished to exploit, also with the support of the viceregal government, which was endeavouring to establish more direct relations with the local merchant class (which was in fact then taking the form of a merchant class in embryo)[16] in order to be able to shake off traditional subordination to foreign merchants (among whom the Genoese took pride of place).[17] Under the rule of Olivares, attempts were also made to conclude a commercial agreement with the Ottoman Empire for the export of silk fabric, and much was made of the role of the public banks, formally in a different world from the commercialism that characterized private finance, in which local capital could find safe investment.[18]

A point to be noted is that de Santis's proposal was largely based on the concern, widespread in the economic thinking of the time, for favourable terms of trade, emerging in the possibility to buy cheap and sell dear (the British author Malynes was facing the same problem in similar terms).[19] The idea was justified by the fact that what counted was not so much the quantity of exports as the overall value seen to depend on the ratio between export and import prices. Currency devaluation or foreign speculation on the exchange rate could result in local goods becoming all too cheap while boosting the prices of foreign goods. "In other words – as Dobb observes – the policy these writers were advocating was not dissimilar to modern policies of currency overvalutation."[20]

Moreover, the emphasis placed on the role of foreign merchants in controlling the exchange rate and trade was not unusual at that time; indeed, the idea that antagonistic countries based their political manoeuvres on the exchange rate was fundamental to what Paul Einzig described as speculation or conspiracy theory.[21] De Santis saw the exchange rate as something "artificial", not "natural", defined "normally" by "a few businessmen (quattro negotianti)", who "are in the habit of fixing the price for exchange every week, more often than not in accordance with their designs, there being no dissent on the part of honourable, disinterested persons, now swelling the currency, now shrinking it".[22] Being "merely artificial",[23] the exchange rate could and indeed had to be regulated by law, to set a limit and restore it to its original function of "convenience", and not ruin.

The belief that a revaluation of the exchange rate would have no effect on the volume of exportation was also held by many, the idea that international demand was inelastic being widespread.[24] De Santis was also well aware that "the systematic enrichment" of the Genoese derived from the monopoly exercised over exchange rates, using an "advantageously oriented and controlled network, in which the superiority of quotation of certainty over uncertainty" allowed the deliverers of bill of exchange (datori) to make considerable profits, exploiting the differences between markets.[25] Furthermore, most of the revenues deriving from financial and commercial intermediation and rents found their way out of the Kingdom, thereby contributing to a worsening of the exchange rate.[26] In the Kingdom, de Santis remarked, "there is nothing left to sell, these foreigners having sucked the blood of all and sundry in the Kingdom, to the extent that hardly a living is left to anyone".[27] He took this line so far as to threaten the interests of the foreign merchants directly, writing that "it would be opportune for

His Majesty, for the good of the Kingdon, to suspend payments of their shares of the rents to foreigners for four or six months, so that they could not make their weekly remittances, and this would bring the exchange rate down to an unprecedentedly low level."[28] Nevertheless – de Santis concluded – this was a strategy that would not prove opportune "for His Majesty".

The model of development proposed by de Santis was based on the opinion that the Mezzogiorno could play its part in international trade by exploiting its alleged absolute advantage in the production of agricultural commodities (de Santis calculated a commercial surplus of five million ducats). This was an opinion based on the fairly widespread belief that Italy's Mezzogiorno was a land endowed with extraordinary fertility[29] and able to satisfy the growing demand from abroad.[30] In reality, the Mezzogiorno, like the other parts of Europe with the exception of the United Provinces and England, was in the throes of a serious agricultural and food crisis that had also filled the coffers of many *hombres de negocios*, both Neapolitan and foreign, as well as feudal lords, engaging in speculative activities concerning supply to the food administration. Given this model of development, the local manufacturing activities, increasingly exposed to the threat of competition from the centres of Northern Italy, remained decidedly secondary.

While the Kingdom's foreign trade had shown a distinctly healthy balance (for grain, oil, raw silk, and silk fabric),[31] it nevertheless remained subordinate to foreign commercial mediation, and a local merchant class was unable to strike out independently. In the early 17th century, things had taken a further turn for the worse with the agricultural crisis, and de Santis's positions appeared unrealistic, mere wishful thinking. His stratagem to control exchange rates, adopted by the viceroy the Duke of Benavente in June 1607, had no better fortune, because this measure was opposed by the foreign merchants who threatened to suspend all trading activities with the Kingdom.[32]

The line taken against foreign finance, backed by de Santis, was contested by an anonymous Genoese,[33] who had a different analysis to offer. As he saw it, the conditions of Neapolitan exchange were the result of: (1) the subtraction of the rents of the "nazion genovese", (2) the public banks' use of paper currency, and (3) the extremely poor quality of the internal currency. To remedy this situation, the anonymous Genoese proposed: (1) leaving the exchange rate free without setting any limits; (2) withdrawing from circulation all the clipped coins, with exchange based on weight; (3) obliging the banks to settle bills of exchange in cash.[34] After the decree on exchange had failed, in June 1609, Viceroy Benavente adopted the measure on currency exchange with the holders, whether private or public banks, bearing the cost of the operation: this time, it was a measure that went against the interests of the local categories, marking a radical change of policy after the failure of the exchange control measures.[35] Another answer to the positions taken by de Santis came with the *Brief Treatise*, published in July 1613 by Antonio Serra, who hailed from Cosenza but was then held prisoner in the Vicaria. His answer seemed to defend the role played by the foreign merchant class, above all Genoese, in the Kingdom of Naples.

Serra confuted de Santis's analysis and rejected the solution of an official exchange price, instead proposing complete deregulation and in practice leaving the domination of foreign finance over monetary flows unaffected. The analysis performed by Serra that led to these conclusions was in radical contrast with that of de Santis, and it was clearly conceived within a broader perspective that showed greater awareness. The fertility of the soil, which de Santis had seen as the element upon which the wealth of the Mezzogiorno was based, represented for Serra only one of the causes accounting for a country's economic success, and not even the most important. For countries that had no mines of precious metals, wealth had to be, rather, the result of a co-functioning of accidental causes, which Serra distinguished between proper accidents, depending on natural conditions, and common accidents, because "they occur, or may occur, in any kingdom".[36] Apart from the fertility of the soil (domestic agricultural surplus), the proper accidents included a favourable geographical position for trade in transit. The common accidents were represented by the "quantità degli artefici" (multiplicity of manufacturing activities), the "qualità della gente" (enterprising population), "traffico grande" (extensive trade), and "provvisione di colui che governa" (effective and good government).

The pattern that was thus delineated reflected the realities well enough.[37] The Kingdom of Naples was totally lacking in common accidents, and of the proper accidents, it enjoyed only the fertility of the soil (the one concession to de Santis), while the ascendancy of Venice and Genoa resulted from a happy combination of proper and common accidents. Venice was a good example of favourable geographical position, which, together with the quality of its manufacturing activities, ensured a conspicuous and particularly rich volume of intermediation commerce, with the support of the appropriate government policies. In the case of Genoa, her success was due to the enterprising population, which had succeeded in finding scope for trading and penetration in all directions. Finally, Rome offered the example of effective government alone, proving a decisive cause of well-being and wealth.

On the basis of this analysis, the development model proposed by Serra for the Kingdom of Naples was the diametrical opposite of de Santis's model. Unlike de Santis, Serra took a more realistic view of the role of the Mezzogiorno in international trade, seeing it as dependent on foreign countries for most of its spices and drugs, metals (iron, lead, and tin), groceries (sugar), manufactured articles, and in particular clothing, as well as glass and mirrors, not to mention art works and even publishing (considered of scant importance) and, finally, despite the fertility of its soil, wheat. Serra was, then, well aware of the peripheral condition of the Kingdom of Naples, although, like de Santis, he made no mention (in his *Treatise*) of the sums that were removed to Madrid and Rome, and which, as we know, constituted the main component of the Kingdom's "loss".[38]

Given this background, the only possibility for rapid development could come from artisanal and manufacturing activities. Manufacturing production could ensure greater wealth than agricultural production because it offered higher returns and absolute certainty of productive outcome.[39] The superiority of industry in this respect had already been expounded by Giovanni Botero at the end of the 16th century, and some direct influence on Serra is undeniable.[40]

> Given that art competes with nature, some may ask which of the two matters more in making a place great and populous: the fertility of the soil or the industry of man. Clearly, it is industry, in the first place because the products of man's creating hand are many more and of much higher price than the things generated by nature, so that nature provides the material and the subject, but the subtlety and art of man bring forth an infinite variety of forms.[41]

The model of development proposed once again by Serra was the very same that had been followed by Italy's mercantile centres since the commercial revolution of the 13th century. At the beginning of the 16th century, the model still seemed to be unbeatable (the Italian economy was going through its *Estate di San Martino, Indian Summer buoyancy*[42]) and even more widely extolled. Here, again, we find an affinity with Botero, who had used very similar terms: the greatness and magnificence of cities such as Venice, Genoa, Florence, and Milan depended, according to Botero, on the manufacturing activities that yielded income for two thirds of the population.[43]

> There is nothing that matters more to make a State great and populous and rich in every commodity than the industry of men and the multitude of arts, some of which are necessary, some conducive to civil life, some desired for show or ornament, and some for delicacy and entertainment for people of leisure: the result is concourse of money and people who work, or traffic with the product, or supply material to the workers, buy, sell, and transport from one place to another the creative skills and labour of men.[44]

However, extension of the manufacturing development model to the Kingdom of Naples could not, according to Serra, rely on the local population, who were unfit to perform this type of activity.

> The inhabitants of the country are so unenterprising that they do not trade outside their own territory – not even with the other parts of Italy, let alone with the other nations of Europe, such as Spain, France and Germany. And such local industries as do exist are run not by the Neapolitans themselves, but by people from other places, chiefly other parts of Italy – Genoese, Florentines, Bergamasques, Venetians and others. But although the Neapolitans see these people running businesses in their own country, they lack the initiative to follow their example and set up businesses in their own homes. In this they are the exact opposite of the Genoese, who have few opportunities at home, but, not content with the business that they do in other parts of Italy, put up which all kinds of hardship and danger, travelling not just through every nation of Europe but through the other parts of the world, even, if they can obtain a license from His Catholic Majesty, as far as the New Indies. The effect of their actions illustrates the importance of this accident of an enterprising population. For although their country is barren, the Genoese have money in abundance, whereas the citizens of the Kingdom of Naples, although their land is fertile, are extremely poor.[45]

This is a fundamental passage in Serra's treatise:[46] if there was this local incapacity, given as a sort of anthropological fact,[47] it was obvious that the void had to be filled by people who were able to organize and manage manufacturing production, namely the foreign merchants who should be given freedom of action to exploit the local resources in order to gain a footing in the international markets. This goal could be achieved by attracting technical and entrepreneurial skills from outside through mercantilistic policies, as had already been done in Tuscany by Cosimo I de' Medici, favouring the immigration of artisans from other parts of the world (*Medicean Economics*);[48] these would constitute the local productive class, filling the gap in entrepreneurial skills.[49] In fact, as pointed out by Francesco Caracciolo, both Serra and Botero evoked "in practice the approach of the sovereigns of the independent kingdom, seeking to promote economic activity and the birth of industries with incentives and allowances for the entrepreneurs".[50]

Again, Botero had made the point in much the same terms:

> The prince who wishes to make his city populous must, then, bring in every sort of industry and manufacturing, which he will do by bringing in skilled workers from other countries and providing them with comfortable and convenient accommodation, and so keep account of the fine crafts and appraise the inventions and works that have singular or rare qualities, and offer rewards for perfection and excellence; but above all this must not entail the need to take the raw materials away from the State, neither wool nor silk, nor timber nor metals or suchlike, because the craftsman also leave with the materials; and many more people live with traffic with the worked material than with the simple material; and the princes' revenues are far richer with the export of products rather than materials, such as velvet, silk, rascia [unrefined woollen cloth], canvas, linen, ropes and hemp.[51]

Serra defended the role of the foreign merchants, and in particular the Genoese, as creators of wealth while at the same time warning them, extolling the supremacy of industrial activities, to avoid investing capital in land and the public debt so as to steer clear of dubious trafficking, against a tendency that seemed to have emerged clearly at the beginning of the 17th century.[52]

Monetary policy was, of course, to be subordinate to the goal of development, and therefore no administrative measures should be adopted on exchange, no restrictive intervention on monetary outflows[53] or the inflow of foreign currencies (which the mint was to evaluate by weight),[54] but a return to the old issue of defending the value of the currency,[55] including the small coin,[56] and maintaining the just proportion of legal value among the various metals minted.[57] It was, according to Serra, upon these principles that the most appropriate monetary policy was to be based for a country that was obliged to import and that sought a place for itself in international trade as producer of industrial goods. Essentially, the emphasis was again on a principle of currency stability, which had been at the basis of the mercantile republics' monetary policy since the 13th century and was particularly appreciated by the Genoese creditors.[58] The monetary system was not, therefore, irrelevant to the process of development – even though it represented a secondary cause, being the result of government provisions.

If this was the background that represented Serra's frame of reference, we can also grant credence to a hypothesis that interprets the scant biographical evidence advanced by Rodolfo Benini at the end of the 19th century,[59] conjecturing that Antonio Serra was a member of a family of Genoese merchants who were particularly active in the closing decades of the 16th century.[60] Apart from the onomastic evidence, his praise of the merits of the Genoese "nation" places him beyond all doubt among the supporters of the Genoese side (with which he seems to have had "intrinsic relations") in the confrontation with the local merchant class. At the same time, his advocacy of stable government as an essential factor for development led him to see in the oligarchic institutions of the Venetian Republic the perfect form of government,[61] which meant that the viceregal institution, with its political discontinuity resulting from the external changeable interests of the Castilian monarchy, could only represent the opposite model.[62]

The advanced industrialism recommended by Serra was in sharp contrast with the backwardness of the Kingdom, which was then in the throes of a generalized subsistence crisis attributable only in part to the normal fluctuations of the agricultural cycle. The seriousness of the problem was to be seen in the recurrent food crises, which repeatedly brought pressure to bear on the city's food administration, showing increasingly grave peaks of emergency as from the beginning of the 17th century (see Figure 4.1).

This problem, totally ignored, as we have seen, in the analysis by de Santis and Serra, actually took a central position in the thinking of certain intellectuals, offering an alternative development model.

Originally, the interest in agriculture arose in response to the food administration crises that took place as early as the 1580s.[63] In 1604, Francesco Imperato, in his *Discorso Politico*, stressed the importance of food administration by the state, including among the major duties of the prince the responsibility "to provide appropriate remedy to poor harvests, and take action on it unreservedly... with his own resources", without levying new taxes, and resorting to import if necessary. The most important task of government, however, lay in being acquainted with the real state of agricultural production, so as to avoid speculation on prices.[64]

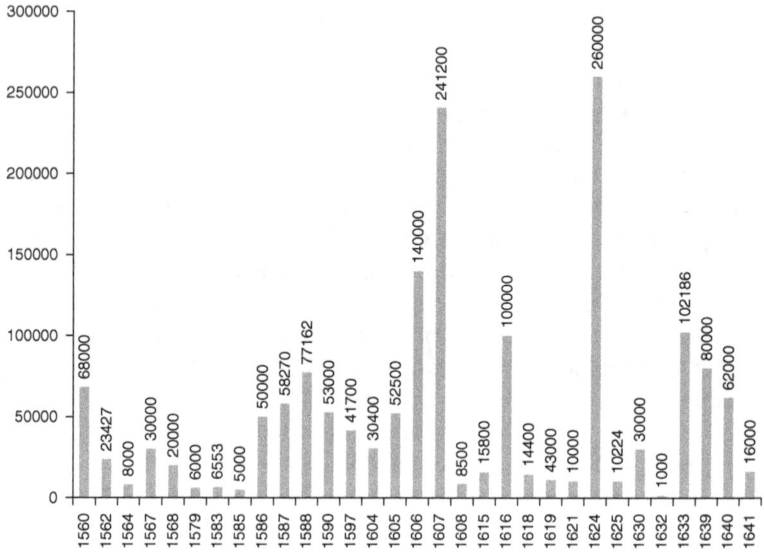

Figure 4.1 Food administration supplies of grain in the city of Naples (in *tomoli*) (vertical axis) 1560–1641

Source: Coniglio (1955, pp. 32–35).

The issue of subsistence was addressed in more decided terms by Tommaso Campanella, in his *Arbitrii sopra le entrate del regno di Napoli*, written in 1605. Campanella proposed drastic solutions[65] to fend off the speculative activity of the merchant class on food administration, calling on the government to take direct charge of the stock of grain, coming to agreements with the merchants and intermediaries before the seeding.[66] In broader terms, in the *Città del Sole*, Campanella reasserted the primacy of agriculture as the basis of wealth and prosperity,[67] contrasting his ideal model of society with the poverty and privilege that characterized conditions in the capital. Carlo Tapia was later to forge a theoretical framework for the issue of subsistence and the primacy of agriculture[68] in his *Trattato dell'abbondanza*. "Of all the industries in human life – Tapia wrote – the farmers' is the most laborious, the most necessary, and calls for the greatest application".[69] Food shortages are due not only to natural causes but also to the wrong choices in production or the speculative activities of the merchant class, considered a natural enemy of the farmworker.[70] Here, too, the solution entailed direct involvement of the state, with institution of public storehouses (in which it would be obligatory to store a tenth or twentieth of the harvest), the necessary price control, severe penalties set for grain hoarders, abolition of fiscal barriers to domestic circulation of grain and a ban on exports.[71]

Over and above the differences, in this area of the literature a development model is proposed based on the capacity of the agricultural sector to generate surplus and ensure abundance. Solving the food problem – an issue also addressed in similar terms in other contexts[72] – becomes central to fostering the growth of the economy. This position, ascribing priority to the agricultural sector, appears to be historically well founded. The general development of the economy in the age of the Renaissance was – Romano observes – "fruit above all of the expansion of agriculture, giving a boost to commerce and industry".[73] At the end of the 16th century, "agricultural support for the commercial and industrial sectors began to wane",[74] bringing on that productive and generalized stagnation that characterized the 17th century as an age of crisis, escaped only by Holland and England.[75]

> Agriculture, then, is the key to understanding the 17th-century crisis (as also the 16th century expansion). ... Is it really still possible today to believe that preindustrial societies found their economic engine in mercantile, banking and industrial activities? If it were so (i.e. possible), a good part of today's underdevelopment would be settled ... The basic fact – which remains fundamental – is that these economies find their real strong point in agriculture. Paraphrasing Colbert, we might say that "when agriculture works, everything works". Gold, silver, banks, galleys and commerce undoubtedly play an important part, but it is agriculture that has the leading role.[76]

The crisis of 1619–1620 was the first effect of decline in agricultural production, characterized by the degradation of the agrarian landscape and the reduction in land reclamation and cultivated areas (with the exception of Holland), to the advantage of stock-breeding and viticulture, with the return of social systems of serfdom, reaction on the part of the lords (refeudalization) and demographic decline brought on by the famine-epidemic cycle.[77] On the other hand, Holland and England showed growth and development trends supported by productive and social innovations in the agricultural sector (a veritable agrarian revolution), as we shall see in detail in the following section.

3 Conclusions: the Dutch Miracle and Italian decline

When placed in its historical context, Serra's *Brief Treatise* appears as one of the possible responses to the economic crisis that characterized the Kingdom of Naples at the beginning of the 17th century.

Serra proposed a development model that favoured industrial activities, seeing them still as a sound and certain source of wealth and power, as demonstrated by the history of the Italian mercantile republics. A strong industrial position would automatically solve the problem of subsistence insofar as the favourable terms of trade would ensure reliable and advantageous supply from abroad. The examples of Venice and Genoa demonstrated that what counted in generating wealth was entrepreneurial and commercial enterprise, even if the land did not suffice to guarantee the necessary subsistence. For the Kingdom of Naples, prospects could have been even more promising in that the "fertility of the location" would have ensured greater independence and based growth on sounder foundations. All it needed was to transplant industrial activities, facilitating the immigration of entrepreneurs and artisans.

The possibility should not have seemed unrealistic at the beginning of the 17th century since the traditional Italian manufacturing centres – Genoa, Florence, and Venice, in the first place – "lacked neither capital nor entrepreneurial spirit, nor insight and commercial organisation".[78] However, it was precisely then that signs of decline began to appear, represented by the tendency to reduce risky investments in favour of safe investments in property rents (real estate and the feuds of the nobles) and finance (state bonds and exchange). Although they were still rich, Italy's merchant classes were no longer prepared to risk their capital, not only because safer investment was possible, but also because the growing competition from the English and Dutch merchants reduced market outlets abroad, while at home there were no more opportunities for profitable investments.[79]

At the end of the 16th century, Botero was already contrasting Venice with Genoa, evidencing the relative decline of the latter:

> In Italy we have two singularly flourishing republics: Venice and Genoa, and between the two Venice is clearly well ahead of Genoa in terms of both state and greatness. If we seek the reasons for this, we will find that this has come about because the Venetians, concentrating on real merchandise, filled their pockets but little individually, and greatly in common, while the Genoese, investing in exchanges,

increased their wealth beyond measure at the individual level, but with extremely impoverished public revenues.[80]

The *industrialist* proposal contained in the *Brief Treatise* appeared to be in sharp contrast with the pursuit of rentable positions and the tendency towards unproductive expenditure that characterized Italy's slow decline. At the beginning of the 17th century, this process did not seem irreversible, and extension to the Mezzogiorno of Northern Italy's manufacturing capitalism could have offered a solution to the stagnation and productive investment, supplying new and profitable openings. Moreover, it was a matter of following through with the traditional role of the Mezzogiorno, subordinate to the manufacturing and financial centres of the North[81] and thereby confirming, in the climate of unity guaranteed by Spanish predominance, the function served by the Mezzogiorno for the northern economy.

His fervent advocacy of the Italian industrial model, however, constituted the greatest limitation to Serra's analysis. Unlike other contemporaries, Serra failed to see what already appeared evident to other attentive observers of economic realities in the first decade of the 17th century: Holland's rapid development, the growing and aggressive presence of the English in the Mediterranean, and loss, for Venice, of the central role in trade with the East.[82]

The Dutch Miracle[83] thus has been termed the rapid development shown by the rebel United Provinces, by then generally recognized, to the extent that even Imperial Spain had given in to Dutch military might, compelled to conclude a truce with the Calvinist heretics. The process of development in Holland exhibited features that differed greatly from the situation in Italy. The United Provinces showed no prevalence of a model of sectoral productive specialization but rather an integrated cycle that went from the production of subsistence goods to financial activities. Holland had solved the problem of feeding its citizens despite its great population density, as from the mid 15th century exploiting agronomic innovations that had boosted the yield of certain crops and livestock,[84] generating a surplus destined for export with the effect of orienting all agricultural production to the market. In the particularly favourable geographical position and scarcity of natural resources lay the incentives to develop entrepreneurial and commercial skills (also boosted by immigration from the Spanish Netherlands). These various factors led the Dutch to extend their trade on a large scale, taking the place of the *Hanseatic League* in the Baltic Sea and the North Sea.

Herring fishing in the North Sea fuelled this trade. The Dutch succeeded in introducing technical innovations thanks to which the herrings could be conserved and subsequently marketed over great distances, providing European diet with a significant contribution of protein in a period of serious general food shortage (known as the *Little Ice Age*). The herring trade and conservation had developed on the strength of innovations in the shipyards, calling for vast quantities of timber coming from the Baltic area (in recognition of the importance of the trade in this area it was in fact termed the *Mother Trade*). From the same area came the grain that ensured food supply in Holland and the rest of Europe, as far as the Mediterranean. In exchange for these products, the Dutch traded manufactured articles (fabrics, gunpowder, precious metals, weapons, and luxury goods), as well as spices and the produce of specialized agriculture (beer, floriculture, fruit and vegetables, and raw materials for textile production) and livestock farming (dairy products). The quest for direct sources of raw materials and groceries drove the Dutch to territorial expansion in the New World and the Pacific, taking advantage of the collapse of Portuguese dominion and Spain's military decline. Thanks to the creation of the Dutch empire, overseas control over the principal resources was guaranteed together with openings for the growing profits. In the beginning of the 17th century, Amsterdam was already enjoying a leading position both in world trade and in the financial and money markets which waxed increasingly strong after the foundation of the *Wisselbank*[85] in 1609.

The development shown by the Dutch did not escape the attention of contemporaries, and "the abrupt rise of a country unendowed by nature to such heights of wealth and power was, indeed, frequently regarded as a miracle".[86] Consideration of "the flourishing state of the Dutch economy has in this way served as an important stimulus to the development of the science of political economy".[87] Holland became a case for "conscious imitation" at the level of economic policy, above all in England and France.

Serra had nothing to say about the case of Holland, although his lucid analysis of the causes of economic development could have been applied to it perfectly well. By the beginning of the 17th century, the Dutch Miracle was well known and widely discussed in Italy, too:[88] as early as 1567, the Florentine author Lodovico Guicciardini wrote an extensive treatise on the economic and political situation in the Low Countries,[89] while detailed descriptions of the warfare involved were provided by the chronicles.[90] In 1610 Venetian Paolo Sarpi extolled the might of the Dutch, and in 1611 Cardinal Guido Bentivoglio, papal nuncio in France and Flanders, wrote a *Relatione delle Province Unite (Report on the United Provinces)*, published in 1629 (to be followed later by the detailed *Storia della guerra di Fiandra, (History of the War of Flanders)* 1637.[91] In Naples in particular, Holland's fortunes found attention, above all because the Dutch theatre of operations had seen the direct involvement of Neapolitan troops under the command of Spanish nobles, who subsequently received important government appointments in Naples (for example, the Viceroy Duke of Osuna, who in his youth fought against the Flemish rebels). Thus, it is hardly surprising that the example of the industry of Flanders had already found mention in a report addressed to the Viceroy don Juan de Zúñiga (Anon. datable 1586–1595) and that Tommaso Campanella, writing in prison, dedicated a chapter of his *Monarchia di Spagna* (1600–1601)[92] to the Low Countries. Moreover, Serra's lavish praise of the Venetian republican oligarchy could also have drawn attention to the successes of the republican state of the United Provinces.[93]

In other economic environments, however, a veritable "fear of the Dutch" began to make itself felt, prompting analysis of the reasons for success in order to bring about imitative processes. Only two years after publication of the *Brief Treatise*, with French society in the throes of economic crisis, Antoine de Montchrétien, in his *Traité de l'Economie Politique*, recognized that the United Provinces had, in the space of a few years, grown from province to empire in a rich and powerful country.[94] Montchrétien attributed the reason for the success to the predominance achieved in maritime trade.[95] He also recognized that challenging Dutch power was no easy task, because there could be no competing with them in costs. He therefore proposed an autarchic policy for France, promoting domestic trade, eschewing international exchange and favouring colonial conquest as a way of acquiring raw materials. Montchrétien was already arguing in terms of the *world-system*, while Serra's reflections, by contrast, were limited to Italy's historical experience, still advanced as a valid model, although it had by then lost relevance with the new power relations coming into play.

A few years later, England's "fear of the Dutch" gave way to irresistible fascination. The example of a small densely populated country, bounded by narrow spits of land wrenched from the sea to become "a port, a bank, a factory where products from the whole world are transformed",[96] inspired emulation and even imitation. Throughout the 17th century, the Dutch Miracle dominated British economic literature. Thomas Mun, Josiah Child, William Temple, William Aglionby, and William Petty tried to account for Holland's extraordinary success.

They all attributed Holland's wealth to the sea, with its predominant role in maritime commerce over great distances. The fullest account was provided by Temple, who described Holland's commercial primacy to its happy geographical position, between the sea and navigable rivers, affording transport at low cost. To these were added to the needs resulting from a densely populated land driving up the prices of foodstuffs and entailing the imperative to obtain the necessities elsewhere through trade.

> Wherever they are so, if it lies upon the Sea, they naturally break out into Trade, both because, whatever they want of their own, that is necessary to so many Mens Lives, must be supply'd from abroad; and because, by the multitude of people, and smalness of Country, Land grows so dear, that the Improvement of Money, that way, is inconsiderable, and so turns to Sea, where the greatness of the Profit makes amends for the Venture.[97]

The rest of Holland's success is accounted for precisely by its entrepreneurial skills and high quality of manufactured articles.[98]

The mythical status acquired by Italy's manufacturing primacy and its mercantile republics, Venice taking on the role of "ideal State",[99] certainly influenced Serra's analysis, coming between him and a critical view of the limits his model was already showing in the face of the new growth factors characterizing development in the United Provinces and England. Proposing a model constructed essentially on economic liberalism, based on the free circulation of currencies and goods, Serra failed to grasp the element that most strongly characterized the commercial policy of the great powers, consisting in mercantilistic protectionism and privileged companies. Although his analysis of the causes of economic development was essentially correct and applicable also to the case of Holland,[100] his policy conclusions are rather more nearsighted – provincial, we might even say,[101] unaware of the irreversible transformations that would leave the economy of Northern Italy on the fringe (as exporter of primary and semifinished products, and no longer as a producer of manufactured articles) and condemn the Spanish Mezzogiorno to an even more marginal role, as a simple reserve for the predatory war economy of the Habsburg Empire and as a market outlet for English and Dutch goods.

Like most of the Italian intellectuals at the beginning of the 17th century, Serra had not yet become aware of the signs of Italy's decline, nor of the new hegemony that was taking shape in the core of the *world-system* economy. Botero tellingly epitomized this limit to Italian culture in a few incisive lines:

> We Italians are too much our own friends and too interested as admirers of our things when we prefer Italy and its cities to all the rest of the world.[102]

Notes

1. Galasso, G., *Alla periferia dell'Impero. Il Regno di Napoli nel periodo spagnolo (secoli XVI–XVII)*, Turin: Einaudi, 1994.
2. Musi, A., *L'impero dei vicerè*, Bologna: Il Mulino, 2013.
3. Galasso, G., *Storia del Regno di Napoli*, vol. II, *Il Mezzogiorno spagnolo (1494–1622)*, Turin: UTET, 2006, p. 951.
4. Coniglio, G., *Il Viceregno di Napoli nel secolo XVII. Nuove notizie sulla vita commerciale e finanziaria tratte dagli archivi napoletani*, Rome: Edizioni Storia e Letteratura, 1955, pp. 190–213; Galasso, G., "Momenti e problemi di storia napoletana nell'età di Carlo V", in *Mezzogiorno medievale e moderno*, Turin: Einaudi, 1965, pp. 201–229; Galasso, G., 1965, p. 156; Muto, G., *Le finanze pubbliche napoletane tra riforme e restaurazione (1520–1634)*, Naples: Edizioni Scientifiche Italiane, 1980.
5. Dell'Erba, N., *La riforma monetaria angioina e il sviluppo storico nel Reame di Napoli*, 1932, ristampa anastatica Forni, estratto dall'Archivio storico per le province napoletane (anno XVIII, XIX, XX e XXI), p. 145.
6. De Rosa, L., *I cambi esteri del Regno di Napoli dal 1591 al 1707*, Naples: Banco di Napoli, 1955, p. 53.
7. Musi, 2013.
8. "Not that economics, finance and money had not been discussed before, but it was only then that consideration of these issues was freed from sociological and moral discussion of a doctrinaire nature, from reference to specific administrative problems of the moment, and from contingent pressures addressed in isolation on every occasion although recurrent. It was only then that the general picture of the problems facing the Kingdom took shape at this level, while at the same time the economic aspects emerged in their more structural characteristics" (Galasso, 2006, p. 931).
9. Colapietra, R. (ed.), *Problemi monetari negli scrittori napoletani del Seicento*, Rome: Accademia Nazionale dei Lincei, 1973, p. 16.
10. de Santis, 1605a, *Discorso intorno alli effetti, che fa il cambio in Regno*, Naples: presso Costantino Vitali, 1605, in L. De Rosa (ed.), *Il Mezzogiorno agli inizi del '600*, Bari: Laterza, 1994, pp. 5–74, p. 29.
11. Ibid., p. 7.
12. Ibid., pp. 13, 32.
13. Ibid., pp. 9–10
14. Ibid., p. 10.
15. de Santis, 1605b, *Secondo discorso intorno alli effetti che fa il cambio in Regno, sopra una risposta, che è stata fatta aduerso del primo*, Naples: stamperia di Felice Stigliola, 1605, in L. De Rosa (ed.), 1994, pp. 5–74, p. 62; On banking

activity in the polls between the 16th and 17th centuries and the failure of the private banks, cfr. Silvestri, A. (a), "Sui banchieri pubblici napoletani dall'avvento di Filippo II al trono alla costituzione del monopolio", *Bollettino dell'Archivio Storico del Banco di Napoli*, 3, 1951, pp. 1–35; Silvestri, A. (b), "Sui banchieri pubblici nella città di Napoli dalla costituzione del monopolio alla fine del banco dei Mercanti", *Bollettino dell'Archivio Storico del Banco di Napoli*, 4, 1951, pp. 1–24.

16. As to whether there was, in fact, some "indigenous" form of bourgeoisie, Giuseppe Coniglio (Coniglio, 1955, pp. 14–17) is somewhat sceptical.
17. On the presence and importance of the Genoese colony in the Kingdom of Naples, cfr. Brancaccio, 2001. Brancaccio, G., *Nazione genovese: Consoli e colonia nella Napoli moderna,* Naples: Guida Editori, 2001. On the Genoese merchants and bankers operating in Naples between the 16th and 17th centuries, cfr. Musi, A., *Mezzogiorno spagnolo: la via napoletana allo stato moderno,* Naples: Guida, 1991, pp. 131–172.
18. Galasso, 2006, pp. 888–890, 899–900.
19. Dobb, M., *Studies in the Development of Capitalism,* Fourth Impression, London: Routledge & Kegan Paul, 1950, p. 202.
20. Ibid., p. 203.
21. Einzig, P., *The History of Foreign Exchange,* New York, NY: St. Martin's Press, 1962, pp. 139–141.
22. de Santis, 1605b, pp. 42–43.
23. Ibid., 1605a, p. 44.
24. Dobb, 1950, p. 203.
25. Boyer-Xambeau, M.-T., G. Deleplace, and L. Gillard, *Monnaie privéè et pouvoir des princes,* Paris: Presses de la Fondation Nationale des Sciences Politiques, 1986; *Banchieri e principi. Moneta e credito nell'Europa del Cinquecento,* Turin: Einaudi, 1991, pp. 149–152.
26. de Santis, 1605a, p. 38.
27. Ibid., p. 39.
28. Ibid.
29. Ibid., 1605a, p. 38.
30. Calabria, A., *The Cost of Empire,* Cambridge: Cambridge University Press, 1991, pp. 9–14.
31. Galasso, 1965, p. 182.
32. Colapietra, 1973, p. 25; Galasso, 2006, p. 938.
33. de Santis, 1605b, pp. 51–56; according to De Rosa, it might have been Giovanni Giacomo Lando, the author of a treatise on trading practices. (De Rosa, L. (ed.), Introduzione a *Il Mezzogiorno agli inizi del '600,* Bari: Laterza, 1994, p. xxxiii; Lando, G.G., *Aritmetica Mercantile,* Naples: Tarquinio Largo, 1604).
34. Colapietra, 1973, p. 25; Galasso, 2006, p. 938.
35. de Santis reasserted his positions, adding that exchange conditions had suffered from the Belmosto operation and the Spanish bankruptcy of 1597 (de Santis, 1605b, pp. 71–72).
36. Serra A., *A Short Treatise on the Wealth and Poverty of Nations,* English translation by Jonatan Hunt of *Breve trattato delle cause, che possono far abbondare li Regni d'oro, et argento Dove non sono miniere. Con applicatione al Regno di Napoli. Del dottor Antonio Serra della città di Cosenza. Diviso in tre parti,* Naples: appresso

Lazzaro Scorriggio, 1613, edited and with an introduction by Sophus A. Reinert, London, New York, Delhi: Anthem Press, 2011, p. 119.

37. Giovanni Botero, too, in the *Cause della Grandezza delle Città (Causes of the Greatness of the Cities)* saw the causes of wealth in the advantages of the location, the fertility of the soil and the favourable position vis-à-vis the communication routes (Botero, G., *Delle cause della grandezza delle città,* Rome: pel Martinelli, 1588, in Botero, G., *Della Ragion di Stato,* a cura di L. Firpo, Turin: UTET, 1948, pp. 341–409, 355–356).
38. De Rosa, 1994, p. xlvi–xlvii.
39. Serra, 1613, p. 121.
40. Reinert, S.A., *Introduction* to Serra (1613), pp. 1–93, 43–46; Firpo, L., Introduzione a Giovanni Botero. *Della Ragion di Stato,* a cura di Luigi Firpo, Turin: UTET, 1948, p. 29.
41. On the "mercantilist" thought of Giovanni Botero, cfr. Descendre, R., "Raison d'Etat, puissance et économie: Le mercantilisme de Giovanni Botero," *Revue de Métaphysique et de Morale,* 3, n. 39, 2003, pp. 311–321; Botero, 1948, p. 247.
42. Thus, Carlo Maria Cipolla defined the short-lived recovery of the economy of northern Italy at the beginning of the 17th century, does tend to decline into stagnation (Cipolla, C.M., *Storia dell'economia italiana. Saggi di storia economica,* Turin: Einaudi, 1959, vol. I, p.17; Galasso, 1965, pp. 172–173; Calabria, 1991, p. 9).
43. Botero, 1948, p. 248.
44. Botero, 1948, pp. 246–247.
45. Serra, 1613, pp. 124–125.
46. Serra, 1613, p. 206.
47. Again, there is an affinity with Botero, who, unlike Serra, offers an explanation of this particular shortcoming of the Neapolitans. "In barren lands industry and diligence thrive, but in fertile lands delicacy and idleness" (Botero, 1948, p. 103). Again, in the *Cause della Grandezza delle Città,* Botero remarks: "Fertile soil is not enough, then, to make a city great: and the reason is that where the land is abundant and copious, the inhabitants, finding everything that is necessary and useful at home, have no reason or interest to go elsewhere, but enjoy it in their birthplace with no effort, and all love ease with the least possible discomfort" (Botero, 1948, p. 355).
48. Reinert, 2011, pp. 38–46.
49. A few years later, Giulio Cesare Capaccio expressed the wish that the foreigners operating in the Kingdom would consider Naples no longer a colony but a homeland. (Capaccio, G.C., *Il Forastiero,* Naples: Gio. Domenico Roncagliolo, 1634, p. 674.)
50. Caracciolo, F., *Il regno di Napoli nei secoli XVI e XVII,* Messina: Università degli Studi, 1966, p. 152.
51. Botero, 1948, pp. 249–250.
52. Calabria, 1991, pp. 5–6; Musi, A., *Mezzogiorno spagnolo. La via napoletana allo Stato moderno,* Naples: Guida, 1991, p. 168; Villari, R., *La rivolta antispagnola a Napoli: le origini (1587–1647),* Bari: Laterza, 1967, p. 173; Antonio Calabria writes: "Constant was the presence of Genoese in the security market (of the Kingdom of Naples). Merchant bankers from the Republic of Genoa were by far the most prominent businessmen in the Kingdom, involved in

all the aspects of its trade and finance. They were the most active grain, silk, oil and wine merchants and exporters: they were important shipping magnates and provisioners to the state fleet, which included the galleys they leased the state, they figured prominently in public administration, as tax farmers and fiscal officials. They were also the most important financiers in the Kingdom, and they supplied the lion's share of the loans raised by the Crown in sixteenth-century Naples. In short, the Genoese held a position in sixteenth-century Naples analogous to the one they captured in sixteenth-century Castille" (Calabria, 1991, p. 118). The Genoese "held a good portion of the state securities and their presence in the bond market was noteworthy throughout the century.... Genoese investors, even in redeemable securities alone, represent what might be termed a flight of capital out of the Kingdom towards Genoa, where many of them resided and received their rents from their agents or factors. The exodus of capital towards the North highlighted the mediation of foreign merchant bankers in the Neapolitan economy, and it symbolized the South's dependent position *vis-à-vis* the Northen Italian economy" (Calabria, 1991, pp. 118–119).

53. "The freedom to export money increases trade, whereas a ban on exporting money reduces it. For it is not always in a merchant's interest to use bills of exchange; often it will be advantageous to use cash. Therefore, if the exportation of money is banned, he will refrain from bringing money into the Kingdom, for the ban would prevent him from having access to it should he need it elsewhere later. So he may well prefer to suffer a disadvantage in other respects and refrain from trading in the Kingdom" (Serra, 1613, p. 213). The ban on exporting money was permissible only if exportation would cause some harm, as in the case of the country having no local production, but this was not the case of the Kingdom, which had in any case local productive capacity (Serra, 1613, p. 215).
54. Serra, 1613, p. 220.
55. Ibid., p. 222.
56. Ibid., p. 224.
57. Ibid., p. 234.
58. Arrighi, G., *The Long Twentieth Century. Money, Power, and the Origins of Our Times*, London, New York, NY: Verso, 1994, p. 155.
59. Benini, R., "Sulle dottrine economiche di Antonio Serra", *Giornale degli Economisti*, vol. 3, no. 5, 1892, pp. 222–248; Colapietra, 1973, p. 28, n. 47.
60. "A man of the same name as our author – Benini wrote – appears among the principal tradesmen and bankers convened in Naples by the consuls of Genoa and Florence to regulate procedure for exchange payments. If the coincidence of first name and surname is no mere chance, the familiarity Serra shows with commercial matters, which seems, on the evidence of many passages in his book, to derive from his frequent occasion of financial institutions, suggests the possibility of some kinship with the homonymous figure (at least a generation older). The practice widespread in various parts of Italy of giving the grandson/nephew the name of the grandfather or paternal uncle would account for the homonymy. In this case the related Serras would be Genoese settled in Calabria for reasons of commerce" (Benini, 1892, pp. 222–223). The merchant Antonio Serra, as Raffaele Colapietra recalls, was very active and influential with the relatives Giambattista and Geronimo

during the 1560s (Colapietra, 1973, p. 28, n. 47). "In 1568 the Genoese Ottobono Grillo and Gio. B. [undoubtedly Giovambattista] Serra received authorisation for transport by land from Cosenza to Naples of 50,000 pounds of silk" (Galasso, 1992, p. 226, n. 171; my thanks to Luca Addante for this last reference). The Genoese Serras feature as investors of capital in the acquisition of feuds (De Rosa, L., *Il Mezzogiorno spagnolo tra crescita e decadenza, Milan: Il Saggiatore,* 1987, p. 60). On the Genoese banker Serras' creditors of the Spanish monarchy, cfr. Calabria, 1991, pp. 2, 65.

61. "Serra" – wrote Luigi Einaudi – "wants the men in his State to be good farmers and industrious tradesmen, and to be governed with Venetian continuity by aged men experienced in public affairs and constantly renewed by fresh young forces" (Einaudi, L., *Saggi bibliografici e storici intorno alle dottrine economiche,* Rome: Edizioni di storia e letteratura, 1953, p. 132; Serra, 1613, pp. 139–145. On the connection between Serra's thought and the Republican myth represented by Venice, cfr. Addante, L., "Repubblicanesimo e mito di Venezia nel *Breve Trattato* di Antonio Serra", *Clio. Rivista trimestrale di studi storici,* Anno XXXVII, n. 1, gennaio-marzo 2001, pp. 117–154.
62. Oscar Nuccio tended to see in this position a political viewpoint favouring independence (Nuccio, O., "Sul significato storico del Breve Trattato di Antonio Serra", *Rivista Storica del Mezzogiorno,* 1967, pp. 46–71).
63. This is evidenced by the *Breve Compendio et particolar notitia de molte cose importanti al Servizio di Sua Maestà et benefitio universale del Regno,* addressed to the Viceroy don Juan de Zúñiga – which opposed the power of the grain speculators, Anonymous manuscript, *Società Napoletana di Storia Patria, XIII D 32.*
64. Imperato, F., *Discorso politico intorno al regimento delle piazze della città di Napoli,* Naples: nella Stamperia di Felice Stigliola, 1604, pp. 30–31; Lepre, A., *Storia del Mezzogiorno d'Italia,* vol. I, La lunga durata e la crisi (1500–1656), Naples: Liguori, 1986, p. 236; much the same points were later to be made by Fabio Frezza, another exponent of the "people". (Frezza, F., *Discorso intorno ai rimedi d'alcuni mali ai quali soggiace la Città, et il Regno di Napoli,* Naples: per li heredi di Tarquinio Longo, 1623).
65. Particularly interesting is Campanella's proposal for the monetary crisis (he noted that "there is great disorder in this kingdom, for almost all the coins are clipped", Campanella, T., *Arbitrii sopra le entrate del Regno,* 1605, in R. Colapietra (ed.), 1973, pp. 85–110, p. 102), recommending that the Viceroy should fix fiscal payments in weight while spending "in number", obtaining an advantage, deeming the operation perfectly legitimate (it is the people who clip, committing an offence).
66. Government monopoly was also to be extended to silk production (Campanella, 1605, p. 87).
67. Firpo, L., *Recensione di: Tommaso Campanella: Città del Sole,* Turin: Einaudi, 1941, p. 85.
68. Lepre, 1986, p. 241.
69. Tapia, C.,*Trattato dell'abbondanza,* Naples: pel Mollo, 1638, p. 31.
70. Ibid., pp. 83–84; Lepre, 1986, p. 242.
71. Ibid., pp. 86–98.
72. Heckscher terms "provision policy" the set of measures aiming to ensure abundance (Dobb, M., *Studies in the Development of Capitalism,* London: Routledge & Kegan Paul, 1963, p. 232).

73. Romano, R., *Opposte congiunture. La crisi del Seicento in Europa e in America*, Venice: Marsilio, 1992, p. 5.
74. Romano, 1992, p. 6.
75. On the role of agriculture in the 17th century crisis, cfr. Wallerstein, I., *The Modern World System II: Mercantilism and the Consolidation of the European World-Economy, 1600–1750*, New York, NY: Academic Press, 1980, chap. 1. On the connection between industrial takeoff and agricultural development, cfr. Johnston, B., "Agriculture and Structural Transformation in Developing Countries: A Survey of Research." *Journal of Economic Literature*, 8, 1970, pp. 369–404; Reynold, L.G. (ed.), *Agriculture in Development Theory*, London: Yale University Press, 1975; Jones, E.L., *Agriculture and the industrial revolution*, Oxford: Basil Blackwell, 1974; O'Brien, P.K., "Agriculture and the Industrial Revolution", *Economic History Review*, New Series. 30, 1977, pp. 166–181; Overton, M., *Agricultural Revolution in England: The Transformation of the Agrarian Economy 1500–1850*. Cambridge: Cambridge University Press, 1998; Tiffin, R. and X. Irz, "Is Agriculture the Engine of Growth?" *Agricultural Economics* 35, 2006, pp. 79–89; Tsakok, I. and B. Gardner, "Agriculture in Economic Development: Primary Engine of Growth or Chicken and Egg?" *American Journal of Agricultural Economics*, Agricultural and Applied Economics Association, vol. 89(5), 2007, pp. 1145–1151.
76. Romano, 1992, pp. 6–7.
77. Wallerstein, 1980, chap. 1; Romano, 1992, p. 12.
78. Pagano de Divitis, G., *Mercanti inglesi nell'Italia del Seicento. Navi, traffici, egemonie*, Venice: Marsilio, 1990, p. 32.
79. Parker, G., *Global Crisis: War, Climate Change and Catastrophe in the Seventeenth Century*, New Haven, CT and London: Yale University Press, 2013.
80. Botero, 1948, pp. 78–79.
81. Abulafia, D., *The Two Italies. Economic Relations between the Norman Kingdom of Sicily and the Northern Communes*, Cambridge: Cambridge University Press, 1977.
82. This was a development that already appeared evident at the beginning of the 17th century, as attested by a dispatch of September 1605 from the Venetian ambassador in London, Nicolò Monin, to the Doge and Senate, denouncing the growing English influence in the Mediterranean and the threat of exclusion for Italian mediation, traditionally exercised in that area (Pagano De Vitis, 1990, p. 15). On Venice's loss of commercial importance, cfr. Romano, 1992, p. 153.
83. Swart, K.W., "The miracle of the Dutch Republic as seen in the Seventeenth Century." Inaugural lecture delivered at University College London, 6 November 1967, London: H.K. Lewis, 1967, p. 2; Huizinga, J.H., *Dutch Civilization in the Seventeenth Century, and Other Essays*, London: Collins, 1968, p. 10; Davids, K. and J. Lucassen, *A Miracle Mirrored: The Dutch Republic in European Perspective*, Cambridge: Cambridge University Press, 1995; Israel, J., "The Dutch Republic: Its Rise, Greatness and Fall, 1477–1806", *Oxford History of Early Modern Europe*, Oxford: Oxford University Press, 1995; Prak, M. and D. Webb, *The Dutch Republic in the Seventeenth Century: The Golden Age*, Cambridge: Cambridge University Press, 2005.

84. "As from the 16th century the very densely populated plains of Flanders and Brabant had become, as noted by Slicher van Bath, the Mecca of Europe's agricultural experts" (Bairoch, P., *Le Tiers-Monde dans l'impasse. Le démmarrage économique du XVIIe au XXe siècle*, Paris: Editions Gallimard, 1971, p. 28).
85. Wallerstein, I., *The Modern World System I: Capitalist Agriculture and the Origins of the European World-Economy in the Sixteenth Century*, New York, NY: Academic Press, 1974, p. 320.
86. Swart, 1967, p. 2.
87. Ibid.
88. Blanco-Morel, M. and M.F. Piéjus (eds), *Les Flandres et la culture espagnole et italienne au XVIe et XVIIe siècle*, Lille: Université Lille III, 1998; Villari, R., *Un sogno di libertà. Napoli nel declino di un Impero (1585–1648)*, Milan: Mondadori, 2012, pp. 493–503.
89. Guicciardini, L., *Descritione di M. Lodovico Guicciardini patritio fiorentino di tutti i Paesi Bassi, altrimenti detti Germania Inferiore: con più carte di geographia del paese, & col ritratto naturale di più terre principali*, Antwerp: appresso Guglielmo Silvio stampatore regio, 1567, 2nd ed. 1585. References to the Low Countries can also be found in Botero, cfr. Botero, 1948, p. 249.
90. Campana, C., *Della guerra di Fiandre*, Vicenza: Appresso Giorgio Greco, 1602; Giustiniani, P., *Della guerra di Fiandra*, Antwerp: appresso IoachimioTrognesio, 1609.
91. Bentivoglio, G., *Relatione delle Province Unite*, Colonia: Pantino, 1629; Bentivoglio, G., *Della guerra di Fiandra*, Venice: Appresso Francesco Baba, 1637.
92. This chapter was subsequently published separately in Antwerp in 1617 as *Discorso sul Paesi Bassi*, and went through seven reprints up to 1632 (Villari, 2012, p. 495; Firpo, L., "Appunti campanelliani XXII. Un'opera che Campanella non scrisse: Il Discorso sui Paesi Bassi", *Giornale critico della filosofia italiana, XXIII*, 1952; Fournel, J.L. "Campanella et la monarchie de France: Empire universel et équilibre despuissances", in AA.VV., *Tommaso Campanella e l'attesa del secolo aureo*, Florence: Olschki, 1998, pp. 5–37).
93. On the myth of the Republic of the United Provinces in 17th century political thought, cfr. Venturi, F., *Utopia e riforma nell'Illuminismo*, Turin: Einaudi, 1970; Addante, 2001, p. 123.
94. Montchrétien, A. de or Montchrestien, A. de (1615), *Traicté de l'oeconomie politique: dédié en 1615 au Roy et à la Reyne mère du Roy par Antoyne de Montchrétien*, avec introd. et notes par Th. Funck-Brentano, Paris: Plon, 1889. "The exercise of commerce, which constitutes a great part of political action, is always practised by peoples that have enjoyed power and glory, and now even more diligently than ever by those pursuing power and expansion. It is also the quickest way to acquire wealth, and with it to rise to the heights of honour and authority. We have Holland as proof and example before our eyes, as our ancestors had had the Republics of Genoa and Venice. Without doubt this country is a miracle of industry.... Never before had a State done so much in so little time; never before did such weak and obscure beginnings lead to such great, evident and sudden progress" (Montchrétien, 1615, p. 142). "If I wanted to leave to posterity an example of the usefulness of commerce, I would first describe the cities of Amsterdam and Mildenburg." Montchrétien, 1615, p. 143.

95. Montchrétien, 1615, p. 250.
96. Dockès, Pierre, *L'éspace dans la pensée économique du XVIe au XVIIIe siècle Nouvelle Bibliothèque Scientifique*, Paris, Flammarion, 1971, p. 105.
97. Sir William Temple served as English Ambassador to the Dutch Republic and provided one of the most penetrating analyses and vivid descriptions of the Republic in his *Observations upon the United Provinces of the Netherlands*, first published in 1673. (Temple, W., *Remarques sur l'Etat des Provinces-Unies des Pays-Bas*. Utrecht: n.p., 1672, pp. 211–212.)
98. In similar terms, William Petty, too, saw the success of the Dutch as the gift of its geographical position, which favoured trade.
99. Addante, 2001.
100. In terms of Serra's scheme, the Republic of the United Provinces possessed not only a favourable geographical position but also a multiplicity of manufacturing activities, an enterprising population, extensive trade and effective government.
101. The provincialism that Italian culture fell into in the late Renaissance is effectively evoked by Antonio Gramsci in his *Note sul Machiavelli sulla politica e sullo Stato modern*, where he contrasts the political thought of Nicolò Machiavelli with the narrower viewpoint of Francesco Guicciardini. "Guicciardini – Gramsci observes – returns to purely Italian political thinking, while Machiavelli had risen to the European level. Machiavelli cannot be understood without taking account of the fact that he reaches beyond Italian to European experience (international at the time): his «will» would be utopian without the European experience" (Gramsci, A., *Note sul Machiavelli sulla politica e sullo Stato moderno*, Turin: Einaudi, 1948, p. 85).
102. Botero, 1948, p. 393.

5
The Influence of Portuguese Economic Thought on the *Breve trattato*: Antonio Serra and Miguel Vaaz in Spanish Naples

Gaetano Sabatini

1

The fourth centenary of the *Breve trattato delle cause che possono far abbondare li regni d'oro e d'argento dove non sono miniere con applicazione al Regno di Napoli*, published in Naples in 1613,[1] has presented an important opportunity to reflect on its content, on its author Antonio Serra, and on the context in which his ideas developed and matured.[2] Although many studies have been written about the volume and its author, analyses of the *Breve trattato*'s theoretical content have as yet failed to examine similarities between Serra's thought and that of early 17th-century Portuguese *arbitristas* in any depth. The relevant points of contact between these two areas deserve to be highlighted, and they can provide crucial insights into the author's life and the circumstances in which his work appeared.

At the start of the 17th century, Portuguese economic culture appears to have been strongly influenced by the formation, across the preceding century, of a trade network that extended from Lisbon to the Indian and Atlantic Oceans and by the introduction of the new commercial and financial practices associated with it. Portuguese economic treatises gradually moved away from formulations inspired by Scholastic philosophy towards a mercantilist vision dictated by the exigencies of commercial capitalism's development, particularly in the form promoted by the Portuguese monarchy, in which royal monopolies and private enterprises coexisted. No longer did the moral character of economic action or the licitness of economic practices lie at the centre of theoretical reflection. They were replaced instead by the organization and financing of an administrative and military apparatus capable of expanding alongside the overseas empire and of promoting the wealth of the state and of the aristocracy that constituted its ruling elite. Population, manufacturing, wealth, money, wages, and trade are the basic ideas around which a discourse began to coalesce, one that, though still in an embryonic and pre-scientific form, was nonetheless able to provide a description of the real workings of the economy by relying on rudimentary analytical instruments, inductive methods, and early attempts at quantifying these phenomena.[3]

The first contribution of Portuguese economic thought that belongs to this period and has significant points of contact with Serra's *Breve trattato* is certainly the *Do sitio de Lisboa: dialogo*,[4] published in 1608 by Luis Mendes de Vasconcelos, who was captain-major of the Portuguese army in Asia and was between 1617 and 1621 the governor of Angola.[5] Written as a dialogue, among various characters – what was common in the humanistic literature – and with quotations from the Greek and Latin classical tradition. *Do sitio de Lisboa* is a learned peroration addressed to Philip III, encouraging him to move to Lisbon the capital city of the Catholic Monarchy, which, at that time, also included the Lusitanian Kingdom and all of its overseas dependencies. With this purpose in mind, the author focuses on the excellent natural endowments of Lisbon and its territory in terms not only of natural ports, healthy climate, and fertile soil[6] but also of the efficiency of the supply networks that from the Kingdom's various regions led to the city, showing the potential for expansion of production and of the Portuguese domestic market and emphasizing the Portuguese vocation towards commerce on a global scale.[7]

In his vision of the Portuguese's natural calling to commerce, Mendes de Vasconcelos maintains that relations with the overseas territories should be of a purely mercantile nature: the wealth of Lisbon and of the entire Kingdom can grow only through a network of exchanges based on the dominions in India and Brazil. On the basis of these assumptions, he is strongly against both the peopling of these territories with inhabitants who come from the Kingdom, since this would reduce the domestic availability of labour, especially in the sectors of agriculture and livestock breeding, as well as the investment of considerable resources in the realization of military and defensive works, because this would equally entail the outflow of resources. The resources for the realization of these works, to the contrary, must come from the trade itself, developed independently in Goa and in the other territories of Portuguese India.[8] The arguments of Mendes de Vasconcelos, then, inspired by a strictly mercantilist vision, to be reached of Portugal's economic self-sufficiency, meant to follow on the one supporting domestic production and import substitution and the strengthening the foreign trade (including through the creation of a private trading fleet along with the limitation of the state's commercial monopolies), with its beating heart in the city of Lisbon. In this treatment of Lisbon, with its natural endowments, and its central role in the provisioning system and trade networks, one can find important assonances with the *Breve trattato*, with reference to the city of Naples, and with its own natural endowments and the special characteristics of its trade.

In the first part of the *Breve trattato*, in fact, Serra explains that the wealth of a kingdom depends primarily on its specific natural characteristics, defined as the endowment of resources unique to a given territory – what he calls *accidenti propri* – namely the fertility of the soil, the geographic position, the climate, and so on. To these factors have to be added what Serra calls *accidenti comuni*: *quantità d'artifici, qualità de genti, trafico grande de negozi e provisione di quel che governa* – that is, the production of manufactures, professional skills, and the moral qualities of people, the volume of trade both domestic and international, and the wisdom of the Kingdom's political leadership. Just as Mendes de Vasconcelos in addressing Philip III boasts of the natural endowments of Lisbon and Portugal and invokes measures for strengthening its trade, so Serra, who not incidentally dedicates his own work to the viceroy of Naples, exalts the abundant resources of Naples and its kingdom as well as comparing them with those of other Italian cities and states, Venice in particular. Indeed, he holds that if the *Serenissima Repubblica* seems to be much richer than Naples, this derives not from a greater endowment of resources but from trade and how it is practised there.

Do sitio de Lisboa concentrates entirely on problems of trade, and it does not give money the central place that it plays in the thought of Antonio Serra; this issue is, though, a major preoccupation in the works of Duarte Gomes Solis, the second Portuguese writer of economic texts whose work, which can be read as complementary to that of Mendes de Vasconcelos, presents important points of contact with the *Breve trattato*.

Born in Lisbon in 1561 or 1562 to a family of new Christians and grown up in Medina del Campo, the most important financial centre in 16th-century Castille, Duarte Gomes Solis sailed from Lisbon in 1585 for Goa, hoping to continue in Portuguese India the commercial activities that his father had engaged in on the Iberian peninsula; his journey, interrupted by a shipwreck off the coast of Mozambique, followed by imprisonment at the hands of indigenous peoples, could resume only when the survivors successfully gained the protection of the *alferes-mor*, commander of the fortress of Mozambique, Jorge de Menezes, and it finally ended only in the spring of 1586 with his arrival in Goa.[9] There Gomes Solis started a vast commercial enterprise and also held positions important for the royal *fazenda*, like that of *administrador geral da pimenta*, contractor of the pepper trade monopoly, which put him in close contact with the governor Manuel de Sousa Coutinho (1588–1591), also becoming his counsellor in monetary matters, an experience that would become the basis for some of his most important later writings.[10]

Likely because of this close relationship, Gomes Solis came to be implicated in the investigation promoted by the viceroy Maties de Albuquerque into the activities of Sousa Coutinho, the governor; arrested, at the beginning of 1592 he was taken aboard the *Madre de Deus* to Lisbon to be put on trial, but in August of the same year, while navigating the waters near the Azores, the Portuguese carrack, also laden with precious metals, was one of the five ships captured by the English corsair Martin Frobisher, commanding a fleet fitted out by Sir Walter Raleigh to intercept gold being transported from the East Indies, and was brought to England. Back to Lisbon in April 1593, in November of that year Gomes Solis left again for India, where he arrived in the middle of 1594, which suggests that he was acquitted of the charges brought against him.[11] Having returned to Portugal in 1601, not without a further incident of attack by English ships, he settled in Lisbon, rich and full of experience. He married in 1604 and lived in Lisbon until his death, which occurred around 1630; during this time he was intensely active as an *arbitrista*, dealing with themes of trade, finance, and money.[12]

Although the two best known works of Gomes Solis, the *Discursos sobre los comercios de las Indias* (1622)[13] and the *Alegación en favor de la Compañía de la India Oriental* (1628),[14] were published in Spanish only at the beginning of the 1620s – amid the general climate of renewal accompanying Philip IV's ascent to the throne, which led many thinkers of the Iberian peninsula to contact the young king, advancing proposals for the economic and political reform of the Kingdom – their writing began, according to the author's explicit declaration, in 1610.[15] Moreover, in the case of the *Discursos*, the dating at the writing to the beginning of the second decade of the 17th century, is confirmed by the presence in the text of the transcription of three letters dated 1612, two from the author to the Duke of Lerma and a third to the Consejo de Estado Juan de Ciriza. Other manuscripts of the same work, also datable to the same period but which remained unprinted, have only recently come to light.[16] This evidence of the manuscript circulation of texts by Gomes Solis before their effective publication at this time is particularly important for establishing a connection between the thought of Antonio Serra and that of the Portuguese *arbitrista*.

A typical exponent of the world of *cristaõs novos* merchant bankers and deeply involved in the economic system of the Portuguese empire, Duarte Gomes Solis shows in his writings primarily the advantages of creating trading companies, not without constant reference to the thought of Botero and Bodin, indicating his interest for mercantilistic subjects. The point of contact with the thought of Serra, especially with the remedies set out in the second part of the *Breve trattato*, however, is to be chiefly found where Gomes Solis treats the circulation of money, credit, and exchange inside the peninsular system and more precisely when he expounds the monetary measures to be adopted in order to solve the chronical problems of silver scarcity suffered by the Spanish empire.[17]

Since all nations had an absolute need of silver for their trade and since Spain alone controlled most of the silver production that fuelled trade in Europe, Gomes Solis held that the continuous outflow of money from Spain was determined by silver's high intrinsic value, which drove foreign operators to try to obtain it in exchange for copper or bullion coins with artificially elevated nominal value (and, according to Gomes Solis, often false). The measure that he proposed to deal with this phenomenon consisted, in the first place, in the monetization, along with a strong copper alloy, of half of all the silver produced in the empire, raising the nominal value of the money by 29% and prohibiting its export outside the Spanish territories and dominions. The remaining half of the silver, kept as pure as possible, would instead be considered as a commodity and thus freely exported; at the same time, all the copper divisional coin and bullion would have to be removed from the market.[18] Additionally, the abundance of silver coin in circulation would have facilitated exchanges and resulted in a decrease of interest rates as well as in the disappearance of usury.[19]

Anticipating objections to his proposal, Gomes Solis similarly argued that this measure (1) would not entail an increase in expenditures for purchasing imports since they would be reduced due to their higher price, reorienting demand towards domestic goods; (2) would not necessarily obligate the sovereign to pay interest on loans or to repay their capital in the same coinage in which he received them; (3) would lead to a reduction in the size of the land forces maintained by the Catholic monarchy that served outside its territories and thus would require upkeep in foreign coin, in favour of the development of naval forces.[20] It is this discussion of monetary issues that establishes an ideal bridge between Naples and Lisbon: many of the problems facing Duarte Gomes Solis can be found in the second and third parts of the *Breve trattato*.

Indeed, as already mentioned, Serra criticized in the *Breve trattato* some of the monetary policy measures taken by the Spanish government in Naples over the preceding years; more precisely, he dedicated the second part of the work to the refutation of the proposals advanced some years earlier by Marc'Antonio de Santis in his *Discorso di Marc'Antonio de Santis intorno a gli effetti, che fa il cambio in Regno* (1605) and later accepted in a pragmática issued in June of 1607 by the viceroy, the Count of Benavente.

This provision was meant to solve the chronic problem of the scarcity of money by having the authorities fix a lower exchange rate for Neapolitan coinage, or, more accurately, a lower price with respect to that prevailing at the time on the market for foreign currency acquired by means of bills of exchange; de Santis believed, in fact, in the existence of a cause-and-effect nexus between higher exchange and the scarcity of money plaguing the Kingdom of Naples. In reality the measure did not bring about the expected benefits and was abandoned in the course of a few months.

Serra, however, was not averse to de Santis's proposal simply because it did not empirically work but because, in point of theory, he held that the true cause of the outflow of money was the disequilibria in the composition of the balance of payments. Although he was in principle not opposed to the use of administrative measures on exchange, he held that fixing the exchange rate alone was ineffective because it did not affect the real causes of the problem but to the contrary could be easily circumvented, while it would still easily create obstacles that disrupt trade. Gomes Solis never reaches the elegance and complexity of Serra's economic reasoning, but like Serra, he held that it was pointless to affect the lowering of the value of exchange and captured the nexus between commercial operations and the overall trend of exchanges.

2

But what relationship could have existed between Antonio Serra and Portuguese *arbitrismo*? To answer this question, it is necessary to remember that at the end of the 16th century there was in Naples a community of Portuguese *cristaõs novos* merchant bankers, that was able, although not especially large in number, to achieve a prominent social and economic position there over the course of just a few years. Miguel Vaaz (ca. 1550, 1622), together with his brothers and in concert with other bankers of Genoese or Flemish origins, inserted himself in a major way into the vast financial speculation on the supplying with wheat of the city of Naples.[21]

The presence of Miguel Vaaz in the Kingdom of Naples is documented from 1585, when he comes to be paid an *entretenimiento* of twenty *scudi* per month (increasing to thirty by 1586), for services rendered during the period of the consolidation of the union of Portugal and Spanish Monarchies.[22] The activities that the Portuguese merchant engaged in in Southern Italy always revolved around two geographic centres – the capital of the Kingdom, Naples, and the Pugliese provinces – and quite often both of the areas were linked together in the same commercial (especially as regards the production, purchase, and sale of wheat) or financial operations, like the payment in Naples of letters of exchange coming from Puglia and vice versa. At the same time, Miguel Vaaz rapidly found out how to play an important role for the families of the Pugliese aristocracy and patriciate, carrying out important intermediary financial functions of various kinds for them. Additionally, the operations that Miguel Vaaz carried out in these years continually intersected with financial brokering and trade as well as the arming of merchant ships; the growing importance of the lattermost activity is demonstrated by his purchase, in 1601 in the port of Naples, of a ship of 2,200 *salme*, equal to a load capacity of around 325 tons.[23]

Among Miguel Vaaz's commercial activities, a special place was occupied, as already mentioned, by the wheat trade exercised especially within the *annona*, the system for provisioning the city of Naples;[24] the first documents that attest the growth of the volume of business carried out in this area by Miguel Vaaz refer to the period around the turn of the century. At the same time, the Portuguese banker continued to be engaged in many financial operations in order to raise capital for the wheat trade, especially dedicating himself to speculation tied to the management of the Neapolitan public debt and to the system of *arrendamenti* – that is, the system of contracts for the sale of the Kingdom's future fiscal revenues, either those to be paid by the Kingdom's communities or from gabelles and customs.

Miguel Vaaz then acted as intermediary in the payment of bills of exchange on behalf of influential members of the nobility who used this financial instrument for the collection of rents. It was likely through this activity, together with being a merchant of luxury goods, including slaves, high-quality wines, and fine fabrics destined for a clientele of the highest rank,[25] that Vaaz's contacts relating to the practices of financial brokering with the representatives of the elites of the Kingdom were strengthened and transformed into an extraordinary network of social relations. From this perspective, one likely needs to include his ties with the Counts of Lemos, present in the Kingdom for more than fifteen years, first with Fernando Ruiz de Castro Andrade y Portugal, VIth Count of Lemos, viceroy of Naples in 1599–1601, and then, after his death, with his youngest son Francisco Fernández de Castro Andrade y Portugal, Count di Castro, lieutenant general of the Kingdom during 1601–1603 (and later the VIIIth Count of Lemos) and finally with Pedro Fernández de Castro Andrade y Portugal, VIIth Count of Lemos, viceroy of Naples between 1610 and 1616.[26]

The first members of the *linaje* of the Counts of Lemos with whom Miguel Vaaz had documented dealings are Catalina Zuñiga y Sandoval, wife of the VIth Count of Lemos, her son Francisco de Castro and daughter-in-law Lucrezia Gattinara of Legnano:[27] Vaaz administered the rents of Francisco de Castro and his wife.[28] The same pattern – purchase of luxury goods and financial operations – would come to be repeated with the arrival as viceroy of Naples of Pedro Fernández de Castro, VIIth Count of Lemos; in the year of the taking possession of the new viceroy, 1610, and probably just in relation to his transfer to Naples, Vaaz saw to the payment for a variety of luxury goods – textiles, hangings, clothes, and more – that Pedro de Castro and his wife, Catalina de la Cerda y Sandoval, bought from Neapolitan merchants.[29]

When in June of 1610 Pedro Fernández de Castro, VIIth Count of Lemos, arrived in Naples to assume the duties of viceroy, the Kingdom was emerging from a cycle of grave famines, which had culminated in 1606.[30] In these years, so difficult for the population of Naples, the operating cost of the *annona* of the city increased tremendously, so much so that the Count himself in 1614 affirmed that during the governments of his predecessors the expenditures for provisioning the city created a burden of more than five million ducats[31] on the patrimony of the Kingdom, this against estimated revenues in 1612 of less than two million.[32]

The Count of Lemos entrusted Miguel Vaaz with reviewing the administration of Naples's system of supply, and in a short time, as he would later write to the viceroy, he found evidence of frauds and mismanagements, thereby increasing the patrimony from around 300,000 to around 550,000 ducats. He affirmed that if from then on this office was not given to wicked men unmindful of the common good, but to a capable and honest man, like himself, it would be possible, with the help of an expert government, to increase the patrimony of the annona up to a million ducats.[33]

Vaaz now enjoyed the almost unlimited confidence of the viceroy; in 1610, the year of his arrival in Naples, the Count of Lemos set up a council to deal with the monetary and financial problems of the Kingdom. Included in this group were six bankers of foreign origins: Giacomo Fornari and Paolo Grillo from Genoa, Benedetto Biffoli from Florence, Pietro Cortone from Bergamo, Antonio Antopel from Flanders, and of course Miguel Vaaz from Portugal. These in addition to the Neapolitan high magistrate Marc'Antonio de Santis, a jurist and expert on monetary problems, lieutenant of the Camera della Sommaria, the Kingdom's chief administrative body.[34] The presence of de Santis guaranteed that the council would not act contrary to the other Neapolitan administrative bodies, but the choice of the six foreign bankers sent a clear message that the new viceroy did not feel himself bound by the Kingdom's traditionally established economic powers and that instead he wanted to have around him a group of *hombres de negocios* whom he could trust absolutely; among them, it was Miguel Vaaz who soon showed himself capable of playing the role with the most political weight. For example, when in 1613 the Count of Lemos intended to intervene on the age-old problem of the state of foreign exchanges of Neapolitan money, subject to constant downward pressure because of the unstoppable flow of gold and silver pouring out of the Kingdom's borders (caused by a trade deficit and by the payment of various kinds of rents to foreigners),[35] it was the Portuguese banker who called together a meeting with the representatives of the main foreign trading colonies that resided in the Kingdom and who spoke, in the viceroy's name, of the grave disadvantages caused by currency imbalances.[36]

The Count of Lemos's high opinion of Miguel Vaaz was not shared by many of his contemporaries, not only because of the New Christian banker's always unscrupulous dealings in the world of Neapolitan business, but also for using for his own benifit his close relationship with the viceroy, for example when he acquired the fief of Mola (the viceroy to obtain from Philip III the title of Count of Mola for him in 1613) or when he sold wheat of bad quality to the city of Naples during the very years of the government of the Count of Lemos.[37] In other words, during the progress of the Count of Lemos's rule in Naples, a gap becomes ever more clearly present between the almost unlimited faith that the viceroy placed in Vaaz, whom he raised to the rank of his chief adviser, especially with respect to the management of the Kingdom's economic resources and the reform of its financial institutions, and the hostility that this privileged position generated among the Neapolitan ruling elite, the other bankers (above all the Genoese ones), and the aristocracy, particularly after the elevation of Miguel Vaaz to the dignity of count.

The hostility towards Vaaz and the aversion generated by the esteem in which he was held by the viceroy are clearly manifest in 1614–1615 in the clash between the Count of Lemos and the aristocracy over privileges of a fiscal nature. The story, reconstructed by Isabel Enciso in her monograph on the Count of Lemos,[38] is here retraced insofar as it involved the Portuguese merchant.

In 1614 the viceroy tried to unify in the royal treasury the collection of the customs duties of Naples, which were until then divided between the royal treasury and the city. The measure promoted by the viceroy would not have injured the city, which would have continued to collect the same income that it previously enjoyed without having to deal directly with the management of the customs, but it directly harmed the interests of those who had invested money in the purchase of the fiscal income that originated in the collection of the city's duties – in other words the interests of the urban aristocracy.[39] The decision to combine the gabelle on the entry and exit of merchandise to and from the city of Naples in the hands of the royal fisc was in effect an expression of the attempt to make fiscal administration more efficient at a time when the *hacienda* of the Kingdom of Naples appears to be particularly suffering.[40]

With the same intention of alleviating the economic problems of the Kingdom, the viceroy advanced a second proposal, which was intended by the Count of Lemos to put an end to speculation on real estate and to the thoughtless growth of the population of the capital, but it came to be interpreted on the part of the aristocratic class as an attack.[41] In this case, the viceroy had revived and harshened already existing regulations on the construction of new houses not conforming to the current standards, decreeing that where the prohibitions had not been respected, they would be charged fines, which in the treasury's expectations would secure for the *hacienda* a yearly income of nearly 100,000 ducats, but since those receiving these sanctions would primarily be the great noble settlements of Naples's city centre, this measure was also soon branded as anti-aristocratic in spirit.[42]

Finally, almost at the same time as the two provisions already mentioned, the Count of Lemos carried out a third, concerning the supply of water for the city of Naples, and in particular a water source located about eight kilometres north of the city on lands that belonged to the Benedictine monastery of Ss. Severino and Sossio: the city had tried to buy the spring by ratifying its right of ownership over it, but this was prevented by the intervention of the Consiglio Collaterale, the highest political advisory body in the Kingdom, chaired by the viceroy himself; the Consiglio Collaterale prevented the city from making an agreement with the monks, but it allowed the royal treasury to reach a compromise with the churchmen if this was necessary for securing a water supply for the city.[43]

It should be noted that ownership of the spring was once again a matter that related to provisioning the city since its control made possible the construction close to the city of new mills capable of grinding as much as 5,000 tomoli of grain every day, thereby avoiding the dangers – as well as the frauds and thefts – associated with transporting grain to mills farther away, in the neighbouring localities of Torre Annunziata, Scafati, and so on. Furthermore, the city had spent more than 40,000 ducats to build the aqueduct that would have channelled water from the spring, without the contribution of the viceroy and Consiglio Collaterale, who were now intervening to stop a deal it had already made with the fathers at San Severino.[44]

The urban nobility, gathered in the *Seggi*, representing the municipal organization of Naples, rose up, and a group of aristocrats – with interests both in customs duties and in new constructions – led by Carlo Caracciolo and the prince of Avellino asked the viceroy to withdraw his decision or to give them a special permission to bring their grievances directly to the court in Madrid. Even though he was willing to concede that the treasury's demands had been excessive in the water incident, the viceroy, strongly supported by some of his most prominent advisers, such as Fulvio Di Constanzo, member of the council of the Cancelleria, the Marquis of Corleto, and of course Miguel Vaaz, decided to take an extremely firm stance in line with the traditionally adopted policy concerning the Consiglio Collaterale, and denied the legitimacy of the request. The dissident aristocrats, however, on 22 and 23 August 1614, called together the *Seggi* and having obtained the support of some fifty members of the city's patriciate chose the duke of Bovino, Jeronimo de Guevara, to serve as their ambassador to the court.[45] The viceroy, in turn, reacted by getting 108 members of the urban patriciate to sign a document that called for Jeronimo de Guevara's mission to be immediately blocked.[46]

The protest of the aristocrats was not, however, directed only against the Count of Lemos but also against the one who was considered the instigator of these and many other acts of the government of the viceroy, namely Miguel Vaaz. Among the various issues that the dissidents brought to the attention of the viceroy in the document demanding licence to send an ambassador to Madrid, there was also in fact the demand that the administration of the *real hacienda* be entrusted only to representatives of the city (namely the same urban aristocrats) and to the king's ministers, not to private persons, and especially that the Count of Mola, Miguel Vaaz, be excluded: "*que no se entremeta en administrar el peculio de la ciudad ninguna persona que tenga tratos y contratos, espacialmente el Conde de Mola, e que este gobierno se dexe a los Ministros de la Ciudad que asistan a el con intervención de los Ministros regios*".[47]

But since when had the Count of Mola taken to nonchalantly managing public funds? The steps of his approach to the Count of Lemos are retraced in the statement written against Vaaz: curiously, his closeness with other members of the same family, which also seems to have been well known, is not recorded, but his link with the viceroy through the lieutenant of the Camera della Sommaria Juan Alonso Suarez is identified.[48] Suarez, who at the very top of the Kingdom's chief administrative tribunal was also directly responsible for the management of the royal patrimony, had presented Vaaz to the Count of Lemos as a person willing to collaborate in bringing order to the Kingdom's financial management.[49]

From another point of view, it was the Count of Lemos himself, intending to deal as soon as possible with the *hacienda*'s grave state of indebtedness,[50] who sought the help of expert counsellors and, as he wrote, the New Christian merchant was recommended to him by the Duke of Vietri, in his capacity as *grasero* in charge, the citizen magistrate tasked with running the *annona* of Naples, and his predecessor, the Marquis of Corleto, knowing of Vaaz's uncommon ability in supplying the city with wheat, affirmed that "*todo lo que no è hallarse en Santo Lorenço con nosotros el Conde de Mola es perder tiempo*", with the Basilica of San Lorenzo being the place where the Seggi convened and thus where the business of the city administration was settled.[51] Once he had gained the Count of Lemos's confidence, Vaaz, according to his detractors, tried to make Suarez look bad in the eyes of the viceroy, accusing him, according to an audit of the accounts, of having cost the treasury 200,000 ducats through errors in the administration of fiscal revenues; he freed himself of other opponents in the same way and forced all of the viceroy's chief interlocutors to deal with him in the affairs of state.[52]

The reforms in accounting and the financial administration of the Kingdom that the Count of Lemos brought about at the suggestion of Vaaz are well known,[53] but each reform brought with it a dose of discontent that ultimately focused on the New Christian merchant. For example, the creation of the *Cassa Militare*, designed to streamline the payment of the militias and subject to the control of the Kingdom general treasury, inevitably brought with it the hostility of the general treasurer, who saw this measure as diminishing the importance of his own office; analogously, and again with reference to the creation of the *Cassa Militare*, to organize the payment of salaries to the Kingdom's soldiers, he required them to declare their past remunerations to the fisc, before their new ones would be paid, and this measure too caused no little resentment.[54] Notwithstanding these reforms, defending against the threat of the Turkish fleet and maintaining the troops engaged in wars in Lombardy continued to weigh heavily on the state coffers, in the amount of more than 500,000 ducats, obliging the *hacienda* to have recourse to new and more burdensome loans with foreign bankers.[55]

In effect, parallel to the intervention on the administrative machinery, Vaaz suggested to the Count of Lemos that he proceed with a drastic reduction of the weight sustained by the state for the public debt by lowering the rate of interest paid; this measure, which was made even more restrictive by refusing to pay back the capital to those who would not accept the lower rate, aroused the strong opposition of the holders of the public debt, who later succeeded in obtaining a concession from the sovereign that there was no obligation to accept such an imposition.[56] The choices in relation to managing the sale of income from the public debt is a particularly thorny issue because it has repercussions on the stability and social cohesion of the Kingdom. The king's intervention sought to ensure the strengthening of internal consensus; the Neapolitan aristocracy, in fact, believed that the measure taken by the viceroy would have excessively penalized their patrimony, while Vaaz, the measure's promoter, continued to support the policy of lowering the interest rate, arguing that, given the small share of the assets possessed by the local nobility, the damage would not have been excessive for the Neapolitan bankers, while the state finances would earn a substantial gain on the rendite sold to foreign merchants and bankers.[57]

As the phrase referring to the Duke of Vietri and the Marquis of Corleto indicates, before the arrival of the Count of Lemos, Vaaz participated informally in the city administration, or, more precisely, in the supplying of all edible goods (*grassa*), as well as in the collection of city revenues (*peculio*), which, as mentioned, took place in a room of the convent annexed to the Basilica of San Lorenzo. Once continuity had been established with the viceroy, his role only came to be strengthened: Vaaz's presence – not incidentally called the "leaven" of every piece of business – became the norm among the administrators who dealt with the city's *grassa* and *peculio* and his opinion, although purely advisory, was nonetheless held in the highest esteem, especially by the viceroy himself.[58] Seeing its power more strongly limited by the awkward presence of the New Christian merchant was the old aristocracy of the *Seggi* ("seats"), so-called for the privilege of sitting in the municipal council, by means of which the great families of the Neapolitan nobility traditionally managed the city's resources, and certainly not to their own detriment.

So this was the context, on the occasion of the 1614 protest against the measures adopted by the viceroy, in which the request to distance Vaaz from the management of public funds developed along with the attempt to send Jeronimo de Guevara on a mission to Madrid. From letters written to Montoya de Cardona, member of the *Consejo de Italia* in Madrid, we know how Vaaz reacted to the accusation made against him, although always with the declared intention of supporting the viceroy's action: he accused the *Seggi* of having been transformed from an expression of the city's good government into tools of oppression and declared the members who sat in them seditious subjects who were not acting for the common good and in service of the king but were instead inspired by their own personal interests; so for every city seat, Vaaz provided a list of the chosen members, reckoning each of them "*el mas infame y de peor calidad y costumbre y de menor substancia*".[59] In the case of Jeronimo de Guevara's mission, then, he identified the responsibility of a small number of members – Carlo Carafa for the *Seggio* of the Quartiere di Nilo, Muzio Carmignano for the *Seggio* of the Quartiere di Montagna, Carlo Antonio Capece Zurlo for the *Seggio* of the Quartiere di Capuana, all held responsible for grave crimes – who had deceived the other members.[60]

But Vaaz never failed to praise the political foresight of his patron, whose prudence in governing the Kingdom had guaranteed a general level of prosperity, both in the supply of foodstuffs and in limiting the fraud and usury that enriched only shopkeepers and barons; before the arrival of the Count of Lemos – and thus, implicitly, of his own arrival – in the Neapolitan government, speculators on the price of wheat obtained high profits, artificially keeping the price of wheat between 50 or 60 *carlini* per *tomolo* in the provinces and between 25 and 30 *carlini* per *tomolo* in Naples, while during the government of the Count of Lemos, price controls kept the price between 10 and 12 *carlini* in the provinces and between 4 and 6 in the capital, an 80% reduction.[61]

But while the clash between the viceroy and the aristocracy was still raging, in May 1615 news arrived that the Count of Lemos would not be given a mandate to serve another mandate of three years in Naples and that his departure loomed in the middle of 1616, which awakened in Vaaz the not unreasonable concern that this decision could signal not only a loss of the sovereign's favour towards his representative but also the beginning of the end of his own fortunes.[62] Vaaz's worries proved more than justified because while the departure of the Count of Lemos from Naples resolved many of the controversies that the viceroy had stirred up, it also increased the pressure on the New Christian merchant.

The document written up against Miguel Vaaz in 1616, a little before or after the turnover of viceroys in Naples, reflects a kind of posthumous absolution of the work of the Count of Lemos, with most of his mistakes put squarely on the back of the New Christian merchant. As such, the list of things to which Vaaz had to answer grew longer: in addition to the charge of having abused his influence over the viceroy and having been seated illegitimately in the tribunal of San Lorenzo, cleverly manipulating things in such a way as to fix the prices of foodstuffs for his own profit, Vaaz was held guilty of the reduction of the number of ships arriving in Naples, in order to thereby exercise a monopoly on the transport and sale of goods, which were bought in foreign markets and sold at higher prices. In a similar way, Vaaz was accused of forcing Pugliese producers to provide grain at below market price so that he could reap big profits from selling their product in Naples; in this way, he was able to root out the competition, even causing Ascanio Delia, a business rival who refused to give in to his blackmail, to be put on trial with false accusations.[63]

Because of Miguel Vaaz's deceptive actions, "many dangers of strife and rioting occurred",[64] says the anonymous author of the 1616 document, which stirred up anxiety and divided the nobility into factions, setting a bad example for the people and creating tragic consequences for the city. Although hated by most, Vaaz, thanks to his economic power, was able to bring over to his cause not only "knights, who perhaps were standing closer to him out of fondness"[65] but also the viceroy himself, who, out of gratitude for the diligent commitment the New Christian banker had lavished on the Kingdom's business, felt obligated to defend him, seeing that "he provoked hatred by having served him, since before he was loved or at least not hated".[66]

If the Count of Lemos felt obliged to show gratitude to Vaaz, all the more so in his debt were those aristocrats whose positions depended on the viceroy and who were unable to leave the favour of his most trusted adviser, like the Prince of San Severo "in debt up to his eyes and also with interests in the wheat trade"; the Duke of Monteleone "obligated to the house of Lemos in many respects as everyone knows"; or finally Tiberio Carafa, "the widower of the lady Giulia Orsini, from which marriage he retains the title of Prince of Bisignano, and who depends for his food on the will of judges, on the viceroy, and others".[67]

Hostility against Miguel Vaaz reached its peak in the months following the entrance in Naples of the new viceroy and was healed with the persecution that the Duke of Osuna, lined up on the opposite side of the Count of Lemos in the struggle between the factions at the court of Philip III, unleashed against all of the closest associates of his predecessor;[68] conspicuous among them was Miguel Vaaz, whom the Duke of Osuna suspected of having tried to thwart his coming to Naples and who himself at the moment of the new viceroy's arrival was publicly accused by the Neapolitan municipal organization of having sold the city spoiled or low quality grain.[69] On 4 May 1617, the viceroy Duke of Osuna ordered the arrest of Miguel Vaaz.

3

For the crucial role played in all the economic and financial questions of the Kingdom of Naples at least in the years between 1610 and 1616, namely those of the government of the VIIth Count of Lemos, it is certain that Miguel Vaaz, through his emissaries, received a copy of everything that could be found, both in print and manuscript, in the principal European markets on the subject of finance, money, exchange, supply, production, trade, and so on. And certainly because of his origins and contacts with Portugal, he would not have missed what was produced on these subjects within the ambit of Lusitanian *arbitrismo*. It is most likely, then, that even the writings of Mendes de Vasconcelos and Duarte Gomes Solis circulated in Naples in the years in which Serra was writing the *Breve trattato* and their content was known.

But is this enough to establish contact between Miguel Vaaz and Antonio Serra? It is possible to make some hypotheses about it. The first is that Vaaz should have been aware of the fact that Serra was preparing a treatise of an economic character, not only because of the limited dimensions of the intellectual circles in the Naples of the early 17th century but also because of the practice common, at that time, that the texts, before going into print, often many years after their composition, enjoyed an ample and sustained circulation in manuscript; the second hypothesis is that Vaaz was not indifferent to this news – to the contrary, he did not look kindly on others wanting to present the viceroy with remedies for the Kingdom's economic troubles, given his position as the principle and nearly only adviser to the Count of Lemos; the third hypothesis is that Vaaz was sufficiently unscrupulous to try to eliminate a potential rival by constructing false accusations against him (something for which, as was already mentioned, Vaaz actually came to be accused).

To corroborate the hypothesis of a less than benevolent relationship between Vaaz and Serra, there is also the fact that, as mentioned, the second part of the *Breve trattato* is essentially dedicated to refuting the proposals concerning money advance some years earlier by Marc'Antonio de Santis in the *Discorso* of 1605 and subsequently accepted by the viceroy of Naples, the Count of Benavente, in June of 1607.[70] These measures, largely corresponding with those that Vaaz would again present during the government of the Count of Lemos, aimed at reducing the exchange rate of the Neapolitan ducat in order to attract foreign currency to the Kingdom, but they were quickly abandoned since they resulted in the opposite effect; in other words, because he was ultimately discussing the same measure, Serra, criticizing de Santis, was also putting on trial the monetary measures suggested by Vaaz.

If these assumptions are true, it partially changes the interpretation of the two dispatches sent from the viceroy's secretariat to the regent of the Vicaria prison on 11 November 1612 and 27 May 1614, which have been published by Amabile, that have made it possible to affirm with certainty that on these dates, and so before and after the publication of the *Breve trattato*, Serra was really locked in prison;[71] these documents need to be understood in the sense that Vaaz managed to put Serra in prison before the publication of his volume, even if he was unable to impede its release, perhaps in the meantime already sent to a printer, and that the charges were fabricated by putting in Serra's dwelling materials for counterfeiting coins, materials that must nonetheless have been meagre or doubtful, since the anonymous redactor of the 1614 dispatch describes them, with a bit of evident scepticism, as "*ese pedacito de oro o alquimia*" – that is, as that little piece of gold or product of alchemy.[72]

Only further thorough and systematic research in the Neapolitan archives might be able to lead to the discovery of documents that prove some form of direct contact or relationship between Serra and Antonio Miguel Vaaz.

Notes

1. After the 1613 Neapolitan edition, the *Breve trattato* was republished in Custodi, P. (ed.), *Scrittori classici italiani di economia politica*, parte antica, vol. I, Milan: Destefanis, 1803, pp. 1–179; Graziani, A. (ed.), *Economisti del Cinque e Seicento*, Bari: Laterza, 1913, pp. 141–235; Colapietra, R. (ed.), *Problemi monetari negli scrittori napoletani del Seicento*, Rome: Accademia dei Lincei, 1973, pp. 163–228 (other more recent editions follow).
2. For a critical framework for Serra's work, cfr. De Rosa, L., *Economisti meridionali*, Naples: Istituto Italiano per gli Studi Filosofici, 1995, pp. 9–32; Roncaglia, A. (ed.), *Alle origini del pensiero economico in Italia. Moneta e sviluppo negli economisti napoletani dei secoli XVII–XVIII*, Bologna: Il Mulino, 1995 (especially Rosselli, A., *Antonio Serra e la teoria dei cambi*, pp. 37–58); Roncaglia, A., "Antonio Serra", in *Rivista italiana degli economisti*, 1999, 4, pp. 421–438; Reinert, S.A., "Introduction", in Antonio Serra, *A Short Treatise on the Wealth and Poverty of Nations (1613)*, London and New Delhi: Anthem, 2011, pp. 1–93.
3. Bastien, C., *A divisão da historia do pensamento económico português em períodos*, Working Paper n° 16, GHES, Gabinete de Historia Económica e Social, ISEG, Lisbon: 2000, p. 9.
4. Lisbon: Oficina de Luys Estupiñan, 1608; successive editions: 1786, 1803, 1974, 1990, and, nearly complete, in Sergio, A. (ed.), *Antologia dos economistas portugueses*, Lisbon: Biblioteca Nacional, 1924, vol. I, the edition that has most contributed to knowledge of this work among contemporary scholars.
5. On Mendes de Vasconcelos, see Bastien, 2000, pp. 9–10; Magalhães, J.C., *História do Pensamento Económico em Portugal. Da Idade Média ao Mercantilismo*, Coimbra: Coimbra Editora, 1967, pp. 183–196.
6. Mendes de Vasconcelos, 1608, pp. 95–113.
7. *Ibid.*, pp. 125–130; see also Curto, D.R., *O discurso político em Portugal (1600–1650)*, Lisbon: Centro de Estudos de História e Cultura Portuguesa, 1988, pp. 195–196.
8. Mendes de Vasconcelos, 1608, pp. 4–5, 73–74.
9. Magalhães, 1967, pp. 513–514.
10. *Ibid.*, p. 514.
11. *Ibid.*
12. *Ibid.*, p. 515.
13. Original edition without place of publication; republished in the edition of Amzalak, M.B., Lisbon: Gráfica Lisbonense, 1943.
14. Original edition without place of publication (Lisbon: n.p., 1628) republished in the edition of Amzalak, M.B., Lisbon: Império, 1955.
15. Gomes Solis, 1622, p. 60.

16. Bourdon, L., "Mémoires inédits de Duarte Gomes Solis", in *Anais do Instituto Superior de Ciencias Economicas e Financieras*, vol. XXIII, 1955, vol. 1, pp. 110–164.
17. A general overview of the work of Gomes Solis, among others, may be found in Torgal, L.R., *Ideologia Política e Teoria do Estado na Restauração*, Coimbra: Biblioteca Geral da Universidade de Coimbra, 1981, vol. I, pp. 397–399, and Studnicki-Gizbert, D., *A Nation upon the Ocean Sea: Portugal's Atlantic Diaspora and the Crisis of the Spanish Empire, 1492–1640*, Oxford: Oxford University Press, 2007, pp. 134–138.
18. Bourdon, 1955, pp. 120, 131, 149; Magalhães, 1967, p. 201.
19. Bourdon, 1955, pp. 150–151; Gomes Solis, 1628, p. 229.
20. Bourdon, 1955, pp. 121–125.
21. On Miguel Vaaz, as well as for previously published literature, see Sabatini, G., "The Vaaz: Rise and Fall of a Family of Portuguese Bankers in Spanish Naples (1590–1660)", in *The Journal of European Economic History*, vol. XXIXX, 2010, pp. 623–655; Id., "Un mercato conteso: banchieri portoghesi alla conquista della Napoli dei genovesi (1590–1650)", in Herrero Sánchez, M., Y.R. Ben Yessef Garfía, C. Bitossi, and D. Puncuh (eds), *Génova y la Monarquía Hispánica (1528–1713)*, Genoa: Atti della società ligure di Storia Patria, Nuova serie, vol. LI, 2011, pp. 141–170; Id. "From Alliance to Conflict, from Finance to Justice: a Portuguese Family in Spanish Naples (1590–1660)", in Cardim, P., T. Herzog, J.J. Ruiz Ibáñez, G. Sabatini (eds), *Polycentrics Monarchies: How Did Early Modern Spain And Portugal Achieve And Maintain A Global Hegemony?*, Brighton: Sussex Academy Press, 2012, pp. 91–107; Huerga Criado, P., "Cristianos nuevos de origen ibérico en el Reino de Nápoles en el siglo XVII", in *Sefarad*, LXXII, 2012, pp. 351–387; Crivelli, B. and G.Sabatini, "La carrera de un mercader judeoconverso en el Nápoles español. Negocios y relaciones políticas de Miguel Vaaz (1590–1616)", soon to appear in *Hispania*. Despite the promising title, Mazur, P.A., *The New Christians of Spanish Naples, 1528–1671*, London: Palgrave Macmillan, 2007, provides no new knowledge and, inexplicably, does not take account of the most recent studies published on the topic.
22. *Al virrey de Nápoles de Alaminos a 6 de febrero de 1585. Entretenimiento de 20 escudos al mes en Nápoles a Miguel Vaez Portugués*, Archivo General de Simancas (AGS), Estado, leg. 1088, doc. 24, *Acrecentamiento de 10 escudos el entretenimiento de 20 que Miguel Vaez tiene en Nápoles. En San [?] a primero de Agosto de 1586*, Estado, leg. 1088, doc. n. 165.
23. *A Michele Vaez 19–10–1601*, Archivio Storico del Banco di Napoli (ASBN), Banco San Giacomo, giornale copiapolizze di banco.
24. On the Neapolitan *Annona*, see Coniglio, G., "Annona e calmieri nella Napoli spagnola", in *Archivio Storico per le Province Napoletane*, LXV, 1940, pp. 105–194; Id., "Note sulla storia della politica annonaria dei viceré spagnoli a Napoli", in *Archivio Storico per le Province Napoletane*, LXVI, 1941, pp. 274–282; Id., "L'Annona", in *Storia di Napoli*, vol. V, t. II, Naples: Società Editrice Storia di Napoli, 1972, pp. 691–718; Alifano, E., *Il grano, il pane e la politica annonaria a Napoli nel Settecento*, Naples: ESI, 1996; Fenicia, G., *Politica economia e realtà mercantile nel regno di Napoli nella prima metà del XVI secolo (1503–1556)*, Bari: Cacucci, 1996; Papagna, E., "Napoli e le città del grano nel Mezzogiorno spagnolo", in *Società e storia*, XX, 1997, n. 75, pp. 127–142;

Sabatini, G., "Carlo Tapia e le proposte di riforma dell'annona e delle finanze municipali nel regno di Napoli alla fine del XVI secolo", in *Storia Economica*, I, 1998, pp. 121–140; Id., "'Il pane di Cerbero'. Aspetti di politica annonaria e demografica nel Regno di Napoli nell'età di Filippo II", in Martinez Millan, J. (ed.), *Felipe II (1598–1998). Europa y la Monarquia Catolica*, vol. I, Madrid: Editorial Parteluz, 1998, pp. 767–776; Sabatini, G., "Carlo Tapia y el abastecimiento de grano en Nápoles", in Martínez Millán, J. and Visceglia M.A. (eds), *La monarquía de Felipe III, La Corte*, vol. III, Madrid: Fundacíon Mapfre, 2008, pp. 931–934.

25. *A Fra Vincenzo de Ponte 18–08–1601*, ASBN, Banco San Giacomo, giornale copiapolizze di banco.
26. On the lineage of the counts of Lemos, see Enciso Alonso-Muñumer, I., *Nobleza, poder y mecenazgo en tiempo de Filipe III. Nápoles y el Conde e Lemos*, Madrid: Actas editorial, 2007, and on Francisco Fernández de Castro in particular, Favarò, V., *Carriere in movimento. Francisco Ruiz de Castro e la Monarchia di Filippo III*, Palermo: Mediterranea – Studi e ricerche, 2013.
27. *A Michele Vaez 07–01–1603* and *A Michele Vaez 28–09–1610*, ASBN, Banco San Giacomo, giornale copiapolizze di banco.
28. *A Ferrante Morfino 07–07–1605*, ASBN, Banco San Giacomo, giornale copiapolizze di banco; *A Epifanio Iubeno 28–04–1603*, ASBN, Banco Spirito Santo, giornale copiapolizze di banco, *A Andres de Tovalina 25–10–1601* and *A Michele Vaez 03–04–1603*, ASBN, Banco San Giacomo, giornale copiapolizze di banco. *A Michele Vaez 26–02–1607*, ASBN, Banco Spirito Santo, giornale copiapolizze di banco.
29. *A Michele Vaaz 28–10–1610*, ASBN, Banco San Giacomo, giornale copiapolizze di banco.
30. Coniglio, G., *Il viceregno di Napoli nel sec. XVII. Notizie sulla vita commerciale e finanziaria secondo nuove ricerche negli archivi italiani e spagnoli*, Rome: Edizioni di Storia e Letteratura, 1955, pp. 149–155; Colapietra, R., *Il governo spagnolo nell'Italia meridionale (Napoli dal 1580 al 1648)*, Naples: Società Editrice Storia di Napoli, 1972, pp. 195–200; Zotta, S., "Momenti e problemi di una crisi agraria in uno 'Stato' feudale napoletano (1585–1615)", in *Melanges de l'École Française de Rome, Moyen Age – Temps Modernes*, vol. XC, 1978, no. 2, pp. 715–779; De Rosa, L., *Il Mezzogiorno spagnolo tra crescita e decadenza*, Milan: Il Saggiatore, 1987, pp. 71–88, 110–127.
31. *Carta de Pedro Fernández de Castro, VII conde de Lemos, sobre la oposición y apoyo a su gobierno, Napoli, 8 de deciembre de 1614*, Biblioteca Nazionale di Napoli (BNN), Manoscritti Brancacciani, V B 10, 16 r-v.
32. Sabatini, G., "La spesa militare nel contesto della finanza pubblica napoletana del XVII secolo", in Cancila, R. (ed.), *Mediterraneo in armi (secc. XV–XVIII)*, Quaderni di "Mediterranea", no. 4, Palermo: 2007, vol. II, pp. 593–635, especially p. 599.
33. *Carta del conde de Mola al regente Montoya, 20 de mayo de 1615*, BNN, Manoscritti Brancacciani, V B 10, fls. 108 r-v.
34. Brancaccio, G., *"Nazione genovese". Consoli e colonia nella Napoli moderna*, Guida, Naples: 2001, pp. 113–114. On the figure of Marc'Antonio de Santis, jurist as well as attentive student of economic phenomena affecting the Kingdom of Naples and author of the celebrated *Discorso intorno a gli effetti*

che fa il cambio in Regno (1605), see Colapietra (ed.), 1973, and De Rosa, L. (ed.), *Il Mezzogiorno agli inizi del Seicento*, Rome-Bari: Laterza, 1994.

35. On this, see De Rosa, L., *I cambi esteri a Napoli dal 1591 al 1707*, Naples: Banco di Napoli, 1955.
36. Brancaccio, 2001, p. 115.
37. *Miguel Vais e le sue pregiudiziali invenzioni 1610–1616*, BNN, Manoscritti, X 10 B 65; on both of these aspects, see Sabatini, 2011.
38. Enciso Alonso-Muñumer, 2007, pp. 383–404.
39. *Carta de Pedro Fernández de Castro, VII conde de Lemos, sobre la oposición y apoyo a su gobierno*, Nápoles, 8 de diciembre de 1614, BNN, Manoscritti Brancacciani, V B 10, fl. 18r. On the system of customs in the Kingdom of Naples in the age of Spanish dominion, see Bianchini, L., *Storia delle finanze del Regno delle due Sicilie*, ed. by L. De Rosa, Naples: ESI, 1971 (original edition, Naples: 1859), pp. 257–261.
40. *Miguel Vais e le sue pregiudiziali invenzioni 1610–1616*, BNN, Manoscritti, X 10 B 65 (at fl. 3 for the citation).
41. On Naples's demographic growth around the end of the 16th century and start of the 17th, with special reference to problems of supply, see Sabatini, 1998.
42. *Carta de Pedro Fernández de Castro, VII conde de Lemos, sobre la oposición y apoyo a su gobierno, Napoli, 8 deciembre 1614*, BNN, Manoscritti Brancacciani, V B 10, fl. 19r.
43. *Ibid.*, fl. 20r.
44. On the arrangement of Neapolitan aqueducts at the start of the 17th century and on the city's water supply problems, see the synthetic work of Montuono, G.M., "L'approvvigionamento idrico della città di Napoli. L'acquedotto del Serino e il Formale Reale in un manoscritto della Biblioteca Nazionale di Madrid", in D'Agostino, S. (ed.), *Storia dell'Ingegneria. Atti del 2° Convegno Nazionale, Napoli, 7–8-9 aprile 2008*, Naples: Associazione Italia di Storia dell'Ingegneria, 2008, vol. II, pp. 1029–1050, especially pp. 1038–1041, which makes use among other things of a very interesting anonymous Neapolitan manuscript from around 1610 entitled *El servicio de aguas en Nápoles* conserved in the Biblioteca Nacional de Madrid (BNM), ms 9610, fl.112r-115v.
45. *Carta de Pedro Fernández de Castro, VII conde de Lemos, sobre la oposición y apoyo a su gobierno, Napoli, 8 de deciembre de 1614*, BNN, Manoscritti Brancacciani, V B 10, *passim*.
46. Jeronimo de Guevara was described by supporters of the ambassadorial mission as "a persona di gran lignaggio, di segnalata virtù, versato in altre ambascerie per la sua religione a Roma, alla Magna alla maestà cesarea in Francia al Cristianissimo è stato causatore dell'elezione del suo Gran Maestro, ed in corte ben conosciuto, e con riscontro che egli ha con il segretario Baldarana per servitio fattogli in "persona di suo figlio dell'istesso abito" (Miguel Vais e le sue pregiudiziali invenzioni, BNN, ms. X B 65, fl. 5r); this eulogistic description should be contrasted with the disparaging one of him made by Miguel Vaaz, who instead insists upon the fact that Jeronimo was the son of Inigo de Guevara, who had in the past been forced to leave the Kingdom on account of positions that he took against the viceroy's policy and that Jeronimo himself had a mercenary disposition, and was persuaded

to complete the mission to Madrid upon payment of 15,000 or 20,000 ducats, a circumstance that helped in characterizing the whole undertaking as venal: *Carta del conde de Mola al regente Montoya, 8 de deciembre de 1614*, BNN, Manoscritti Brancacciani, V B 10, fls. 36v-37r.

47. *Carta de Pedro Fernández de Castro, VII conde de Lemos, sobre la oposición y apoyo a su gobierno, Napoli, 8 deciembre 1614*, BNN, Manoscritti Brancacciani, V B 10, fl. 15v.
48. Juan Alonso Suarez, appointed in 1602 lieutenant of the Camera della Sommaria, the highest administrative court of Justice of the Kingdom of Naples, participated in this capacity in the inspection of offices conducted by Juan de Herrera in the years of the government in Naples of the count of Benaventa and was then, at the behest of the count of Lemos, put in charge of the Consiglio Collaterale (Coniglio, 1955, p. 159; Comparato, V.I., *Uffici e società a Napoli, 1600–1647*, Florence: Olschki, 1974, p. 116; Intorcia, G.,*Magistrature del Regno di Napoli. Analisi prosopografica, secoli XVI–XVII*, Naples: Jovene, 1987, pp. 229, 384).
49. *Miguel Vais e le sue pregiudiziali invenzioni 1610–1616*, BNN, manoscritto X B 65, fl. 3.
50. *Ibid.*
51. *Carta de Pedro Fernández de Castro, VII conde de Lemos, sobre la oposición y apoyo a su gobierno, Napoli, 8 de deciembre de 1614*, BNN, Manoscritti Brancacciani, V B 10, fl.16r.
52. *Miguel Vais e le sue pregiudiziali invenzioni 1610–1616*, BNN, Manoscritti, X B 65, fl. 3r and v.
53. Galasso, G., *Alla periferia dell'impero. Il Regno di Napoli nel periodo spagnolo (secc. XVI–XVII)*, Turin: Einaudi, 1994, pp. 157–184; Enciso Alonso-Muñumer, 2007, pp. 420–448; Sabatini, 2011, pp. 155–157.
54. *Ibidem.*
55. *Carta del conde de Mola al regente Montoya, 8 de deciembre de 1614*, BNN, Manoscritti Brancacciani, V B 10, fl. 38v. The rate of interest for the *asientos* was calculated at 14%.
56. Coniglio, 1955, pp. 159–199; Sabatini, 2011, p. 157.
57. According to a statement of Michael Vaaz in his petition, the lowering of interest rates would have weighed down the patrimony of the Neapolitan nobles only in the amount of 19,000 ducats, while it would guarantee the state a savings of 95,000. Moreover, the renegotiation of interest on the public debt would guarantee the aristocracy the ability to resell their assets to obtain a relative gain. *Carta del conde de Mola al regente Montoya, 8 de diciembre de 1614*, Manoscritti Brancacciani, V B 10, fl. 40r. On the subject of public debt in the Kingdom of Naples, see Mantelli, R., *L'alienazione della rendita pubblica e i suoi acquirenti dal 1556 al 1583 nel Regno di Napoli*, Bari: Cacucci, 1997 and Sabatini, G., "Nel sistema imperiale spagnolo: il debito pubblico napoletano nella prima età moderna", in De Luca, G. and Moioli A. (eds) *Debito pubblico e mercati finanziari in Italia, secoli XII–XX*, Milan: Franco Angeli, 2007, pp. 287–304.
58. *Carta de Pedro Fernández de Castro, VII conde de Lemos, sobre la oposición y apoyo a su gobierno, Napoli, 8 de deciembre de 1614*, Manoscritti Brancacciani, V B 10, fl. 19r.

59. *Carta del conde de Mola al regente Montoya, 8 de diciembre de 1614*, Manoscritti Brancacciani, V B 10, fl. 33v.
60. *Ibid.*
61. *Ibid*, fl. 34v.
62. *Carta del conde de Mola al regente Montoya, 20 de mayo de 1615*, BNN, Manoscritti Brancacciani, V B 10, fls. 108r-v.
63. *Michele Vais e le sue pregiudizievoli invenzioni, 1610–1616*, BNN, manoscritto X B 65, fl. 9r.
64. *Ibid.*, fl. 13r.
65. *Ibid.*, fl. 10v.
66. *Ibid.*, fl. 11r.
67. *Ibid.*, fl. 10v.
68. On the duke of Osuna, see Linde, L.M., *Don Pedro Girón, Duque de Osuna, la hegemonía española en Europa a comienzos del siglo XVII*, Madrid: Encuentro, 2005, and on his government in Naples, see Schipa, M., *La pretesa fellonia del Duca d'Ossuna (1619–1620)*, Naples: Pierro, 1911, and Colapietra, 1972, pp. 201–208.
69. Zazzera, F., "Giornali dell'Illustrissimo ed Eccellentissimo Signor Pietro Girone duca d'Ossuna", in Palermo, F. (ed.), *Narrazioni e documenti sulla storia del regno di Napoli dall'anno 1522 al 1667*, in *Archivio Storico Italiano* IX, 1846, pp. 471–617, especially pp. 478–482.
70. Colapietra (ed.), 1973, pp. 24–28.
71. Amabile, L., *Fra Tommaso Campanella, la sua, i suoi processi e la sua pazzia*, Naples: Morano 1882, vol. III, pp. 646–648.
72. *Ibid.*, p. 648.

6
Authority and Expertise at the Origins of Macro-economics

Sophus A. Reinert

When the Norwegian Nobel laureate in economics Ragnar Frisch first drew the distinction between "micro-dynamic" and "macro-dynamic" analyses in 1933, ostensibly "founding" the modern field of macro-economics, his contribution was linguistic rather than conceptual.[1] Theorists and practitioners had been engaged with the analysis of aggregate economic phenomena for millennia, but only in early modern Europe did this perennial preoccupation take on the form and structure of an increasingly codified discourse.[2] The reasons for this were many and varied, but they were intimately connected to the mounting demands of international competition between solidifying political communities; the growing importance of increasingly global patterns of long-distance trade and transoceanic imperialism; and a rising and progressively educated public sphere.[3] This chapter revisits the founding role played by the Neapolitan lawyer and economics writer Antonio Serra (f. 1613) in a widespread debate over the theorization of macro-oeconomic phenomena in early modern Europe.[4]

Within this emerging discourse, evident in Italy at least as early as the 15th century, an important discussion surfaced regarding exactly whom to trust, about what, and why – one in which plausible sources of authority and expertise in economic debates were both formalized and contested.[5] It was a time of protean possibility, the nature and purpose of what in time would be known as "political economy" and eventually "economics" still to be crystallized. In this context, Serra's 1613 *Short Treatise on the Causes that Can Make Kingdoms Abound in Gold and Silver Even in the Absence of Mines* has long enjoyed a privileged position in the historiography of economics, and it should come as no surprise that it also played an important and uniquely self-conscious role in theorizing the nature of authority in discussions regarding the economic affairs of a political community.[6] Yet its memorability derives less from the work's immediate impact – it was, famously, ignored for nearly a century and a half before its rediscovery in the Neapolitan Enlightenment – than from the extraordinary sophistication of its engagement with the question.[7]

There can be little doubt that the application of methodologies born in the neighbouring disciplines of the history of political thought and of the history and philosophy of science has changed the historiography of political economy in recent decades.[8] Looking beyond what Joseph A. Schumpeter would have called the "history of economic analysis", new traditions of interpretation are flourishing that, from different perspectives, consider economic ideas and their concomitant policies in wider historical contexts rather than primarily approaching them as either bygone aberrations or brilliant antecedents of contemporary doctrine.[9] Working on the seminal foundations laid by Steven Shapin and Simon Schaffer, historians of science have now come to accept that the construction of "scientific" knowledge essentially depends on the generation or mobilization of consensus.[10] The problem, of course, is that consensus regarding the reasonable and the true in economic affairs – as in most fields of knowledge – changes more often than many practitioners would like, not merely in terms of the results themselves but also regarding how they should be reached and for what purposes. There exists a growing literature on the ways in which "scientific rigor" in economics went from meaning empirical to mathematical in the wake of World War II for example, and the extraordinary professional successes of econometrics in the last decades of the 20th century have veiled the extent to which dramatic changes periodically appear in the accepted parameters of economic discourse.[11] And just as the financial crisis that began in 2008 dramatically challenged many of the foundational assumptions of economics as it had progressed since the 1980s, so the sources of authority in economic debates were many, varied, and competing in early modern Europe.[12]

Not only did very different sorts of people claim to harness expertise in the area, ranging from merchants to military officers, religious figures, scholars, and statesmen, but they summoned a wide and often mutually exclusive range of arguments to do so, from the ever-present authorities of "history", plausibly the most influential at the time, and "experience" both in mercantile and political endeavours, to personal "genius" and of course variations of providence, whether expressed as an "obvious and simple system of natural liberty", the "invisible hand", or, as one Jesuit put it rather bluntly, "the economic hand of God".[13] The spectrum ranged, in short, from the deeply empirical and materialist to the virginally abstract and deific. This breadth of possibilities resulted, in part, from the lack of an established professional or vocational identity at the time; there was no title, systematic recognition, or institutional home, let alone a guild or university affiliation, for knowledge about aggregate economic phenomena.[14] Before the rise of the "scientific" expert, notions of expertise were associated most commonly and most clearly with lawyers and physicians, who had inherited the vocabulary and trappings of *peritia* – literally expertise – from antiquity.[15] Proto-economists could appeal to no such inheritance. The only thing that most observers agreed upon from the late 16th century onwards was that political economy itself had come to be of cardinal importance in domestic as well as international affairs.[16]

Yet, the importance of economic expertise was not always that clear-cut, and it is worth remembering how and why such a change came about; when, in short, the knowledge necessary to manage – and, it turns out, *survive* – international trade regimes was theorized as such. Illustrative examples abound, but for economies of space, that of the ill-fated English Muscovy Company will suffice. Shortly before succumbing to consumption during the summer of 1553, the Tudor boy King Edward VI of England penned a missive for his loyal knight Sir Hugh Willoughby, recently selected to lead a bold new expedition to foreign lands.[17] The letter, plausibly dictated by someone in the circle of the great lawyer, humanist, and sometime Secretary of State Sir Thomas Smith, was addressed to all the world's notables, and justified such exotic voyages by invoking the ancient trope about the power of commerce to unite a divided humanity:

> For the God of heaven and earth greatly providing for mankinde, would not that all things should be found in one region, to the ende that one should have neede of another, that by this meanes friendship might be established among all men, and every one seeke to gratifie all.

Therefore, Edward VI continued, he hoped foreign rulers would show "humanitie" towards these brave English merchants, whom he encouraged to venture out

> to countreis to them heeretofore unknowen, aswell to seeke such things as we lacke, as also to cary unto them from our regions, such things as they lacke. So that hereby not onely commoditie may ensue

> both to them and us, but also an indissoluble and perpetuall league of friendship be established betweene us both.[18]

International trade could, the argument went, strengthen the bonds of sociability across the earth by resolving the geographical discrepancy between the world's resources and people's needs, forging, so to speak, a global economic community to mitigate humankind's political and linguistic fragmentation. Edward VI expressed an ancient ideal – one which continues to enjoy ever greater purchase – of restoring harmony to humanity through the encouragement of international trade and the creation of a worldwide commercial society.[19] The questions, of course, were, how exactly can this be achieved, and what sort of knowledge might be necessary to initiate, maintain, and expand such a global system?

The 1550s were a particularly precarious decade in English history, and behind Edward VI's noble vision hid the spectre of grim necessity. At home, religious turmoil was brewing, and the greatest economic crisis in memory was a reality, with surplus merchandise accumulating in dockside warehouses and cloth exports in precipitous decline following the Tudor revocation of Hanseatic trading privileges; from 132,660 cloths in 1550 to a mere 84,968 in 1552.[20] Abroad, competing powers had discovered a veritable cornucopia in the New World through technical sophistication in war and navigation, not to mention outright daring, the tall tales surrounding which were gradually being translated into endless streams of precious metals.[21] And, to make matters worse, the new empires of Spain and Portugal in the East and West Indies had been enshrined by Pope Alexander VI's 1493 so-called Bulls of Donation, making it hard for latecomers such as England to catch up.[22] "There is left one way to discover", the Bristol merchant Robert Thorne wrote to Henry VIII already in 1527, "which is into the North".[23]

And north is where Englishmen would go. In reaction to the 1550s crisis, at once domestic and geopolitical, a new joint-stock company was formed under the leadership of Sebastiano Caboto, son of the more famous Venetian explorer of Newfoundland Giovanni Caboto: *The Mystery, Company, and Fellowship of Merchant Adventurers for the Discovery of Regions, Dominions, Islands, and Places Unknown*, or *The Company of Merchant Adventurers* for short. Its explicit aim was to emulate the great powers of the age, to bravely go where no European had gone before and procure for England new markets as well as resources.[24] On 11 May 1553, Willoughby set sail with three ships and 115 souls from London harbour. Following the Thames out to sea, he proceeded to map an intrepid northward course up the coast of Norway, their ultimate aim, as the alchemist and geographer Richard Eden would put it, being nothing short of "by the north seas to discover the mightie and riche empire of Cathay".[25] They sought, in other words, to reverse England's precarious situation in the European economic theatre by finding a market for their surplus manufactures by way of the as yet undiscovered Northeast Passage to China.[26]

In concordance with contemporary logics of patronage, Willoughby had been chosen to lead the expedition for his loyalty, good birth, and statesmanlike demeanour, not to mention his military valour during recent Scottish campaigns, but it is plausible that he had never set foot on a ship before, let alone seen the *Aurora Borealis*, and it seems that nobody told him winters might get cold north of the Arctic Circle.[27] Caboto wrote detailed instructions for the voyage, but theory only got the expedition so far in the North Atlantic.[28] Arctic storms separated the ships off the coast of Finnmark, in Northern Norway, and while one ship made its way around the North Cape and into the White Sea, from which it eventually made contact with Muscovy near present-day Arkhangelsk and opened regular trading relations between the two growing empires, Willoughby led two ships aimlessly around the Barents Sea. Prey to the winds and ignorant leadership, they eventually hit Novaya Zemlya in September, from which they returned westwards across the Barents Sea, via the equally "uninhabitable" Kolguyev Island to winter in an estuary of the Varzina River on the Kola Peninsula.[29] Their safe harbour revealed itself a "Ha[ven] of Death", as a manuscript note on Willoughby's log put it, and Russian fishermen eventually found their frozen corpses with the spring thaw, still bundled in the colourful woollen cloths that the merchant adventurers had hoped to peddle in far-away Cathay.[30]

Willoughby's end highlights the unforgiving nature of early modern economic globalization – in which living or dying was often a coin toss – with disconcerting clarity, and it helps explain why useful knowledge soon was institutionalized as a necessity for its realization.[31] Willoughby had been considered "trusty and faithfull", but as it turned out, these were necessary but not sufficient conditions for leading hyperborean missions through the long night of arctic winter.[32] A 1576 admiralty hearing on the failure of the expedition put the matter succinctly: it had been "for lacke of knowledge" that Willoughby's crews "were frozen to deathe".[33] They had died, in short, because he was no "expert in navigation", to use the Genoese Jesuit and Statesman Giovan Pietro Maffei's term for the likes of Christopher Columbus and Ferdinand Magellan, masters of what was becoming known as "the art of navigation".[34]

This is not to say that there had been no good navigators who had been appreciated for their talents before this field of knowledge was conceptualized, but now Tudor advisers realized that England's future depended on its ability to consistently export its manufactures and capture foreign markets.[35] And it learned the hard way that this in turn demanded certain clusters of knowledge in need of nurture, not only in terms of navigation and arctic survival but in the judicious selection of middlemen, envoys, and more generally the logistics and management of economic agents and resources on an imperial scale. This was, in short, one of many moments in early modern European history in which the *politics of knowledge* came to the forefront and the need for "expertise", as it was called, became paramount as a means of succeeding, not merely in international competition but in interaction itself, whether predatory or reciprocal.[36]

The idea that relevant "experience" made "experts" in early modern Europe is today generally accepted, though the historiography of the Renaissance "expert" of course is venerable. [37] Already, Alfred von Martin's 1952 *Sociology of the Renaissance* presented the "expert" as a major protagonist in the period's "will to economic power" and quest to achieve "mastery over nature".[38] Yet much ink has since been spilled over the appropriate "labels" and "categories" in this history, addressing questions of whether seekers and masters of knowledge in early modern Europe should be called scientists, natural philosophers, or experts; when the word "expertise" itself became a noun; and generally, the virtues and vices of anachronism in the history of science.[39] This recent scholarship would have been enriched by considering also the Italian context at the time, as Italian varieties of "*peritia*" were discussed explicitly during the Renaissance in relation to other words such as "*arte*", "*scienzia*", "*esperienza*", and "*disciplina*" to define not merely artisanal skills but the politics of economic administration and reason of state.[40] The great 1612 *Vocabolario* of the Florentine *Accademia della Crusca* in effect defined a "*perito*" as an "expert, scholar, scientist [*esperto, dotto, scienzato*]" and "*perizia*" as "experience, knowledge [*esperienza, sapere*]".[41]

The main interest here, however, is less in the terms that were used than what said terms were meant to convey. Just as "reason of state" was a poly-categorical concept, for example, so "good government" could be both a "practice" and an "art" in the early modern period, and many terms and categories related to political and economic questions were far from sequential in chronological terms. Well into the late 18th century, phrases such as "the art of good government" could serve as an umbrella term in Italian debates embracing, among other things, "the science of money" regarding "the economy of the state", understood in this context to mean the state's territory rather than the ruler's household; and "the great art of commerce" similarly remained synonymous with "political economy" and "civil economy" long after one might have assumed economic discourse to take on more consistent labels.[42] Clearly, "the economy" was an aspect of life to be studied and understood long before some scholars argue that it ostensibly came into being in 19th-century Britain or the 20th-century United States, though the exact terminology varied, and it was not, one might add wisely, conceptualized in disembedded and self-regulatory terms.[43]

Is it then dangerously anachronistic to argue that the more coherent discipline of political economy, later known as economics, gradually emerged from a broad historical tradition preoccupied with the political art, practice, and expertise of economic affairs? Adam Smith famously proclaimed "the great object of the political economy of every country" to be "to increase the riches and power of that country".[44] In practice, that "object" preceded "political economy" by millennia, much as wars were won long before people began calling military expertise an "art of war". Scholars are of course right to warn against projecting present categories onto an unsuspecting past.[45] But by ardently wishing to escape anachronism, say by claiming that Adam Smith was not an "economist" because there was no "economy" for him to discuss, one risks not merely quixotic antiquarianism, which has many charms, but the downright obfuscation of historical processes. As Herbert Butterfield put it, "we are in error if we imagine that we have found the origin of... liberty when we have merely discovered the first man who talked about it".[46]

Literally thousands of early modern historical actors thought and theorized about issues that today would appertain to the discipline of "macroeconomics", whether they did so under the rubric of "reason of state", "political economy", or something entirely different, and while it certainly is worthwhile to approach their ideas on their own terms and in their own vocabulary, their endeavour to understand and master aggregate economic phenomena should be respected as such. Of course, Smith was not a 21st-century macroeconomist, and of course, his world is not ours, but few would claim that either of these statements was true in any case. Indeed, given that a state of general equilibrium has never existed, and indeed *can* never exist, the real act of anachronism is to hold such an idealized vision of an abstract "economy" up as a necessary measure for economic thinking in the first place – a surprisingly common crime.[47]

In medieval and Renaissance Italy, knowledge of such aggregate matters was often classified as an "art", which the *Vocabolario della crusca* later defined as "a habit derived from experience, enabling one to perform with reason in any given subject, such as the seven liberal arts, or the mechanical ones".[48] Art, in short, was a habit of excellence born from experience in some field that already by the 13th century had expanded from its practical and artisanal origins to incorporate more purely intellectual endeavours such as "civic wisdom".[49] By the late Renaissance, the term had come to also retroactively convey broader fields of expertise in new words, if not in new ways. Not only would Antonio Cornazzano pen his *Beautiful Work on the Military Art*, followed by better known examples such as Niccolò Machiavelli's *The Art of War*, but ancient authorities on the ageless subject of warfare were similarly recast in this new terminology at the time; Polyaenus' *Stratagems for War* were translated in Italian as *The Stratagems of the Art of War*, and Publius Flavius Vegetius Renatus' *De Re Militari*, literally *On Military Matters*, came to be known as *On the Military Art*.[50] And such "military art", eventually known also as "Reason of War", could, in line with contemporary theories of the necessary relationships between microcosm and macrocosm, even find individualist expression, as the case was with the writer and man-at-arms Pedro Monte's works on martial arts.[51]

The relationship between Monte and Machiavelli, between self-defence manuals and guidebooks for leading armies and winning wars, mirrored that between the individual and political arts of commerce. The distinction between the two harked back to antiquity, as evident from Plutarch's statement in his *Life of Crassus* that "economy, which in things inanimate is but moneymaking, when exercised over men becomes policy", but the discourse regarding individual economy developed a more widespread and coherent discourse of expertise and authority first, long known as the "*ars mercatoria*".[52] One of the most influential texts in this tradition was doubtlessly the frequently republished 1458 handbook *On Commerce and the Perfect Merchant* by the Ragusan merchant, humanist, and diplomat Benedetto Cotrugli, long-time resident at the court of Naples. "Everybody", he assured his readers, "runs to the merchant" for "counsel" regarding the "government of money, on which all human states depend".[53] By 1540, a Venetian translation of Xenophon's *Oeconomicus* explicitly argued that one could be an "expert" in the "accumulation of wealth".[54] Yet, though the politics of administering an economy – and veritable industrial policies – were institutionalized across Italy already in the late Middle Ages, there were few self-conscious attempts before Serra to achieve what Richard A. Goldthwaite has called "a theoretical understanding of economic activity" in aggregate terms during the Renaissance.[55] By the time that Antonio Genovesi claimed his chair in political economy at the University of Naples in 1754, however, such a distinction between "the practice of merchandizing" or the "art of commerce" on the one hand and the "political science of commerce" or "political economy" on the other was taken for granted.[56] The 16th and 17th centuries, in other words, witnessed the gradual formalization of Ragnar Frisch's divide between micro and macro, as mercantile practices increasingly were codified and older forms of political household management and the politics of international trade came together to form a new field of expertise regarding the economic affairs of political communities.

The colourful reign of Cosimo I of Tuscany (1519–1574) can fruitfully be considered a watershed in this process, both theoretically and practically.[57] Having stumbled into power after the 1537 assassination of Alessandro de' Medici, the young and untested Duke – from a provincial lineage of the Medici dynasty – quickly imposed his will on Tuscany, ruthlessly eliminating his enemies, conquering nearby cities, and consolidating his control over territories. And much like the famous Uffizi he built centralized administrative structures under his government, so his economic policies were systematically aimed at empowering his state.[58] Cosimo I perfected the Italian tradition of inviting artisans to settle in his territories as part of a larger plan to domesticate foreign expertise and establish new industries in his territories, across the board from German engineers for the new silver mines at Pietrasanta to Flemish tapestry workers, Venetian glassmakers, and silk-weavers from Lucca.[59] And it was through his personal involvement that Tuscany successfully developed a silk industry to replace its declining woollen manufactures.[60] Wishing to "do something useful for merchants", Cosimo I had institutionalized a series of economic reforms, particularly in the 1550s, aimed at long-term structural development of his territories rather than short-term fiscal gains, and authors in the reason-of-state tradition soon presented his array of policies as a coherent "art" or "model" for others to follow in early works on the politics of economic policy.[61]

However venerable – if implicit – such preoccupations with individual and aggregate phenomena were, a certain rhetoric of novelty, explicitly bound to the revolutionary "discovery" of a veritable New World across the Atlantic, characterized economic debates on both extremes of this spectrum in the late Renaissance.[62] Leonardo Fioravanti argued in his 1564 *Mirror of Universal Science*: "When the art of navigation was discovered, and peoples saw that one could so easily traverse the sea from one place to another, and bring different goods where they were worth the most: one began to pursue the art of commerce".[63] According to his 16th-century editor, Cotrugli had done to the merchant what Xenophon and Cicero had done to kings and orators respectively – that is, creating an ideal type "perfect in all parts" – something that nobody had done "from the beginning of the world until him".[64] In spite of trade's timeless nature, the scale of modern commerce had come to represent an entirely new phenomenon, featuring new actors mastering new forms of expertise. Serra would harness a very similar rhetoric to present his "new" field of macroeconomic knowledge, the novelty of which he perhaps was too cognizant of, both as an "art" and as a "science" in his epochal 1613 *Short Treatise*.[65]

We know, of course, very little about Serra's life, except that he was a lawyer and wrote in jail, but from the nature of his argument he was clearly learned and of a humanist orientation, familiar not merely with ancient philosophy and Roman law but with Italian literary giants like Petrarch.[66] He probably published his treatise in an attempt to ingratiate himself with the Spanish viceroy and acquire a pardon, plausibly following the recently successful example of the revolutionary magus and polymathic writer Tommaso Campanella, but his immediate justification was to address an ongoing economic crisis in the Kingdom of Naples, refute policy proposals recently offered by the financier and international merchant Marc'Antonio de Santis, and finally present a general economic theory of competitive development and underdevelopment.[67] Their differences were substantial not only in terms of how the crisis could be overcome – whether through interventions in the financial or real economy – but also, and importantly, in terms of the acceptable sources of authority and expertise in macroeconomic affairs, and more specifically whether trust should be placed in personal experience in international trade or in a deeper and more generalized form of learned knowledge derived from conscious study.

Serra's humanist predilection towards scholarship served to simultaneously downplay the achievements of modern knowledge and accentuate his own innovation. The ancients, he argued, were unsurpassable in all areas that had interested them and that they had cared about, but long before Nicholas Barbon or David Hume came to define "Trade" a "Matter of State", Serra theorized that the dynamics of the modern world had unveiled an entirely new sphere of human life and therefore of learning to be charted.[68] Hence, Serra did not want to discuss politics or the "art of government in general", because whether one preferred monarchies or republics, one could not deal with such issues better than

"Plato and Aristotle" had done, nor would he struggle with jurisprudence and how to "distinguish just from unjust", because in that one could not supersede Emperor Justinian's codifications of Roman law. What Serra *did* want to turn the attention of the reader towards was a third, hitherto neglected aspect of statecraft, an aspect, however, which was of painful relevance for contemporary Naples:

> My aim is to discover the causes that can make a kingdom abound in money even if it possesses no gold or silver mines, a subject on which not a single word has been written by any of the ancient or modern writers on the ideal disposition of the political state.[69]

But in trumpeting its originality, he also underlined the universal interest and relevance of what soon would be known as political economy:

> This subject is an important and a complex one. Everyone knows what a difference it makes to the prosperity of the population in general and the prince in particular whether or not a state abounds in gold and silver. Everyone knows how many people yearn for riches and how few attain them. Everyone knows what an extraordinary number of measures have been taken in our own kingdom by those responsible for this area of government because they saw the kingdom growing poorer and poorer, and realized the gravity of the situation. Yet all their efforts have been in vain – even though, as we have seen, there existed in the kingdom the most powerful cause for it to abound in gold and silver – and the situation seems beyond all hope of recovery.[70]

In fact, in line with Serra's formation and the humanist tradition on which he drew, his argument was also rhetorical: just as "everyone" knew how important good government was, so "even the most ignorant bumpkin" would pronounce himself on the matter:

> There is a widespread conviction that the art of organizing a republic or governing a kingdom, and of remedying any disorders that may arise or defects that may exist in them, is common to all people, and everyone presumes to understand it. Whatever danger may threaten, however difficult it may be, even the most ignorant bumpkin will suggest a remedy, declaring that such and such a measure should be taken or such and such a law passed, and that if he were the ruler, he would adopt such and such a course of action. The opposite happens

> in any other science or art: no one dreams of discussing them unless he has first acquired practice and experience in them, either in whole or in part; this may be seen in philosophy, astrology, mathematics and other disciplines, and in all the arts.[71]

Hence "Marco Antonio de Santis, a man of great experience in commerce", as Serra introduced him, had mistakenly supposed that his personal success in matters of trade and finance equipped him with the insight, and importantly the authority, to intervene in macroeconomic affairs. But didn't he have "practice and experience" on the basis of which he could express himself with regard to some "science or art"?[72]

The issue was in effect not that nobody had produced an aggregate equivalent to Cotrugli before; it was that nobody had done so convincingly and with real authority derived from scholarship. De Santis, of course, had already written on the subject, and his argumentative logic with regard to macroeconomic questions of interest rates, exchange rates, and what we would understand as the balance of payments was derived obsessively from his understanding of how "merchants" acted and reacted in the world. Mercantile experience trumped even "eminence" in debates, a striking statement in light of early modern tropes regarding the synergy between social status and scientific authority.[73] "My opinion", de Santis explained, "is rather based on experience, sole master of all human actions, than on subtle arguments", and he forcefully argued that such experience should "shut everyone's mouths" because it was generalizable to the point where what happened in Genoa could dictate policies "to everyone", no matter the contextual differences.[74]

Serra acknowledged that de Santis had published on the topic before him, but Serra insisted that de Santis had not

> done so adequately, for in the first place he does not proceed with scholarly rigour, and in the second he does not discuss all the causes in general, but only presents one particular notion of his own (and individual cases, as the philosopher [Aristotle] says, can never generate scientific knowledge).[75]

Serra, on the other hand, proposed to examine the generalizable causes of the wealth and poverty of nations "in due order", to bring his training and expertise to bear on problems some might have thought outside erudite jurisdiction.[76] After all, as it turned out, "the science of government" was not something that just any merchant could pick up, because it was as "difficult and uncertain" as "medicine", an analogy Serra elucidated with a quote from Hippocrates: "Art is long, life is short, judgment difficult, experience dangerous and occasion sudden". Medicine was among the most difficult yet important of fields, in which practical expertise and scholarly learning uniquely were intertwined, and the preface to Serra's *Short Treatise* reads like a sustained case for the unique expertise of scholarly learning for understanding *also* the economic realm. Serra himself clearly had personal business experience, evident from his usage of technical terms relating to contemporary mercantile practices, but he argued that, like in medicine, this was not enough to grasp the whole picture. To make his case, he wove together contemporary economic practices, sacred and secular history, ancient philosophers, Roman law, and of course Petrarch's *Sonnets* to produce a general theory of why some political communities were wealthy while others were poor – a theory, in short, explaining the dynamics of macroeconomic phenomena. But he explicitly did not limit his analysis to what could be derived from singular experience in the way that de Santis had done. Learning, in the end, provided useful knowledge with necessary perspective.

Serra's holding fast to the notion that the ancients remained authoritative on everything but the politics of making a nation wealthy, *while* simultaneously arguing for the relevance of his intellectual tradition for tackling these issues, had powerful repercussions also for his theory of economic growth and the substance of his policy recommendations:

> And since navigation – the only art in which the moderns surpass the ancients – has been so greatly facilitated that trade is carried on not merely between east and west and north and south, but even between one hemisphere and the other, and goods can be easily transported from one to the other, who will deny that the sale of manufactured products is more certain and more profitable than that of agricultural produce?[77]

Where many of the most cherished authorities of antiquity had favoured virtuous bucolic idylls to the corruption of urban life, Serra's methodology – generalizing theories based on the different and, in the cases of Naples and Venice, divergent historical experiences of the Italian city-states, and importantly recognizing the revolutionary consequences of long-distance trade in the modern world – led him to embrace the transformative power of urban industry and manufacturing.[78] By putting his faith in industry, and indeed in the ideal of economic development itself over autonomous cultural achievement, Serra drew on a Renaissance tradition of urban bias to significantly qualify the humanist paradigm.[79] The specific idea that Serra harnessed to do so, that the moderns had overcome the ancients in knowledge of geography and navigation by discovering the compass – precisely the expertise that Willoughby fatally had not possessed – was a common trope not only in the more learned circles of the Renaissance but also among practitioners. The ancient "philosophers" had been mistaken, the Italian explorer and financier Amerigo Vespucci related from personal experience in 1500, to think that the Southern Hemisphere was uninhabitable, "and thus", he concluded somewhat arbitrarily, "it is certain, that practice is of more value than theory".[80]

Significantly, Serra did not follow in Vespucci's footsteps by dismissing the ancients, for that would in practice have meant joining de Santis in attempting to "generate scientific knowledge" from "individual cases" of practical experience.[81] Instead, he found ways of justifying new political possibilities and preoccupations by recourse to information and ways of thinking which had simply not been available to the canonical authors of antiquity, perhaps most importantly of all the rich and comparative history of the Italian city-states since the Middle Ages. Unlike other notable works of early modern economic theorizing, and indeed of scientific inquiry in general, Serra took care to pay his dues to erudition while staking out the new areas of analysis revealed by the commercial revolution.[82] And in turning to such base matters as trade and production, Serra in no way abandoned the scholastic and Renaissance political vocabulary of virtue, liberty, and the common good. He merely participated – in an admittedly extraordinary and innovative way – in the broadening of its conceptual horizon. Contrary to what was often presumed, a flourishing economy was not simply the consequence of good government for Serra; it was itself a vital aspect of civic life, on equal footing with politics and the law and therefore the direct subject of human agency. Though venturing beyond the interests of the ancients, Serra in important ways relied both on their vocabulary and their values to do so.

Not surprisingly, the main theoretical consequence of Serra's humanist claim to expertise through broad learning lay in the relationship that he proposed between theory and practice. Having discussed numerous "Natural" and "Accidental" "Causes" of the wealth of nations, from geography to industry, he argued that the most "powerful cause of all" was "effective government", which on the necessary basis of profound contextual knowledge uniquely could tailor "remedies" to the specific needs of a situation in order to allow a polity to "abound in gold and silver". Yet this was a "very difficult" task because in matters of political economy" it was

> necessary to pay attention to more than one thing, for the same cause often has different effects on different subjects, as the sun hardens mud but softens wax, and as a soft whistle excites a dog but soothes a horse.[83]

In other words, Serra argued that the complexities of human experience tended to preclude universalist claims in matters of political economy like those proposed by de Santis; theories had to be grounded in, and policies carefully tailored to, contexts that invariably were unique if they were to do any good, but it was ironically only through deep knowledge of numerous such contexts that good theories could be formulated.[84]

Though the common ground shared by both writers was large, including the commitment to a pragmatic and contextual politics, a contrasting comparison with one of Niccolò Machiavelli's most famous letters is here enlightening. Whereas the Florentine Secretary could proclaim, "[b]ecause Fortune has determined that, not knowing how to talk either about the silk business or the wool business or about profits and losses, I must talk about politics", it was impossible for Serra to talk of one without the other.[85] Just as politics could not ignore the limits imposed on it by economic concerns in the modern world, so the economy itself demanded – indeed *incarnated* – politics, and both were intertwined with a polity's legal system. To consider any one of them in isolation was quintessentially oxymoronic and indeed dangerous for Serra and the neglected tradition that he has come to represent.[86]

The debate between de Santis and Serra was echoed across Europe, as writers and statesmen increasingly realized that the rise to prominence of economic affairs had changed the nature of politics itself.[87] In line with Francis Bacon's insistence on the importance of "observation and experience" in increasing factual knowledge, to mention only the most famous example, merchant pamphleteers in 17th-century England began to openly flaunt their familiarity with commerce as an exploitable source of authority in economic affairs, at times even expressing their observations with experimental vocabularies. William Carter, writing on the importance of woollen manufactures for England's progress and warning of their plausible decline in his 1669 *England's Interest Asserted*, noted: "I shall confine my self to those things only, whereof I have had not only credible information, but a considerable (though a sad) experimental knowledge", and the Bristol best-seller John Cary gradually adopted a more legalistic and scientific terminology of "proof" and "evidence" across the editions of his famous *Essay on the State of England*, eventually calling tariffs and voyages "experiments" and "trade" itself a "science" with "principles".[88]

Both men claimed authority on the same foundations as de Santis had, namely their personal experience in international trade, but Cary went one step further by not merely adopting a more generalized "scientific" vocabulary but by actively seeking to present a holistic analysis of political economy, also to avoid accusations of being a "Projector" set at propagandizing for his own branch of trade or finance.[89] But practitioners also made more creative claims to expertise and therefore influence. The merchant and writer Sir Dudley North – posthumously famous as an ostensible predecessor of modern libertarianism – is a good example. He too had sought to avoid being dismissed for his "interest", but he was not merely praised, in the introduction to his pamphlet, for his "Knowledge and Experience of Trade", which "could not be attained, unless he were a Trader himself", but also for being representative of the "new Philosophy" emanating from "*Des Carte's* excellent dissertation *de Methodo*", by which he "reduceth things to their Extreams". The introduction to North's *Discourse of Trade* concluded that "Knowledge in great measure is become Mechanical", meaning "built upon clear and evident Truths", on "Principles indisputably true", but lamentably, this approach had been monopolized by the "studious and learned", to be contrasted with the "Common-Seaman, [who] with all his Ignorance, proves a better Mechanick, for actual Service, than the Professor himself, with all his Learning". In other words, in order for the organization of aggregate economic dynamics to become a Cartesian, mechanical knowledge, it had to be based on the experiences and empirical observations of practising merchants rather than on scholarship and learning.[90]

The paradox inherent in this Cartesian argument against learning did not seem to bother anyone, but its purpose was anyway to claim authority for North's remarkably politicized arguments at all costs, not to formulate coherent theoretical postulates. Though the substance of his arguments for government non-intervention fell on barren ground, his methodological insistence on the authority of experience as such echoed widely held beliefs. The problem of course was agreeing on whose experiences were informative and why, as well as the extent to which contemporaries simply disagreed on what said "experience" actually taught is remarkable. Contemporaries such as Cary and North both drew on their own experience in international trade to propose nearly diametrically opposite theories of political economy, as did merchants with equally divergent viewpoints who were brought together in the developing institutions known as boards of trade or chambers of commerce throughout early modern Europe.[91] The question that Andre Wakefield has so rightly reminded scholars to ask regarding their sources – namely "why should we trust them?" – was as valid then as now.[92] Yet it is striking that the rhetorical strategy that seemed to work best at the time, if we are to judge by market outcomes for proposals of political economy, chose to emphasize less the practical experience of individual merchants in specific branches of trade – though those too continued to enjoy currency – than the historical experiences of polities themselves to make arguments regarding economic affairs. In the end, the cluster of greatest consensus in England in the wake of the Williamite Settlement, and of the very practice of 18th-century British imperialism itself, developed on the assumption that the historical "experience" of polities had taught precisely the contrary of what North had argued.[93] Indeed, English and later British political economists proceeded, most probably unknowingly, precisely in the interventionist, industrialist spirit championed by Serra's humanist political economy.[94]

With time, of course, historical consensus shifted again, and Adam Smith's dictum that merchants were mainly vectors of "interested falsehood" rather than useful expertise long came to prevail in economics.[95] The problem of authority and expertise in economic debates remains more crucial than ever, and one can hardly argue that we have found a satisfactory answer. Or, rather, the answers that have been found satisfactory never remain so for very long. Theoretically, macroeconomic thinking now benefits from armies of highly educated economists whose technical sophistication was undreamt of until recent decades, and the scale of the discipline has grown exponentially to the point where what is at stake is no longer two crews of wayward merchantmen in the Barents Sea, or a southern Italian Kingdom in crisis, but the very sustainability of human life on earth.[96] Yet, and in spite of being entrenched in, and empowered by, a solidly established network of validating institutions, the methodological legitimacy – not to mention normative politics – of mainstream economic "expertise" finds itself challenged again after several decades of increasing, if nonetheless always contested authority, by disgruntled students and alternative theoretical paradigms; by distraught politicians and angry demonstrators; and not to mention by what most people would understand to be events themselves.[97]

This is to be expected. Even the most solidly entrenched scientific theories, from biblical chronology through bloodletting and the phlogiston theory to eugenics, have seen their legitimacy abruptly and dramatically erode, if only to reappear in another guise, and economic knowledge has been no less prone to such sudden reversals of fortune in the face of changing scholarly and popular opinion.[98] Consensus changes, particularly in democratic polities, and the truisms of economics past, from shock doctrines to bans on capital controls, are not those of economics present any more than the category of what constitutes commercial goods – human beings, needless to say, were included in this list for millennia – has remained unaltered across the ages.[99] Often, these disciplinary changes have resulted from real-world economic crises exploding the assumed correspondence between theory and practice. And from Serra's Naples through the disastrous Physiocratic reforms of the 1760s to the Great Depression to our contemporary predicament, the muse Clio is frequently called upon in such circumstances for guidance and perspective; invoked as ultimate arbiter of economic expertise and authority of last resort, history tragically finds fertile ground in barren times.[100] As no exception, Serra's fame across the centuries has derived significantly from the usages to which he was put by – and guidance he gave to – later readers in contexts of crisis; whether as a great citizen of a marginalized Cosenza; a symbol of Italy's lost greatness and its claim to fame as the homeland of political economy; an Italian patriot writing under Spanish mismanagement; or the first theorist of "the Southern Question" who sought to find explanations for the divergent development trajectories of the Italian peninsula.[101]

And there remain many reasons to study Serra four centuries after he wrote his *Short Treatise*. One is of course antiquarian and aesthetic, by which the study of his writings is no different from our appreciation of a painting or an opera. Yet as Quentin Skinner has argued, even the most rigorously antiquarian approach to the past can help us "reappraise" current "assumptions and beliefs", history serving as a "repository of questions we no longer ask".[102] This was one of the central arguments in Schumpeter's praise of the history of economic analysis as such, through which any economist could experience a "widening of his [or her] own horizon", and Istvan Hont argued similarly that history was the "tool of skeptics", bringing necessary perspective to debates about political economy.[103]

At our current moment of theoretical crisis, the question remains whether the history of economic thought and Serra's *Short Treatise* in particular cannot teach us something more concrete and more lasting – or, better, whether Serra's "expert" humanist warning against universal theoretical propositions might not, ironically, itself contain a lesson of perennial purchase: context matters for the conceptualization as well as the application of political economy, a universal claim that, ironically, precludes most other claims to similar status. The expertise of history is not merely cautionary but proactive; it can, indeed should, actively inform the formulation of economic theories and policies. We still long for a world of peaceful commercial collaboration like that adumbrated by Edward VI, and Willoughby was only one of countless sacrifices on the altar of that noble ideal. Yet now, as so many times before, we are reminded of the technical difficulties of realizing such an obvious scheme and the myriads of ways in which the world's complexity voids dogmatic solutions to our problems, however virtuous their intent or expert their execution.[104] So as the embeddedness of "the economy" yet again reasserts itself with a vengeance across the world, an awareness of, if not a return to, the humanist origins of what Frisch called "macro-dynamic" thinking in Antonio Serra is not just an aesthetic luxury but a practical necessity.

Notes

1. Frisch, R., "Propagation Problems and Impulse Problems in Dynamic Economies", in Koch, K. (ed.), *Economic Essays in Honor of Gustav Cassel*, London: Allen & Unwin, 1933, pp. 171–205. See also Schumpeter, J.A., *A History of Economic Analysis*, Oxford: Oxford University Press, 1954, p. 278, elaborated in Murphy, A.E., *The Genesis of Macroeconomics: New Ideas from Sir William Petty to Henry Thornton*, Oxford: Oxford University Press, 2009, p. 2. It is noteworthy that Frisch had relied on a similar vocabulary of "mikrokosmos og makrokosmos" already in his "Statikk og dynamikk i den økonomiske teori", *Nationaløkonomisk Tidsskrift*, vol. 3, no. 37, 1929, pp. 321–379, pp. 323f3. On Frisch, see among others Munthe, P., *Populister og originale økonomer*, Oslo: Aschehoug, 1999. On the "micro-macro divide", see Biltoft, C., "On a Certain Blindness in Economic Theory: The Firm, the State, and the Macro-Micro Divide, 1926–1937", in Fredona, R. and S.A. Reinert (eds), *The Legitimacy of Power: New Perspectives on the History of Political Economy* (forthcoming).
2. This is not the place to resurrect the venerable quarrel over whether the ancient economy was "primitive" or "modern", through which scholars often seem to ventriloquize arguments regarding modern capitalism. For key texts that argue opposite positions, see Finley, M.I., *The Ancient Economy*, Berkeley, CA: University of California Press, 1999 and Cohen, E., *Athenian Economy and Society: A Banking Perspective*, Princeton, NJ: Princeton University Press, 1992. The very existence of Xenophon's treatise on the ways and means of increasing the revenues of Athens makes arguments regarding the nonexistence of economic thought in antiquity spurious, though, needless to say, he was no rational choice automaton: see *Xenophon's Poroi: A New Translation*, trans. and ed. R. Doty, Lewiston, NY: Edwin Mellen, 2003.
3. See, on these processes, Reinert, S.A., "Rivalry: Greatness in Early Modern Political Economy", in Stern, P. and C. Wennerlind (eds), *Mercantilism*

Reimagined: Political Economy in Early Modern Britain and its Empire, Oxford: Oxford University Press, 2014, pp. 348–370.

4. On "oeconomics" and "economics" at the time, as well as different perspectives on how to approach the tension between the two, see Schabas, M. and N. De Marchi (eds.), *Oeconomies in the Age of Newton*, Durham: Duke University Press, 2003.
5. On the exceedingly long history of the problem of authority, see Furedi, F., *Authority: A Sociological History*, Cambridge: Cambridge University Press, 2013.
6. Serra, A., A Short Treatise *on the Wealth and Poverty of Nations (1613)*, translated by J. Hunt, edited and with an introduction by S.A. Reinert, London: Anthem, 2011 [henceforth] Serra, 1613. On its historiography see particularly pp. 5–8.
7. The earliest known "reception" of Serra was in Doria, P.M., "Relazione dello Stato Politico, Economico, e Civile del Regno di Napoli nel tempo, ch'è stato governato da i Spagnuoli, prima dell'Entrata dell'Armi Tedesche in detto Regno [post-1712]" and his "Del Commercio del Regno di Napoli... [1740]", both in *Manoscritti napoletani di Paolo Mattia Doria*, ed. Belgioioso, G. et al., 6 vols, Galatina: Congedo, 1981–1986, vol. I, pp. 49–139 and pp. 141–208, respectively (references to Serra on pp. 119 and 146). On Doria's use of Serra, see Reinert, S.A., "The Sultan's Republic: Jealousy of Trade and Oriental Despotism in Paolo Mattia Doria", in Paquette, G. (ed.), *Enlightened Reform in Southern Europe and its Atlantic Colonies, c. 1750–1830*, Farnham: Ashgate, 2009, pp. 253–269. It should further be added that Serra's methodology had clear repercussions, in this context, for Doria's *Vita civile*, Naples: Vocola, 1729, pp. 315–316 and *passim*. The first printed reference to Serra was, famously, in Galiani, F., *Della moneta*, 2nd ed., Naples: Stamperia Simoniana, 1780, note XXIX.
8. For the case of the history of political thought, see the foundational essays in Hont, I. and M. Ignatieff (eds), *Wealth & Virtue: The Shaping of Political Economy in the Scottish Enlightenment*, Cambridge: Cambridge University Press, 1986. In terms of the history of science, the breakthrough text here was Shapin, S. and S. Schaffer's extraordinarily influential *Leviathan and the Air-Pump: Hobbes, Boyle, and the Experimental Life*, Princeton, NJ: Princeton University Press, 1985. For a particularly influential application of methodologies derived from the history and philosophy of science to economics, see Mirowski, P., *More Heat than Light: Economics as Social Physics, Physics as Nature's Economics*, Cambridge: Cambridge University Press, 1989; and, for methodological statements, see Schabas, M.L., "Breaking Away: History of Economics as History of Science", *History of Political Economy*, vol. 24, no. 1, pp. 187–203 and id. "Coming Together: History of Economics as History of Science", in Weintraub, E.R. (ed.), *The Future of the History of Economics*, Durham, NC: Duke University Press, 2002, pp. 208–225.
9. Sir W.J. Ashley's critique of the historiography of economics as "a museum of intellectual odds and ends, where every opinion is labeled as either a surprising anticipation of the correct modern theory or an instance of the extraordinary folly of the dark ages" still rings partly true; see his *An Introduction to English Economic History and Theory*, 2 vols., New York, NY: G.P. Putnam, 1888, vol. II, p. 381, discussed in Magnusson, L., *Mercantilism: The Shaping of an Economic Language*, London: Routledge, 1994, p. 13.

10. On science as mobilization of consensus, see Shapin and Schaffer, 1985; Shapin, S., *The Social History of Truth: Civility and Science in Seventeenth-Century England*, Chicago, IL: University of Chicago Press, 1995.
11. Hodgson, G.M., *How Economics Forgot History: The Problem of Historical Specificity in Social Science*, London: Routledge, 2001; Weintraub, E.R., *How Economics Became a Mathematical Science*, Durham, NC: Duke University Press, 2002; but see now the eloquent account in Backhouse, R.E., *The Puzzle of Modern Economics: Science or Ideology?* Cambridge: Cambridge University Press, 2010, pp. 99–116. For the pre-history of this, see Reinert, S.A., "'One Will Make of Political Economy…what the Scholastics did with Philosophy': Henry Lloyd and the Mathematization of Economics", *History of Political Economy*, vol. 34, no. 4, 2007, pp. 643–677.
12. A growing literature is seeking to explain the nature and consequences of the crisis for economic theory; see among others Backhouse, 2010; Roncaglia, A., *Why the Economists got it Wrong*, London: Anthem, 2010 and, on how the discipline closed ranks in the face of its extraordinary failures, Mirowski, P., *Never Let a Serious Crisis go to Waste: How Neoliberalism Survived the Financial Meltdown*, London: Verso, 2013.
13. On the importance of "history" and "experience", see Reinert, 2011, p. 204 and *passim*; on "genius", see among many others Foscarini, M., *Relazione fatta dal Marchese Foscarini gia Ambasciadore Veneto presso la Corte di Torino nel 1742. Dopo il suo ritorno a Venezia*, f. 36r, Biblioteca Civica "G. Canna", Casale Monferrato, Italy, *091 93*; for Adam Smith's argument, see his *An Inquiry into the Nature and Causes of The Wealth of Nations*, ed. Cannan, E., 2 vols., Chicago, IL: University of Chicago Press, 1976, vol. II, p. 208; for the "economic hand of God", see Ferdinando Facchinei to Francesco Antonio Zaccaria, addendum to letter of 17 April 1763, Archivo Histórico de la Casa de Loyola, Sanctuary of Loyola, Azpeitia, Spain, *Fondo Zaccaria*, b. 19, 1v.
14. On the rise of other vocations at the time, see McClure, G.W., *The Culture of Profession in Late Renaissance Italy*, Toronto, ON: University of Toronto Press, 2004. On the roles of guilds and universities in conferring authority and expertise, see among many others Nummedal, T., *Alchemy and Authority in the Holy Roman Empire*, Chicago, IL: University of Chicago Press, 2007, p. 17 and *passim*.
15. The lawyer in classical Rome and his heir in medieval and Early Modern Europe was, for example, called *iurisperitus* (expert in law) and, along the same lines, the *medicus* could be called *medicinae peritus*. Long before similar discourses emerged in what we now call "science", lawyers not only established complex rules for identifying and disseminating juristic consensus but also thought explicitly and practically about expertise in other *artes* (especially as regards "expert testimony"); for the former, see the masterful discussion of "*communis opinio*" in Lombardi, L., *Saggio sul diritto giurisprudenziale*, Milan: Giuffrè, 1967, pp. 164–182, and for the latter, see the cases and opinions cited in Toschi, D., *Practicae conclusiones iuris*, volume 6, Rome: Zanetti, 1606, pp. 202–206, and volume 8, Rome: Mascardi, 1608, p. 184.
16. Hont, I., *Jealousy of Trade: International Competition and the Nation-State in Historical Perspective*, Cambridge, MA: Harvard University Press, 2005, p. 2 and *passim*.

17. On Edward VI, see the eminently readable Skidmore, C., *Edward VI: The Lost King of England*, London: Weidenfeld & Nicolson, 2007.
18. Edward VI of England, "The copie of the letters missive, which the right noble Prince Edward the sixt sent to the Kings, Princes, and other Potentates, inhabiting the Northeast partes of the worlde, toward the mighty Empire of Cathay, at such time as Sir Hugh Willoughby knight, and Richard Chancelor, with their company, attempted their voyage thither in the yeere of Christ 1553. and the seuenth and last yeere of his raigne", in Hakluyt, R., *The Principal Navigations, Voyages, Traffiques and Discoveries of the English Nation...* 3 vols., London: George Bishop, Ralph Newberie, and Robert Barker, 1599–1600, vol. I, pp. 231–232. Smith was probably also the author of *A compendious or briefe examination of certayne ordinary complaints of diuers of our country men in these our dayes which although they are in some part vniust & friuolous, yet are they all by vvay of dialogues throughly debated & discussed*, London: Thomas Marshe, 1581 [written c. 1549], which echoed this letter neatly on f24r: "for God hath ordeyned that no countrey shoulde haue all commodities, but which that one lackes another brings forth: and that, that one countrey lacketh this yere, another hath plenty thereof commonly the same yere, to the intente men may knowe that they haue neede one of anothers healpe, and thereby loue and societie to growe among all men the more". On its authorship, see *A Discourse of the Commonweal of This Realm of England*, ed. Dewar, M., Charlottesville, VA: University Press of Virginia for the Folger Shakespeare Library, 1969. On the classical roots of this popular early modern trope, see Pagden, A., "Human Rights, Natural Rights, and Europe's Imperial Legacy", *Political Theory*, vol. 31, no. 2, 171–199, particularly p. 186.
19. See also, on such projects, Reinert, 2011, p. 34.
20. Brenner, R., *Merchants and Revolution: Commercial Change, Political Conflict, and London's Overseas Traders, 1550–1653*, London: Verso, 2003, p. 7.
21. On the different imperial experiences at play, see among others Elliot, J.H., *Empires of the Atlantic World: Britain and Spain in America 1492–1830*, New Haven, CT: Yale University Press, 2007.
22. On the consequences of the Papal Bull for English imperialism, reorienting it, among others things, towards the North East as a means of reaching Cathay, see among others MacMillan, K., *Sovereignty and Possession in the English New World: The Legal Foundations of Empire, 1576–1640*, Cambridge: Cambridge University Press, 2009, pp. 70–78. See also the classic Baum, A., *Die Demarkationslinie Papst Alexanders VI un ihre Folgen*, Cologne: J.B. Heinmann, 1890; van der Linden, H., "Alexander VI, and the Demarcation of the Maritime and Colonial Domains of Spain and Portugal, 1493–1494", *The American Historical Review*, no. 22, 1916, pp. 1–20; Giménez Fernández, M., "Nada más sobre las Letras Alejandrinas de 1493 referentes a las Indias", *Anales de la Universidad Hispalense*, vol. 16, 1956, pp. 3–37.
23. Thorne, R., "A Declaration of the Indies and Lands Discovered, etc", in Hakluyt, 1599–1600, vol. I, pp. 212–216.
24. The classic account of the foundation of what soon would be known as the "Muscovy Company" remains; see Willan, T.S., *The Early History of the Russia Company 1553–1603*, Manchester: Manchester University Press, 1956, particularly pp. 1–5.

25. Eden, R., *The Decades of the Newe Worlde or West India…*, London: Powell [for Sutton], 1555, Preface to the Reader.
26. Though long famous, the episode has recently generated interest among popular historians; see Mayers, K., *North-East Passage to Muscovy: Stephen Borough and the First Tudor Explorations*, Stroud: The History Press, 2005 and Evans, J., *Merchant Adventurers: The Voyage that Launched Modern England*, London: Weidenfeld & Nicolson, 2013.
27. J. [Iosif Khristianovich] Hamel, *England and Russia; comprising the Voyages of John Tradescant the Elder, Sir Hugh Willoughby, Richard Chancellor, Nelson, and Others*, trans. J.S. Leigh, London: Richard Bentley, 1854, pp. 5–6.
28. Cabot, S., "Ordinances, instructions, and advertisements of and for the direction of the intended voyage for Cathay…", in Hakluyt, 1599–1600, vol. I, pp. 226–230.
29. The logbook is reproduced in Hakluyt, 1599–1600, vol. I, pp. 234–237. Not much is known regarding Kolguyev Island, but see still Trevor-Battye, A., *Ice-Bound on Kolguev: A Chapter in the Exploration of Arctic Europe to which is Added a Record of the Natural History of the Island*, Westminster: Archibald Constable and Company, 1895.
30. For the note, see British Library, London, United Kingdom, "Sir Hugh Willoughby's voyage for the discovery of Cathay, in 1553", *Cotton MS, Otho E VIII*, f. 16r. The event eventually became the stuff of legend across Europe, particularly given accounts that the corpses had been found frozen in a variety of statuesque postures around the ship, as if flash-frozen while going about their quotidian tasks. See Palmer, D.W., *Writing Russia in the Age of Shakespeare*, Farnham: Ashgate, 2004, pp. 28–29. It has been suggested that the crews in effect died of carbon monoxide poisoning rather than cold, see Gordon, E.C., "The Fate of Sir Hugh Willoughby and His Companions: A New Conjecture", *The Geographical Journal*, vol. 152, no. 2, 1985, pp. 243–247. Its grizzly end did not keep Hakluyt from presenting Willoughby's voyage as matching Columbus' venture to the New World (though admittedly "not with the like golden successe, not with such deductions of Colonies, nor attaining of conquests"), see Hakluyt, 1599–1600, vol. I, A Preface to the Reader.
31. For a cogent argument regarding the fruitful use of the term "globalization" in the early modern period, see Cheney, P.B., *Revolutionary Commerce: Globalization and the French Monarchy*, Cambridge, MA: Harvard University Press, 2010. As Jan de Vries has shown, half of the about two million Europeans who sailed East round the Cape of Good Hope in the period 1500 to 1795 "died a premature death" before making it back home, see de Vries, J., "Connecting Europe and Asia: A Quantitative Analysis of the Cape-Route Trade, 1497–1795", in Flynn, D.O., A. Giráldez, and R. von Glahn (eds), *Global Connections and Monetary History, 1470–1800*, Aldershot: Ashgate, 2003, pp. 35–106, p. 72.
32. Edward VI of England, "The copie of the letters missive", in Hakluyt, 1599–1600, vol. I, pp. 231–232.
33. See the deposition of James Alday relating to the expedition of Sir Hugh Willoughby, The National Archives, Kew, UK, *High Court of Admiralty, 13/22 ff. 99d -101v.* The passage is often quoted from Willan, 1956, p. 5, but the reference there given is wrong.

34. Maffei, G.P., *Delle Indie orientali*, translated by F. Serdonati, Venice: Zenaro, 1589, pp. 13, 16, 126. Unsurprisingly, A. Pigafetta had used the same term to describe Magellan in his account of the circumnavigation; see id., *The First Voyage Around the World, 1519–1522: An Account of Magellan's Expedition*, ed. T. J. Cachey, Toronto, ON: University of Toronto Press, 2007, p. 131. On "the art of navigation" see furthermore de Medina, P., *Arte de navegar*, Valladolid: Francisco Fernandez de Cordova, 1545, for the Italian edition of which, see id., *L'arte del navegare*, translated by V.P. da Corzula, Venice: Gioanbattista Pedrezano, 1555.
35. The literature on the early history of navigation is vast, but see, for an overview, Ash, E.H., *Power, Knowledge, and Expertise in Elizabethan England*, Baltimore, MD: Johns Hopkins University Press, 2004, pp. 250–251.
36. For analysis and historiographical references, see Ash, 2004, as well as the essays in Ash, E.H. (ed.), *Expertise: Practical Knowledge and the Early Modern State*, Chicago, IL: University of Chicago Press, 2010 and Klein, U. and E.C. Spary, *Materials and Expertise in Early Modern Europe: Between Market and Laboratory*, Chicago, IL: University of Chicago Press, 2010. For caveats, see Wakefield, A., "Butterfield's Nightmare: The History of Science as Disney History", unpublished manuscript.
37. Classic statements are Dear, P., "Mysteries of State, Mysteries of Nature: Authority, Knowledge and Expertise in the Seventeenth Century", in Jasanoff, S. (ed.), *States of Knowledge: The Co-Production of Science and Social Order*, London: Routledge, 2004, pp. 206–224; Rabier, C., "Introduction: Expertise in Historical Perspective", in id. (ed.), *Fields of Expertise: A Comparative History of Expert Procedures in Paris and London, 1600 to Present*, Newcastle-upon-Tyne: Cambridge Scholars Publishing, 2007, pp. 1–33.
38. von Martin, A., *Sociology of the Renaissance*, trans. W.L. Luetkens, London: Routledge and Kegan Paul, 1952, pp. 20–24.
39. See, for an overview, Wakefield, "Butterfield's Nightmare".
40. See, for a particularly extended discussion, Bonaventura, F., *Della ragion di stato et della prudenza politica*, Urbino: Alessandro Corvini, 1623, pp. 5–14. Even the elegant Appuhn, K., *A Forest on the Sea: Environmental Expertise in Renaissance Venice*, Baltimore, MD: Johns Hopkins University Press, 2009, p. 321f4 curiously relies on the Oxford English Dictionary for an 1825 definition of "expert" to make sense of early modern Venice.
41. Accademia della Crusca, *Vocabolario degli Accademici della Crusca*, Venice: Giovanni Alberti, 1612, p. 614.
42. Diodati, L., *Dello stato presente della moneta nel regno di Napoli e della necessità di un alzamento*, Naples: M. Stasi, 1790, p. iv; Donaudi delle Mallere, I., *Saggio di economia civile*, Turin: Eredi Avondo, 1776, p. 52, on which see Monestarolo, G., *Negozianti e imprenditori nel Piemonte d'antico regime: La cultura economica di Ignazio Donaudi delle Mallere (1744–1795)*, Florence: Olschki, 2006.
43. For arguments that "the economy" emerged in much later periods, see, among others, Foucault, M., *Les Mots et les choses: Une archéologie des sciences humaines*, Paris: Gallimard, 1966; Tribe, K., *Land, Labour and Economic Discourse*, London: Routledge & Kegan Paul, 1978; Schabas, M.L., *The Natural Origins of Economics*, Chicago, IL: University of Chicago Press, 2005; Mitchell, T., *Rule of Experts: Egypt, Techno-Politics, Modernity*, Berkeley, CA: University of

California Press, 2002, pp. 81–82, 298–303; Schabas, M.L., "Constructing 'The Economy'", *Philosophy of the Social Sciences*, vol. 39, no. 1, 2009, pp. 3–19.
44. Smith, *Wealth of Nations*, vol. I, p. 397.
45. E.g. Mitchell, T., *Rule of Experts: Egypt, Techno-Politics, Modernity*, Berkeley, CA: University of California Press, 2002, pp. 81–82.
46. Butterfield, H., *The Whig Interpretation of History*, London: G. Bell, 1931, p. 43, on which see Sewell, K., *Herbert Butterfield and the Interpretation of History*, Houndmills: Palgrave Macmillan, 2005, p. 34. Or, as Alfred Zimmern argued so long ago regarding historical economics, "to refuse to apply economics to Greek history because economic activity was only one side of Greek life would be like refusing to admit that meteorological laws were valid for Sheffield because it is difficult to discern the sky there". See Zimmern, A.E., "Suggestions Towards a Political Economy of the Greek City-State", in id., *Solon & Croesus: And other Greek Essays*, Oxford: Oxford University Press, 1928, 165–199, p. 172. On Zimmern, see Morefield, J., *Covenants without Swords: Idealist Liberalism and the Spirit of Empire*, Princeton, NJ: Princeton University Press, 2004.
47. In this I agree wholeheartedly with the sentiment expressed in Schumpeter, J.A., "Preface to Japanese Edition of 'Theorie der Wirtschaftlichen Entwicklung'", in id. *Essays on Entrepreneurs, Innovations, Business Cycles, and the Evolution of Capitalism*, ed. by R.V. Clemence with an introduction by R. Swedberg, New Brunswick: Transaction Publishers, 1989, pp. 165–168.
48. Accademia della Crusca, *Vocabolario*, p. 80.
49. Najemy, J.M., "The Medieval Italian City and the 'Civilizing Process'", in Guglielmotti, P., I. Lazzarini, and G.M. Varanini (eds), *Europa e Italia/Europe and Italy: studi in onore di Giorgio Chittolini/Studies in Honour of Giorgio Chittolini*, Florence: Firenze University Press, 2011, pp. 355–369.
50. Cornazzano, A., *Opera bellissima del arte militar*, Venice: C. da Mandello, 1493; Machiavelli, N., *Dell'arte della guerra*, Florence: Bernardo Giunti, 1521; Polyaenus, *Stratagemi dell'arte della guerra*, translated by N. Mutoni, Venice: al segno d'Erasmo, 1551; Publius Flavius Vegatius Renatus, *Del arte militare*, translated by G. Tizzone, Venice: Bernardino di Vitale, 1524.
51. Bonaventura, F., *Della ragion di stato et della prudenza politica*, Urbino: Alessandro Corvini, 1623, p. 16; Monte, P., *Exercitiorum atque artis militaris collectanea*, Milan: Scinzeler, 1509. On Monte, see Fontaine, M.-M., *Le condottiere Pietro del Monte, philosophe et écrivain de la Renaissance, 1457–1509*, Geneva: Slatkine, 1991. On the Neo-Platonic microcosm-macrocosm tradition, see, among many others, Conger, G.P., *Theories of Macrocosms and Microcosms in the History of Philosophy*, New York, NY: Columbia University Press, 1922.
52. Plutarch, *Lives of Illustrious Men*, trans. A.H. Clough, Boston, MA: Little, Brown, & co., 1928, p. 384. On this tradition, see Hoock, J., P. Jeannin, and W. Kaiser (eds), *Ars mercatoria: Handbücher und Traktate für den Gebrauch des Kaufmanns, 1470–1820*, 3 vols, Paderborn: Schöningh, 1991–2001. On the mirroring of private and public economy in Cotrugli, see Romano, D., *Housecraft and Statecraft: Domestic Service in Renaissance Venice, 1400–1600*, Baltimore, MD: Johns Hopkins University Press, 1996, p. 16.
53. Cotrugli, B., *Della mercatura*, Venice: All'Elefanta, 1573, p. 66. On Cotrugli, see Jouanique, P., "Three Medieval Merchants: Francesco di Marco Datini,

Jacques Coeur, and Benedetto Cotrugli", *Accounting, Business and Financial History*, vol. 6, no. 3, 1996, pp. 261–275.

54. Xenophon, *La economica di Xenofonte*, trans. A. Piccolomini, Venice: Al segno del [P]lozza, 1540, p. 28v. For a later discussion of the role of experience in providing expertise in a similar context see also de Herrera, G.A. (ed.), *Agricoltura tratta da diversi antichi et moderni scrittori*, trans. M. Roseo da Fadriano, Venice: Nicolò Polo, [1592], [p. ix].
55. Molà, L., "Stato e impresa: privilege per l'introduzione di nuove arti e brevetti", in Braunstein, P. and L. Molà (eds), *Il Rinascimento italiano e l'Europa*, vol. III: *Produzione e techniche*, Treviso-Costabissara: Angelo Colla Editore, 2007, pp. 533–572; Goldthwaite, R.A., *Economy of Renaissance Florence*, Baltimore, MD: Johns Hopkins University Press, 2011, p. 591.
56. Reinert, 2011, p. 205
57. Brown, J.C., "Concepts of Political Economy: Cosimo I de' Medici in a Comparative European Context", in Anonymous (ed.), *Firenze e la Toscana dei Medici dell' Europa del '500*, Florence: Leo S. Olschki, 1983, pp. 279–293; Reinert, "Introduction", pp. 38–46.
58. Cochrane, E., *Florence in the Forgotten Centuries, 1527–1800*, Chicago, IL: University of Chicago Press, 1973, particularly pp. 1–92; Van Veen, H.T., *Cosimo I de' Medici and His Self-Representation in Florentine Art and Culture*, Cambridge: Cambridge University Press, 2006, p. 81.
59. On his economic policies and their results, see among others Adelson, C., "Cosimo I de' Medici and the Foundation of Tapestry Production in Florence", in *Firenze e la Toscana dei Medici*, Florence: Leo S. Olschki, 1983, pp. 899–924, p. 913 and id., "The Tapestry Patronage of Cosimo I de'Medici: 1545–1553", PhD Dissertation, New York University, 1990; Goldthwaite, R.A., *Wealth and the Demand for Art in Italy, 1300–1600*, Baltimore, MD: Johns Hopkins University Press, 1993, pp. 16–19, 44; Ilardi, V., "Renaissance Florence: The Optical Capital of the World", *European Journal of Economic History*, vol. 22, no. 3, 1993, pp. 507–541, particularly pp. 534–535; Kempers, B., *Painting, Power, and Patronage: The Rise of the Professional Artist in the Italian Renaissance*, London: Allen Lane, 1992, p. 275; Litchfield, R.B., *Emergence of a Bureaucracy: The Florentine Patricians, 1530–1790*, Princeton, NJ: Princeton University Press, 1986, pp. 35–36, 206–213; Malanima, P., *La decadenza di un'economia cittadina: L'industria di Firenze nei secoli XVI–XVIII*, Bologna: Il Mulino, 1982, pp. 104, 111–112, 314–315; id. "L'industria fiorentina in declino fra '500 e '600", in *Firenze e la Toscana dei Medici*, pp. 295–308, p. 299; id., "An Example of Industrial Reconversion: Tuscany in the Sixteenth and Seventeenth Centuries", in Van der Wee, H. (ed.), *The Rise and Decline of Urban Industries in Italy and the Low Countries*, Leuven: Leuven University Press, 1988, pp. 63–74, p. 67; McCray, W.P., *Glassmaking in Renaissance Venice: the Fragile Craft*, Aldershot: Ashgate, 1999, pp. 127–128; Morelli, R., "The Medici Silver Mines (1542–1592)", *Journal of European Economic History*, vol. 5, no. 1, 1976, pp. 121–139, particularly pp. 123 and 135; Parigino, G.V., *Il tesoro del principe: funzione pubblica e privata del patrimonio della famiglia Medici nel Cinquecento*, Florence: Leo S. Olschki, 1999, pp. 84–85; Rolova, A., "La manifattura nell'industria tessile di Firenze del Cinquecento", in *Firenze e la Toscana dei Medici*, pp. 309–325, particularly p. 310.

60. Goodman, J., "Tuscan Commercial Relations with Europe, 1550–1620: Florence and the European Textile Market", in *Firenze e la Toscana dei Medici*, pp. 327–341, p. 331; Litchfield, 1986, pp. 212–213; Malanima, 1982, pp. 314–315.
61. "Disteso della deliberazione de Magnifici Signori Luogotenenti e consiglieri", 8 April 1551, Archivio di Stato di Firenze, Florence, Italy, *Pratica Segreta, 1, 126 inserto*, 1r. See for example the Earl of Monmouth's 1656 English translation of Boccalini, *I ragguagli di Parnaso: Or Advertisements from Parnassus…*, London: Humphrey Moseley, pp. 66, 416, but most influentially Botero, G., *The Reason of State and The Greatness of Cities*, translated by P.J. and D.P. Waley, New Haven, CT: Yale University Press, 1956, p. 133 and *passim*. See on his "art" of managing internal and external relations and the resources and happenings of his lands also Baldini, B., *Vita di Cosimo Medici: primo Gran Duca di Toscana*, Florence: Bartolomeo Sermartelli, 1578, p. 16. On Cosimo I's eulogists generally, see Menchini, C., *Panegirici e vite di Cosimo I de' Medici: Tra storia e propaganda*, Florence: Leo S. Olschki, 2005.
62. For perspectives on the revolutionary consequences of this discovery, see among others Abulafia, D., *The Discovery of Mankind: Atlantic Encounters in the Age of Columbus*, New Haven, CT: Yale University Press, 2008 and, for a more popular account, Appleby, J., *Shores of Knowledge: New World Discoveries and the Scientific Imagination*, New York, NY: W. W. Norton & Company, 2013.
63. Fioravanti, L., *Dello specchio di scientia universale*, Venice: Andrea Ravenoldo, 1564, ff. 30v-33v, particularly 30v.
64. Cotrugli, 1573, pp. 4–5.
65. Serra, *Breve trattato*, pp. 1–2.
66. On humanism, see particularly Hankins, J., "Humanism and the Origins of Modern Political Thought", in Kraye, J. (ed.), *The Cambridge Companion to Renaissance Humanism*, Cambridge: Cambridge University Press, 1996, pp. 118–141 as well as Nauert, C.G., *Humanism and the Culture of Renaissance Europe*, Cambridge: Cambridge University Press, 2006. For the strain of humanism which has come to be known as 'civic humanism', see Baron, H., *The Crisis of the Early Italian Renaissance*, Princeton, NJ: Princeton University Press, 1966; Pocock, J.G.A., *The Machiavellian Moment: Florentine Political Thought and the Atlantic Republican Tradition*, with a new afterword by the author, Princeton, NJ: Princeton University Press, 2003; and, for revisions, the essays in Hankins J. (ed.), *Renaissance Civic Humanism: Reappraisals and Reflections*, Cambridge: Cambridge University Press, 2000.
67. For Tommaso Campanella's more successful strategy to escape jail through economic writings, see his "Arbitrii sopra l'aumento dell'entrate del regno di Napoli (1608)", in Colapietra, R. (ed.), *Problemi monetari negli scrittori napoletani del Seicento*, Rome: Accademia Nazionale dei Lincei, 1973, pp. 85–101, p. 101. Compare to Serra, *Breve trattato*, p. 133. On Campanella see Ernst, G., *Tommaso Campanella: Il libro e il corpo della natura*, Bari-Rome: Laterza, 2002.
68. Barbon, N., *A Discourse of Trade*, London, 1690, pp. A3v-r; Hume, D., *Political Essays*, ed. Haakonssen, K., Cambridge: Cambridge University Press, 1994, p. 52
69. Serra, 1613, p. 6; discussed also in Schefold, B., "Antonio Serra: Der Stifter der Wirtschaftslehre?", in id. (ed.), *Antonio Serra und sein Breve Trattato: Vademecum zu einem Unbekanten Klassiker*, Düsseldorf: Verlag Wirtschaft und Finanzen GMBH, 1994, pp. 5–27.

70. Serra, 1613, p. 6.
71. Serra, 1613, pp. 1–2.
72. *Ibid.*
73. de Santis, M.A., "Discorso di Marc'Antonio de Santis intorno alli effetti che fa il cambio in regno [1605a]", in Colapietra (ed.), 1973, pp. 111–141, particularly pp. 111, 116–122, 129; de Santis, M.A., "Secondo discorso di Marcantonio de Santis intorno agli effetti che fa il cambio in regno. Sopra una risposta, che e' stata fatta avverso del primo [1605b]", in Colapietra (ed.), 1973, pp. 143–162, particularly p. 143. On science and civility, see Shapin, 1995.
74. de Santis, 1605b, pp. 154–155.
75. Serra, 1613, pp. 1–7. He might well have been aware also of the Neapolitan D. Carafa's "I doveri del principe", in id, *Memoriali*, ed. Nardelli, F.P., Rome: Bonacci editore, 1988, pp. 97–209, particularly pp. 195–197, on which see Bentley, J.H., *Politics and Culture in Renaissance Naples*, Princeton, NJ: Princeton University Press, 1987, pp. 26–27, 141–147.
76. Serra, 1613, pp. 1–7. This was, of course, at best a rhetorical strategy, for Serra might not have been entirely unfamiliar with the rather serious works of Jean Bodin and Giovanni Botero, not to mention the rich sixteenth-century Spanish debate on the issue, on which see Perrotta, C., "Early Spanish Mercantilism: The First Analysis of Underdevelopment", in Magnusson, L. (ed.), *Mercantilist Economics*, Boston, MA: Kluwer, 1993, pp. 17–58.
77. Serra, 1613, p. 12.
78. The literature on this bucolic dream is immense. On the ancient Greeks, see Hanson, V.D., *The Other Greeks: The Family Farm and the Agrarian Roots of Western Civilization*, Berkeley, CA: University of California Press, 1999. On the pastoral tradition as a whole see Alpers, P., *What is Pastoral?*, Chicago, IL: University of Chicago Press, 1997; for land-holding conservatism in the Western tradition, see Pocock, 2003. On its modern incarnation in the Slow Food movement, see Honoré, C., *In Praise of Slow: How a Worldwide Movement is Challenging the Cult of Speed*, London: Orion, 2004.
79. On this, see Martines, L., *The Social World of the Florentine Humanists, 1390–1460*, Princeton, NJ: Princeton University Press, 1963, pp. 34–37.
80. Amerigo Vespucci to Pier-Francesco de' Medici, 18 July 1500, published as 'First letter of Americus to Lorenzo di Pier-Francesco de' Medici', in Lester, C.E. and A. Foster, *The Life and Voyages of Americus Vespucius...* New York, NY: Baker & Scribner, 1846, pp. 151–174, 160–161. See also Guicciardini's analysis of navigation in *The History of Italy*, translated by S. Alexander, New York, NY: Phaidon, 1969, pp. 177–182, discussed in Marino, J.A., 'Economic Structures and Transformations', in id. (ed.), *Early Modern Italy, 1550–1796*, Oxford: Oxford University Press, 2002, pp. 51–68, 51–53. On Campanella's exaltation of the three inventions of modernity – gunpowder, the printing press, and the compass – see his *La Città del Sole: Dialogo Poetico – The City of The Sun: A Poetical Dialogue*, translated with an introduction and notes by D.J. Donno, Berkeley, CA: University of California Press, 1981, p. 121. A similar statement appeared already in the sixteenth-century autobiography of Girolamo Cardano, *The Book of My Life*, translated by J. Stoner, London: J. M. Dent & Sons, 1930, p. 190. On the issue generally, see Grafton, A., *New Worlds, Ancient Texts: The Power of Tradition and the Shock of Discovery*,

Cambridge, MA: Harvard University Press, 1992, p. 63 and *passim* as well as Pagden, A., 'Plus Ultra: America and the Changing European Notions of Time and Space', in Marino, J.A. (ed.), *Early Modern History: Testing the Limits of Braudel's Mediterranean*, Kirksville, MO: Truman State University Press, 2002, pp. 255–273.

81. Serra, 1613, p. 7.
82. On these larger issues, see Grafton, A., *Defenders of the Text: The Traditions of Scholarship in an Age of Science, 1450–1800*, Cambridge, MA: Harvard University Press, 1991.
83. Serra, 1613, pp. 19–22.
84. For an antithesis of Serra's approach, see again de Santis, 1605b, pp. 154–155.
85. Niccoló Machiavelli to Francesco Vettori, 9 April 1513, in Machiavelli, *Tutte le Opere*, ed. M. Martelli, Florence: Sansoni, 1971, pp. 1131–1132.
86. The tradition is not unlike what Werner Sombart once defined as the "activistic-idealist" tradition in economics; see his *Der Moderne Kapitalismus: Historisch-systematische Darstellung des gesamteuropäischen Wirtschaftslebens von seinen Anfängen bis zur Gegenwart*, 3 vols Munich-Leipzig: Duncker & Humblot, 1928, vol. II, p. 919. For a similar modern argument, see Foley, D.K., *Adam's Fallacy: A Guide to Economic Theology*, Cambridge, MA: Harvard University Press, 2006.
87. Neapolitan and English debates have been taken to be comparatively representative before, though for different purposes, see for example Schumpeter, 1954, p. 353 and *passim.*
88. Carter, W., *England's Interest Asserted...* London: Printed for Francis Smith, 1669, p. 2; Cary introduced the term "science" in the third edition of his 1695 *Essay on the State of England*, entitled *An Essay, towards Regulating the Trade, and Employing the Poor, of This Kingdom*, London: Collin and Mabbat, 1717. More generally on the "scientific" nature of contemporary political economy, see Reinert, 2011, pp. 120–125.
89. John Cary to John Locke, 9 May 1696, in Locke, J., *The Correspondence of John Locke*, ed. E.S. de Beer, 8 vols, Oxford: Oxford University Press, 1976–1989, vol. V, pp. 633–635; see also John Cary to Thomas Long, 19 August 1696, in British Library, London, United Kingdom, *Add. MS. 5540*, 76v. Though Locke thought Cary had succeeded in a letter of 2 May 1696, in Locke, V, pp. 625–627, and Edmund Bohun followed suit in his letter to John Cary of 2 January 1695–1696, in *The Diary and Autobiography of Edmund Bohun, Esq.*, ed. by Rix, S.W., Beccles: Privately Printed, 1853, pp. 131–132, consensus was not reached, and Anonymous, *Some Considerations Offered to the Citizens of Bristol Relating to the Corporation of the Poor in the Said City*, N.P.: n.p, 1711, p. 12 called Cary a "Great Projector", though on different grounds. On this, see Reinert, 2011, p. 132.
90. North, D., *A Discourse on Trade*, London, 1691, Preface. The reference is to Descartes, R., *A Discourse on the Method* [1637], trans. I. Maclean, Oxford: Oxford University Press, 2008. On North, see Finkelstein, A.L., *Harmony and the Balance: An Intellectual History of Seventeenth-Century English Economic Thought*, Ann Arbor, MI: University of Michigan Press, 2000, pp. 186–204. For a rather more positive reading, see for example Backhouse, R.E., *Economists and the Economy*, 2nd ed., Piscataway, NJ: Transaction Publishers, 1994, pp. 201–202.

91. The crucial history of the emergence of such institutions in the European world has yet to receive apt comparative treatment, but see for examples Borgherini-Scarabellin, M., "Il magistrato dei Cinque Savi alla Mercanzia dalla istituzione alla caduta della Repubblica", *Miscellanea di storia veneta*, vol. 4, no. 2, 1925, pp. 1–146; Laslett, P., "John Locke, the Great Recoinage, and the Origins of the Board of Trade: 1695–1698", *The William and Mary* Quarterly, third series, vol. 14, no. 3, 1957, pp. 370–402; Schaeper, T., *The French Council of Commerce, 1700–1715: A Study of Mercantilism after Colbert*, Columbus, OH: Ohio State University Press, 1983; Bennet, R.J., *Local Business Voice: The History of Chambers of Commerce in Britain, Ireland, and Revolutionary America, 1760–2011*, Oxford: Oxford University Press, 2012.
92. Wakefield, A., *The Disordered Police State: German Cameralism as Science and Practice*, Chicago, IL: University of Chicago Press, 2009, p. 90.
93. On the failure of North's vision to materialize as a theoretical atrocity (however salubrious for the history of British economic development), see Appleby, J.O., *Economic Thought and Ideology in Seventeenth-Century England*, Princeton, NJ: Princeton University Press, 1978.
94. Unless, of course, Mario Nigro was right in arguing that Thomas Mun had encountered Serra's *Breve trattato* while working in Livorno, see his "Antonio Serra", *Almanacco calabrese*, 1953, pp. 79–88, particularly p. 82.
95. Smith, *Wealth of Nations* vol. I, p. 522. On the topic, see also Krugman, P., *A Country is not a Company*, Boston, MA: Harvard Business Press, 2009.
96. For an influential statement of the scope of economics in face of the climate crisis, see Gore, A. *The Future: Six Drivers of Global Change*, New York, NY: Random House, 2013, p. 4 and *passim*.
97. See, from vastly different perspectives, Backhouse, 2010; Breckman, W., *Adventures of the Symbolic: Post-Marxism and Radical Democracy*, New York, NY: Columbia University Press, 2013, pp. 283–288; Easterly, W., *The Tyranny of Experts: Economists, Dictators, and the Forgotten Rights of the Poor*, New York, NY: Basic Books, 2014, particularly pp. 6–7. On such networks and how they confer authority to knowledge, see among others Latour, B. and S. Woolgar, *Laboratory Life: The Construction of Scientific Facts*, Princeton, NJ: Princeton University Press, 1986. On how the logic of this specific economics network – of universities, institutes, journals, Clark Medals, and so on – gradually narrowed the confines of "scientific" economics, simultaneously marginalizing and galvanizing heterodox schools of thought (many of which simply developed currents that once had been mainstream, whether historical, institutional, evolutionary, or other), see Lee, F., *A History of Heterodox Economics: Challenging the Mainstream in the Twentieth Century*, London: Routledge, 2011. For notable calls for greater economic pluralism *before* the crisis, see among others Reinert, E.S., *How Rich Countries Got Rich…And Why Poor Countries Stay Poor*, London: Constable: 2007; Rodrik, D., *One Economics, Many Recipes: Globalization, Institutions, and Economic Growth*, Princeton, NJ: Princeton University Press, 2008.
98. The literature on such scientific revolutions is, needless to say, immense, but see for a milestone Kuhn, T.S., *The Structure of Scientific Revolutions*, Chicago, IL: University of Chicago Press, 1962. For a famous example of "scientific" refashioning, see still the case of eugenics and sociobiology in Sahlins, M.D., *The Use and Abuse of Biology: An Anthropological Critique of Sociobiology*, Ann Arbor, MI: The University of Michigan Press, 1977.

99. On the convoluted history of recent economic dogmas, see, among others and from different perspectives, Abdelal, R., *Capital Rules: The Construction of Global Finance*, Cambridge, MA: Harvard University Press, 2007; Piketty, T., *Capital in the Twenty-First Century*, Cambridge, MA: Harvard University Press, 2014. For one take on the decommodification of humankind, see Draper, N., *The Price of Emancipation: Slave-Ownership, Compensation and British Society at the End of Slavery*, Cambridge: Cambridge University Press, 2013. On the complex relationship between political liberty and intellectual authority, see among others Furedi, 2013.
100. See, for influential examples by non-historians in the economic realm, Galiani, F., *Dialogues sur le commerce des blés*, Paris: Delalain, 1770; Keynes, J.M., *The General Theory of Employment, Interest and Money*, London: Palgrave Macmillan, 1936; Lee Kuan Yew, *The Grand Master's Insights on China, the United States, and the World*, Cambridge, MA: MIT Press, 2012, p. 100.
101. See, for historiographical discussion, Reinert, "Introduction", pp. 77–82.
102. Skinner, Q., *Liberty Before Liberalism*, Cambridge: Cambridge University Press, 1997, pp. 108, 112.
103. Schumpeter, 1954, p. 4; Hont, 2005, p. 156.
104. See, for one of endless examples, the cautionary moral tale in Munk, N., *The Idealist: Jeffrey Sachs and the Quest to End Poverty*, New York, NY: Doubleday, 2013, particularly pp. 11–19, 230–232.

7
The Republic of Wealth and Liberty: The Politics of Antonio Serra

Luca Addante

It is the text itself of the *Breve trattato* that calls out for analysis from the political perspective, not only because the book advanced various proposals in economic policy, but also because it postulated the primacy of politics over economics, suggesting "between the line" proposals for reform that were decidedly radical given the institutional organization of the Kingdom of Naples.[1] Serra's political argument is developed – or, better, dissimulated[2] – in particular in the *Proem* and then in chapters VI and X of the first of the three parts into which the *Breve trattato* is divided. As the reader of this book may know, he formulated a complex typology of causes which he held to promote a country's wealth, applying a method that already foreshadowed the modern scientific approaches and which still surprises even today. Over a century before the development of political economy, this Italian economist, perfectly aware that he was presenting "a subject that is both great and new",[3] did not limit his scope to analysis of the practical aspects of economic and financial issues – in which he had been preceded by other Italians – locating them within a theoretical setting by means of a method that based rational investigation on empirical foundations, and in particular on comparison.[4] Of this, Serra was fully aware: in criticizing Marc'Antonio de Santis, (the main target of his polemics) he observed that the latter had not proceeded "with scholarly rigour, and ... he does not discuss all the causes in general, but only presents one particular, practical notion of his own" which things, "as the Philosopher says, can never generate scientific knowledge".[5]

The *Breve trattato* was based on analysis of concrete realities: a realistic approach that shows Serra's debt to the method adopted by authors like Niccolò Machiavelli.[6] Serra[7] expressed his preference for the kind of doctor who based his cure on "experience" rather than the other kind who worked on the basis of "guesswork". At the same time, he stressed the need to construct a rational theoretical framework of "causes in general" within which to fit his empirical findings, seeking to base his theories both on reason and on experience.[8] Indeed, he challenged his adversary de Santis "to prove his theory with reason and real facts, rather than imaginary ones, and not with mere assertion"[9] but with awareness that "experience is the mistress of all things, and all arguments, however powerful, must yield to her".[10] This approach was coherent not only with Machiavelli but with the epistemological perspectives widely adopted in the most advanced Neapolitan naturalism of the 16th and17th centuries too, from Scipione Capece to Bernardino Telesio and Tommaso Campanella.[11] These natural philosophers (and others) had argued the need to investigate natural phenomena with the perception of the "senses" (primarily), but also with "reason". There is no coincidence that Serra made explicit reference to "natural philosophy", in two cases: at the beginning of the treatise, observing in the dedicatory letter that "wonder, as the natural philosophers tell us... can be produced by two causes"; and in the *Proem*, where he invokes "natural philosophy".[12]

Serra argued that the wealth of a state – and not only the monetary wealth – was assured by two types of general factors, which he defined as "natural" and "collateral". The former lay essentially in the presence of metal mines in the state yielding the material to mint coins – gold and silver. In this respect, there were obviously no reforms that could be of any use – either the mines were there or they were not. However, Serra did not see mines as incomparable factors for the accumulation of wealth, and to show this, was not the case he went on to enumerate the second group of causes – the collateral causes, classifying them as "particular" and "common factors". The former were once again major factors peculiar to a given country, like mines impossible to export, and Serra subdivided them into two categories: surplus of agricultural produce, which could be exported to procure coin; and the geographical position of the country, decisive importance attaching to whether or not the "site" was traversed by the international trade routes. To these two elements, however, the Calabrian theoretician added four "common factors" which lay at the core of his reasoning since they, and only they, could find their way into a country through measures of reform. These factors, according to Serra, were: "A multiplicity of manufacturing activities, an enterprising population, extensive trade", and, finally, institutions and political choices.[13]

Serra looked into the reasons why the Kingdom of Naples, despite a surplus of agricultural produce, forever foundered in a sea of financial troubles. The Republic of Venice, too, like the Kingdom, was devoid of mines, and moreover, unlike the Southern State, the *Serenissima* had to import foodstuffs, to the effect, he observed, that considering the "conditions in the two cities, those in Naples are, or should be, a cause and a powerful occasion for creating an abundance of money, whereas those in Venice should be a cause and occasion for making the city poor". "And yet", he pointed out, "the opposite is the case: Venice abounds in money and Naples is poor".[14] Looking into this apparent paradox, Serra pointed out that the Queen of the Adriatic enjoyed a key geographical position for trading operations, in contrast to the peripheral Kingdom of Naples. However, he did not see this advantage as sufficing to account for the disparity between the fortunes of the Republic and the Kingdom. It was here that the common factors came in, in that the shores of the Lagoon displayed a great many factories while, despite the availability of raw materials, he noted a lack of transformation and production plant in the Kingdom – apart from the silk factories and a few rare examples monopolized by foreigners – with the result that the Kingdom was obliged to import practically all the manufactured products. In turn, Serra associated industrialization with keen enterprising spirit, and these factors, together with geographical position, he saw as favouring international trade. With trade now shifting in the direction of the Atlantic, Naples found itself irrevocably left on the periphery of the great international routes, and the propensity of the Neapolitans for an easy life and sweet idleness, aggravated yet further the scant productivity and meagre volume of trade. Thus, according to Serra, geophysical, anthropological, and economic factors contributed to the wealth of the country, but taking prime position over all these "causes" was the fourth "common factor", politics:

> Government is a kind of agent cause which stimulates, causes and preserves the other accidents; it is what maintains order, without which nothing in the world can work well... When [this factor] occurs to perfection in any Kingdom, it will undoubtedly be the most powerful cause of all of making it abound in gold and silver, for it may be described as the efficient cause and .superior agent of all the other accidents. [15]

The primacy of politics over economics was thus peremptorily asserted as "efficient cause and superior agent of all the other accidents". But if it's true that the economist invoked state intervention to encourage the citizens to set up factories and engage in trade, any such intervention, he deemed, had to be in a context of free circulation of money and goods,[16] and not of a market enjoying the artificial support of privileges and customs barriers. This is certainly not to say that Serra was a precursor of economic liberalism: indeed, the very logic implied by the term "precursor" belongs to an old approach to the history of ideas by now obsolete. Nevertheless, the fundamental proposals set out in the *Breve trattato* included attributing freedom to currency exchange: it was not the state that could fix the level, as did the Kingdom of Naples and as was common opinion: "Exchange... is and must be free".[17] Such opinions may have seemed non-conformist in an age ignorant of economic science with states taking on increasingly all-embracing roles, and Serra was well aware of the fact, for in Naples not only the authorities but even the economic agents were wondering why exchange must be or is free, observing "that no one was able to give an answer".[18] But the Italian economist, who had studied law,[19] answered that "the reason is not so far to seek... in fact nothing could be easier", since, he remarked, it was "clearly stated in Justinian's *Codex*", in "the chapter *De actionibus et obligationibus*", where the general rule is set "that contracts are voluntary at first, but become binding once they have been made. Therefore, since the will is of its nature free, it follows that contracts are all free at first".[20] Clearly, then, the strength of Serra's convictions derived from a vigorously libertarian spirit, an approach that contrasts with any absolutist policy (including mercantilism). Serra so defined the natural essence of human freedom, as in those years it was also beginning to be defined by theoreticians of natural law such as Althusius and Grotius, but also by natural philosophers like Campanella.

Moreover, this was by no means all, for he went as far as to claim freedom of speech, for the sake of principles that – at a time when the *Index* of Prohibited Books and censorship reigned triumphant – were simply subversive, Serra advocating the open exchange (and clash) of opinions as ultimately fruitful. It was an approach that he championed de facto, publishing from a prison cell (and, furthermore, in the vernacular) a book replete with proposals for radical reform, also writing in perfectly explicit terms that "it is characteristic of the truth to reveal itself through discussion".[21] In the Baroque period, such a way of thinking was a symptom of extreme anti-conformism,[22] although not many years before, it had found significant circulation in circles associated with Neapolitan culture, and in particular among the 16th-century radical heretics and libertines whose cult of individual freedom had matured under the influence of the teaching of Juan de Valdés.[23] Significantly, a compatriot of Serra, also associated with the Valdesians, namely Valentino Gentile, had from 1558 to 1566 braved two sentences of death (finally passed, of course) wandering around Catholic and reformed Europe asserting the right to proclaim his radicals views.[24]

Apart from economic issues and the value attached to freedom of speech, the libertarian culture underlying the *Breve trattato* also emerged at the political level, right from the *Proem*, where the author indicts those "modern" thinkers who departed from the paths of the "ancients", taking politics in a direction that he saw as bordering on tyranny, "depicting and approving tyrannical government as politically expedient" – noxious attitudes symptomatic of crass "ignorance" which, he sadly remarked, "has been embraced by no small number of rulers and their advisers".[25] For our Calabrian writer, then, the situation of the Kingdom of Naples was disastrous not only at the economic level but more generally in political terms. To counteract this, the prisoner Serra proposed a very particular kind of political primacy, quite opposite to the perspectives running to absolutism, *ragion di Stato*, or the myths of royal majesty, which dominated the debate at the time, but, rather, he based it on the natural freedom of people and the "myth of Venice", the great Republic.[26] Of the *Serenissima* he admired the burgeoning of factories, the enterprising aptitude of the citizens, and also the good fortune of enjoying a geographical position that, together with other factors, evidently favoured a great volume of trade and wealth accruing to state and population alike. Besides all this, however, Serra sang his paean to the political wisdom of the Republic's elites and, above all, celebrated its political-institutional structures. We may therefore reasonably ascribe Antonio Serra to the republican culture of the 17th century, as defined in particular by Franco Venturi (1971), and to a more general climate of libertarian thinking, to that 17th century "culture of opposition" discussed by Rosario Villari. A culture of dissent which, although often veiled in dissimulation, contributed to the revolutionary ferment of the mid 17th century, from Catalonia to Great Britain to Naples itself. And it is a culture that in the more radical cases, and in a century that saw the rise of absolutism and survival of the myth of royalty, manifest itself – more or less openly – in the republican choice, closely associated with libertarian claims and, often, assertions of a patriotic spirit, also recurrent in the *Breve trattato*.

Of course, one can always object that admiration of the Venetian system did not invariably take the form of a republican position. In fact, many writers point out that the Republic of Saint Mark actually represented an exemplary case of "mixed government":[27] monocratic in that the figure of the doge was seen to surmount all; aristocratic in institutions such as the senate (or "Pregadi") and other offices; and democratic in the vast assembly of the Great Council. This was the position taken by, among others, the paradigmatic texts in defining the myth of Venice, such as *De magistratibus et republica Venetorum* by Gasparo Contarini (1543)[28] and the *Libro della Republica de' Viniziani*[29] by Donato Giannotti (1540), although it is also to be seen even in the medieval roots of the myth.[30] But this was not the case with Serra, who, as we will see, dwelt on the senate alone in his considerations on the Venetian institutions, mentioning neither the doge nor the Great Council.

Over and above this aspect, some preliminary observations are called for to make clear the meaning he attributed to the word "republic". The term was, of course, often used to translate *res publica* – Bodin's *République* – as was the practice in juridical, historical, and political science treatises in medieval and early modern times, apart from a few odd cases, such as that of Machiavelli[31] – Republic as a synonym for state, a political system connoted in the broad sense with no inherent definition of its particular, collective form. In any case, perusal of Serra's text suffices to dispel all doubts. At a certain point, he observes: "No other *dominion* or *republic*[32] in the world has ever lasted as long as Venice".[33] He then goes on to say more clearly: "no such system of appointing magistrates has ever been adopted in any other *seigniory* or *republic*".[34] Finally, in the *Proem* to the treatise, Serra averred that "the art of organizing a *republic* or governing a *kingdom*, and of remedying any disorders that may arise or defects that may exist in them, is common to all people, and everyone presumes to understand it".[35] Thus, it appears evident that Serra differentiated between two basic forms of government – republics and kingdoms (or seigniories) – as indeed did Machiavelli in the celebrated opening of the *Prince*: "All the States, all dominions that have command over men, have been and are either republics or principalities".[36] The Machiavellian typology had revolutionized theoretical work on forms of government; departing from the Aristotelian classification, *politìa* and aristocracy had in fact converged in the Republic typology, which then came to form a system with a character of its own, contrasting with the monarchy by virtue of its pluralist government, based on law and freedom.[37]

Having sorted out these preliminary points, we can now bring the focus on the view of Venice offered by the *Breve trattato*. To begin with, there is actually nothing very surprising about the fact that Serra looked to Venice as a state to take as an example. Examining the persistence of republican ideas in the 17th century, Franco Venturi has demonstrated that the libertarian aspirations that pervaded the political concepts and endeavours of those years were to a great extent based upon the concrete example of the United Provinces, on the one hand, and the Italian republics (Venice foremost among them), on the other: "It was they who preserved an alternative model to monarchy, and denied the latter its final triumph, not only on the political and military level, but also on the ideological".[38] In the course of the 16th century, in fact, after a centuries-long gestation, a veritable "myth of Venice" had swept through Europe; the essence of its constitution and the shrewdness with which the state was run by the elites of the Republic had become an obligatory reference point not only at the political level, but in European culture as a whole, to the extent that a number of political theoreticians of the 16th and 17th centuries saw the Venetian system as a sort of ideal state. It is a way of thinking that is perfectly understandable in the case of the Venetian authors, who would tend to magnify the fortunes of their "dominion". At the same time, however, the admiration for Venice was significantly exceptional among authors of other Italian states including Florence: suffice it to recall Giannotti, but also Savonarola, Guicciardini or the Orti Oricellari circles, and although we must not lose sight of the distance taken from this cult by Machiavelli[39], there can be no underrating the fact that in Florence both the institution of the Great Council (1494) and that of the life Gonfaloniere (1502) were inspired by the Venetian institutions.[40] Even odder was the circulation the myth found in the currents of ideas flowing through Europe, apart from the interest understandably shown by the republicans of the Netherlands: Montaigne[41] appreciated the institutions of the *Dominante*, as did various authors writing in English.[42] Even Jean Bodin, although highly critical of the system of the *Serenissima* in his *Six livres sur la République*, and while remaining a theoretician of absolute "monarchie royale", went as far as admitting that Athens, Rome, and Venice were "des républiques les plus illustres qui aient existé sous l'état populaire".[43]

Thus, for anyone speaking of Republic in the first years of the 17th century in Italy, reference to Venice was imperative. From this point of view, the *Serenissima* was a happy island in Italy's straits, hemmed in between counterreformation and absolutism. Nor is it any wonder that Serra himself, to revive the fortunes of the state, set his sights in the direction of the Lagoon. Besides the geophysical, anthropological, and economic factors, the success and efficiency of the Queen of the Adriatic – he wrote – derived above all from its good government and stability, aspects which he saw as being guaranteed by the political structures of the Republic. It was not only the geographical position but also the institutions that constituted an authentic "speciality". In Venice, in fact, unlike all the other republics and principalities,

> the government is in effect always the same. Such continuity has never been possible in other seigniories or republics. In seigniories, a government will last about fifty years at most, assuming that the king is resident in the country and – a large assumption, this – that from beginning to end of his reign he possesses the same wisdom and judgement and the same amount of experience. If the king does not reside in the country, the government, as is well known, will only last as long as the viceroy's term of office. In effect, a single form of government can last in a kingdom for the lifetime of the king; afterwards, when he dies, whether he is succeeded by one of his sons or by someone else, the government that ensues will not be the same as that which existed before; hence the proverb 'new lords, new laws': the new king will not agree in every detail with his predecessor's opinions, nor in any case can he know what the former king regarded as disorders in his kingdom, not what measures he would have taken in a given situation, nor what measures he did in fact take to remedy past disorders. This is why the subjects of the Papal States, with their continual changes in regime, do not receive the good government that they might receive if the government was stable.[44]

Thus, we see that stable government constituted a fundamental value for our economist. Here he might be seen to be falling in with the more traditional political position of the 17th century, averse to all upheavals and any factor that might in one way or another foment them. Stability of governments was in fact an essential theme in political writings of the Baroque age.[45] However, the majority of writers settled the matter elaborating ever more refined and forceful absolutist theories – suffice it to consider the champion in the field, Bodin,[46] who saw stability as consubstantial with royal monarchy. And yet the theme of stability was also an essential ingredient of the Venice myth, and it was in fact in this respect that Serra took his place among the proponents of the republican (and not of mixed government) version of the myth. His main argument, in fact, was that stability was in itself an attribute peculiar alone to the republican political system. He observed that stability was rendered impossible in principalities and monarchies by the continual changes that monocratic regimes inevitably went through. "New lords, new laws", he remarked with a commonsensical argument, since a king could at the best reign for about fifty years, and even if he took pains to be consistent throughout his reign (the likelihood of which Serra doubted), once he was dead his heir would bring changes to his choices and the directions he pursued since, he went on, stretching the point, perhaps, the same "government can last in a kingdom for the lifetime of the king". This was a "systemic" flaw which accounted for the wretched government of the Pontifical State: "This is why the subjects of the Papal States, with their continual changes in regime, do not receive the good government that they might receive if the government was stable". The point came over all the more forcefully seeing that some pages before he had placed Pope Sixtus V among the very few heads of government that had achieved "excellence".[47] All this depended on factors that derive wholly from human will, if not indeed from chance, and an inferior successor could ruin all the good work: the reign of Sixtus V fell not long before the time when Serra was writing, but by then papal government had already become a paradigm of the structural instability of monarchies. Having established these characteristics, therefore, it was obvious enough to point out that this was all the more so in the case of those states (like his Kingdom of Naples) where the sovereign did not reside in his dominion but delegated power to a viceroy, with continual, counterproductive shifts in the political line.

In a word, the criticisms which this prisoner took the liberty of levelling at the monocratic government were nothing short of crushing. Such opinions could find their like in European political culture only in the rare cases of such exceptional figures, and in any case only in republican regimes. A further critique that emerged from Serra's text, moreover, was directed against hereditary governing powers (at least in the case of monocratic powers), which saw him alongside that rebel of the age par excellence, Tommaso Campanella. The latter, in fact, argued that in order to build the "optimal republic", the need was to pursue close connection between political roles and the social and natural inclinations of people (their talent), while "the republic always faces ruin ... when [individuals] come into office by chance, because the sons of kings are kings, the sons of nobles officials, or because they are relatives of the rulers or friends, or because they are rich and buy distinction, and not because they are good and wise".[48] However, despite these criticisms of hereditary (and venal) entry into office, Campanella did not see the republic as necessarily the best form of government. He maintained (with Machiavellian arguments) that "monarchy for acquisition and republic for maintenance are generally the best" and that "the rule of one is better in wartime, and of many in times of peace".[49] The best form of government, according to the philosopher, was to be chosen between elective monarchy and republic – in any case with a senate occupying a central role and under the sovereignty of the law;[50] thus Campanella placed some emphasis on the advantages of an elective monarchy, as in the papal state.[51] For Serra, on the other hand, who came up with explicit criticism of the papal monarchy, the other monarchical system was by its very nature riddled with structural flaws, whether by heredity, election, or delegation. As he saw it, monarchy, and even more viceroyalty, were incapable of solving the problems of such a complex organism as the state, nor could they contribute to promoting the wealth of the citizens.

Another noteworthy aspect of the *Breve trattato* is the thoroughly secular approach taken to politics and economics. Even the pontifical state was seen by Serra from a totally secularized viewpoint, judged purely in terms of the effectiveness of the organization of government and political choices, with a method that left no room for religious or metaphysical digressions. The author contemplated no place for spiritual elements at the basis of state organization or economic dynamics. While such an attitude found some support in the well-known Venetian jurisdictional system, due attention must also be paid to the fact that even the fundamental authors of the "myth of Venice" canon had some mention to make of Divine Providence[52], and yet more importantly, the republican symbology (from Saint Mark to the doges' rites) was not lacking in references to transcendental dimensions, closely interwoven into the political dimension. The only concessions that Serra made were two vague references to Thomas Aquinas and "Saint John", but in connection with thoroughly earthly values[53], otherwise building his argument solely on the basis of "reason", "proof", "sense" and, above all, "experience". While bringing Solomon into the *Proem* as one who received *elettione da Iddio* ("election by God"), at the same time he pointed out that the wise king had asked God "simply in order to be able to rule his people well, for his seemed to him the most important and difficult thing".[54] Immediately after this he did not hesitate to remark that even "Moses ... even though he continually conversed with the Lord as if with a member of his own family, and even though he was able to consult him, and was his representative in that task" had nevertheless not been able to "perfectly attain" the wisdom of good government.[55]

Skill in government was, then, extremely difficult to achieve, guaranteed neither by the monarchic system nor by God or religion, but

> in the development of the Venetian constitution, ... great attention was paid from the very beginning to good government ... Several different laws were passed at once, and new ones were constantly

> added thereafter, the old ones being improved on or removed as appropriate. Particular care was devoted to the election of magistrates and to control over electoral procedure; no such system of appointing magistrates has ever been adopted in any other seigniory or republic; and yet no other dominion or republic in the world has ever lasted as long as Venice... So well regulated is the system of electing magistrates that it is impossible for anyone to be appointed through coercion or favouritism, as so often happens elsewhere; no one can be appointed to high office unless he has first gained experience in the lower and middle ranks and has acquitted himself well in both.[56]

Having established stability as a primary, incomparable factor in republican government, Serra goes on in much the same vein to point out that in the Republic the primary object of the governors is to pursue "the public good" and not personal advantages, in accordance with the canonical (and patriotic) image of the myth of Venice. It is a position that has much in common with Campanella[57] and which was to become widespread among the Neapolitan revolutionaries of 1647–1648.[58] Its origins, however, lay in the republican patriotism of the Machiavelli of the *Discourses*, who held that "without doubt this common good is thought important only in republics",[59] whereas the absolutist Bodin[60] would assert that the principle of the common good was peculiar to sovereignty (i.e. royal monarchy) as such.

Continuing with his analysis of the political system of Venice, and going into greater detail than the general features and principles, Serra noted that its exceptionality was also due to the way the political class was chosen: before reaching the peaks the power, every Venetian enjoying political rights was trained in more humble offices, thereby acquiring the experience necessary for government of the state machinery. Moreover, appointments were made through a complicated electoral system that involved both the drawing of lots and election proper, with the result that, on the strength of this procedure and the primacy of the public good, Serra held that there could be no possibility of coming into any office of importance "through coercion or favouritism", evidently in contrast with practice elsewhere, and particularly in his Naples. Here, then, Serra was already pointing out how institutional features were able to provide the necessary foundations, together with the patriotic culture of the common good, for the extraordinary stability and wealth of the time-honoured Republic. Thanks to the institutional system and the political culture on which it was based, it was always the best citizens who entered upon political office. The pivot of that system, "the highest organ of all" he identified in the

> Council of the *Pregai*, wich is comparable to the Senate in ancient Rome. This body has the power to pass and repeal laws, to declare war and to make peace; it comprises about one hundred and fifty members ... No magistrate can hold supreme power even for a short period without the consent of the Council of the *Pregai*.[61]

The Venetian Senate, the Council of "*Pregadi*" (the Council of "*Pregai*", as Serra, like Machiavelli, called it[62]) was thus the secret, the pivot of that amazing system, able to guarantee political stability and wealth for its lucky and virtuous citizens. Significantly, Serra compared it with the senate of Rome, defined it as "the highest organ of all", without the least reference to the doge or the Great Council, nor to the other institutions that shared power in a system of mixed government, with the merest mention of the various other, lower-ranking powers, which he did not name in detail but held to be inferior to what he deemed the "supreme" power of the state: the senate. Very significant is the silence on the figure of the doge, and it is interesting to see what Contarini had to say on the subject, remarking that "there is no one who is unaware that the Prince of the City of Venice shows all the bearing of the king, and a sort of royal government",[63] although he also pointed out that "this power is so constrained by the laws that he can do nothing on his own".[64] Attributing important political significance to the doge, then, inevitably lead to support for the system of mixed government because it meant that the republican model was largely conditioned by the monocratic type, and although this was mainly of symbolic import, there can be no underrating the political weight of symbols at the time when Serra was writing his *Breve trattato*.

In effect, it should not be hard to detect some budding conservatism in these remarks in the *Breve trattato*. And, after all, at the time of Serra, the myth of Venice was decidedly characterized more by a spirit of conservation than of change.[65] Basically, the Republic of Saint Mark remained the model to look to for policies asserting the power of the nobility, which had come to represent the norm throughout the 16th century in the length and breadth of Italy. Access to public office had been limited far and wide, and in particular in Serra's South, to those of noble birth, which naturally brought the cities' aristocracies moving in the direction of oligarchy.[66] The foreign policy of Venice itself was by now geared to conservation of the Republic, not expansion of its dominions. So it was that, at a time when power politics predominated in the sphere of international relations, if there was any idea of reform it would tend to be in the direction of reinforcing national states along the lines of absolutism and *ragion di Stato*, in keeping with the example of the great monarchies such as France. This appeared to be the most promising way of limiting the excessive power of the feudal nobility and fostering the development of the middle class, and this should of course have applied even more to the Kingdom of Naples, an extreme case of feudal monarchy where the problem was to reduce the power of the nobility, and certainly not to enhance it, according it further powers through a parliament to be raised anew from its increasingly wilting condition. But precisely here is the point that needs stressing if we are to appreciate the full measure of novelty represented by the political proposal in the *Breve trattato*.

Proceeding with his treatise, Serra never made any reference to a society founded on status, with only fleeting reference to the nobility (not to mention clergy), any distinction in the population being between "citizens" and "foreigners".[67] The one more explicit reference is to be found in the dedicatory letter where, referring to the reforms of the viceroy, Count of Lemos (dedicatee of the work), he expressed the wish that "the cult of justice [be] reformed, the abundance of life [grow], and the peace [be] preserved, by rooting out those who disturb it, protecting the weak by striking fear in the great",[68] although no social specification of what was meant by the "great" was forthcoming. The keystone of his proposal was to favour free enterprise, free trade, and free finance unless of course they clashed with the public interest, which he patriotically held to be supreme. An aspect one cannot fail to remark is that the "manufacturers" and "merchants", who were to lead the way to resurgence with the support of the enlightened elites never qualified as aristocrats: they were "citizens", so it was they who would become the economic backbone of the middle class. And, in particular, it was they who were to invest in the most remunerative activities like trade and "production of woollens, especially the finer fabrics" and then in "the production of linen, silk, weapons, paintings, sculptures, books and the medical drugs, as well as in an infinity of other things".[69] This is not to say that Serra meant the leaders in the economic and financial activities to go on to become leaders of the political government. And yet it is surely significant that not even when dealing with Venice did he mention that access to government was by succession because it was a rigidly patrician society: to the government of Venice by nobles he dedicated not a single word, unlike the canonical authors of the "myth".

And this helps account for his silence on the Great Council in the *Breve trattato* because this was the constitutional body from which the aristocratic nature of the Republic emerged, issuing forth the other institutions like the senate and reserving access solely to the offspring of patrician families by right of birth, under no constraint in the form of election or drawing of lots, but only with the threshold of a certain age (25 years, with a few exceptions).

In this respect, therefore, it seems reasonable to associate Serra with the Southern Italian movement of reformers discussed by Rosario Villari,[70] represented by historians like Giovanni Antonio Summonte, scientists like Nicola Antonio Stigliola and Ferrante Imperato, jurists or lawyers like Francesco Imperato, and, later, Giulio Genoino, future leader of the Revolution of 1647–1648. In practice, the "reform movement" looked to the reinforcement of the state on the basis of an agreement to be pursued with the monarchy. However, the central object of the battle – the reason for favouring a state with greater powers and decisive initiative on the part of the monarchy – was to sap the power of the feudal nobility in response to the claims of a composite middle class that was, however, already clearly identifiable, with a certain awareness of its role. And here again we find accord with Campanella, who lashed out both at the hereditary and feudal nobility, on the one hand, and at the plebs, on the other,[71] in the hope that between these two poles "the people in the middle, between the plebs and the Senate of nobles, might win out".[72] Their victory was to be based on the principles of meritocracy and the love of "equality" since "the excessively poor are rapacious, insidious and perjurers, the excessively rich overweening and licentious",[73] aiming at equality between nobles and the people, in accordance with principles much like those of the reform movement, upon which the Neapolitan revolution would germinate. As we have seen, however, the reformers had a penchant for monarchy, and Campanella himself wavered between preference for elective monarchy and republic, although he too would have liked to see the institution of a senate endowed with extensive powers. In this respect, then, Serra turned out to be even more radical, and in the light of the position that he took, we can better understand why republican ferment was soon to develop in Naples, too, in the circles of the *Accademia degli Oziosi* (the Idlers' Academy) with writers like historian and jurist Francesco de' Pietri, who, like Serra and Campanella, celebrated the role of the middle class and the senate. Mobilizing arguments much like those set out in the *De antiquitatae Reipublicae Batavicae* by Grotius,[74] he also elaborated the myth of the truly ancient (extremely long-lived) republican constitution of Naples, of the free "Neapolitan Republic",[75] a thesis which had already found voice in de' Pietri's master, the historian and reformer Giovanni Antonio Summonte,[76] and then found new life in the Neapolitan revolution, in works like *Partenope liberata* by the chemist and pharmacologist Giuseppe Donzelli[77] or the anonymous *Il Cittadino Fedele*[78] as also in the demands of the radical leaders of the Republic such as Vincenzo D'Andrea.[79]

Of course, now we are no longer surprised by the fact that such myths invoked ancient traditions and apparently conservative ideals (although not going as far as what might be taken to be desire for "restoration") instead of change. Actually, however, as has been pointed out by leading scholars of the 17th century like John H. Elliott, Christopher Hill and Rosario Villari[80], the idea of progress as it was to grow and spread as from the 18th century was unknown to the Baroque age, and the most useful approach in proposing changes and reforms was to hark back to how things had stood before the situation to be changed had set in.[81] Frequently, moreover, this process involved inventing a past which had never existed, or at any rate bending the historical facts to the present needs. Bearing these points in mind, in fact, we can read Serra's apparent political conservatism in a different light in that it was nothing like conservatism in present-day terms. Elliott, Hill, and Villari themselves have made it clear that beneath the veil cast by invoking the past could emerge truly innovative and reforming contents.[82] And indeed, considering the specific case of Antonio Serra, in terms not only economic-financial but also political-institutional, the objectives set out in the *Breve trattato* certainly did not rest on ideals of conservation. Suffice it to recall the virtually unfathomable abyss between the institutions of a collective and independent state like the Republic of Venice and the institutions of a feudal monarchy under the control of Spain like the Kingdom of Naples[83], to make no more specific mention of the concrete role attributed in the two systems to the parliamentary institute so keenly pursued by Serra, Campanella, and other reformers.[84] What, in fact, was at stake were proposals for reform that, if fully implemented, would have undermined the Spanish viceroyalty, as was later to be seen with their partial implementation in the course of the Neapolitan revolution, when an independent republic was proclaimed and the idea was to concentrate the sovereignty of the state in a senate.[85]

In short, in the light of all the evidence examined here, we may justifiably recognise a place for Antonio Serra alongside the most advanced exponents of the European political culture of his time – figures such as Tommaso Campanella, Johannes Althusius, Hugo Grotius, and, more generally speaking, all those who came out against systems that reflect the liberticidal principles of statolatry, protagonists of that "opposition culture" that – by giving due circulation in writing and in speech to dissent (overt or under less evident guise) against absolutism, *ragion di Stato*, the myths of regality, and the political theologies of the Counter-Reformation – would lead to what has been tellingly defined as the "revolutionary conscience of Europe".[86] Like Campanella, Serra envisaged a desperate attempt to bring about a "truly great reform". And both were doomed to failure, to rot in a prison cell. But the stony silence with which the monarchy would continue to respond to projects for reform (like the project aired by Giulio Genoino, also destined to have a taste of prison) was a decisive factor in bringing on a far more dramatic turn of events, with nothing short of revolution – rapidly taking a separatist, republican bent – showing various significant points in common with the most radical ideas of reform cherished by Campanella, and indeed by Serra himself.[87]

Notes

1. Addante, L., "Repubblicanesimo e mito di Venezia nel *Breve trattato* di Antonio Serra", *Clio*, XXXVII, 1, 2001, pp. 117–154.
2. On dissimulation in Serra see Addante, 2001. More in general see Villari, R., *Elogio della dissimulazione. La lotta politica nel Seicento*, Rome-Bari: Laterza, 1987; Cavaillé, J.-P., *Dis/simulation. Jules-César Vanini, François La Mothe Le Vayer, Gabriel Naudé, Louis Machon et Torquato Accetto. Religion, morale et politique au XVIIe siècle*, Paris: Honoré Champion, 2002.
3. Serra, A., *A Short Treatise on the Wealth and Poverty of Nations* (1613), translated by J. Hunt, edited and with an introduction by S.A. Reinert, London: Anthem, 2011, p. 105.
4. Serra, 1613, pp. 117, 133–135 and *passim*.
5. Serra, 1613, p. 115.
6. "Since my intent is to write a thing that is useful for whoever understands it, it seemed to me more appropriate to go after the effectual truth of the thing than the imagination of it" (Machiavelli, N., 1532, p. 87), *Il Principe*, English trans. W.J. Connell, Boston, MA-New York, NY: Bedford-St. Martin's, 2005.
7. Serra, 1613, pp. 143 and *passim*.
8. Serra, 1613, pp. 159, 193.
9. Serra, 1613, p. 175.
10. Serra, 1613, pp. 169, 171.
11. Addante, L., *Eretici e libertini nel Cinquecento italiano*, Rome-Bari: Laterza, 2010.
12. Serra, 1613, pp. 101, 111. Actually, however, it is worth noting that the connection that Serra makes between wonder and ignorance, and indeed the importance he ascribes to wonder as a stimulus to scientific investigation, had already found a place in Aristotle (*Metaphysics*, I, 2, 982b).

13. Serra, 1613, pp. 119 and *passim*. The expression used by Serra ("la provisione di quel che governa") would appear to refer only to policies. Actually, as we will see later on, Serra took the quality of policy decisions and the institutional organization of the state to be inextricably interwoven.
14. Serra, 1613, pp. 137–139.
15. Serra 1613, pp. 129–131, 139. See also p. 239, where he notes that "all [...] inevitably depends on the last common accident, which must stimulate, organize and conserve the other accidents."
16. See, for example, Serra, 1613, part III, ch. 2 (209ff.), where he considers the efficacy of *the remedy of prohibiting the exportation of money*.
17. Serra, 1613, p. 199.
18. *Ibid.*
19. That Serra held a degree in Law we learn from the frontispiece of the *Breve trattato*, where he qualifies himself as "doctor": as we know, at the time in Southern Italy the term was generally applied to graduates in juridical disciplines.
20. Serra, 1613, p. 201.
21. In the edition of *Breve trattato* that I used, J. Hunt translates the word "discuterla" as "reasoning". I prefer "discussion" (Serra, 1613, p. 159).
22. But see Villari, 1987.
23. On Valdés and valdesianism, see Firpo, M., *Juan de Valdés and the Italian Reformation*, Farnham: Ashgate, 2015. On the radical upshots of the Valdesian movement, see also Addante 2010; Addante, L., *Valentino Gentile e il dissenso religioso nel Cinquecento. Dalla Riforma italiana al radicalismo europeo*, Pisa: Edizioni della Normale, 2014.
24. Addante, 2014.
25. Serra, 1613, p. 111. Anti-tyrannical, libertarian demands continued to circulate in Baroque Europe despite the absolutist, counter-reformation clampdown, particularly through the "monarcomachs" and the culture of the Netherlands. Elsewhere, too, however, similar phenomena were to be seen, as in England and indeed in Italy, with a significant contribution by the radical heretics and libertines, and the more radical theoreticians of natural rights, as well as republican culture in general. Besides the texts cited below on the myth of Venice and 17th-century republicanism, see Skinner, Q., *The Foundation of Modern Political Thought*, 2 vols, Cambridge: Cambridge University Press, 1978; Tuck, R., *Natural rights theories. Their origin and development*, Cambridge-London-New York, NY-Sydney: Cambridge University Press, 1981; Tuck, R., *Philosophy and government 1572–1651*, Cambridge: Cambridge University Press, 1993; Villari, R., *Ribelli e riformatori dal XVI al XVIII secolo*, Rome: Editori Riuniti, 1983[2]; Villari, 1987; Villari, R., *Politica barocca. Inquietudini, mutamento e prudenza*, Rome-Bari: Laterza, 2010; Villari, R., *Un sogno di libertà. Napoli nel declino di un impero 1585–1647*, Milan: Mondadori, 2012; D'Addio, M., "Il tirannicidio", *Storia delle idee politiche economiche e sociali*, Firpo, L. (ed.), vol. 3, Turin: UTET, 1987, pp. 511–609; Bobbio, N., "Il giusnaturalismo moderno", *Il pensiero politico. Idee teorie dottrine*, vol. 2, Andreatta, A. and A.E. Baldini (eds), Turin: UTET, 1999; Benigno, F., *Specchi della rivoluzione. Conflitto e identità nell'Europa moderna*, Rome: Donzelli, 1999; Turchetti, M., *Tyrannie et tyrannicide de l'Antiquité à nos jours*, Paris: Puf, 2001; Zancarini, J.-C. (ed.), *Le Droit de résistance, XIIe-XXe sèicle*, Paris: Ens,

2001; Testoni Binetti, S., *Il pensiero politico ugunotto. Dallo studio della storia all'idea di contratto (1572–1579)*, Florence: Cet, 2002; Cavaillé 2002; Mellet, P.-A. (ed.), *"Et de sa bouche sortait un glaive". Les Monarchomaques au XVI siècle*, Geneva: Droz, 2006; Mellet, P.-A., *Les Traités monarchomaques: confusion des temps, résistance armée et monarchie parfaite (1560–1600)*, Geneva: Droz, 2007. As for the Italian states, it is of course worth recalling the figure of Campanella, who was in the times of Serra a fierce opponent of every form of tyranny. It suffices to recall the celebrated lines: "Io nacqui a debellar tre mali estremi: / tirannide, sofismi, ipocrisia" ("I was born to conquer three great evils: tyranny, sophism, hypocrisy) ("Delle radici de' gran mali del mondo", Campanella, T., *Le poesie*, Giancotti, F. (ed.), Turin: Einaudi, 1998, p. 49).

26. On the circulation of the myth of Venice between the 16th and 17th centuries, see Fink, Z.S., "Venice and English political thought in the seventeenth century", *Modern Philology*, XXXVIII, 1940, pp. 155–172; Fink, Z.S., *The Classical Republicans. An Essay in the Recovery of a Pattern of Thought in Seventeenth-Century England*, Evanston, IL: Northwestern University Press, 1962[2]; Chabod, F., *Scritti sul Rinascimento*, Turin: Einaudi, 1967; Gaeta, F., "Alcune considerazioni sul mito di Venezia", *Bibliothèque d'Humanisme et Renaissance*, XXIII, 1961, pp. 58–75; Lane, F.C., "At the Roots of Republicanism", *Venice and History. The collected papers of Frederic C. Lane*, Foreword by F. Braudel, Baltimore, MD: John Hopkins University Press, 1966, pp. 520–539; Matteucci, N., "Machiavelli, Harrington, Montesquieu e gli Ordini di Venezia", *Il Pensiero politico*, III, 3, 1970, pp. 337–369; Bouwsma, W.J., *Venice and the Defense of Republican Liberty. Renaissance Values in the Age of the Counter-Reformation*, Berkeley, CA-Los Angeles, CA: California University Press, 1968; Bouwsma, W.J., "Venice and the Political Education of Europe", in Hale, J.R. (ed.), *Renaissance Venice*, London: Faber and Faber, 1973, pp. 445–466; Gilbert F., "The Venetian Constitution in Florentine Political Thought", *Florentine Studies. Politics and Society in Renaissance Florence*, Rubinstein, N. (ed.), London: Faber and Faber, 1968, pp. 463–500; Pocock, G.A., *The Machiavellian Moment. Florentine Political Thought and the Atlantic Republican Tradition*, Princeton, NJ: Princeton University Press, 1975; Skinner 1978; Haitsma Mulier, E.O.G., *The Myth of Venice and Dutch republican thought in the seventeenth century*, Assen: Van Gorcum, 1980; Muir, E., *Civic Ritual in Renaissance Venice*, Princeton, NJ : Princeton University Press, 1981; Pecchioli, R., *Dal "mito" di Venezia all'"ideologia americana". Itinerari e modelli della storiografia sul repubblicanesimo dell'età moderna*, Venice: Marsilio, 1983; Fasano Guarini, E., La crisi del modello repubblicano: patriziati e oligarchie, Firpo, M. and N. Tranfaglia (eds), *La Storia*, vol. 3, Turin: UTET, 1986, pp. 553–584; Silvano, G., "Repubblicanesimo e repubblicanesimi all'inizio dell'età moderna. La rivolta delle Province Unite e il De Republica Emendanda di Ugo Grozio", *Il pensiero politico*, XX, 3, 1987, pp. 395–404; *Storia di Venezia, Dalle origini alla caduta della Serenissima*, vol. IV, *Il Rinascimento. Politica e cultura*, Tenenti, A. and U. Tucci, (eds), Rome: Istituto della Enciclopedia italiana, 1996; Conti, V., *Consociatio civitatum. Le repubbliche nei testi elzeviriani (1625–1649)*, Florence: Cet, 1997; Martin, J. and D. Romano (eds), *Venice Reconsidered. The History and Civilization of an Italian City-State 1297–1797*, Baltimore, MD-London: Johns Hopkins University Press, 2000; Crouzet-Pavan, É., *Venice Triumphant. The Horizons of a Myth*, Baltimore, MD-London, Johns Hopkins University Press,

2002; Hill, C., *Intellectual Origins of the English Revolution Revisited*, Oxford: Clarendon Press, 2001; Schreiner, P. (ed.), *Il mito di Venezia. Una città fra realtà e rappresentazione*, Rome: Edizioni di storia e letteratura, 2006; Fenlon, I., *The Ceremonial City. History, memory and myth in Renaissance Venice*, New Haven, CT-London: Yale University Press, 2007.
27. On the mixed government, see De Mattei, R., *Il pensiero politico italiano nell'età della Controriforma*, 2 vols, Milan-Naples: Ricciardi, 1982; Pocock, 1975.
28. Contarini's text was written between the 20s and 30s of the 16th century: Gilbert, F., "The Date of the composition of Contarini's and Giannotti's books on Venice", *Studies in the Renaissance*, XIV, 1967, pp. 172–184; Gilbert, F., "Religion and Politics in the Thought of Gasparo Contarini", in Rabb, T.K. and J.E. Seigel (eds), *Action and Convinction in Early Modern Europe. Essays in memory of E.H. Harbison*, Princeton, NJ: Princeton University Press, 1969, pp. 90–116; Bouwsma 1968; Fragnito, G., *Gasparo Contarini. Un magistrato veneziano al servizio della cristianità*, Florence: Olschki, 1988; Cavazzana Romanelli, F. (ed.) *Gaspare Contarini e il suo tempo*, Venice: Stamperia di Venezia, 1988; Silvano, G., *La "Republica de' Viniziani". Ricerche sul repubblicanesimo veneziano in età moderna*, Florence: Olschki, 1993; Gleason, E., *Gasparo Contarini. Venice, Rome and Reform*, Los Angeles, CA-Berkeley, CA-London: University of California Press, 1993.
29. Giannotti, D., *Libro de la Republica de Vinitiani*, Rome: Per Antonio Blado, 1540. Giannotti's book came out in Rome in 1540 but it had been written mainly between 1525 and 1527: Gilbert, 1967; Pocock, 1975; Cadoni, G., *L'utopia repubblicana di Donato Giannotti*, Milano: Giuffrè, 1978; Silvano, 1993.
30. Gilbert, 1968. On the medieval roots of the myth, see also Fasoli, G., "Nascita di un mito", *Studi storici in onore di Gioacchino Volpe*, 2 vols, Florence, Sansoni, 1958, I, pp. 445–479; Gaeta, F., "Storiografia, coscienza nazionale e politica culturale nella Venezia del rinascimento", *Storia della cultura veneta*, vol. III, t. 1, Arnaldi, G. and M. Pastore Stocchi (eds), Vicenza: Neri Pozza, 1980, pp. 1–91; Gaeta, F., "L'idea di Venezia", *Storia della cultura veneta*, vol. III, t. 3, Arnaldi, G. and M. Pastore Stocchi (eds), Vicenza: Neri Pozza, 1981, pp. 565–641.
31. Bobbio, N., *La teoria delle forme di governo nella storia del pensiero politico*, Turin: Giappichelli, 1976.
32. Here, as in the other quotations, the italics are mine.
33. Serra, 1613, p. 143.
34. *Ibid.*
35. Serra, 1613, p. 109.
36. Machiavelli, 1532, p. 41.
37. On theory of forms of government, see Bobbio 1976; Bobbio, N., *Stato, governo, società. Frammenti di un dizionario politico*, Turin: Einaudi, 1985; Matteucci, N., "Governo, forme di", *Enciclopedia delle scienze sociali*, vol. IV, Rome: Istituto della enciclopedia italiana, 1994. It is in any case worth recalling that Savonarola had long before differentiated forms of government between monarchies and republics, to begin with, only to return to Aristotle's classification later on (Gilbert, 1968). On the use of the term "republic" in modern-age political vocabulary, see also Isnardi Parente, M., "Appunti per

la storia di État, Républicque, Stato", *Rivista Storica Italiana*, LXXIV, 2, 1962, pp. 372–379.

38. Venturi, F., *Utopia and Reform in the Enlightenment*, Cambridge: Cambridge University Press, 1971, p. 22. On republicanism in the 17th century, see also Durand, Y., *Les républicques au temps des monarchies*, Paris: Puf, 1973; Schöffer, I., "The Batavian Myth during the sixteenth and seventeenth Centuries", *Britain and the Netherlands*, vol. V, Bromley, J.S. and E.H. Kossmann (eds), The Hague, M. Nijhoff, 1975, pp. 78–101; Skinner, Q., *Liberty before Liberalism*, Cambridge: Cambridge University Press, 1998; Nuzzo, E., *La superiorità degli Stati liberi. I repubblicani inglesi*, Naples: Esi, 1984; Mastellone, S., "I repubblicani del Seicento ed il modello politico olandese", *Il pensiero politico*, XVIII, 2, 1985, pp. 145–163; Silvano, 1987; Haitsma Mulier, E.O.G., "The language of seventeenth-century republicanism in the United Provinces: Dutch or European?", in *The Languages of political theory in early-modern Europe*, Pagden, A. (ed.), Cambridge: Cambridge University Press, 1987, pp. 179–195; Koenigsberger, H.G. (ed.), *Republiken und Republikanismus im Europa der Frühen Neuzeit*, Munich: Oldenbourg, 1988; Scott, J., *Algernon Sidney and the English Republic, 1623–1677*, Cambridge: Cambridge University Press, 1988; Scott, J., *Commonwealth Principles. Republican Writings of the English Revolution*, Cambridge: Cambridge University Press, 2004; Secretan, C., *Les privilèges berceau de la liberté. La Révolte des Pays-Bas: aux sources de la pensée politique moderne (1566–1619)*, Paris: Vrin, 1990; Bock, G., Q. Skinner and M. Viroli (eds), *Machiavelli and Republicanism*, Cambridge: Cambridge University Press, 1990; Appleby, J., *Liberalism and Republicanism in the Historical Imagination*, Cambridge, MA: Harvard University Press, 1992; van Gelderen, M., *The Political Thought of the Dutch Revolt 1555–1590*, Cambridge: Cambridge University Press, 1992; Wootton, D. (ed.), *Republicanism, Liberty and Commercial Society, 1649–1776*, Stanford, CA: Stanford University Press, 1994; Peltonen, M., *Classical humanism and republicanism in English political thought 1570–1640*, Cambridge: Cambridge University Press, 1995; Procacci, G., *Machiavelli nella cultura europea dell'età moderna*, Rome-Bari: Laterza, 1995; Armitage, D., A. Himy, and Q. Skinner (eds), *Milton and Republicanism*, Cambridge: Cambridge University Press, 1995; Adamo, P., "Immaginario puritano e repubblica: la Rivoluzione inglese", *Etica e religione nella tradizione repubblicana. Aspetti storici e teorici*, Turin: Fondazione Agnelli, 1996, pp. 41–71; Norbrook, D., *Writing the English Republic: Poetry, Rhetoric and Politics, 1627–1669*, Cambridge: Cambridge University Press, 1999; Glover, S.D., "The Putney Debates: Popular versus Élitist Republicanism", *Past and Present*, no. 164, 1999, pp. 47–80; De Michelis Pintacuda, F. and F. Francioni (eds), (2002), *Ideali repubblicani in età moderna*, Pisa: Ets, 2002; de'Pietri, F., *Dell'Historia napoletana…*, Naples: Nella Stampa di Gio. Domenico Montanaro, 1634; Skinner, Q. and M. van Gelderen (eds), *Republicanism: a Shared European Heritage*, 2 vols, Cambridge: Cambridge University Press, 2002; Nelson, E., *The Greek Tradition in Republican Thought*, Cambridge: Cambridge University Press, 2004; Fasano Guarini, E., R. Sabbatini and M. Natalizi (eds), *Repubblicanesimo e repubbliche nell'Europa di antico regime*, Milan: Angeli, 2007; Rahe, P.A., *Against Throne and Altar. Machiavelli and Political Theory under the English Republic*, Cambridge: Cambridge University Press, 2008.

39. Gilbert, F., *Machiavelli e il suo tempo*, Bologna: Il Mulino, 1977, pp. 319–334; Cervelli, I., *Machiavelli e la crisi dello Stato veneziano*, Naples: Guida, 1974; Sasso, G., *Machiavelli e gli antichi e altri saggi,* vol. I, Milan-Naples: Ricciardi, 1986, pp: 499–530.
40. Gilbert, F., *Machiavelli and Guicciardini. Politics and History in Sixteenth-Century Florence*, Princeton, NJ: Princeton University Press, 1965; Gilbert, 1968.
41. Montaigne, M. Eyquem de, *Journal de voyage en Italie par la Suisse et l'Allemagne*, P. Faure (ed.), Paris: Bordas, 1948, p. 81.
42. For the English texts, see notes 25, 26 and 38.
43. Chabod, 1967, pp. 682–683. It is worth recalling that Bodin praised the religious tolerance prevailing in Venice in the *Colloquium heptaplomeres*. See also Gianturco, E., "Bodin's Conception of the Venetian Constitution and his Critical Rift with Fabio Albergati", *Revue de littérature comparée*, XVIII, 1938, pp. 684–695.
44. Serra, 1613, p. 141.
45. Villari, 2010.
46. Bodin, J. *Les six livres de la Républicque*, Lyon: Du Puys, 1580, pp. 688 and *passim*.
47. Serra, 1613, p. 129.
48. See Campanella, T., *Aforismi politici. Con sommari e postille inedite integrati dalla rielaborazione latina del* De Politica *e dal commento di Ugo Grozio*, Firpo, L. (ed.), Turin: Giappichelli, 1941, p. 99; see also pp. 125, 130–131 and *passim*. The *Aforismi politici* (or *De Politica*), the first version of which dated back roughly to 1601, subsequently to be re-elaborated at various times up to the editions in Latin of 1623 and 1637, were seen by Campanella himself as being his most important work of political theory, maintaining that with it he had founded political science: "Scripsi praeterea *Aphorismos politicos*, quos deinde in capitula distinxi, et politicam scientiam condidi" (Campanella, T., *De libris propriis et recta ratione studendi syntagma*, (ed.), Brissoni, A., Soveria Mannelli: Rubbettino, 1996, p. 43). It is, moreover, worth recalling that the far more famous *Città del sole* was published by Campanella himself as appendix to *De Politica*.
49. Campanella, 1941, pp. 97, 122.
50. On these Campanella's political ideas see Addante, L., *Patriottismo e libertà. L'*Elogio di Antonio Serra *di Francesco Salfi*, Cosenza: Pellegrini, 2009, p 78ff.
51. Campanella, T., *Discorsi ai principi d'Italia*, Firpo, L. (ed.), Turin: Chiantore, 1945; Campanella, T., *La monarchia del messia*, Frajese, V. (ed.), Rome: Edizioni di storia e letteratura, 1995.
52. Silvano, 1993, p. 126.
53. Thomas Aquinas was mentioned with regard to the pre-eminence among the virtues of justice: "Justice, according to Aquinas, contains the other virtues within itself". As for Saint John, Serra refers to a moral consideration: "Let him who is in filth remain in it" (Serra, 1613, pp. 131, 179).
54. Serra, 1613, p. 113.
55. In the index of topics of the original version, the point is indicated thus: "Moses did not attain perfect skill in governing the Jewish people".
56. Serra, 1613, pp. 141–143.
57. Addante, 2009, pp. 82–83.

58. Villari, R., *Per il re o per la patria. La fedeltà nel Seicento*, Rome-Bari: Laterza, 1994; Villari, 2012.
59. Machiavelli, 1531, p. 329.
60. Bodin, 1580, p. 654.
61. Serra, 1613, p. 143.
62. Machiavelli, N. (1531, p. 297), *Discorsi sopra la prima deca di Tito Livio*, English trans. A. Gilbert, 2 vols, vol. I, Durham, NC and London: Duke University Press, 1999. Note that for Machiavelli, too, the senate was the "greatest council" of the Venetian Republic: *ibid.*
63. Contarini, G., *De magistratibus et republica Venetorum*, Paris: Ex officina Michaëlis Vascosani, 1543, p. 52. See also pp. 58 ff.
64. Contarini, 1543, pp. 57 and *passim.*
65. Berengo, M., *L'Europa delle città. Il volto della società urbana europea tra Medioevo ed Età moderna*, Turin: Einaudi, 1999.
66. Visceglia, M.A. (ed.), *Signori, patrizi, cavalieri in Italia centro-meridionale nell'Età moderna*, Rome-Bari: Laterza, 1992; Berengo, 1999.
67. Serra 1613, pp. 163, 177.
68. Otherwise, Serra (1613, pp 105, 147) made reference to the nobles and clergy observing the fact that "clothes are imported", and the categories that tended most to purchase clothes of "fine fabrics" were the "nobles, merchants and wealthy citizens", to which were added "priests, friars and monks".
69. Serra, 1613, pp. 121 and *passim.*
70. Villari, 2010; Villari, 2012.
71. See the previous observations on hereditary qualification for office. But see also the sonnets "Della nobiltà e suo' segni veri e falsi" ("On nobility and its true and false signs"); and "Della plebe" ("On the Plebs"): Campanella, 1998, pp. 182, 185.
72. Campanella, 1941, p. 136.
73. Campanella, 1941, pp. 136, 138.
74. Grotius, H. (1610), *The antiquity of the Batavian Republic. With the notes by Petrus Scriverius*, Waszink, J. et al. (eds), Assen: Van Gorcum, 2000.
75. De'Pietri, 1634, pp. 33–50; de' Pietri, F., I problemi accademici..., Naples: Francesco Savio, ad istanza di Giovan Dominico Montanaro, 1642; *Proem.*
76. Summonte, G.A., *Historia della Città e Regno di Napoli...*, Naples: Appresso Gio. Iacomo Carlino, 1602, pp. 108ff. and *passim.*
77. Donzelli, G., *Partenope liberata...*, Naples: Ottavio Beltrano, 1647, pp. 205–206.
78. *Il cittadino fedele (1647). Discorso breve della giusta, generosa, e prudente risolution del valoroso, e fedelissimo Popolo di Napoli per liberarsi dall'insoportabili gravezze impostegli da Spagnuoli*, ed. Villari, 1994, pp. 39–57, especially pp. 53–54.
79. See Comparato, V.I., "Società civile e società letteraria nel primo Seicento: l'Accademia degli Oziosi", *Quaderni storici*, 2, 1973, pp. 359–388; Comparato, V.I., *Uffici e società a Napoli (1600–1647). Aspetti dell'ideologia del magistrato nell'età moderna*, Florence: Olschki, 1974; Villari 1983^2, 1994, 2010, 2012; Messina, P., "Giuseppe Donzelli e la rivoluzione napoletana del 1647–1648", *Studi storici*, XXVIII, 1, 1987, pp. 183–202; Musi, A., *L'Italia dei vicerè. Integrazione e resistenza nel sistema imperiale spagnolo*, Cava de'Tirreni: Avagliano, 2000; Rovito, P.L., *Il viceregno spagnolo di Napoli*, Naples: Arte tipografica, 2003.

80. Elliott, J.H., "Revolution and Continuity in Early Modern Europe", *Past and Present*, 42, 1969, pp. 35–56; Villari, 1983², 2010; Hill, 2001². See also Kamen, H., *The Iron Century. Social Change in Counter-Reformation Europe. 1550–1660*, London: Weidenfeld and Nicolson, 1971.
81. Villari, 1987, p. 56.
82. Villari, 1983², p. 35. Villari also points out that "the compatibility between invocation of the past and modernizing aims was made clear by Machiavelli in chapter XXV of the first book of the *Discourses*" (*Ibid.*, p. 50).
83. I made a broad comparison between the two systems of government in Addante, 2001.
84. For extensive treatment of the Venetian Senate and its powers, the essential reading remains: Besta, E., *Il senato veneziano (Origine, costituzione, attribuzioni e riti)*, Venice: Visentini, 1899; and Maranini, G., *La Costituzione di Venezia*, vol. 2, *Dopo la serrata del Maggior Consiglio*, Florence: La Nuova Italia, 1974. On the parliament in the Kingdom of Naples, see D'Agostino, G., *Parlamento e società nel Regno di Napoli. Secoli XV–XVII*, Naples: Guida, 1979; Villari, 2012.
85. Villari, 1983, 2012; Conti, 1983; Rovito. 2003.
86. Villari, 2010.
87. Villari, 2012.

8

External Imbalances and the Money Supply: Two Controversies in the English "Realme" and in the Kingdom of Naples

Lilia Costabile

1 Introduction

Many scholars have noted the similarity between the controversy entered upon by Gerard Malynes, Edward Misselden, and Thomas Mun in England in the early 1620s and the debate that only few years earlier had flared up between two economists active in the Kingdom of Naples: Marc'Antonio de Santis and Antonio Serra, to whom, as I will argue in this paper, we should add Giovanni Donato Turbolo.[1] However, still lacking in the literature is a systematic comparative study of the arguments that these writers developed on the common subject of their disputes, namely the causes of, as well as the remedies for, the massive specie outflows then plaguing their countries. This paper contributes to fill this gap, in the belief that such comparison may be rewarding for the following reasons.

First, the similarity between the two debates sheds interesting light on how economists conceptualized in similar terms certain empirical regularities characterizing their respective economic systems. These regularities occurred in spite of the two countries' different positions and trajectories in the international hierarchy of power. At the beginning of the 17th century England was emerging "as a unified and self-conscious state... entering the full flood of a period of aggressive and irritable nationalism".[2] The English ruling classes considered economic dominance over rivals as a basic precondition for national welfare, and they were accordingly moving towards imperial expansion via both military and economic warfare. The commercial downturn in the 1620s could not stop the country's ascending march towards triumphant capitalism. By contrast, the Kingdom of Naples, then part of the Hispanic Monarchy, had long since lost its independence and was now a subordinate province within a declining empire. Yet, in spite of their opposite economic trajectories, the Kingdom of Naples and the English "Realme" suffered from the same problem, namely a drain on their metallic coin and, consequently, severe liquidity constraints biting on economic activity. This hit particularly hard because the money supply in those times was mainly metallic. Thus, one good reason to take an interest in these old debates lies in the picture that they reveal of converging theoretical efforts to understand the causes of liquidity constraints under the national and international arrangements of the time.

Second, these economists correctly linked the money supply with the balance of payments. To illustrate this link, they developed a useful accounting framework and interesting theoretical and applied studies of open monetary economies. Underlying their analytical interest was a political concern. As much as their situations differed, both the English and the Neapolitan writers viewed the balance of payments and the related money flows as reflecting power in economic relations, the former being interested in securing England's economic power in the international arena,[3] the latter in promoting development by escaping dependence, or at least by slackening its hold on the Kingdom's economy. Both groups of writers required an analytical framework for their basic concepts, and it is here that we see a theoretical convergence between the ascending "Realme" and the declining Kingdom, as a common set of analytical tools and diagnoses emerged "above national context".[4] Thus, comparing these early models of the balance of payments helps clarify the polycentric origins of economic thought in the pre-Smithian period.

The idea of a conceptual convergence is buttressed by the transnational network of virtual theoretical alliances emerging from this literature. The similarities strikingly cut across nationalities: to explain the international money flows, de Santis and Malynes[5] described in similar terms the complex technology of international exchanges operating in Europe and its distorting effects on exchange rates, terms of trade, cash flows, and the money stock. By contrast, Serra, Mun, and Misselden underlined the competitiveness, or lack thereof, of the "real" economy. Thus, de Santis and Malynes would have been on the same side in a hypothetical supranational controversy, with the other three sharing the opposite position and the wise Turbolo, with his interest in both real and monetary determinants of external imbalances, occupying the middle ground between them.

In spite of these dividing lines, all the disputants accepted a basic accounting framework, which the present essay illustrates in Section 2. Their heated controversies concerned the way in which the monetary and real side of the economy should be integrated in a comprehensive conceptual architecture and how the macroeconomic variables were related to financial markets and the structure of production. These controversies are illustrated in the next two sections. More specifically, Section 3 investigates the links that connect the balance of payments to the operation of financial markets in the works of de Santis and Malynes, while Section 4 illustrates the links between external equilibrium, competitiveness, and the sectoral composition of output described by Misselden, Mun, and Serra.[6] This section also includes a summary of Turbolo's original position. Section 5 concludes by relating the results of our investigation to some current interpretations of mercantilism.

2 Open monetary economies: the accounting framework

The protagonists of our story wanted to help remedy the "great scarcity of cash" that affected their economies, a real problem that was well documented by both contemporary documents and historical studies.[7] Consequently, they became interested in the macroeconomics of open monetary economies and, more specifically, in the links between the balance of payments and the money supply.

The money supply is linked to the balance of payments because any external imbalance must be settled in money – a task performed through specie flows under the monetary arrangements of their time and through movements in international reserves under our modern international monetary system. In modern parlance, money flows out of the country whenever the balance of payments (i.e. the sum of the current account balance, plus the capital account balance, plus the non-reserve component of the financial account balance) is less than zero.

It was precisely the experience of monetary drains that led these economists to develop their analyses of the balance of payments and the related accounting framework, which they correctly framed in terms of the specie flows between the national economy and the rest of the world. In their accounting systems, both the English and the Neapolitan writers presented listings of the relevant items. However, while the former put their emphasis on imports and exports of merchandise and services, the Neapolitans went further, including a wider range of items in the current account, such as factor income receipts (profits and rents) and net unilateral transfers; moreover, they investigated international capital movements in what we now call the financial account more thoroughly than their English counterparts.

Serra and de Santis had reason to and did in fact disagree on the numerical value of the merchandise account, which was in substantial surplus according to de Santis but was balanced, or showed at most a small surplus, in Serra's opinion.[8] However, they both recognized the other items in the current account and agreed on their negative sign.

First, huge amounts of money left the country as "unilateral transfers" in the form of taxes and "donations" to the Spanish monarchy and, to a lesser extent, as remittances to Rome. Second, the "factor income receipt" item was negative as a consequence of the "income from investments and profit from businesses that foreigners receive in the Kingdom".[9] In 1619, Turbolo estimated the amount of rents paid to foreigners at two million *ducati* per year.[10] The foreign *rentiers* were mostly Genoese businessmen, the traditional bankers of the Hispanic monarchy, which rewarded them for their services with unique opportunities for profits in many commercial and financial activities, both in the private sector and in the public sector.[11] In the public sector, these Genoese operators mostly profited from the mortgaging of future public revenues.[12] This made for the "vicious circle of indebtedness", which burdened both the central Neapolitan government and the municipalities.[13] Serra denounced the crushing weight of this immense debt, which multiplied "by the hour".[14]

As for the financial account, the Neapolitan economists included foreign investments in their accounting framework. Serra correctly considered them as an item with a positive sign, though he deemed them able to offset only a minimum portion of the deficit items in the current account.[15] In this connection, he went beyond mere accounting to theoretical propositions, explaining these capital inflows as a function of the positive interest-rate differential between domestic and foreign interest rates.[16] De Santis, who also took foreign investments into account, was pessimistic about their effects, stressing the other side of the coin, namely the profit and rent payments owed by the country to foreign investors, who "suck the blood of all the private citizens in the Kingdom". Moreover, he denounced the negative consequences of sudden stops and reversals when direct investment opportunities were exhausted,[17] or when financial speculation took them away from the country. In this connection, he investigated short term speculative capital flows. This phenomenon, it must be added, was also considered by Malynes. We will go back to this point in Section 3.

Having offered a fairly complete listing of the relevant items,[18] the Neapolitans correctly concluded that specie outflows had to make up not only for the current account but also for the total external deficit. By contrast, the English writers blamed specie outflows mostly on the trade account imbalance. As Mun said, "we lose those monies only which are made of the over-balance of our general trade, that is to say, that which we spend more in value of forraign wares, than we utter of our own commodities".[19] True, he added some minor remittances to Rome by local priests and Jesuits, as well as gifts to ambassadors and other foreigners to the current account balance,[20] thus showing some awareness of the "unilateral transfer payment" item. But, all in all, the English economists were lucky enough to have very limited experience with taxes and rents to be paid abroad. As for capital flows, they referred to neither inward nor outward foreign investment. They may have disregarded them on account of the fact that foreign investments at the time were "meagre",[21] and did not affect sovereign powers, while, as we have seen, they had strong impact on the unlucky Neapolitan province of the Spanish empire.

Thus, there is an interesting difference between the two groups of economists, reflecting the historical circumstances of their respective homelands: the Neapolitan Kingdom was a dependent economy, and for this reason it was open to foreign investment, both directly and financially, both in the private sector and in the public sector; consequently, it was burdened with taxes and rents to be paid abroad. By contrast, the English writers lived in an independent economy connected to the rest of the world almost exclusively through trade and war. The Neapolitan economists paid a high cost – fraught with long-lasting consequences for Southern Italy's future history – for their superior understanding of the complexities of the balance of payments.

These differences notwithstanding, the Neapolitan and the English economists had the same accounting framework in mind, registering with a negative sign all the items generating money outflows and with a positive sign all inward payments. While the specific items that they registered in their accounting systems testify to their awareness of the factual conditions of their respective countries, the emergence of a common accounting framework interestingly illustrates the supranational characteristics of political economy in the early stages of its formation. Going on, now, from accounting frameworks to theoretical explanations, let us look at the transnational network of virtual interpretative alliances emerging from these two controversies.

3 Malynes and de Santis: the no-silver-flow condition, financial markets, and the "abuse of the exchange"

Gerard De Malynes (fl.1583–1641) and Marc'Antonio de Santis (fl. 1596–1605) blamed the scarcity of cash on the system of international payments, which was based on the coexistence of two distinct financial instruments, namely metallic money and letters (or bills) of foreign exchange. They argued that as a result of the practices of foreign exchange dealers, the exchange rate set in the market for letters of exchange was made independent of the metallic parity and thus diverted from its equilibrium level, stimulating destabilizing international flows of metallic money.[22]

Some introductory remarks are necessary in order to understand the similarities and differences between their respective arguments. First, London and Naples usually quoted the exchange rate in different ways: in London, it was commonly defined as the variable amount of foreign currency per *pound sterling*, according to the practice by which London had "the head of the exchange" with many markets in Northern Europe, especially the Low Countries.[23] By contrast, in Naples the exchange rate was quoted as the price of the foreign currency in terms of the domestic currency – that is, the units of *carlini* that Neapolitan citizens had to give up for a unit of the foreign currency. Consequently, when Malynes complained about an exchange rate that was too low, and de Santis about an exchange rate that was too high, they meant the same thing, namely a depreciated national currency: English tradesmen, said Malynes, were receiving too few foreign coins – for example, Dutch *florins*, for a *pound*; the Neapolitans, said de Santis, were paying too many *carlini* for, e.g., a Florentine *florin*. Both statements meant that the external value of the domestic currency was below what they regarded as its equilibrium level.

Second, according to a common continental practice, the Neapolitans usually quoted the exchange rate in terms of an international *numéraire* or money of account:[24] the gold *écu* or *scudo d'oro* in use in the "Bisanzone fair" (actually held in Piacenza). Obviously, once each currency was quoted in terms of a common international *numéraire*, bilateral exchange rates between any two currencies were also determined. Thus, the "aerial exchange rate", as de Santis called it,[25] was the price of the Piacenza gold *écu* in units of Neapolitan *carlini*, or in other subdivisions and multiples of the national currency: a *carlino* was equal to ten *grana*, and to 1/10 of a *ducato*. By contrast, Malynes considered the exchange rate between currencies in actual circulation, without reference to any international *numéraire*.[26]

Finally, and most importantly, economic operators had access to two alternative means of international payments: silver coins and letters (or bills) of exchange. For instance, a Neapolitan (English) merchant could either send cash abroad or pay cash for a bill of exchange that entitled him/her to a given amount of the foreign currency in the foreign market – for example, *florins* in Florence (in Amsterdam). The foreign currency was readily available because the exchange dealer had a correspondent in Florence (Amsterdam), whom he instructed to pay the merchant (or their correspondent) a number of *florins*, corresponding to the exchange rate stipulated in the contract, at a specified term, usually after a standardized *usance* period. As a result of the latter, bills of exchange also involved the extension of credit. Interest charges were incorporated into the quoted exchange rates, which Malynes brought attention to, arguing against the usury element that foreign exchange dealers hid under the appearance of compensation for "discrepancies and distances of time and place".[27]

With these provisos in mind, let us look at the logic of our two authors' arguments, which came in four steps. As first step, they defined the equilibrium level of the nominal exchange rate (dubbed "fair" by de Santis and "right" by Malynes) as the level at which the flow of the precious metals between countries would come to a halt. According to Malynes,[28] the equilibrium exchange rate would be given by the *Par pro Pari* or *value for value* condition – that is, by the mint parity between national and foreign currencies taking account of their respective weight and fineness.[29] De Santis incorporated into the fair rate of exchange some consuetudinary and legal elements, such as the exchange rate ruling in recent years and the quotations fixed by the monetary authority: consequently, in his view, the *equilibrium* exchange rate could deviate somewhat from strict metallic parity.[30] The two essential points are for both authors that the equilibrium exchange rate represented the "no-silver-flow condition", as we may call it, and that any deviation of the exchange rate from its equilibrium level would generate specie movements: a depreciation in exchange rates would lead to export of metallic coins, while, on the contrary, specie would come into the country following an appreciation.[31] "To avoide the cariage of money, a certaine exchange was devised, grounded upon the weight, fineness and valuation of the money of each country, according to value for value", said Malynes.[32] De Santis added specific numbers to his definition:

> The fair price of the gold scudo at the exchange, people should know, is 130 [*grana*]... Therefore, the exchanges which the Kingdom makes with the markets in Italy, and these with it, at the said fair price of 130, determine that no hard cash comes into the Kingdom, and at the same time that the cash that is in the Kingdom stays in it, and does not go out. Changing at a price higher than the said fair price entails not only that no cash comes into the Kingdom, but also that all that is in goes out; changing at a lower price than the said fair price brings an uncountable amount of cash into the Kingdom, and at the same time keeps it inside.[33]

The second step taken by our authors was to establish the reasons why the actual exchange rate often diverged from its equilibrium ("fair" or "right") level. Both blamed the divergence on the operation of the market for letters of exchange, although they both recognized that, if properly used, these instruments could prove useful in international trade. "The right use of the exchange", said Malynes, "is very needfull and convenient";[34] consequently, he had no objections to the "permutation" of foreign commodities "for our money",[35] but only if and when trade occurred at the "due course of the exchange rate".[36] In the same vein, de Santis defined an exchange operation as "a permutation of money that is given in one place to receive the fair amount of currency in another".[37] Thus, what the two authors objected to was not the use of these financial instruments but "the abuse of the exchange". They both conceived that under the circumstances of perfectly competitive markets, the forces of supply and demand would bring the actual exchange rate into equality with the equilibrium exchange rate.[38] But, they argued, under the current circumstances dealers exploited some degree of market power in the market for letters of exchange. Ultimately this was a microeconomic problem, which lay in the oligopolistic structure of the financial markets, which allowed the exchange dealers ("bankers" for Malynes and "negotianti" for de Santis) to collude and set the price for these letters as high as possible, as is in the interest of any oligopolistic seller.

In this connection, Malynes contented himself with blaming the heads of the banks, who set exchange rates according to their interests when they convened in the "*ferias*, or faires onely for monies... kept at *Madril, Lyons, Civil, Bisanson, Florence*". These rates were then imposed on England, which had little autonomy since "in the maine sea of exchanges", the exchange of England runs only "as a river or branch".[39]

De Santis proposed a more detailed analysis. He argued that exchange rates were set in a two-stage process. In the first stage, a selected group of financial operators met quarterly at the Bisanzone fair[40] and set exchange rates on the basis of the supply and demand of the different currencies. De Santis did not object to the operation of this group of wise men, conceding that the financiers in Piacenza "took the rule" from the markets.[41] Unfortunately, though, these centrally-set exchange rates were only the basis upon which decentralized negotiations took place in the second stage. In Naples, for instance, a very limited number of financial operators (or "negotianti", as he called them) were active on the supply side of the market. On the other side of the market, demand for letters of exchange was high, and highly inelastic. As a consequence, the negotianti were able to adopt collusive practices in order to make the supply of bills of exchange artificially scarce and set their price artificially high. "Suffice it to say that four negotianti every week have the habit of setting the price of the exchange, and most of the time, exception being made for some honourable and unselfish individuals, according to their purposes make the money now increase and now become tight".[42] Apparently, the negotianti were doing more than simply exploiting arbitrage opportunities when they happened to occur:[43] they exploited a market power that simply would not exist in competitive markets.[44] With his analysis, de Santis was responding to these negotianti and their spokespeople, who had criticized his proposal of regulating the exchange rate by law, arguing that such regulation would amount to "ravishing" the exchange rate.[45] In fact, he was returning that charge to sender.

Our two authors then proceeded to their third analytical step by elucidating in detail why silver would flow out of the country. This was simply a matter of individual responses to economic incentives: domestic traders would settle their payments abroad by sending coins (by "shipping" or sending them "on the back of mules", as de Santis explained)[46] if letters of exchange were more expensive than metallic money or, put the other way around, if their purchasing power over foreign currencies was lower. As Malynes clarified with flawless logic, if "more will be given for our money being caried in *specie* then [*sic*] by bill of exchange can be had, then our money is transported; whereas otherwise no man would adventure the money...if by a simple bill of exchange he might have as much payde him beyond the seas: for in truth gaine is the cause of exportation of our monies".[47]

Elaborating on the same concept, de Santis clarified that a depreciated currency would induce not just one but three categories of agents to send silver coins out and paper into the Kingdom, thus leaving it "deprived of coins and, I may say, left with virtually none".[48] These three categories were domestic importers of foreign goods, foreign importers of Neapolitan goods, and, most importantly, financial speculators, whose activity, "cambio per arte", consisted in buying cheap and selling dear.

Consider the Neapolitan importers of foreign goods: by sending cash abroad, they would pay 13 *carlini* per *écu* at the mint par. Alternatively, by sending letters at the current exchange rate they would pay 14.5 *carlini* per *écu*. Obviously, they would choose to send cash. By contrast, foreign importers of Neapolitan goods preferred to send letters of exchange into the Kingdom because by so doing they would pay only 0.069 of an *écu* for a *carlino* rather than 0.076. Finally, but most importantly, financial speculators would create a major drain on the Kingdom's money stock by sending silver coins abroad to gain from variations in the exchange rate. They would obtain speculative gains if, as they wagered, the *carlino* depreciated in the future; they would then realize their profits by sending the money "back by way of exchange" – that is, by bills of exchange. Such bearish speculation was the most powerful cause of the scarcity of silver since "gaining from the exchange" was the "cause of most exchanges" in the Kingdom.[49] Malynes, too, was aware of financial speculation in England. He called this speculative trade "a merchandising exchange" and severely condemned it.[50]

The fourth and final step taken by de Santis and Malynes was to elucidate the consequences of the specie outflow on the *real* exchange rate, or the "terms of trade", which we define as: $R=e\ P^f/P$ (e being the domestic price of the foreign currency, P^f the price level in the foreign country, and P the domestic price level). De Santis focused his analysis of worsening terms of trade on the depreciation of the domestic currency – that is, on the rise in e in our formula.[51]

In Malynes's more complete analysis, the terms of trade would turn against England (foreign goods would be bought "too deare")[52] as a consequence of the combined effects of a weakening pound (a rise in e) and of a rise in the ratio P^f/P, this rise being determined by the flow of specie out of the domestic and into the foreign country that would be set in motion by the depreciation itself:

> But this due course being abused, causeth ... our monies to be transported, and maket scarcitie thereof, which abated the price of our home commodities: and on the contrary advances the prices of

> forreine commodities beyond the seas, where our money concurring with the monies of other countries causeth plenty, whereby the price of forrein commodities is advanced.[53]

Because Malynes saw this effect of money flows on the ratio between foreign and domestic price levels, some modern interpreters have credited him with an understanding of the "self-regulating mechanism" (i.e. the Humean price-specie flow mechanism).[54] However, Malynes rejected the idea that these price movements re-equilibrate the external balance. Far from being a remedy, these changes meant deteriorating terms of trade:[55] "the overballancing of forrain commodities with our home commodities, which consisteth in the price of commodities, not in the quantity or qualitie of them".[56] In other words, the deficit was not determined by the excess of imports over exports in volumes but by relative price effects.

Coherently with their diagnoses, both authors recommended that the monetary authorities should revalue the domestic currency. De Santis explained that re-evaluations have positive welfare effects on consumers, as well as positive effects on tax revenues via import tariffs.[57] Because of these proposals, the two economists were, and still are, criticized for their *dirigiste* attitude towards the exchange rate. But the weight of this allegation is uncertain because the question of the relative advantages of fixed vs flexible exchange rates is still a matter of debate today.[58]

Summing up, de Santis and Malynes were acute observers of financial markets and provided interesting accounts of the microeconomics of specie export points and the macroeconomics of monetary drains. My interpretation contrasts with the viewpoint of those who see these two enemies of oligopolistic dealers merely as "medievalists", as Spiegel[59] considers Malynes to be. We need not necessarily take the critics of financial capitalists' malpractices for backwards-looking conservatives.

4 Misselden, Mun, Serra, Turbolo: the real side of the economy and the "product mix"

On the opposite side of the two controversies, we find Misselden and Mun in England and Serra in Naples. Here is another example of transnational theoretical convergence. These authors shared the idea that the drain on metallic coin had little to do with financial factors, believing instead that the drain was determined by the trade deficit, in turn a consequence of uncompetitive productive structures.[60]

Misselden (fl. 1608–1654) blamed the deficit on excessive imports of luxury goods due to people stepping "into one anothers rankes".[61] He argued that social mobility, in addition to threatening the stability of the social hierarchy, also resulted in external imbalances.[62] As causes of the trade deficit, he also mentioned wars, the obstacles to commerce determined by the pirates in the Mediterranean sea,[63] and "the encroaching of strangers, in fishing upon our coasts",[64] the latter of which displaced domestic production of consumption goods and pulled "the bread out of the natives mouthes".[65]

Thomas Mun (1571–1641) provided a much more sophisticated analysis of the competitive advantage of nations in his book *English Treasure by Foreign Trade,* written during the 1620 controversy but not published until 1664. His treatment included some of the factors in Misselden's list, such as wars (chapter VI), the fishing problem (chapter XIX), and excessive consumption of foreign luxuries (chapters III, VI, and XIX). He argued that luxury goods should be produced at home, with great advantage for job creation and employment opportunities for English workers. But the most interesting part of his analysis concerns export promotion strategies. He opposed the hindering of exports by unduly "endearing" their price abroad, including through export duties.[66] Prices should be tailored to the specific demand elasticity of each product in foreign countries: English exporters should charge high prices for necessaries, because the foreign demand for these goods was inelastic. By contrast, export prices should be kept low for goods characterized by elastic foreign demand. As an example, Mun recalled that by reducing the price of clothes, England had recently registered a large increase in the volume of sales to Turkey, and in revenues thereof. Well acquainted with cunning commercial practices, Mun went so far as to recommend cuts in selling prices as a long-term strategy of import penetration in foreign markets. The resulting crowding out of competitors would increase England's market share in world markets and, in due time, allow English exporters to raise prices "and so in time obtain our dear price again".[67]

Our clever merchant knew very well that such aggressive commercial policies required the support of a strong industrial and commercial structure, which in turn called for a far-sighted industrial policy based on strategic choice of the product mix. The crucial objective in this strategy was to move the country up the value-added chain through the promotion of domestic industry. Mun celebrated the apotheosis of industrial and manufacturing activities as creators of value-added:

> ... Iron oar in the Mines is of no great worth, when it is compared with the employment and advantage it yields being digged, tried, transported, bought, sold, cast into Ordnance, Muskets, and many other instruments of war for offence and defence, wrought into Anchors, bolts, spikes, nayles, for the use in Ships, Houses, Carts, Coaches, Ploughs, and other instruments for tillage. Compare our Fleece-wools with our Cloth, which requires shearing, washing, carding, spinning, weaving, fulling, dying, dressing and other trimmings, and we shall find these arts more profitable than natural wealth.[68]

Following this logic, Mun argued that industrial progress requires that raw materials be imported and then re-exported as finished products.[69] This policy amounted to changing the country's international specialization from traditional sectors, such as raw materials and agricultural products, to advanced manufacturing.

In Mun's view, a nation that aspires to international economic hegemony should also devote great care to the development of commercial activities, with special reference to the carrying trade. Moreover, the country would greatly benefit from displacing other nations in the provision of transport and insurance services. This would lead to both sizeable cost savings and new employment opportunities in industrial sectors like shipbuilding. He saw the industrial sector and the service sector as an integrated whole, promoting economic progress at home and dominance over competitors internationally. In Mun's words, this promotion amounted to favouring the development of artificial wealth "which consists in our manufacturing and industrious trading with forraign commodities" over "Natural wealth", constituting the original endowment of each country.[70] In this context, Mun was well aware of the positive synergies between a favourable international specialization, on the one hand, and, on the other, the competitive advantage offered by a large population employed in cutting-edge sectors. As he argued, "people which live by the Arts are far more in number than they who are master of the fruit", and "where the people are many, and the arts good, there the traffique must be great, and the Countrey rich".[71]

In Mun's approach, the aggressive pursuit of national interests went hand in hand with opposition to restrictions on trade and with the promotion of multilateralism.[72] He condemned as inefficient the bilateral balanced trade imposed by the statute of "Imployments", requiring that foreigners use the money earned by their imports into England to buy English goods (chapter X).

Mun was a prominent, well-respected merchant and a director of the East India Company. As early as 1623, Misselden had extolled his virtues and those of his first book, *Discourse of Trade unto the East Indies*.[73] Mun had an inside knowledge of commercial practices and went beyond the individual merchant's point of view by elucidating the structural and macroeconomic conditions and consequences of successful commercial expansion. In view of these merits, it is even more striking that in 1613 Antonio Serra (fl. 1613), a "poor devil"[74] languishing in the Vicaria jail in Naples, had developed a system of thought which, while anticipating Mun's approach in many essential respects, surpassed it in profundity and comprehensiveness.

This mysterious writer, a doctor from Cosenza about whom almost nothing is known,[75] wrote a book entitled *A short treatise on the causes that can make kingdoms abound in gold and silver even in the absence of mines (Breve trattato delle cause che possono far abbondare li regni d'oro e d'argento dove non sono miniere)*.[76] Serra concentrated on the economic problems of the Neapolitan Kingdom, but his lucid analysis, transcending the local dimension, goes to the heart of the structural determinants of economic development and underdevelopment.

His starting point was, once again, the balance of payments. He recognized that the external deficit was determined by two elements, namely the trade deficit, on the one hand, and, on the other, the payment of taxes plus rents and profits abroad, the latter element being the joint result of political and economic dependence. As he saw the situation, given the Kingdom's subordinate position within the Spanish empire, it was impossible to escape political and economic dependence,[77] but it was possible to work on the trade balance by strengthening the nation's productive structure.

Rejecting de Santis's argument on exchange rates, Serra started his bleak diagnosis of the Kingdom's economic problems with a distinction between "proper accidents" and "common accidents".[78] Proper accidents were idiosyncratic factors related to natural conditions, such as land fertility, geographical position, and so on. These "accidents", partly responsible for the country's dire economic conditions, could not be changed by policy intervention. It was more fruitful to concentrate on "common accidents" – that is, the causes of national wealth amenable to policy-induced change.

The first of these common accidents was the sectoral composition of output. Successful countries relied on "a multiplicity of manufacturing activities",[79] while the Kingdom's product mix was defective in this respect, leading to unfavourable international specialization. The Kingdom was in fact a net exporter of agricultural products, thanks to the natural fertility of its soil,[80] but it had to import all its industrial and manufactured products, the only exception being silk. Serra's treatment of this point marks genuine theoretical innovation because he went beyond the mere definition of a hierarchical order between economic branches and enquired into the reasons for the superiority of manufactures. Unlike agriculture, he argued, the manufacturing sector yields reliable profits because of both its independence from the weather and the less perishable nature of its products. Above all, the manufacturing industry is able to multiply its products "at proportionally lower cost".[81] This is the first known statement of the law of increasing returns "in the form of decreasing unit costs"[82] – an innovation that sets Serra apart from contemporary writers as a theorist of structural analysis.

The second "common accident" was "an enterprising population".[83] Serra thought that the citizens of the Kingdom of Naples were defective in this respect, being "so unenterprising that they do not trade outside their territory…and such local industries as do exist are run not by the Neapolitans themselves, but by people from other places – chiefly other parts of Italy – the Genoese, Florentines, Bergamasques, Venetians and others".[84] As a modern interpreter has noted, this statement was not merely "pedagogic and academic"; rather, it should be interpreted in the light of the politics of the Spanish empire at that moment and possibly with Serra's own personal objectives in mind:[85] in line with Viceroy Lemos's projects, by so severely denouncing the Neapolitan businessmen's lack of entrepreneurial abilities, Serra was trying to pre-empt the revival of a Neapolitan entrepreneurial "party" and make room for a large new wave of Genoese investments in the Kingdom.[86]

Serra's third common accident was "extensive trade".[87] In this respect, Serra noted that the Kingdom was at a disadvantage owing to its "very bad" peripheral geographic position. This prevented the country from developing as a hub of international trade as Venice had done and from having its own transport industry.[88]

The fourth common accident was "good government", "the most powerful of all in making the Kingdom abound in gold and silver, for it may be described as the efficient cause and superior agent of all the other accidents".[89] It was indicative of Serra's courage – or recklessness – that he asserted the superiority of republican governments over monarchies, particularly if one considers that his book was dedicated to the Spanish viceroy, the above-mentioned Count of Lemos. Be that as it may, he praised republican governments because of the institutional continuity that they provided. Kings could in fact last for fifty years at most, and the Kingdom's policies and strategic objectives would then change with the advent of the new monarch. In republics, by contrast, the coexistence of old and new generations in the governing institutions, such as the senate, ensured continuity and – simultaneously – constant rejuvenation of the governing body. Venice was again the example to admire and possibly to imitate.[90]

We may sum up Serra's position by saying that good institutional design is the main foundation of a healthy economic system: good government would create the conditions and provide the incentives to develop a modern manufacturing sector and thereby generate a positive external account, which in turn would make the Kingdom rich in silver and gold, "even in the absence of mines".

Before concluding this section, we should devote some attention to the contribution by Giovanni Donato Turbolo (fl. 1594–1629) to the analysis of the balance of payments in this early stage of economic theorizing. With regard to the international adjustment process, it is to be noted that Misselden and Mun saw the exchange rate as moving in response to external imbalances, and they accordingly argued that the level of the exchange rate was not the cause but a consequence of that balance. Mun's analysis of competitiveness focused more on relative prices than on the equilibrating role of the exchange rate. Serra explicitly denied this equilibrating role and bluntly argued that changes in the level of the exchange rate "would not make any difference" to the external deficit.[91] Malynes and de Santis, for their part, considered the exchange rate to be determined in the market for letters of foreign exchange and to be relatively unresponsive to the overall balance of payments.

In this respect, Giovanni Donato Turbolo was the only author who recognized the effects of depreciations on the trade balance. In a series of discourses delivered between 1618 and 1629,[92] he argued that a weaker domestic currency not only stimulates exports[93] but also reduces the real value of rent payments abroad, these payments now being made in a depreciated domestic currency.[94] Thus, depreciation would make domestic products more competitive and, at the same time, promote redistribution from foreigners to natives. For both reasons, the external balance would improve.

Moving from theoretical analysis to the specific conditions of the Neapolitan Kingdom, Turbolo raised the following question. The Neapolitan currency had indeed depreciated in the market for letters of exchange over the last couple of decades, just as de Santis had argued.

Nevertheless, this depreciation had not brought about the deficit reduction that theory predicted. How could this paradox be explained? As master of the Neapolitan mint, Turbolo was well aware of the complications of international adjustment in a metallic system. Consequently, he proposed the following answer. The positive effects of currency depreciation had not come into operation, because the government had refused to debase the silver coins at the rate of the depreciation,[95] thus preventing the mint parity from converging to the level now ruling in the market for letters of exchange, and all for the sake of "prestige". In that period, the weak Kingdom was in fact trying to buy credibility with its creditors by keeping the currency strong.[96] But the government's refusal to debase the metal coins led to dramatic losses for the Kingdom because the price paid for the imported bullion was higher than its value when minted into silver coins. This had caused a loss of "more than 400,000 *ducati* in few years".[97] Under these circumstances, the money drain could not be remedied, the Kingdom was "exhausted of money",[98] and no re-equilibrating process came in operation.[99] Our competent mint master earnestly lamented this.

5 Conclusions

The Kingdom of Naples was on its way to economic involution when Serra, de Santis, and Turbolo wrote their essays. As we read in their works, the silver fetters within which their Kingdom was floundering were the result of dependence, the bitter fruit of the alliance between the local barons, foreign merchants, and a Spanish monarchy made rapacious by the cost of war finance. By contrast, the English authors experienced the external constraint as a limitation to their nation's prosperity and progress towards worldwide commercial empire and industrial pre-eminence.

These differences notwithstanding, the Neapolitan and the English authors adopted similar accounting frameworks for their analysis of open economies. At the theoretical level, they offered two alternative interpretations of how real and financial forces affect the external balance of nations. On one hand, Serra, Mun, and Misselden gave priority to forces operating on the real side of the economy, such as the structure of production and the product mix; on the other hand, Malynes and de Santis focused on the international payments system and the role of financial speculation within it. These alternative explanations offer a fascinating example of how theoretical fault lines cut across nationalities. Finally, Turbolo, thanks to his insider's knowledge of the operation of the monetary system, provided an original contribution with his real and monetary analysis. Through comparative investigation into the two controversies that these economists were involved in, the present paper has tried to clarify the polycentric origins of economic analysis.

By illustrating how these economists conceptualized the link between money supply and the balance of payments, this paper also corroborates the rejection by modern interpreters[100] of the old idea that mercantilists identified money and wealth. This misleading criticism was the fruit of prejudices developed when economists still believed in a dichotomy between real and monetary variables. In those times, the role of money as the liquid asset par excellence was underestimated and money was considered as a representation of real commodities or capital.[101] But money as a means of payment does not *represent* other entities, because what buyers need in advance of their desired transactions is money, rather than other commodities or assets.[102] It is indeed significant that Keynes,[103] whose theoretical work may be interpreted as a far-reaching attempt to differentiate monetary economies from barter economies, proposed a rehabilitation of mercantilism in *The General Theory*. Our analysis shows that the mercantilist writers we have dealt with here were well aware of the distinction between money and wealth, but they were also aware that a permanently negative external balance is not sustainable. Consequently, they offered shrewd analyses of the causes of these external imbalances and proposed thoroughly pondered remedies.

A further criticism that is sometimes raised against these writers points to their ignorance of the automatic adjustment mechanisms operating via the "price-specie flow mechanism"[104] or via the equilibrating role of the exchange rate.[105] This line of criticism is theoretically valid (though it does not apply to Turbolo), but it ignores the justification that international adjustment does not necessarily come into operation and that international imbalances may last for long periods of time. This point has been made with reference to both the time when our economists were active[106] and to more recent periods. For instance, even under the gold standard, considered to be the "self-regulating" monetary system par excellence, the United Kingdom ran persistent and growing surpluses for very long periods of time.[107] Again, long-lasting and growing deficits on the current account have been registered in the dollar-based international payment system.[108] Moreover, and most importantly, the resolution of international imbalances may require more than the automatic operation of market forces.

Finally, these authors have been criticized on the grounds that their elasticity approach to the balance of payments is incomplete and does not meet the test of the Marshall/Lerner conditions expressed in mathematical equations,[109] which is after all hardly surprising given the stage of development of economic theory at their time.[110] But they were reasonably aware that there were elasticity conditions for the validity of their reasoning: for instance, Malynes and de Santis explicitly considered the foreign demand for their countries' exports to be inelastic[111] – a circumstance that, in their view, prevented England and Naples from losing sales abroad when their currencies appreciated. Moreover, de Santis also considered the Kingdom's imports to be elastic (and hence to fall with exchange-rate appreciations). Summing up, de Santis and Malynes may be charged with excessive "elasticity optimism" but certainly not with complete neglect of the elasticity conditions in their balance of payment analysis. And, as we have seen, Mun carefully calibrated price strategies to the specific demand elasticities of individual products.

Bottom line, I submit that, in looking back to the founding fathers of economics, a positive attitude may be more rewarding than simply faulting them for not having gained full command of the sophisticated tools and models of modern economic analysis. Rather, these tools are useful for *our* understanding of what they saw in the world that they lived in and of the ways in which, in attempting to understand that world, they built the conceptual basis of economics.

Notes

I wish to thank Cosimo Perrotta, who read and commented on the present version of this work, and the participants at the session of the ESHET conference where this paper was presented (Rome, 14–16 May 2015). For comments on a previous partial version, I am grateful to the participants at the Cambridge Research Seminar in Political Economy held at Emmanuel College on the 21 of May 2013, and in particular to Ivano Cardinale, D'Maris Coffman, Craig Muldrew, and Roberto Scazzieri.

1. See Schumpeter, J.A., *History of Economic Analysis*, London: George Allen & Unwin, 1954, p. 355; Rosselli, A., "Early Views on Monetary Policy: The Neapolitan Debate on the Theory of Exchange", *History of Political Economy*, 32(1), 2000, pp. 61–62; Reinert, E.S. and S.A. Reinert, "An Early National Innovation System: The Case of Antonio Serra's 1613 Breve Trattato", *Institutions and Economic Development/Istituzioni e Sviluppo Economico*, 1, 3, 2003, pp. 87–119; Roncaglia, A., *The Wealth of Ideas: A History of Economic Thought*, Cambridge: Cambridge University Press, 2005. This literature ignores Turbolo (Turbolo, G.D., *Discorso della differenza e inegualità delle monete del Regno di Napoli, con l'altre monete di potentati convicini, e della causa della penuria di esse*, Naples: Tarquinio Longo, 1616, as reprinted in R. Colapietra (ed.), *Problemi monetari negli scrittori napoletani del Seicento*, Rome: Accademia Nazionale dei Lincei, 1973, pp. 289–297 and Turbolo, G.D., *Discorso sopra le*

monete del Regno di Napoli, Per la renouazione della lega di esse monete, ordinata e eseguita nell'anno 1622. E degli effetti da quella proceduti. E se il cambio alto per extra Regno sia utile, o danno a' Regnicoli, con diverse relationi e copie d'altri discorsi dati fuora nell'anni 1618, 1619 & 1620 pertinenti alla medesima materia, Naples: n.p., 1629, as reprinted in R. Colapietra (ed.), 1973, pp. 297–377), who actually did not directly take part in the controversy engaged in by Serra against de Santis but, a few years later, had interesting things to say on the same issues. See Costabile, L., "Monetary Analysis, Financial Innovation, and Institutions before the Industrial Revolution: a Paradigm Case", in M. Baranzini, C. Rotondi, R. Scazzieri (eds), *Resources, Production and Structural Dynamics*, Cambridge: Cambridge University Press, 2015, pp. 213–231 for an analysis of the Neapolitan debate, including de Santis, Serra, and Turbolo.

2. Angell, J.W., *The Theory of International Prices. History, Criticism and Restatement*, Cambridge, MA: Harvard University Press, 1926, pp. 10–11.
3. Reinert, S.A., *Translating Empire: Emulation and the Origins of Political Economy*, Cambridge: Cambridge University Press, 2011.
4. I borrow part of the title of J. Robertson's 1997 article. The present paper illustrates a case of theoretical convergence before the age of illuminism dealt with by Robertson. (Robertson, J., "The Enlightenment above National Context: Political Economy in Eighteenth Century Scotland and Naples", *The Historical Journal*, 40, 3, 1997, pp. 667–697.
5. de Santis, M.A., (1605a), *Discorso di Marc'Antonio De Santis intorno alli effetti che fa il cambio in Regno*, Naples: appresso Costantino Vitale, 1605; (1605b), *Secondo Discorso di Marc'Antonio De Santis intorno alli effetti che fa il cambio in Regno. Sopra una risposta, che è stata fatta avverso al primo*, Naples: nella stamperia di Felice Stigliola, 1605 (both as reprinted in Colapietra, R. (ed.), 1973, pp. 111–162); Malynes, G., *The Canker of England's Common Wealth*, London: by Richard Field for William Iohnes, 1601; reprinted in Amsterdam, Norwood, N.J.: W.J. Johnson, Theatrum orbis terrarum, 1977; Malynes, G., *The Maintenance of Free Trade*, London: by I.L. for William Sheffard, 1622; reprint New York, NY: Kelley, 1971; Malynes, G., *The Center of the Circle of Commerce*, London: William Iones, 1623; reprint Clifton, N.J: 1973.
6. Misselden, E., *Free Trade, or the Means to make Trade flourish*, London: printed by Iohn Legatt for Simon Waterson, 1622; reprint New York, NY: Kelley, 1971; Misselden, E., *The Circle of Commerce or the Balance of Trade, in Defence of Free Trade*, London: printed by Iohn Dawson for Nicholas Bourne, 1623; reprint New York, NY: Kelley, 1971; Mun, T., *A Discourse of Trade: From England unto the East-Indies, Answering to Diverse Objections which are Usually Made against the Same*, London: printed by Nicholas Okes for Iohn Pyper, 1621; reprint New York, NY: Kelley, 1971; Serra, A., *Breve trattato delle cause che possono far abbondare li regni d'oro e d'argento dove non sono miniere*, Naples: Appresso Lazzaro Scoriggio, 1613, as reprinted and as translated by J. Hunt, in A. Serra, *A Short Treatise on the Wealth and Poverty of Nations*, bilingual edition, ed. by S.A. Reinert, London-New York, NY-Delhi: Anthem Press, 2011.
7. The reader is referred to the relevant literature for the historical and institutional context, e.g. De Rosa, 1987, pp. 95–98; Muldrew, C., *The Economy of Obligation: The Culture of Credit and Social Relations in Early Modern England*, Basingstoke: Macmillan, 1998, p. 100. For the English context, see among others Johnson, E.A.J., "Gerard De Malynes and the Theory of the Foreign

Exchanges", *American Economic Review*, 23, 3, 1933, pp. 441–455; Gould, J.D., "The Trade Crisis of the Early 1620's and English Economic Thought", *Journal of Economic History*, 15, 2, 1955, pp. 121–133; Muchmore, L., "Gerrard de Malynes and Mercantile Economics", *History of Political Economy*, 1, 2, 1969, pp. 336–358 and Muchmore, L. "A Note on Thomas Mun's 'England's Treasure by forraign Trade'", *The Economic History Review*, New Series, 23, 3, 1970, pp. 498–503; Gomes, L., *Foreign Trade and the National Economy. Mercantilist and Classical Perspectives*, Basingstoke and London: Macmillan, 1987; Wennerlind, C., *Casualties of Credit: the English Financial Revolution 1620–1720*, Cambridge, MA: Harvard University Press, 2011. For the Neapolitan side, see Fornari, T., *Studi sopra Antonio Serra e Marc'Antonio De Santis*, Pavia, Fratelli Fusi, 1879; Colapietra (1973); De Rosa, L., *I cambi esteri del Regno di Napoli dal 1591 al 1707*, Naples: Biblioteca dell'Archivio Storico del Banco di Napoli, 1955; De Rosa, L., *Il Mezzogiorno spagnolo tra crescita e decadenza*, Milan: Il Saggiatore, 1987; Calabria, A., *The Cost of Empire. The Finances of the Kingdom of Naples in the Time of the Spanish Rule*, Cambridge: Cambridge University Press, 1991; Galasso, G., *Alla periferia dell'impero. Il Regno di Napoli nel periodo spagnolo (secoli XVI–XVII)*, Turin: Einaudi, 1994; Villari, R. (2014), *Un sogno di libertà. Napoli nel declino di un impero. 1585–1648*, Milan: Mondadori, 2014. For the international financial context, see the two classics: de Roover, R., *Business, Banking and Economic Thought in Late Medieval and Early Modern Europe, Selected Studies*, Chicago, IL and London; University of Chicago Press, 1974; and Neal, L., *The rise of financial capitalism*, Cambridge: Cambridge University Press, 1990.
8. Serra, 1613, pp. 150–151.
9. Serra, 1613, pp. 230–231, 204–205; see also de Santis, 1605a, p.136; Turbolo, 1629, pp. 304, 317.
10. Turbolo, 1629, p. 354.
11. Serra, 1613, pp. 150–151.
12. Thanks to this financial expedient, the administration was able to secure a lump sum equal to the current discounted value of a series of future incomes (e.g. the revenues from a tax). The mortgaging of future public revenues led to the creation of a government bond market in the second half of the 16th century (Calabria, 1991, pp. 52, 104–129).
13. Calabria, 1991, p. 51.
14. Serra, 1613, pp. 104–105, 150–151.
15. Serra, 1613, pp. 152–153.
16. Serra, 1613, pp. 136–137.
17. de Santis, 1605a, p. 136; 1605b, p. 147.
18. Benini, R., "Sulle dottrine economiche di Antonio Serra", *Giornale degli Economisti*, 3, 5, 1892, pp. 222–248, p. 232.
19. Mun, T., *England's Treasure by Forraign Trade*, London: printed by F.G. for Thomas Clark, 1664; reprint: Oxford: Basil Blackwell, 1928, pp. 9–10, 12, 42, 83–84.
20. Mun, 1664, p. 85.
21. Blitz, R.C., "Mercantilist Policies and the Pattern of World Trade, 1500–1750", *Journal of Economic History*, vol. 27, no. 1 (Mar.), 1967, pp. 39–55, p. 50.
22. Reference was mainly to silver coins when they mentioned metallic money. Gold was costly and hence almost absent from both the domestic and the

intra-European circulations. Thus, a shortage of silver impacted strongly on the domestic circulation (Muchmore, 1970, p. 498).

23. Malynes (1601, pp. 28–29) gave a clear definition of the concept: "the head of the exchange is taken to bee [*sic*] at such a place or places where the price doth not alter, as for example: We have the head of the exchanges with Hamborow, Middleborough, Emden, Amsterdam…And on the contrarie, for as much that the price for Roan, Paris and other places in France, and for Venice, and other places in Italie or elsewhere, doth for time to time alter with us according to their Crowne or Ducat, therefore does the head of those exchanges rest with them".
24. It was common practice on the continent to use as *numéraires* "imaginary moneys", i.e. money that either had never existed, or had been out of circulation for centuries. On imaginary moneys, see Bloch, M., Esquisse d'une Histoire Monètaire de l'Europe, *Cahiers des Annales*, n. 9, Paris: Librarie Armand Colin, 1954, pp. 7–96.
25. de Santis, 1605a, p. 114.
26. The system of quoting the sterling pound in imaginary *écus* had been in use in London in the Middle Ages, too (De Roover, 1974, p. 186).
27. Malynes, 1601, p. 32.
28. Malynes, 1601, pp. 14–15.
29. As a purely abstract example, let us suppose that the Neapolitan mint would issue one hundred *carlini* in return for one ounce of silver, compared to fifty *florins* for one ounce in Florence; thus, the two currencies would exchange for 100/50=2. More generally, if X is the price paid for one ounce of silver by the national mint, and Y is the price, measured in units of the foreign currency, paid for one ounce of silver by the foreign country's mint, then the mint parity between the two currencies is $E = X/Y$ (adapting McKinnon, R.I., "The Rules of the Game: International Money in Historical Perspective", *Journal of Economic Literature*, 31, 1, 1993, pp. 1–44). This mint par could not be permanently violated because of arbitrage. The necessary assumptions are free capital mobility, free conversion of coins into silver at the mints, and zero transaction costs (insurance, shipping, and foregone interest). The formula presented above is easily modified into $E = X/(Y - T_N)$, where T_N stands for the transaction costs of transferring silver, e.g. from Naples to Florence.
30. *Seignorage* and debasement were possible causes of divergence from the mint parity (Rosselli, 2000, esp. pp. 68–71).
31. Malynes, 1601, pp. 34–35; 1622, pp. 14–15; de Santis, 1605a, pp. 138–140.
32. Malynes, 1601, p. 14.
33. de Santis, 1605a, p. 132.
34. Malynes, 1601, p. 55.
35. Malynes, 1601, p. 89.
36. Malynes, 1601, p. 35.
37. de Santis, 1605, p. 130.
38. Malynes, 1622, pp. 14–15, 28; de Santis, 1605, pp. 138–139.
39. Malynes, 1601, p. 33.
40. de Santis, 1605a, p. 116.
41. de Santis, 1605a, p. 123.
42. de Santis, 1605a, pp. 138–139.

43. On arbitrage in 17th-century capital markets, see Neal, L. and S. Quinn, "Networks of information, markets, and institutions in the rise of London as a financial centre, 1660–1720", *Financial History Review*, 8, 2001, pp. 7–26. doi: 10.1017/S0968565001000130.
44. Malynes and de Santis are generally looked down upon by commentators, both contemporary with them and of our own day, for their "conspiracy" approach to exchange-rate determination. But they were in fact discussing price setting in oligopolistic markets.
45. de Santis, 1605a, pp. 119, 139.
46. de Santis, 1605a, p. 114.
47. Malynes, 1601, pp. 16, 34, 35.
48. de Santis, 1605a, p. 28.
49. de Santis, 1605a, p. 114–115, 151.
50. Malynes, 1601, p. 55.
51. Rothbard, M., *Economic Thought Before Adam Smith. An Austrian Perspective*, vol. 1, Auburn, AL: 2006, p. 287 [electronic edition; original edition Cheltenham: Edward Elgar, 1995] overlooked de Santis when he assigned to Malynes "the dubious credit for the emergence of the spurious and pernicious "terms of trade' fallacy" (de Santis, 1605a, p. 116). Not every economist would agree that it is a fallacy.
52. Malynes, 1601, p. 3.
53. Malynes, 1601, p. 35.
54. Viner J., *Studies in the Theory of International Trade*, New York, NY: Kelley, 1965, p. 76.
55. If we consider real, rather than nominal, exchange rates, it is untrue that "exchange rates, according to Malynes, were independent of commodity prices and specie flows" (de Roover, 1974, p. 364), because he maintained that these flows affected price levels and consequently the real exchange rate.
56. Malynes, 1601, p. 17.
57. de Santis, 1605a, p. 116.
58. It must be admitted, however, that both Malynes's and de Santis's proposals were repealed soon after having been adopted because they were recognized to have failed.
59. Spiegel, H.W., *The Growth of Economic Thought*, Durham, NC: Duke University Press, 1983, p. 101.
60. Serra, 1613, p. 164; Mun, 1664, p. 42; Misselden, 1623, p. 21.
61. Misselden, 1622, pp. 12–13.
62. Wennerlind (2011, p. 33 ff.) illustrates the static, hierarchical view of society underlying what he describes as Malynes's, Misselden's, and Mun's "Neo-Aristotelian" approach to political economy.
63. Misselden, 1622, pp. 17–18.
64. Misselden, 1622, p. 35.
65. Misselden, 1623, p. 48.
66. Mun, 1664, p. 12.
67. Mun, 1664, p. 8.
68. Mun, 1664, p. 13.
69. Mun, 1664, p. 11.
70. Mun, 1664, p. 7.

71. Mun, 1664, p. 12.
72. Kindleberger, C.P., *Historical economics: Art or science?* Berkeley, CA: University of California Press, 1991.
73. Misselden, 1623, pp. 36–38.
74. Schumpeter, 1954, p. 354.
75. Did he take part in Tommaso Campanella's conspiracy to establish a republic in Calabria, then part of the Spanish-dominated Kingdom of Naples? Or was he, less heroically, merely guilty of counterfeiting? The doubt has not been resolved, and it probably never will be: many regard his involvement in the revolt led by Campanella as a myth.
76. Serra, 1613.
77. Serra, 1613, pp. 238–239.
78. Serra, 1613, pp. 118–119.
79. Serra, 1613, p. 119.
80. Serra, 1613, pp. 154–155.
81. Serra, 1613, pp. 120–121.
82. Schumpeter, 1954, p. 258.
83. Serra, 1613, pp. 122–123.
84. Serra, 1613, pp. 122–123.
85. He was trying to obtain the viceroy's favour and get out of jail.
86. Colapietra, 1973, p. 30.
87. Serra, 1613, pp. 124–125.
88. Serra, 1613, pp. 126–127.
89. Serra, 1613, p. 176.
90. Serra, 1613, pp. 176–177.
91. Serra, 1613, pp. 152–153, 230–231.
92. Turbolo, 1629.
93. Turbolo, 1629, pp. 302, 313.
94. Turbolo, 1629, pp. 304–305.
95. Turbolo, 1629, pp, 311–312, 317.
96. Bulgarelli, L.A., *L'imposta diretta nel Regno di Napoli in età moderna*, Milan: Franco Angeli, 1993, p. 28.
97. Bulgarelli, 1993, p. 311.
98. Bulgarelli, 1993, pp. 299–300.
99. Note that the scarcity of money problem was opening the way to financial innovation both in England, where it took the form of private credit (Muldrew, 1998), and in the Kingdom, where the circulation of paper money was introduced by the "Public Banks" of Naples (De Rosa, L., Gli inizi della circolazione della cartamoneta e i banchi pubblici napoletani, in id. (ed.), *Gli inizi della circolazione della cartamoneta e i banchi pubblici napoletani*, Naples: Istituto Banco di Napoli-Fondazione, 2002, pp. 437–459; Costabile, L., "The value and security of money. Metallic and fiduciary media in Ferdinando Galiani's Della moneta", *European Journal of the History of Economic Thought*, doi: 10.1080/09672567.2014.916730; Costabile, L., "Monetary Analysis, Financial Innovation, and Institutions before the Industrial Revolution: a Paradigm Case", in M. Baranzini, C. Rotondi, R. Scazzieri (eds), *Resources, Production and Structural Dynamics*, Cambridge: Cambridge University Press, 2015, pp. 213–231.

100. Magnusson, L.J., "Mercantilism", in W.J. Samuels, J.E. Biddle, and J.B. Davis (eds), *A companion to the history of economic thought*, Oxford: Blackwell, 2003, p. 53; Perrotta, C., "Thomas Mun's England's Treasure by Forraign Trade. The 17th Century Manifesto for Development Economics", *History of Economics Review*, 59, 2014, pp. 94–106, p. 95.
101. Heckscher, E., *Mercantilism*, London: George Allen & Unwin, 1935, vol. II. p. 209.
102. Clower, R., "A Reconsideration of the Microfoundations of Monetary Theory", *Western Economic Journal*, 6, 1967, pp. 1–8.
103. Keynes, J.M., *The General Theory of Employment, Interest and Money*, as reprinted in *The Collected Writings of John Maynard Keynes*, ed. by Moggridge, D., vol. VII, London and Basingstoke: Macmillan, 1936.
104. Angel, 1926, pp. 13–15.
105. Rosselli, 2000, p. 74.
106. Gould, 1955, p. 125.
107. Triffin, R., "The myth and realities of the so-called gold standard" in B. Eichengreen (ed.), *The Gold Standard in Theory and History*, New York, NY and London: Methuen, 1985, pp. 121–140, p. 126.
108. Costabile, L., "Current Global Imbalances and the Keynes Plan. A Keynesian Approach for Reforming the International Monetary System", *Structural Change and Economic Dynamics*, 20, 2, 2009, pp. 79–89.
109. Allen, W.R., "Modern Defenders of Mercantilist Theory", *History of Political Economy*, 2, 2, 1970, pp. 381–397.
110. Coats, A.W., "The Interpretation of Mercantilist Economics: Some Historiographical Problems; with a rear-guard Response", *History of Political Economy*, Fall, 5, 2, 1973, pp. 485–495.
111. de Santis, 1605a, pp. 132–133; Malynes, 1622, pp. 46–47.

9

Real and Monetary Factors in the de Santis–Serra Controversy

André Tiran

1 The financial actors at play in Serra's time

Understanding the work of Antonio Serra requires some knowledge, however basic, of the economic, monetary, and banking situation in the Kingdom of Naples at the time when Serra wrote his *Breve trattato*.[1] The history of ideas consists all too often in making authors say what they ought to have said, what they are thought to have said, or what we imagine anticipates some later theory or another. Serra's treatise, it is helpful to remind ourselves, was published in 1613. So it was probably written a few years before then. The two *Discorsi* of Marc'Antonio de Santis, against which Serra explicitly reacts, were written and presented in 1605 and 1606.[2] The time lapse between their interventions, of more than six years, raises the question of what the real purpose of Serra's *Breve trattato* actually was.

Serra's text is, indeed, a work of economic analysis, but it is also one of economic policy.[3] This fact obliges us to focus on the political and institutional conditions in the Kingdom of Naples in the period. The main actors at the time were, on the monetary and financial level, the Genoese who controlled Catholic international finance, the viceroy who represented the authorities in Madrid, and the merchants and traders of Naples. Nor should we forget, in the background, the Church and the Papal States, the Republic of Venice, the aristocracy of the Kingdom of Naples, and finally the mass of poor Neapolitan peasants and the relatively limited artisan class in the country.

Between the 13th and 16th centuries, Italy was the battlefield on which the hegemonic ambitions of France and Spain ceaselessly clashed. This was a period also dominated by antagonism between the Christian states (including Venice, Naples, Rome, and Malta) under Spain's banner and expansionist Ottoman Islam. Italy, fragmented into multiple republics and despotic states, fell under the influence of Spain. Upheavals, insecurity, and the plague – still capable of virulence nearly three centuries after the first outbreak – which struck in Venice (1575–1577), Lyon (1628), Nijmegen (1635), and London (1665), caused cascades of currency revaluations. And, as in every period of crisis, hoarding was also accentuated at the time. All of this reduced the velocity of the circulation of money and contributed to a "currency shortage" to which many states fell victim and which served as the immediate context for the debate between de Santis and Serra.

2 The Republic of Genoa[4]

The history of the Genoese Republic is one of a community of adventurers and merchants who, at the beginning of the 12th century, created a chain of trading posts along the Mediterranean's main commercial routes. In the 16th century, 60,000 of the Republic of Genoa's 390,000 inhabitants lived in Genoa itself. Genoese sailors, traders, and bankers embodied a spirit of entrepreneurship and displayed exceptional business management skills.[5] The main business region for the Genoese was Europe, and especially Italy, where, with the support of Spain, they controlled the financial market for nearly 70 years (1557–1627), granting short-term credit to the Spanish monarchy, buying the right to levy taxes, and settling international payments at the Bisenzone (named for its former locale in Besançon) trade fair in Piacenza.[6]

Remarkably, Genoa was able, in spite of a weak government that was threatened by constant internal political conflicts, to maintain some economic stability and incredible financial strength. State creditors concentrated within the city's Bank of Saint George nonetheless implemented a short-sighted foreign policy in terms of the management of the republic's debt and taxes.[7] In this way, they brought all of Corsica and Sardinia to ruin.

The financial dominance exerted by the Genoese made them referees for payments in Europe, handling matters of capital and credit.[8] They succeeded in controlling the export of Sicilian grain at the source and organizing the production of sugar and silk in Sicily. Genoa was able to dominate these markets because of the superiority of its ships (with Genoese galleys exceeding 1000 tons), the business acumen of its merchants, and its strategic investments. Its control of international financial markets allowed it to finance Spain's national debt.

The wealth of early modern Genoa was neither gold nor silver but its ability to raise credit all over Europe and thereby *attract* the world's gold and silver. Genovese trading related "to white metal, yellow metal and bills of exchange".[9] The powerful system of fairs allowed capital from Italian and Spanish cities to flow towards Genoa, against only minimal compensation. Genoa's control over international finance was to last for a little more than 70 years. Genoese, Florentine, and Tuscan merchant bankers did not, for the most part, engage in speculative investments, preferring to lend against future tax revenues, acquire concessions of state monopolies, and supply armies.[10]

The power of the bankers was such that, when the king of Spain decided to do without their services and denounced all their contracts (*asientas*), they succeeded in stopping the flow of gold into the country. Unpaid Spanish troops rebelled, and this resulted in the looting of Antwerp in November 1576. Ultimately, the king had to yield. For Braudel, the aristocratic republic of Genoa (1528–1797), born under Spanish protection, incarnated the spirit of capitalism better than any other.

3 The Republic of Venice

The Most Serene Republic of Venice, or *La Serenissima*, was the most formidable Italian state and the only one to stand as a major power in the 15th century. Venice's might was due to its geographical position, its fleet, its control of maritime trade routes, its insurance skills, and a financial and commercial network that stretched all over Europe. During the 16th century, in spite of the external threat represented by the Turks, and even though maritime trade had become more risky and thus less profitable, industrial production expanded – in wool, glassmaking, leather, mirrors, and cabinetwork – and the agricultural progress was significant.

With 168,500 inhabitants in 1563, and because of its unique political constitution, Venice was a state particularly open to international currents, hosting trading communities of German, Greek, Albanian, and Jewish merchants. Money handling was an important source of revenue for the *Serenissima*, but its merchants also controlled major flows of goods, salt in particular, along Mediterranean trade routes. From 1314 on, Venice had been building galleys *da mercado*, trading ships capable of transporting the equivalent of a fifty-car freight train. At the end of the 16th century, the Venetian mint was coining nearly two million ducats every year, suggesting an enormous and continuous monetary flow of perhaps forty million through Venice.[11]

4 Papal States and the Church

The Papal States were closely bound up with the Kingdom of Naples, geographically, politically, and religiously. The power of the Papal States relates to the important historical role played by the Catholic Church throughout Europe. Beginning in the 10th century, it was ecclesiastical institutions (abbey, convents, bishoprics, etc.) that developed an almost completely monetized taxation system, which led to the great pontifical system that would cover all of Christian Europe and would tax all incomes, small and large.[12] Revenues from convents, parishes, and bishoprics and from the Church's immense landed property all over Europe, not to mention from tithes and alms, flowed into the Papal States. In addition to alms, which represented considerable revenue, Church property benefitted from tax immunity everywhere. A significant portion of the rents in the Kingdom of Naples, in the hands of the clergy, went to the Papal States. Of course, the Church was at the same time responsible for the needs of the poor and the sick and for providing religious services, and these expenditures required considerable monetary resources.

When discussing the taxes collected by the pope, distinction must be made between taxation based on temporal incomes and taxation based on spiritual incomes, like alms – the latter being the more important. The sums transferred were ensured as credit transactions by Florentine, Sienese, and Pisan bankers. When revenues were insufficient to pay the papal tax, religious institutions gave away a share of their income, or the value of their landed property, to these traders and bankers. Inside the states of the Church, the levying of taxes relied on direct taxation and on indirect taxes on the consumption, trade, and management of the public domain. The pontifical tax system was the most efficient and most extensive, and it boosted the trend towards monetizing the European economy.

5 The Kingdom of Naples[13]

After the Treaty of Cateau-Cambrésis in 1559, the whole history of the Kingdom of Naples was marked by imperial domination exerted by military control, the Inquisition, and the Counter Reformation.[14] Spain's sphere of influence, with borders that essentially did not vary until 1713, extended into Italy. The representative of the occupying power was the viceroy. He represented the king of Spain and exerted administrative, legal, economic, and military powers. Although enjoying great power in theory, his exercise of it was closely supervised by Madrid and limited by the local authorities under his administration. The problem facing the two viceroys, those of Naples and Sicily, was to bring the most silver (*donativo*) and men-at-arms possible to Madrid without confronting any more than necessary an idle aristocracy that feared for its own income. The peasants were reduced to utter misery by the government and their feudal lords. The middle class was reduced to legal professionals, large-scale exporters, and bankers living off the government debt. The Church, immensely rich, and the Inquisition nonetheless continued to enjoy exorbitant privileges. Generally, the era of Spanish domination under the viceroys, from 1415 to 1713 in Sicily and from 1504 to 1713 in Naples, was one of decline.

Two thirds of the inhabitants of the Kingdom of Naples were living on feudal lands. The clergy owned nearly one third of the land, half of which was uncultivated. The country lacked roads, and the inhabitants were subjected to hundreds of customs and tolls. Armed robbery was a general concern. The middle class of lawyers (the Kingdom had some 26,000 *dottori*) was not very productive. It would be impossible to quantify with any precision the gigantic size of the Neapolitan bureaucracy since the majority of public offices were sold or conceded to private persons. The financial impact of these privileges relating to finance, customs, and supply was very heavy. With its system of rents, the state was giving away most of its income to financiers or to the Church in order to cover its debts.[15] This system provided the state treasury with an advance on specific future tax revenues, less a certain percentage, in exchange for the right to collect that tax for some period of time.

Budgetary flexibility for the common person was sharply limited in this period. Food costs absorbed the greatest part of their expenditures, and there remained little afterwards for the purchase of durable and semi-durable commodities. The purchase of silk and colonial products played a marginal role at best for most people. It was only the affluent elite that benefitted from them.[16] In years when crops were plentiful, the caloric intake of an adult man was around 3,200 calories, mostly from cereals and a little meat. Much more so than today, the standard of living in Asia and the West was similar. At lower levels, life was beset by disproportionate taxation, the greed of landowners, debt, and the property loss for peasants, the lattermost of whom, as in Calabria and elsewhere, suffered from the double scourge of debts and land rents.[17]

The system of customs administration eliminated, with variable duties, any competition for products coming from the provinces. Smuggling represented a quasi-official and unchecked activity against which armed forces were seldom deployed. Smugglers were protected by the right of asylum in holy places, and the clergy took part in smuggling operations to their own benefit. The Kingdom's foreign trade consisted largely of manufactured imports and raw material exports.

The corporate structures of the craft industry prevented harmful social tensions while also curbing the emergence of a strong entrepreneurial class. The solidarity and mutual aid that characterized the guilds sufficed to justify their continued existence. They often had a common fund called a *Monte*, to which members contributed, that would be distributed according to very precise hierarchical rules.[18] In this way, the contributing members ensured the protection of themselves and their families from the costs of illness, death, imprisonment, and abduction by Arab pirates. The monopolization of the Kingdom's sources of wealth by foreigners – Aragonese, Venetian, Florentine, and Genoese – furthermore prevented the growth of a substantial middle class.

6 The Neapolitan economy in an international context[19]

Grain, oil, and especially silk, which the Kingdom of Naples produced in large quantities, were its prevalent agricultural products. Important manufactures included wool, silk, linseed, leather, and paper. Manufacturing was conducted in the small and large towns of the Kingdom, in Calabria and Campania. Even rural areas could be very productive in this area, as in Abruzzi with wool, silk, and linseed. They generally produced for regional and local markets or, as in the case of silk, for the other provinces of the Kingdom. Imported products included finely woven fabrics and wool, along with spices: pepper, cloves, and others. Sugar was imported from Sicily, Venice, Crete, and Zaragoza because of the lack of qualified personnel to refine it on site in the Kingdom. Paper came from Genoa and glass from Venice. Most of the trade and manufactures were under the control of foreigners (the Genoese especially). This was also true of financial transactions. Foreigners had acquired most the real estate in the major cities, tax farming, and credits in the Kingdom's government debt. They controlled the grain and silk trades, which, anyway, were closely connected with finance. They were enriched by manufactures, but it was the spectacular growth of government debt and their interests in it that allowed them to chalk up enormous profits. And Madrid's insatiable demand for funds enabled them to offer a wide range of financial services.

Synergies developed between their financial and the commercial transactions, enabling them to acquire financial privileges and to influence the administrative structures of the state. Foreigners, and the Genovese in particular, acted as agents for the levying of taxes, as ship owners and as suppliers for stock breeding. They invested the profits from trade, manufacturers, and monetary speculation in government bonds; in 1598 the Genovese held 20% of all of these bonds. Convents and abbeys invested much of their income in the acquisition of Neapolitan municipal revenue sources. Madrid's military expenditures after 1550 resulted in a heavier tax burden and increased debt for the financing of the huge deficit of the Spanish monarchy's treasury. Generally speaking, levied sums could never be used as productive capital for investment. In this context, the exchange rate between Naples and other financial centres was a crucial variable of analysis. This exchange rate, established on the basis of the supply and demand of domestic currencies and bills of exchange, was the product of three criteria: the level of legal parity; the market price of gold and silver coins; and supply and demand in the foreign exchange market.[20]

The money specified in bills of exchange was always money of an "imaginary" account. All payments consisted in converting the prices expressed in the money of the imaginary account into real money. The foreign exchange market was highly organized, with very few operators. The "*Bisenzone*" fair held in Piacenza every three months determined the "account" under the oversight of the senate of Genoa, the list prices of the Piacenza scudo with the major financial centres in Europe, and were valid for all contracts for three months. These markets for bills of exchange were not always liquid. The merchant bankers were very active and essentially practised "exchange through art", which will be explained below.

Let us imagine that the merchant Cavalli bought a bill of exchange because he had to pay a foreign supplier or because he hoped to make a profit when the corresponding vendor reimbursed him with credit under one of two possible forms: as a bill of exchange for Naples or by sending metal money and the authorization to borrow in Naples by making a bill of exchange on the vendor in Naples. In Naples, the form of payment most used was a credit issued by the banks, namely the "*fede di credito*", as it was called. These notes were exchangeable in coins with the holder upon presentation. They enjoyed a high level of confidence and circulated like currency. The government accorded legal value to these notes for transactions between citizens and the government, as well as among citizens. For nearly two centuries, from 1550 to 1794, these credit notes (which had an expiration date registered in the books of the banks on issuance and on liquidation when presented) circulated and mitigated the lack of cash, even for very small sums. They represented the major part of the means of payment in circulation.[21]

"An operation of exchange *per arte*" (fictitious exchange) was considered effective when Cavalli came into possession of the anticipated amount, possibly with a premium. The premium for the purchaser of a bill of exchange for "exchange *per arte*" was based on the difference between the exchange rate set at the time of contract and the exchange rate prevailing abroad at the time of the "return".

It was taken for granted that the Kingdom of Naples listed "uncertain" price quotations and that more important financial centres abroad listed "certain" volume quotations. In general, for the country which quoted price, the currency of the country that quoted volume was systematically more unfavourable. With certain volume quotation, the exchange rate was quoted in foreign currency on the basis of a fixed unit in local currency. One unit of local currency = x foreign currency units. With uncertain price quotation, the exchange rate varied in local currency as compared to a constant amount in foreign currency. One unit of foreign currency units = y local currency units. The bill of exchange – a form of payment that involved two dealers in one country and their respective correspondents in another country – was then the preferred form of international trade, and the "Bisenzone" fair was the international financial centre for all assets and liabilities for an annual amount of around sixteen million ducats, without a single coin circulating.[22]

7 The controversy

In Italy, between the years 1603 and 1613, a controversy erupted that pitted Antonio Serra against Marc'Antonio de Santis. Antonio Serra's work, the *Breve trattato delle cause che possono far abbondare li regni d'oro e d'argento dove non sono miniere*, is a response to de Santis's *Discorso intorno alli effetti che fa il cambio in Regno*. These two texts show a remarkable understanding of the exchange-rate mechanism and of the effects of general economic conditions on foreign trade and money supply. In this controversy, the major questions of international payments all coalesced: the structure of the trade balance, speculation on exchange rates, long- and short-term capital flows, and the terms of international payments. The controversy may thus to be set in the context of the time marked by a chronic shortage of trading currency and by the belief that an abundance of money was an indirect sign of the health of the economy. There were five main disadvantages that resulted from a shortage of specie:

(1) The mint, whose activity involved consolidating foreign currencies for transformation into Neapolitan currencies, had very little demand, resulting in a loss of activity and seigniorage.
(2) Public banks in the Kingdom no longer received cash deposits. The reserves were reduced because of the risk that this implied for stability and for the trust of a public relying on paper money.
(3) The amount of money circulating in the Kingdom could not meet the fixed need for cash payments. This was a major impediment to economic activity and to contracts.
(4) In particular, the government was deprived of metal resources to deal with demands from Madrid, which continued to grow in urgency.
(5) Taxes were paid in either forged or paper money.

It should be noted that, between the 14th and 18th centuries, when authors spoke of "trade balance", under that umbrella they included not only what we understand by the term balance of trade but also elements of the balance of payments, in particular short-term movements of capital. The "trade balance" of two nations was the balance resulting from the payment of their mutual debts. If they were not equal, the surplus, which is what the authors of the time called trade balance, was to be paid in cash. When discussing this issue, authors in this period implicitly inferred payment balances from trade balances. They would know if the overall trade balance of a country was positive by comparing its exchanges with all other states during a given period. Any excess of debt between two nations would have to be settled in metal or through bills of a third nation.

The authors of this era, characterized as "mercantilist" by historiography, considered a positive trade balance desirable because it was usually accompanied by an influx of gold and silver. Their goals in trade policy were warranted by a very narrow domestic money market and by constant need of financing, which required liquidity in gold and silver, but it is wrong simply to infer from this that these authors were theorists of protectionism. Earlier discussions allowed theoretical advances in this period regarding the identification of the factors that determine the exchange rate of national money. Discussions of the relationship between exchange rate and trade balance, which showed the futility of banning the export of money, opened the way to inquiries into other related factors. All the arguments developed by Serra and de Santis attest to an understanding of the relationship between the balance of payments and the exchange rate, between the behaviour of agents at the microeconomic level and macroeconomic consequences. We will first present the theses of the two authors, starting with de Santis and then moving on to Serra. We will then return to the issue of the exchange rate, which is at the centre of the debate between the two authors. This will lead us to examine in detail the terms of international payments at the time.

The validity of the theses remains untested by figures from the time. Moreover, there are a number of underlying theoretical problems in this debate, such as the monetary character of bills of exchange. Serra considered bills of exchange solely as an instrument of credit while de Santis considered them an instrument of payments. Bills of exchange only allowed payment by compensation or settlement at maturity and not by simple circulation. It appears that considering exchange in isolation would be detrimental to the position taken up by de Santis. But, in fact, monetary units of exchange were no more independent of metal than were the local units of account.[23] Monetary units and their exchange rates, traders knew well, were affected by the external constraint, more or less direct, of the metal on which these units were based.

In such a system, merchant bankers are constrained; their monetary power was an expression of politics, of their influence on the decisions of princes. The private coinage of merchant bankers, through the issuance of bills of exchange, simply allowed for greater liquidity of credit and the conversion of assets denominated in foreign currencies into assets denominated in local ones. There was a direct link between the enrichment of merchant bankers and the seigniorage of coins, and this link built up in the evaluation process of the bills of exchange. But it is also true that the existence of bills of exchange virtually eliminated the use of cash in international trade in Europe, keeping it in reserve for internal trade. It is important to bear in mind that the writings of the time are not helpful in clarifying exactly what exchange entails. Many of them designate as exchange any banking or credit transaction that converts one sum of money into another, whether the difference is due to time, space, or the physical form of the instruments being used.

The issues that will be discussed emerge very clearly from Serra's work. Should we classify Serra as a mercantilist or as a proponent of the free market? Was the debate about issues of pure theory or economic policy? Given the assumptions underlying their texts, is it possible to reassess the two authors' contributions to understanding the relationship between the real sphere and the monetary sphere, between the short and long term? What was the historical situation in the Kingdom of Naples when the two texts were written, and how faithfully did their arguments reflect this? Is it possible to reconstruct the analytical apparatus employed by the authors in the debate? How can we judge their opposing arguments?

8 Marc'Antonio de Santis[24]

We know little about Marc'Antonio de Santis other than the fact that he was a very active businessman between the late 16th century and early 17th century. His writings of 1605 gave him an unofficial position in the viceroy's palace. This appears to be confirmed by the fact that on 10 March 1610, the *Collaterale* referred to de Santis as a Neapolitan representative in an international committee charged with analysing the financial issues of the Kingdom. A law of June 1607, which would be revoked just a few months after its implementation, was inspired by his views. The importance of the office held by de Santis is underlined by the fact that the first *Discorso* was delivered orally before being printed by order of the president of the *Sacro Consiglio* in order for it to be reviewed by the highest Spanish authorities and the most important traders who operated in Naples.

His whole argument revolved around the problem of exchange rates. He writes: "In our Kingdom the price of exchange with the other financial centres in Italy, and of these financial centres with the Kingdom, is the reason that cash does not enter our kingdom, and that cash which exists in the Kingdom goes out".[25] De Santis developed his analysis of the scarcity of cash after presenting a relatively positive description of the economic situation of the Kingdom of Naples, which should lead to an abundance of gold and silver. Instead, however, a cash shortage had reigned for fifteen years. To explain this discrepancy between the Kingdom's natural conditions and the scarcity of money, de Santis maintained the following:

(1) The volume of exports of the Kingdom was very high, to the extent that the Kingdom of Naples was the richest in the world for the production of silk, wine, oil, wheat, cattle, and many other things.
(2) Neapolitan exports were essential goods for which demand was inelastic because other countries could not do without Neapolitan products.

(3) Imported goods were mostly luxury goods, subject to changes in price and taste. Their demand was, as such, elastic depending on price levels.
(4) Naples had a hugely positive balance of trade, which should have resulted in a large influx of gold and silver. But this was not the case, and a shortage of money reigned.

De Santis concludes from the foregoing that Naples' shortage of money was a result of problems with the exchange rate rather than with the real economy of the Kingdom. In his demonstration of this, de Santis focuses on the existence of two forms of payment, bills of exchange and coinage, and the temporary and monetary factors acting on them to cause the cash shortage. The proposed remedy was to set a legal exchange rate for foreign currencies in order to reverse the market-driven actions of agents. There were, nonetheless, some obstacles that stood in the way of implementing this reform. These were the difference between the country's legal tender and its market value, on the one hand, and the difference between the country's legal tender and that of neighbouring countries, or those countries with which intense trade relations were maintained, on the other.

It should be noted that, in the short term, bills of exchange worked as a means of payment and could be endorsed as many times as one wished even if they were inherently credits. The proximity of the Papal States resulted in a flux of revenue towards the Kingdom of Naples and a return to the Papal States by exchange with a 10% profit for the operators; the same was true with regard to Genoa. For de Santis, this was the main reason for the economic difficulties of the Neapolitan Kingdom:

> The Kingdom is almost totally deprived of money as a result of three main causes. The first being that purchases of goods (exports) that are produced are not paid in cash. Second, that those who bring goods (imports) for sale withdraw price in cash. Third is the profit that is removed by bringing the money of the Kingdom of Rome or elsewhere in Italy and which they get back through exchange. In my opinion, these are the causes that lead to the lack of cash in our kingdom, and the causes come from a disorder in the exchange that the Kingdom today engages in with other financial centers in Italy and vice versa, as I have clearly demonstrated.[26]

Exports were mainly paid for with bills of exchange and with outflows of metal specie from the Kingdom. To this, de Santis added the speculation led by the merchant bankers who transported the Kingdom's metal specie and made returns through exchange, thus gaining the difference between the scudo of Piacenza and the legal tender in Naples.[27]

For de Santis, the market exchange market rate did not reflect conditions in the real economy. All his efforts were therefore aimed at establishing a legal tender. He believed it was possible, by opposing the anarchy of the marketplace and through informed action, to do so and to set it at a level that would benefit the Kingdom. He considered the market rate less an expression of the free economic forces than the result of speculative action by private operators and the monetary policies of neighbouring countries, the Genoese in particular. To remedy the situation in the Kingdom, he proposed imposing an exchange rate of 125 grains per coin instead of 130 by law. The ducat, in other words, had to be exchanged at a lower effective scudo rate of gold.

The aim was to reverse the flow of metal between the Kingdom and other financial centres. De Santis was quick to clarify that these measures were not intended to force a change on all the financial centres in Italy but simply to protect the Kingdom. The poverty and economic weakness of the Kingdom were primarily due to inadequate financial structures. De Santis pointed out that the financial centre of Naples was subject to that of Piacenza and the latter to the Genoese, who dictated the terms of exchange. The shortage of money, which was a widespread phenomenon in Italy, brought de Santis to reflect on terms and conditions that went beyond the issue of exchange and which led him to judge the situation of the Kingdom of Naples in terms of market exchange as abnormal. Behind the argument itself, there was a political question that related to the Genoese, who held almost 70% of the public debt of the Kingdom but no longer re-invested the incomes they received from these investments locally as they had previously done.

De Santis's solution was simple. It consisted of imposing a revalued exchange rate by passing a law (decree):

> Whether we issue a decree which makes the otherwise serious convictions, no merchant in the Kingdom can change, or demand, or pay the scudo of exchange of Rome and Piacenza more than 125 grains, that of Florence over 115, and that of Venice, and Milan over 98 grains, notwithstanding the fact that in bills of exchange that come from these and other financial centers in Italy, the price of the crown and the ducat is higher, and that we should make the same observation in all financial centers and in all fairs of the Kingdom. That nobody can change during the fair of Lyon, as is the case for many

> years, or that one can change to other financial centers where, since the establishment of the decree, a change hasn't taken place. And that one cannot demand nor pay bills of exchange in the Kingdom, whatever they may be, so-called financial centers of Italy.[28]

All the points raised by de Santis converge in the same direction: to end the financial subordination of Naples vis-à-vis foreigners and especially the Genoese, who exported the profits they made locally by way of the exchange rate. Beyond his technical arguments regarding exchange rates, this is the essential merit of de Santis's work. On the approach developed by de Santis, we can say in conclusion that for him the shortage of specie in the Kingdom of Naples had an exclusively monetary cause. In the causal relationships that he set up between exchange rates, international flows of precious metals, and the balance of payments, the real factors, the productive structure of the Kingdom of Naples and that resulting from the trade balance, played no role. Indeed, we shall soon see how Antonio Serra demonstrated that de Santis's analysis, and even more so the reform he proposed, were both wrong, even though they had the merit of emphasizing the role of exchange rates in international commercial transactions as well as in capital flows, which Serra in turn neglected.

De Santis's point of view was, as such, only short term, monetary, and microeconomic. The crucial point where de Santis stumbled was when he took into account only the trade balance and the speculation on bills of exchange. This point led him to wrongly conclude that the Kingdom's international balance of trade was largely positive, unlike Serra, who would take into account short- and medium-term capital movements, particularly related to the public debt held by the Genoese, to arrive at a clear deficit in the balance of payments. On the other hand, Serra's argument about the mechanism of the exchange market described by de Santis was not very convincing, as it completely ignored the effect of the exchange rate on the balance of payments and, in particular, on the trade balance.

9 The anonymous Genoese

In July 1605, an intervention in the debate, attributed to a Genoese gentleman, was published in Naples. Its argument was simple: the exchange rate reflected a voluntary agreement between parties and not the law. The anonymous Genoese sided with de Santis while establishing a link between the shortage of specie and high rates of exchange, but he affirmed that the decree requested by de Santis would lead only to a reduction in foreign exchange transactions. The Genoese author then advanced another cause of the problems that related to the monetary system in Naples. "*Everything is done at the bank, in writing without money.... And with the convenience of paying, one does not feel the lack of money that exists*".[29] The anonymous Genoese suggested that all existing money be recoined without openly saying that this was being done and that its weight and real value be reduced so as to solve the problem of the money shortage and thus facilitate the financing of the state. In order to keep the income paid to the credit holders of the Kingdom within it, a "low exchange rate" would have to be imposed and debased money would have to be strictly controlled to prevent it from leaving the Kingdom, according to the Genoese.

The Genoese identified several factors to explain the situation in the Kingdom of Naples. First, he observed the deficit of the balance of payments, particularly with reference to the repatriation of profits by foreign investors like the Genoese who did not find opportunities for reinvestment of profits in Naples. Second, he blamed the resultant deterioration in the Neapolitan exchange rate vis-à-vis other financial centres and the concomitant outflow of metal coins in gold or silver.

This discussion on the financial situation of Naples spearheaded by de Santis and the anonymous Genoese was cut short by the disastrous harvest of 1606, the worst of the past (at that time) forty years. Viceroy Benavente's reform programme, which planned a large reduction of the public debt held by foreigners, was never implemented; instead, the authorities followed the above advice. First with a decree of June 1607, which fixed and lowered the exchange rate as suggested by de Santis, and then by another one later that month that followed the proposals of the anonymous Genoese and organized an overhaul of the country's entire money supply, which had to be taken to the mint to be exchanged and recoined, with the exception of very low value coins like the half carlini (the Zanette) and the "tre cinquine". All other money, reduced to a quarter of its value, was exchanged by weight. That said, good money continued to circulate at its superficial value in weight. Only with the Count of Lemos's famous decree of 15 October 1612 was a comprehensive reform of the state's political economy attempted.

10 Antonio Serra[30]

Though Serra's treatise was a truly unique work, we know very little of its author's fate or background. Yet, the book's dedication to the Count of Lemos, viceroy of the Kingdom of Naples, suggests the two might have shared similar views on the necessity and nature of economic reforms. Struck by the plight of the Kingdom of Naples, Serra investigated the reasons for the wealth of Venice and Florence, formulating an economic theory from these comparisons. The Kingdom's situation with regard to international trade, characterized by the importation of manufactures and the export of commodities, was typical of what still can be observed in underdeveloped countries. He found the explanations for the outflow of gold and the negative trade balance in the conditions of the real economy of the country rather than in the realm of finance. In essence, the entire treatise focuses on real factors: natural resources, the nature of the population, the development of industry and commerce and the efficiency of the administration.

During his engagement with de Santis's work, Serra developed an analysis of the general conditions of economic growth, foreign trade, balance of payments, and money supply. His analysis led him far beyond the topics discussed by the other authors of the time to the organization of the monetary system and the stability of international commercial relations; his approach is not that of a merchant or of the master of the mint. The structure of Serra's work is simple:

(1) Conditions for growth designated by the term *accidenti propri*;
(2) the different economic policies a government might adopt;
(3) a comparison of the actual conditions of economic growth in Venice and Genoa compared to the Kingdom of Naples, with a focus on questions of space and human capital, which are designated *accidenti comuni*;
(4) The inability to control the ebb and flow of money by intervening in foreign exchange rates and de Santis's errors in this regard;
(5) then, having developed a sharp criticism of Marc'Antonio de Santis's theses, Serra develops his own approach – that is, the stabilization of the monetary and financial situation in the Kingdom can only be achieved by addressing root causes and not just symptoms;
(6) said root causes can be resolved only by developing domestic manufacturing and encouraging import substitution, but it is also necessary to promote the inflow of foreign capital by mandating the reinvestment of profits;
(7) finally, it would be necessary to reorganise the administration of the state.

The debate between de Santis and Serra focused first on the issue of the trade balance. According to de Santis, trade was booming, and the trade balance should therefore ensure the Kingdom of Naples an influx of gold and silver. Serra began by challenging the importance that de Santis invested in this balance. He also radically challenged de Santis's claim that demand for products from the Kingdom of Naples was inelastic and that the Kingdom could do without the products of other countries. The argument, then, seems to have revolved around the question of what policies might ensure an influx of money into the Kingdom. But by analysing the writings of the two authors, one can further show that their opposition was based on different assumptions about the relationship between the monetary sphere and the sphere of the real economy, and between a short-term perspective and a long-term one.

For Antonio Serra, the scarcity of money was but a symptom of a much greater evil, the structural situation of the economy of the Kingdom. Beyond the apparent causes on which de Santis focused, Serra identified the natural and artificial causes that explained the situation of the Kingdom. He first mentioned the quality of people (i.e. their more or less industrious qualities), noting their positive aspects while highlighting their widespread passivity and lethargy, arguing that human capital had no value without the spirit of initiation and entrepreneurship.

To this is added the low volume of foreign trade, since Naples did not serve as a transit point for any country in international trade, the poor state of national manufactures (often in the hands of the Genoese), and last but not the least the policy of those who governed (*la provisione di chi governa*). This, of course, was more than just a simple reason like the others for Serra, who considered it *"an active cause that drives the others, which causes them, and retains them; it is also one that establishes the entire order, without which nothing in the world can be established"*.

Serra considered cyclical factors (mainly monetary) to be completely incapable of explaining the crisis in the balance of payments. Indeed, his emphasis on finding explanations in long-term structural factors and more generally the real economy set him apart from other authors of the time. From this point of view, Serra's analysis had little to do with mercantilism as it is often understood. But to fully back up his theses, he dedicated an entire section of his book to showing that de Santis's argument was based on wrong assumptions and on an incorrect analysis of the effects of exchanges on the balance of payments. He therefore did not deny that the crisis in the payment system, made manifest by the scarcity of specie, had to be fought – but he was certain that it could not simply be explained by the factors put forth by de Santis.

Serra's analysis focused on the relationship between flows of precious metals, the exchange rate, and a review of the balance of payments. For him, and contrary to de Santis, the balance of payments (both authors use the expression trade balance) of the Kingdom of Naples ran a deficit because "it is true that there are no other inputs, and if money actually does come in; since the inputs are an amount other than the said sum, rents and incomes of foreign manufactures, together with products from outside far exceed the actual quantity, and it follows that de Santis's opinion is false".

Assuming a starting point for de Santis at which the balance of trade (for us, goods and services) was largely positive, Serra showed that he omitted all the other components of the balance of payments, including the interest and amortization of the public debt held by the Genoese, and the repatriation of profits by the Genoese who had factories in the Kingdom. He also noted that Venice's surplus was not found in its external monetary position because sequins (zecchini) were commodity money whose value was higher in the Turkish Empire than at home and were therefore exported on a large scale. The international distribution of precious metal stocks thus varied according to the possible speculation on gold-silver ratios in different countries.

11 Conclusions

Whether we consider Serra's or de Santis's analysis, there are missing elements in the causal chain that links the deficit in the Neapolitan balance of payments to an excessive demand for foreign exchange, the depreciation of the Neapolitan currency, and the increasing incentives to export specie from the Kingdom. De Santis established no link between the exchange rate and the balance of trade (by way of the balance of payments), and he then assumed that foreigners were forced to make exchanges at the mint's legal parity, resulting in a loss for them because they received less money (by weight and value) compared to when their contracts were made because of seigniorage. In Naples, however, it was possible, despite the ban, to find buyers for foreign currencies for a higher price than that allowed by the mint. He further ignored the possibility of adjusting the trade balance due to the variation of the exchange rate, assuming that a considerable surplus in the trade balance of nearly six million ducats was compatible with a permanent depreciation of the national currency. He similarly attributed the outflow of specie to the fact that the exchange rate was too high and considered that the high exchange rate had consequences such as imports being paid in cash and metal and exports in bills of exchange, and he considered that this absorbed any surplus in the trade balance. He unquestionably pointed out the gains at the microeconomic level that the merchants and bankers, who largely were Genoese, could achieve in this context.

Serra, on the other hand, denied that the exchange rate had any influence on the choices made by merchants and on whether payments were made with metal coins or bills of exchange. Having shown that the surplus in the trade balance failed to compensate for the deficit in what we today would call the financial account because of the repatriated revenues from Genoese investments in Naples, de Santis's thesis thus seemed unacceptable to him. He denied the means of payment any influence on the balance of payments, ignored the intermediation of the foreign exchange market, and ignored the fact that individual agents had a choice in their method of international payment. Finally, he completely ignored the role of speculation.

Of course, neither of the authors recognized anything like self-correcting mechanisms affecting exchange rates and trade balances, nor did they mention the consequences of Spanish taxation. De Santis considered the exchange rate to have an impact on the balance of payments without considering the fact that the latter in turn affects the former, and he completely neglected the macroeconomic and structural dimensions of the problem. For Serra, on the other hand, the balance of payments and the exchange rate had no mutual relationship at all. Legal parity became ineffective when merchants did not take into account the actual market price and the theoretical price set by the mint. Yet the actual parity deviated sharply from the legal parity with transition from an official bimetallic system to a monometallic system; the metal that no longer represents the effective unit of account disappears and becomes a mere commodity. As Serra put it,

> the deception consists in this: that the price of the gold scudo in Naples has changed and increased, and in the other places that I have mentioned it has remained almost always the same, nor has the scudo ever circulated in Naples as money, but only trade, and so it has increased in value, and the exchange that is made between the above-mentioned places and Naples is made from gold to silver and not from gold to gold or from silver to silver.[31]

As soon as the reference unit of account became silver in Naples and gold in Venice and Genoa, de Santis's comparison between the legal parities of the three countries ceased to be relevant.

Contemporaries of de Santis and Serra disagreed over whether to revalue or devalue their currencies. Those who defended devaluations proposed acting on the legal parity through two alternative means: by increasing the value of foreign specie by adding a premium to their metal value or by reducing the precious metal content of Neapolitan monetary units while increasing the seigniorage. Serra opposed these proposals because they involved the renunciation of seigniorage and meant accepting foreign currencies flowing into the Kingdom. As creditors, citizens of the Kingdom would be wronged because they would be paid in carlini, which had a lower metal content than those of their debtors. This would result in an effect opposite to that sought by de Santis. Neapolitans would be encouraged to spend Neapolitan money abroad in exchange for foreign specie and to bring other currencies to the Kingdom to exchange for local coins. It would create incentives to export even more specie from Naples. On the other hand, debasing the Neapolitan coinage would lead it to being kept within the Kingdom because its domestic purchasing power would now be greater than its external one.

De Santis was well aware of the effects of a revaluation on the trade balance. He was consistent to the extent that he assumed that the demand for Neapolitan goods was inelastic. In such a scenario, Naples would be able to set prices on exports while its imports were sensitive to price effects resulting from the revaluation. But in order to work, de Santis's measure assumed remarkable control over the foreign exchange market well beyond simply fixing the formal exchange rate. He had a rather naïve take on the situation, knowing that the foreign exchange market of Naples was controlled by a small number of Genoese merchant bankers. He thought that the threat of legal sanctions would suffice for the Kingdom of Naples to take control of foreign exchange markets. Nevertheless, we must always bear in mind that for de Santis and for Serra alike, the Genoese were enemies of the Kingdom of Naples: for de Santis, because they controlled the foreign exchange market and imposed an unfavourable exchange rate; for Serra, because they controlled the finances of the Kingdom, through their involvement with the public debt, and especially with exports. The monetary policy advocated by de Santis implied a major conflict with Genoa; and, without the support of the king of Spain and the viceroy under the influence of Genoese financiers, it was doomed to fail.

De Santis's proposal was, in effect, followed by the law of 1607, which set an official and reassessed exchange rate, and it was, unsurprisingly, a fiasco. We have no evidence to say whether or not it might ever have been possible to control the foreign exchange market at the time, but the Genoese control over all exports and a large part of the imports, as well as the public debt of the Kingdom of Naples, made it a hopeless proposition. This was what Serra reported in his analysis, while adding that even *if* the measures had been effectively implemented, they would have been ineffective. For him, the serious deficit in the balance of payments was the result of structural concerns that could not be overcome by monetary policy alone. Rather, Serra maintained that the monetary crisis ultimately had to be resolved through policies to encourage domestic manufacturing, import substitution, and the mandatory reinvestment of profits in the country, as well as above all by reorganizing the administration of the state.

Notes

1. Serra, A. *Breve trattato delle cause che possono far abbondare li regni d'oro et d'argento, dove non sono miniere, con applicazione al regno di Napoli; del Dr. Antonio Serra,... diviso in tre parti*, Naples: L. Scorriggio, 1613.
2. de Santis, M.A., "Discorso intorno alli effetti che fa il cambio in regno" (1605), in Colapietra, R. (ed.), *Problemi monetari negli scrittori napoletani del Seicento*, Rome: Accademia Nazionale dei Lincei, 1973, pp. 111–141, and "Secondo discorso intorno agli effetti che fa il cambio in regno. Sopra una risposta, che è stata fatta avverso del primo" (1605), in Colapietra (ed.), *Problemi monetari*, pp. 143–162.
3. See Serra, A., *Breve trattato sulle cause che possono far abbondare d'oro e d'argento i regni privi di miniere, con applicazione al regno di napoli diviso in tre parti*, Italian translation by G. Nicoletti, notes and commentary by O. Parise and A. Scarcello, Soveria Mannelli: Rubbettino Editore, 2015; and Serra, A., *A "Short Treatise" on the Wealth and Poverty of Nations* (1613), Reinert, S.A. (ed.), London: Anthem, 2011.
4. Kirk, T., "A Little Country in a World of Empires: Genoese Attempts to Penetrate the Maritime Trading Empires in the Seventeenth Century", *Journal of European Economic History*, 25, 1996, pp. 407–424.
5. Tracy, J. (ed.), *The Political Economy of Merchant Empires: State Power and World Trade*, 1350–1750, Cambridge: Cambridge University Press, 1990.
6. Mandich, G., *Le Pacte de Ricorsa et le marché Italien des changes au XVIIe siècle*, Paris: S.E.V.P.E.N,, 1953, pp. 54–62; and Martinez Ruiz, J.J., "The Credit Market and Profit from Letters of Exchange: Ricorsa Exchange Operations between Seville and The Besançon Fairs, 1589–1621", *Journal of European Economic History*, 33, 2004, pp. 331–358.
7. Grendi, E., "Counterfeit Coins and Monetary Exchange Structures in the Republic of Genoa during the Sixteenth and Seventeenth Centuries", in, Muir, E. & G. Ruggiero (eds), *History from Crime*, Baltimore: Johns Hopkins University Press, 1994, pp. 170–205.
8. Lovett, A., "The General Settlement of 1577: An Aspect of Spanish Finance in the Early Modern Period", *Historical Journal*, 25, 1982, pp. 1–22; De Maddalena, A. and H. Kellebenz, *La Repubblica internazionale del denaro tra XV e XVII secolo*, Bologna: Il Mulino, 1986.

9. Braudel, F., *Civilisation matérielle et capitalisme*, 3 vols, Paris: Armand Colin, Paris, 1979, vol. 3, p. 112.
10. Aymard, M., "La fragilità di un economia avanzata: l'Italia e le trasformaioni dell'economia europea", in Romano, R. (ed.), *Storia dell'economia Italiana,* vol. II, Turin: Einaudi, 1991, p. 77.
11. Braudel, F., *Civilisation matérielle et capitalisme*, 3 vols., Paris: Armand Colin, 1979, vol. 3, p. 100.
12. *Storia d'Italia, Annali* 6, Einaudi, Turin, 1983, pp. 530–540.
13. De Rosa, L., "Economic Crisis in the Kingdom of Naples in the Days of Philip II", *Journal of European Economic History*, 28, 1999, pp. 511–534.
14. de Ruble, A., *Le Traité de Cateau-Cambrésis (2 et 3 Avril 1559)*, Paris: Éditions Labitte & Émile-Paul, 1889; L. Romier, L., *Les origines politiques des guerres de Religion.* Vol. II: *La Fin de la magnificence extérieure, le roi contre les protestants (1555–1559)*, Paris: Perrin et Cie, 1913–1914.
15. "Arrendamenti" are tax collection rights given to private firms (tax farming) in exchange for an advance on the amount of the taxes to be collected, an amount that generally proved much lower than the amount ultimately recovered by the tax contractors.
16. Léon, P., *Histoire économique et sociale du monde*, vol. 2, *Les hésitations de la croissance 1580–1730*, Paris: A. Colin, 1978, p. 19.
17. Léon, *Histoire économique et sociale du monde*, p. 37.
18. A letter patent belonging to a corporation is much more than a simple degree or title due to the rights it confers not only on its owner but also to its beneficiary. In the second half of the 18th century, these institutions were to some extent hit by crisis precisely because of their helper function, which was the object of veritable speculation.
19. De Rosa, L., "The De-Industrialization of the Kingdom of Naples in the Sixteenth and Seventeenth Centuries", in Van der Wee, H. (ed.), *The Rise and Decline of Urban Industries in Italy and the Low Countries (Late Middle Ages – Early Modern Times)*, Leuven: Leuven University Press, 1988, pp. 121–138; Galasso, G., "Trends and Problems in Neapolitan History in the Age of Charles V", in Calabria, A. and J.M. Marino (eds), *Good Government in Spanish Naples*, New York: Peter Lang, 1990, pp. 13–78.
20. Rosselli, A., "Early Views on Monetary Policy: The Neapolitan Debate on the Theory of Exchange", *History of Political Economics*, 32, 2000, p. 61 and "Antonio Serra e la teoria dei cambi", in Roncaglia, A., (ed.), *Alle origini del pensiero economico in Italia*, vol. 1, *Moneta e sviluppo negli economisti napoletani dei secoli XVII–XVIII*, Bologna: Il Mulino, 1995, pp. 37–58
21. De Rosa, L., *I cambi esteri del Regno di Napoli dal 1591 al 1707*, Naples: Banco di Napoli, 1955, p. 3; Palmieri, N., *La fede di credito del Banco di Napoli*, Rome: Officina poligrafica italiana, 1905; Capobianco, R., "La fede di credito", in *Rassegna economica* 11, 1941; de Simone, L., *La fede di credito*, with a preface by A. Marghieri, Naples: Borrelli, 1922; Maroni, G., "La fede di credito", in *Enciclopedia giuridica*, Milan: Società editrice libraria, 1889. The most important work is Ajello, P., "I depositi, le fedi di credito e le polizze dei Banchi di Napoli", *Il Filangieri*, Year 7, part 1, 1882, 641–665, 713–755.
22. De Roover, R., *L'évolution de la lettre de change, XIVe-XVIIIe siècles*, Paris: A. Colin, 1953, p. 76; Goschen, *The Theory of the Foreign Exchanges*, London: E. Wilson, 1926, p. 2.

23. Fournial, E., *Histoire monétaire de l'Occident médiéval*, Paris: F. Nathan, 1970, p. 27.
24. See Casella, A., "de Santis, Marc'Antonio", in *Dizionario Biografico degli Italiani*, vol. 39 (1991).
25. de Santis, M.A., *Discorso intorno alli effetti che fa il cambio in regno*, Naples, 1605, pp. 2–4.
26. de Santis, *ibid.*
27. Avallone, P., *Stato e Banchi Publici a Napoli a Metà del 700*, Naples: Edizioni scientifiche italiane, 1995, pp. 12–18.
28. de Santis, *Discorso intorno alli effetti che fa il cambio*, pp. 2–4; see also Spufford, P., "Le rôle de la monnaie dans la révolution commerciale", in Day, J., *Études d'Histoire monétaire : XIIe-XIXe*, Lille: Presses Universitaires de Lille, 1985, pp. 378–380.
29. de Santis, M.A., *Secondo discorso intorno agli effetti che fa il cambio in regno. Sopra una risposta, che è stata fatta avverso del primo*, Naples, 1605.
30. Roncaglia, A., *The Wealth of Ideas: A History of Economic Thought*, Cambridge: Cambridge University Press, 2005, p. 48; Sumberg, T.A., "Antonio Serra: A Neglected Herald of the Acquisitive System", *American Journal of Economics and Sociology*, vol. 50, no. 3, 1991, pp. 365–373.
31. Serra, *"Short Treatise"*, p. 181.

10
Serra and Underdevelopment

Cosimo Perrotta

1 Underdevelopment in Serra and as a general concept

This paper is in some respects a continuation of a previous article,[1] in which we set out to demonstrate that Antonio Serra took a fully mercantilist approach; that – on examining the Kingdom of Naples – he was the first to investigate economic backwardness; and, finally, that he was also the first to analyse economic dependence (together with Luis Ortiz,[2] but more in depth). Here we mean to show that Serra's analysis is also useful to understand both the origin of Southern Italy's backwardness and some basic processes of underdevelopment in general.

Backwardness in Southern Italy (Serra's country) began four centuries before his publication. It is remarkable that the economic phenomena he analyses and those described by historians of the Middle Ages for this region are much the same. Even more striking is the fact that the same pre-modern situation – in its structural elements – lasted for another three and a half centuries after Serra's book, until the middle of the 20th century.[3] On the other hand, the basic processes that Serra describes are very similar to those which development economists addressed in the second half of the 20th century and which they labelled as underdevelopment.

To begin with, we should stress that underdevelopment is not a synonym for backwardness. While the development economists of the 1940s and 1950s used the two terms interchangeably, later on a conceptual distinction emerged. In general, an economy is considered backward when it is poor and has not yet been touched by industrialization, and this distinction is based mainly on traditional agriculture. In the 1960s and 1970s, economists began to use underdevelopment in the sense of an economy which – although still poor and little industrialized – is transformed by a relationship with a stronger, more developed economy. The two economies develop a dependence on each other, in which the stronger one reshapes the other to its own advantage. It is a spontaneous, although not necessary, process.[4]

Both concepts – backwardness and underdevelopment – are relative. The situations that they describe are definable only in comparison with developed economies, where steady growth is a normal trend and a shared value. The idea of backwardness first arose, although not as a theoretical category, among the mercantilists, notably including Starkey,[5] Ortiz,[6] and Serra,[7] as well as, later on, P.M. Doria,[8] Uztáriz,[9] and Ulloa.[10] In the period of the Enlightenment, Genovesi[11] and his pupils, above all Galanti,[12] proposed a more articulated version of the concept, taking an essentially historical perspective. List adopted a similar line, in contrast to the classical approach. This concept gradually took shape through the combined efforts of all these authors. They lamented the relative backwardness of their own country, taking other countries as positive examples and calling for a policy of modernization and industrialization.[13]

The idea of underdevelopment – although already adumbrated in some contexts – emerged as a category in the 1960s, but underdevelopment itself had come about very early. It began not long after economic development – that is, that process of steady growth in the production of wealth which started in Western Europe around the year 1000. When two economies of very different strength and advancement come into contact, the tendency towards diffusion of development is stymied by the opposite tendency towards polarization. The former tendency was best explained by Smith, who wrote that capital in mature economies yields ever less as it increases, with progressive saturation of the market. A part of capital then migrates towards new countries, which have yet to develop.[14] A similar view is implicit in many versions of the classical (Ricardian) law of comparative advantages and in general in the neoclassical approach, which tends to see underdevelopment as a consequence of the lack of free trade.

The tendency towards polarization has been illustrated by some of the most important development economists, such as Singer, Prebisch, Hirschman, Perroux, Furtado, and Balogh,[15] and it was best expressed in Myrdal's application of the cumulative process model to poor economies.[16] However, the idea was already present in Marx's concept of capitalist accumulation, which implies the centralization of capital and of wealth in general. Marx's followers maintained this approach.[17]

The cause of polarization is that factors of production (especially capital) tend to go where their remuneration is higher – that is, towards the more developed countries. In backward areas, there is often such poverty among economic factors that the cost of production is higher than in rich areas. The early development economists described this situation as the vicious circle of poverty, in which factors hinder one another, producing a general immobility. The vicious circle refers to skilled labour, technologies, efficiency in administration, effective demand for products, and so on.[18] In general the lack of supply also produces a lack of demand and vice versa.

Serra does not employ a concept like polarization, but his way of connecting the different factors of development or lack thereof recalls the idea. In his analysis, as in those of many development economists, it clearly appears that polarization is not only a spontaneous tendency but is often implemented or reinforced by human will. More often than not, it is difficult to separate the objective aspect from the efforts made by the agents of the stronger economy to turn economic processes to their advantage. On this aspect, it is important to read the pioneering article of Erik and Sophus Reinert, which uses Serra's categories to analyse today's literature about underdevelopment and dependence.[19]

However, polarization is not the only feature of underdevelopment. Equally important are the internal factors which block potential growth, converging in conservative defence of the existing social structure. Privileges, rents, and corporate interests are in general very strong in the weaker economies. People who have vested interests oppose the transformations produced by development because the latter would harm them.

Thus, we can say that underdevelopment derives from the combination of external and internal factors. Quite often, such a connection produces an alliance, covert or manifest, between outer and inner social groups, who aim to impede changes or manage them to their own advantage. This kind of process came under way as early as the 12th century in Southern Italy; in the 16th-17th century in Spain; in Ireland from the 17th century to 19th century; in post-colonial countries; in Eastern Europe, intermittently; and so on. And Southern Italy was most probably the first underdeveloped economy in history.

Serra does not, of course, distinguish between backwardness and underdevelopment. He starts by describing four factors ("accidents") that he holds necessary for the enrichment of a country – that is, for development (he expresses development in the mercantilist way, as an inflow of gold and silver – of monetary capital). The four factors are these: manufacturing activities, extensive trade, an enterprising attitude ("people's quality", as the original text says), and good government. The Kingdom of Naples, he repeats time and again, is poor because it lacks all of these factors. In the second half of the book, Serra associates this lack with the hold that foreign merchants had on the Kingdom's economy. Thus, he goes on from description of a backward situation to analysis of dependence.

In Section 2 we will examine the natural causes of Southern Italy's backwardness both in Serra's reflection and in reality. We will then show the convergence between Serra, later historians, and development economists on the internal causes of this standstill. First, we will examine the economic causes (Section 3), and then go on to the political and social ones (Section 4). The same convergence will clearly appear in Serra's treatment of the basic role that foreign merchants played in the origins of underdevelopment (Section 5) and in his projects for remedies to the standstill (Section 6).

2 Natural poverty of Southern Italy

The first "accident" (i.e. factor) that Serra mentions as an obstacle to the Kingdom of Naples' development is a natural one: the geographical position, which, he states, is worse than that of any other region. Unlike Venice, for instance, the Kingdom is far away from both central-northern Europe and Asia (p. 119),[20] and it is not a place of transit to go to other countries (p. 127).

Although Serra overrates this shortcoming, there can be no denying it. In the medieval period, given its peripheral position, Southern Italy not only found it difficult to trade with Europe but was also occupied time and again by new invaders. This created a situation of permanent disorder and instability, which stood in the way of a flourishing economy.[21]

In the Dark Ages, this region had maintained a strong connection with Byzantium and Byzantium's maritime trade, which, unlike western trade, never ceased.[22] This is why the first maritime republics in Italy were from the south (together with Venice). In the 9th century, Amalfi's trade was more important and extensive than that of Venice.[23] However, such trade was always confined to exchange between luxuries from the eastern Mediterranean countries and agricultural goods from Southern Italy. In contrast with the consequences it led to in the northern cities, this trade never gave rise to an increase in craft activities and growth in production.[24]

Another natural factor mentioned by Serra, "agricultural surplus", seems to contrast with the first. Following his adversary, Marc'Antonio de Santis, on this point,[25] Serra states that the Kingdom's agricultural products "exceed the amount required for the needs or comforts of the inhabitants" (pp. 119, 135) and that the accident of agricultural surplus in Naples "occurs to perfection" (p. 133). The paradox expressed by de Santis is that, despite the export of this huge surplus, the Kingdom lacks money.

Here Serra confuses the surplus relative to the population's needs with the surplus that goes to the great landowners. The latter did exist in Naples, while the former did not. In fact, Southern Italy has always been somewhat thinly populated, and up to the mid 20th century the peasants and labourers there had always gone hungry.

Serra is to some extent conditioned by the time-honoured myth of the prosperous and generous nature of Southern Italy. This myth, which de Santis clung to, was created by the first southern dynasties and demolished as late as 1904 by Giustino Fortunato.[26] In any case, Serra takes for granted de Santis's paradox: why is there such scarcity of money in the Kingdom despite such a large volume of exports?

De Santis – as is well known – saw the cause of this situation in the excessively low exchange value of the Kingdom's currency, thanks to which foreigners importing goods from the Kingdom could speculate on the difference in value between currencies. Serra, however, came up with a challenging answer. He shifted the question from the familiar monetary level to a new level: the economy as a whole.

All the historians whose judgement has not been marred by the anti-mercantilist bias have greatly appreciated Serra's view of the problem,[27] which had a wider scope and went deeper than de Santis's. However, Zagari and Rosselli rightly note that, as far as the short run is concerned, de Santis's empirical analysis is not totally unfounded.[28]

Before examining Serra's answer, we have to stress that de Santis's supposed paradox did not exist. The land of Southern Italy was in general far from fertile, consisting mainly of mountains, with extensive Karst or clayey soil, poor in water, with torrent-like rivers.[29] Since the Dark Ages, the nature of the territory had favoured the persistence of the long-established latifundia (large estates), concentrating the surplus in the hands of the big landowners,[30] hindering the formation of cities in the internal areas and rendering transport and communications extremely difficult.

With political and military unrest coming on top of all this, artisanal activities and the consequent export of manufactured commodities hardly stood much chance of growing. Thus, the export of agricultural goods alone could hardly match the import of manufactured goods that the Kingdom needed.

Note that the situation was just the opposite in Northern Italy. There, exceptionally fertile land rich in rivers favoured the breakup of ancient latifundia, to the advantage of communities in the internal areas. This breakup allowed cities to control – and increase – their agricultural surplus, which in turn extended artisanal activities and developed trade, thanks also to easy river transport.[31] Serra overlooks the scant fertility of the Kingdom's soil, and yet he hints at the main issue – that is, the lack of manufactured production. His book is dedicated to accounting for de Santis's supposed paradox. His explanation is divided into three parts. In part 1 of the book, Serra shows that the Kingdom lacks money because it lacks the above-mentioned four factors of development, while in part 2 he confutes de Santis's monetary arguments. Part 3, devoted to the "remedies", is in fact dominated by Serra's thesis that the inflow of money from exports is overwhelmed by an enormous outflow of money as a result of three types of payment: interest on the public and private debt, plus other rents (financial or from estates) paid to foreigners; profits produced by foreigners' businesses in trade or production; and imports.

3 The lack of economic factors for development

Serra, with a typical mercantilist approach, maintains that agricultural surplus is in any case far less important for development than manufactured products. The latter are more important because they do not depend on the variable weather and other natural conditions; can be multiplied indefinitely and at decreasing costs; do not deteriorate and so will sooner or later be sold; and generally yield higher earnings (p. 121).

Manufacturing activities, Serra stresses, are the first cause of wealth in a state. Venice and Genoa have no agricultural production at all, but they enjoy great riches because they abound in manufactures of several types, while Naples, practically devoid of manufactures, remains poor (pp. 123, 133–135).

Serra's thesis is fully confirmed by historians and development economists. Manufactured production has always been the driving force for transition from a static backward economy to a developed one. In medieval times, this came about through the extension of artisanal production (for example, in Northern Italy, Flanders, Barcelona, etc.); in the modern era, through manufactures (for example, in 16th-century Holland and England, and then in France). Later, this transition was accomplished thanks to industrialization (in 19th-century Germany, in 20th-century Asian "tigers", and finally in today's emerging economies).

Development economists have shown that, when a backward country – for lack of manufactured production – exchanges its raw materials and agricultural products for manufactured (industrial) products, it does not achieve development. This is the ultimate meaning of Singer's and Prebisch's explanation of the deterioration of poor countries' terms of trade.[32] This kind of exchange generates a negative cumulative process in the backward country which, needing manufactured goods, is forced to concentrate entirely on agricultural production to buy manufactured goods from the developed countries.

All the development economics authors have stated from the very outset that development can only be based on industrialization.[33] Mercantilists had expressed the same thesis for more than two centuries.[34] Serra is one of the most brilliant representatives of their approach.

On Southern Italy, Serra's description perfectly reflects the state of affairs in the Kingdom in the previous centuries. Most historians agree that it was condemned to backwardness because its artisanal production did not grow and the exportation of manufactured goods was never implemented. These, they say, were the necessary conditions for development.[35]

The Kingdom's main income remained agricultural rent from the large estates, obtained with primitive methods of cultivation. The lack of other activities was the result of the mistaken policy of the state. As soon as Southern Italy was unified (by the Normans in the 11th and 12th centuries), the sovereigns squeezed the cities by imposing very heavy taxes and by severely restricting their autonomy.[36] The maritime cities struggled hard to preserve their autonomy, but in the end they were defeated.[37]

This policy was implemented not only for fiscal reasons. The sovereigns were afraid of losing control over the cities with weakening of the central power. In the end, they destroyed the cities' foreign commerce. If there had been any chance for artisanal activities to develop, it was definitely precluded by the state.

After Serra, the preference for manufactures vanished. The 18th century authors thought that both agriculture and manufactures needed a great deal of attention to develop the economy.[38] In the second half of the 19th century, the authors on the "Southern question", as it is called, believed that Southern Italy's development depended solely on the modernization of agriculture.[39] However, this project failed. Then, at the beginning of the 20th century, Francesco Saverio Nitti finally called for the industrialization of the region.[40] Much later, after World War II, the Italian governments sought to bring industrialization to the south, with ambiguous results.

* * *

The other economic factor which is necessary for development, according to Serra, is extensive trade. Here, too, the model is Venice, whose extensive trade is largely due to manufacturing activities. Thus, Serra depicts, in elementary terms, a cumulative process, in which an increase in trade and increase in production reinforce each other. Later, he repeats this concept and adds effective government to the factors which reinforce one another (pp. 139–141).

On the contrary, in Naples, besides the unfavourable geographical position, there is an indolent population and a lack of industries. All this necessarily leads to the lack of extensive trade. The only possible trade is internal, but this – Serra maintains – cannot produce wealth (pp. 125–127). The sterility of domestic trade was a conviction shared by all 17th century authors. This is the main shortcoming of early mercantilism. At that time, foreign trade was the driving force of development, and the authors consequently rejected internal demand as an outlet for domestic production. Only at the end of the century did the idea slowly gain ground that the domestic market also could foster development.

4 Internal causes of the standstill

The other two factors which are necessary for development (although not strictly economic), according to Serra, are an enterprising population and effective government, again lacking in the Kingdom; and their absence, we may say, leads in turn to the lack of the factors already examined (manufacturing activities and extensive trade).

Let us begin with effective government. Serra does not say explicitly that Naples lacks it, but the comparison with Venice means precisely that Naples does. This element – the author states – is the most powerful factor of development; it is the efficient cause which contains the other causes (pp. 129–131).

An effective government singles out what every economic activity needs, sees the obstacles that must be removed, and finds the ways to reach the respective goals. It must be aware of the consequences of its decisions. First of all, it must prevent any disorder (pp. 127–133). In Venice, Serra writes, there is a collective government, made of several bodies, the election and functions of which are strictly regulated in detail. The republican organization of the government endows norms and policies with stability and offers economic agents certainty. It also takes advantage of the experience of the body members and allows the continuity of governance (pp. 139–145). This is not the case for Naples, whose policies last only for the term of office of the viceroy (p. 141).

In sum, Serra suggests that Venetian government is stable and efficient because it is performed by the local population and represents the interests of the people (or at least of most of them). This is why the institutions act so carefully and appropriately and why they are concerned about the wealth of the community. Thus, in Venice – Serra implies in his analysis – the interests of the common people and those of the elite converge, so that the public interest is shared as the basic value of the commonwealth. Enriching society is the common aim.

The inadequacy of the Kingdom's government suggested by Serra is fully confirmed by most historians, who date it back to the period of the formation of the southern state. The general opinion is that the unified state, far from favouring development, became an insuperable obstacle in the way of it.[41]

It would not be appropriate to interpret Serra's reflection on effective government as commitment to democracy or political independence (as in fact some have).[42] Such aspirations were completely extraneous to his times. However, our author seems to grasp one of the most basic causes of Southern Italy's underdevelopment: the hiatus between the people and the state. From the outset, the sovereigns of the southern kingdom perceived themselves, and were perceived, as invaders and dominators rather than as representatives of the local population. This was also due to the lack of cultural homogeneity in Southern Italy's regions, which varied greatly in religion, customs, and even language.[43]

The sovereigns were not accountable to the people for their decisions, nor did they care about their approval. Rather, they relied on feudal landlords, many of whom were changed when the dynasty changed. They also relied on the Church (whose institutions were, in great number, among the big landowners) and on foreign merchants (see below). This explains why the sovereigns were so callous towards the cities and so indifferent to the wretched conditions of the common people.

This attitude gave rise to deep reciprocal distrust and bitter hostility between the institutions and the people. The institutions were rightly seen as instruments in the hands of the rich and the privileged. Rules and public decisions were interpreted as hypocritical ways of asserting the interests of the powerful. Distrust of the institutions has proved the most lasting factor of southern underdevelopment, even nowadays, and it also characterizes underdeveloped societies in general.

* * *

The last factor of development mentioned by Serra is an enterprising population – that is, people who are industrious, diligent, inventive, who look out for opportunities for their investments and often travel abroad for their business. This, says the author, is the main factor for private enrichment. He mentions, as positive examples, the people of Genoa, Venice, Florence, and Bergamo, as well as Spain, France, and Germany. On the other hand, the Kingdom of Naples' population is indolent and lazy. Even the local industries in Naples are run by foreigners from Northern Italy. This is why Genoa, a barren state, is so rich, while Naples, with its fertile land, is poor (pp. 123–125, 155).

Serra appears obsessed by this attitude of the local population (pp. 153, 163, 193, 207). He never tries to develop the concept or look into the causes, but he is certain that this feature is decisive for all the other aspects of the Kingdom's backwardness. Bearing in mind the origins of Southern Italy's underdevelopment, we may say that the indolence that Serra witnesses is the result of centuries-long processes. We know that the original attitude of the southern cities was very different. Their populations were enterprising, keen to struggle for their autonomy, and ready to travel abroad and risk their business.[44] What made the people indolent was the tendency of the state to impede any economic activity by the locals and tax it heavily, and to be suspicious of any initiative from the bottom.

On top of these problems, the landlords were greedy. They reduced the peasants to bare survival; privatized the common land; dominated the cities;[45] and made alliances with foreign monopolies for the export of their agricultural products. The prevalence of landlords and agricultural rents was the millstone of Southern Italy's backwardness.[46]

While in the rest of Western Europe the sovereigns, in alliance with artisans and merchants, struggled against feudal landlords, marginalized them, and so started economic development, in Southern Italy an unnatural alliance was built up between sovereigns and feudal landlords against the new productive classes, namely merchants and artisans. In fact, it was an alliance against development.

Under the sway of rents, indolence also became an attitude of the rich, driven to protect their own parasitic revenues while abandoning all entrepreneurial initiative. Finally, distrust of the institutions even extended to the elite. The historians tell us that this was a state of affairs that led Southern Italy's society, taken as a whole, to despise the modern world, its rules and its values. Economic backwardness in the end also became civic and cultural backwardness.[47]

Serra concludes that the above-mentioned four factors are the only causes of the wealth of a country. There are no other causes, implying that the monetary processes are irrelevant (p. 133). Thus, in the rationale of Serra's book, the prime causes of the Kingdom's malaise appear to be internal. Although he never refers to social structure, he ultimately ascribes the economic standstill to a political and cultural element: the lack of effective government and the indolence of the local population.

The last part of the book is devoted, by contrast, to the external factors which contribute to creating an underdeveloped economy. The external processes appear to be a consequence of the internal flaws, although their negative influence makes it very difficult to escape standstill.

5 Foreign merchants, the external cause of backwardness

Chapter XI of part 1 marks the crucial passage from the internal causes of the Kingdom's malaise to the external ones. As usual, Serra puts the question in de Santis's terms of inflow and outflow of money. De Santis maintains that the Kingdom annually exports commodities for six million ducats, while it pays six hundred thousand ducats to the foreigners for their revenues in the Kingdom, and another six hundred thousand for imports (pp. 135, *passim*). In the final balance, an inflow of 4.8 million ducats should arrive into the Kingdom; but, on the contrary, there is great scarcity of money.

Serra's answer, let us recall, is that the cause of such a situation is not the exchange rate but rather the outflow of money, which exceeds the inflow. As we have seen, this outflow is due to three causes: the revenues that foreigners obtain from the country, the profits they earn from their enterprises in the country, and imports. Serra repeats these three causes tirelessly: "The total value of these causes," he explains, "is far higher than that of the exported goods, even if the level of exportation were increased, and this is why money does not enter the Kingdom in exchange for exports" (p. 237).

Let us start from imports. This is the only cause that Serra describes with a certain detail. The number of imports, he says, is seriously underrated by de Santis. Because of the lack of manufactures and the people's indolence, the Kingdom is forced to import all manufactured goods. He then gives a remarkable list of examples. What strikes in the author's list is that the Kingdom imports even the most insignificant manufactured goods and the easiest to produce internally, such as clothes, sugar, dyes, and wax. On the other hand, it imports books; glasses of every type; manufactured items made of iron, copper, or brass; spices; medicines; chemicals; weapons; and so on (pp. 147–151).

The author also remarks on a process – typical of underdevelopment in any historical period – which had led Starkey to call for an import substitution policy in England, namely the export of raw materials which are then re-imported as manufactured goods.[48] Many products, Serra says, "which occur naturally in the Kingdom have to be imported from elsewhere at a price equivalent to double the value of the raw materials themselves" (p. 151). On the "rare occasions" when foreigners encouraged some internal production, the initiative failed because of the idleness of the locals (*ibid.*).

As for the other two factors in the outflow of money, they too were greatly undervalued by de Santis: "If the foreigners exported as much as was possible by the sole use of the money they earn from their investments and businesses in the Kingdom, the total value of those exports would equal or exceed" the inflow due to agricultural export (p. 153; see also p. 163). In fact, a small part of these incomes is invested by the foreigners inside the Kingdom. Otherwise, the country would lack even the little money it has (p. 153).

Thus, besides the export of raw materials, Serra insightfully describes the other most important factor to be seen in underdeveloped economies throughout the ages: what we today call the export (or repatriation) of profits by foreign enterprises. He states, "the true cause of money not coming into the Kingdom in exchange for exports is precisely this – the foreigners' income from investments and earnings from business and imports" (p. 197). He repeats this thesis time and again (see pp. 205, 207, 219, and 237). And he adds: if foreigners could, "they would necessarily export their money by any means possible" (p. 215).

Now the question is, were these two processes – export of agricultural products (especially raw materials), and export of profits – new in Serra's time? Actually, they were not. Once again, their roots go back to the very beginning of Southern Italy's Kingdom. If we put together the many pieces of the jigsaw puzzle that the historians leave us with, we can understand the whole process that generated underdevelopment in this region.

The sovereigns, by repressing economic life in the cities and leaving production to the feudal landlords, condemned the economy to poverty.[49] Then, in order to fuel their disproportioned ambitions of conquest – in addition to the normal expenses of administration – they had to turn to foreign merchants from Northern Italy and later also from other countries.[50] These merchants were able to lend the sovereigns enormous sums of money at high interest rates. In order to pay these interest rates or in exchange for the loans, the sovereigns gradually handed over to the foreign merchants all the Kingdom's revenues: export and import duties; taxes on transports, on state monopolies as well as on trade-licences for any activities; taxes on banks, enterprises, and manufactures; tax collection monopolies; and in the end, even total control over public finance.[51]

All this generated what Serra generically calls revenues (*entrate*, translated in the English version as "investments") of foreign merchants. They include the interests rates paid by the state on the loans, which had formed an immense public debt over the centuries; the interest on loans paid to merchants by private citizens – for example, by landlords or professionals; all the financial rents which derived from the monopolies on public duties; and, finally, the commission on tax collection.

Beside these revenues, there were the profits that foreign merchants received from their activities, ranging from collection and export of agricultural products, which they bought from the landlords and import; distribution and sale of manufactured goods to all the businesses involved in internal trade; exchange; and some little manufacturing activities (p. 151). The people, says Serra, referring to the locals, "are so indolent, that far from exporting those commodities, they do not even sell them within the Kingdom itself" (p. 193). Serra calls earnings of this type gains from *industrie* (trades), usually translated in the English version as "businesses".

This overall picture frequently leads Serra to explain that this is why the foreigners do not convert their final bills of exchange into capital. In the Kingdom, there is nothing left to be sold (pp. 153, 195, 215, 237): no agricultural products, no duties, no monopolies. The foreigners have "sucked the very lifeblood from the citizens of the kingdom" (p. 153; for repetitions, see pp. 195, 207, 237. The latter is an expression used by de Santis that Serra agrees with).

Note also that the foreign merchants who lived in the southern cities never mixed with the locals,[52] which explains why they exported nearly all their profits and earnings. Significantly, even in the 17th century, Serra still saw them as a body alien to local society. And the northern merchants maintained their economic domination throughout the Modern Age.[53]

There is yet another aspect of dependence that Serra singles out with great insight. He contests de Santis's observation that the foreign states need the Kingdom's exports because they consist of necessaries and that their price can therefore be raised without negative consequences. It is quite the opposite, Serra says. Since these states export manufactured products, which are not subject to deterioration, they can exchange them even at great distances, while the Kingdom depends on their buying its agriculture goods (p. 193).

6 The remedies

In part 3, Serra shows some perplexity over the hard task of finding a remedy to that situation. The causes of the malaise are very powerful, he says, and even if we know them, there can be no certainty of finding a remedy (pp. 207, 235–237).

First of all, the author suggests a ban on the exportation of money. If we took this proposal superficially, we should suspect Serra of being a chrysohedonist (the old accusation against mercantilists),[54] even more than de Santis. In fact, here Serra expresses another idea typical of development economists, to the effect that, as Myrdal puts it, a temporary protectionist policy is necessary for the weak economy in its trade with a stronger economy.[55]

Serra's argument is cogent. In normal circumstances, a ban on the export of money would harm the Kingdom, but since foreigners find nothing more to buy internally, they export all their earnings, and, because of its backwardness, "there is no need for the money that leaves the Kingdom ever to return" (p. 215). In our case, says Serra, money is not exported in order to make a profit – that is, for investment or for trade (which would enrich the state) – but, on the contrary, consists of profits made internally that are taken out. This represents a total loss for the state (p. 231).

He then stresses that different situations call for different policies: "certain medicines are beneficial to some people but harmful to others". The lack of extensive trade means that the Kingdom's needs differ from those of a normal situation. This difference turns the exportation of money from beneficial to damaging (p. 229).

His observation reveals another basic principle, later to be adopted by development economists. While classical and neo-classical theories suggest that "economic laws" hold in any context, development economics states that the same policies can have different effects in different conditions. What is good in a normal situation – for example, free trade – can be harmful in underdeveloped economies (Myrdal and Balogh elaborate brilliantly on this point).

In sum, the export of capital must be obstructed, as many poor countries tried to do in the 20th century. Serra recalls once again that the malaise of the Kingdom's economy is due first of all to the export of capital by the foreigners: "These are the very causes that have impoverished the Kingdom". Therefore, "the more opportunities one gives [the foreigners] to trade with advantage and profit and to buy shares and assets, the less money will enter the country in exchange for the exported goods" (p. 219).

In this case, the author notes, limiting export does not contradict the idea that extensive trade is necessary for the country's wealth. Foreign trade, he maintains, favours development only if the imported goods are again sold abroad. If it is confined to imports, it even "causes poverty rather than wealth" (p. 219). The comparison with Venice returns. Venice exports the fruits of its enterprising attitude; it does not trade out of necessity, like Naples. This is why Naples remains poor, while Venice enjoys wealth (pp. 219–221).

However, Serra perceives that it is "extremely difficult", "if not impossible", to remove the whole economic network implemented by foreigners. This "remedy might have a disastrous effect on the Kingdom as a whole and on countless private citizens" (pp. 237–239). Moreover, it would be illegal to take away the foreigners' rents and profits (*ibid.*), and failing to pay the interest rates would be harmful (p. 241). Here Serra appears to be acutely aware of a difficulty that affects all the underdeveloped economies, which have been organized according to external interests. All former colonies, for instance, have found it very difficult, "if not impossible", to eliminate monoculture, to stop state borrowing despite the increasing public debt, to substitute manufactured imports, or to limit the exploitation of their own resources by foreigners. Short-run necessity usually forces these economies to retain the very causes of their poverty.

The only radical remedy, Serra concludes, would be to introduce the factors of development that are now lacking. But even this, although it is "not strictly impossible", is "extremely difficult in practice" – the main obstacle being the indolence of people. All this depends on the possibility to have an effective government (p. 239). This pessimistic analysis is powerful and rigorous. It stresses that the true long-lasting obstacles to development in Southern Italy are cultural and institutional, impediments in the Middle Ages and in Serra's times, and even more so today. In the very last page of his book (p. 249), Serra repeats once again that "all it would need is…effective government", which is "the controlling superior cause of all other accidents" (development factors). This is still the core problem of Southern Italy's underdevelopment.

However, the author continues his quest for possible remedies. A part of the foreigners' businesses and the importation of manufactured goods can be removed and then substituted by introducing manufacturing activities in the state (p. 241). The essential goods that we cannot help importing, instead of being paid for in cash, "could be paid for with commodities of equivalent value" – that is, with goods produced inside (p. 247). In sum, these policies call for the introduction of the development factors now lacking. By doing so, we can enrich the state "even without the help of…a domestic agricultural surplus", Serra says, "as the experience of many Italian cities has shown" (pp. 247–249).

Thus, although the foreigners' rents and profits cannot be removed, their harmful effects can be reduced (pp. 243–245). On this latter point, Serra was very cryptic because he hoped to use the promise of his suggestions to be freed from prison.

7 Conclusions

We leave the conclusions to Serra's own words, which eloquently express a call to struggle for development in Southern Italy (a call which still holds). On the introduction of manufactures in the country, he writes: "These aims are not merely possible but…vital. They must therefore be pursued as energetically as possible". "Difficulties", he adds, "may daunt the weak and faint-hearted, but not a strong, courageous prince" (p. 241).

The courage he is talking about is above all an intellectual attitude: "It is the intellect's function to make difficult things easy, and it can often achieve things that most people think impossible" (*ibid.*). He criticizes that kind of mind "which holds that anything it does not already know is impossible, not considering that all the inventions of ancient and modern times would no doubt have seemed impossible until they were invented" (p. 249).

Serra's call for cultural change – as a pre-requisite for development – was to be revived during the Enlightenment by Genovesi,[56] who passed it on to his followers.

Notes

1. Perrotta, C., "Antonio Serra's development economics: mercantilism, backwardness, dependence", *History of Economic Thought and Policy*, 2, 2013, pp. 5–19.
2. See Ortiz, L. (1558), "Memorial a Felipe II", *Anales de Economia*, XVII, 63, January 1957, pp. 117–200.
3. See Perrotta, C. and C. Sunna (eds), *L'arretratezza del Mezzogiorno. Le idee, l'economia, la storia*, Milan: Mondadori, 2012.
4. See e.g. Furtado, C. (1961), "Desenvolvimiento e subdesenvolvimiento", partly included in his *Théorie du développement économique*, Italian trans. Bari: Laterza,1972, especially ch. IV.
5. Starkey, T. (1529–1532), *A Dialogue between Pole and Lupset*, London: Royal Historical Society & University College, 1989.
6. Ortiz, L., *Memorial del contador Luis Ortiz a Felipe II* [1558], Madrid: Instituto de España, 1970.
7. Serra, A. (1613), *A Short Treatise on the Causes that Can Make Kingdoms Abound in Gold and Silver Even in the Absence of Mines* (in the cover: *A Short Treatise on the Wealth and Poverty of Nations*), trans. from Italian by J. Hunt, ed. by S.A. Reinert, London-New York, NY-Delhi: Anthem Press, 2011.
8. Doria, P.M., "Relazione dello stato politico, economico, e civile del Regno di Napoli", in his *Manoscritti napoletani*, vol. I, Galatina: Congedo, 1709, pp. 49–139.
9. Uztáriz, G. (1724), *Theórica y práctica de Comercio y de Marina*, Madrid: Sanz, 1742.
10. Ulloa, B., *Restablecimiento de las fábricas y comercio español*, 2 vols, Madrid: Marin, 1740.
11. Genovesi, A. (1765–1767), *Delle lezioni di commercio o sia di economia civile*, Milan: Vita e Pensiero, 2013.
12. Galanti, G. (1781–1794), *Della descrizione geografica e politica delle Sicilie*, 2 vols, Naples: ESI, 1969.
13. Besides Ortiz and Serra, cited, see Starkey (1529–1532), Doria (1709), Uztáriz (1724), Ulloa (1740), Genovesi (1765–1767), Galanti (1781–1794), List, F., *System der politischen Ökonomie*, Italian trans. Milan: ISEDI, 1972. (1841).
14. Smith, A., *The Wealth of Nations*, E. Cannan (ed.), London: Methuen, 1904, online ed. Library of Economics and Liberty (1776), I, pp. 9, 10–15.
15. Prebisch, R. (1949), 'El desarrollo económico de la América Latina…', now in *Desarrollo económico*, 1986, No. 103, pp. 479–502; Singer, H.W., "The distribution of gains between investing and borrowing countries", *American Economic Review*, vol. 40, no. 2, 1950, pp. 473–485; Hirschman, A., *The Strategy of Economic Development*, New York, NY-London: Norton, 1958, ch. 7; Furtado 1961; Balogh, T. (1963), *Unequal Partners*, Italian trans. Turin: Einaudi, 1967; Perroux, F. (1964), *L'économie du 20.me siècle*, Italian trans. Milan: Comunità, I, chs 1–3, pp. 33–100, II, chs 2–6, pp. 145–272, VI, chs 6–7, pp. 584–590.
16. Myrdal, G. (1957), *Economic theory and under-developed regions*, Italian trans. Milan: Feltrinelli, 1966, esp. chs 2–3.
17. See e.g., Marx, K. (1867), *Das Kapital*, Buch I, Italian trans. Rome: Editori Riuniti, 1964, ch. 23, secs 1–4, pp. 671–709; Luxemburg, R. (1912) *Die*

Akkumulation des Kapitals, Italian trans. Turin: Einaudi, 1960, 3rd part; Sweezy, P. (1942), *The Theory of Capitalist Development*, Italian trans. Turin: Boringhieri, 1970, ch. 12, pp. 253–280.

18. Cfr. Nurkse, R. (1951), *Problems of Capital Formation in Underdeveloped Countries*, Italian trans. Turin: Einaudi, 1965. ch. 1.
19. Reinert, E.S. and S.A. Reinert, "An Early National Innovation System: the Case of Antonio Serra's 1613 *Breve Trattato*", *Institutions and Economic Development*, Milan: Franco Angeli, 2003, I/3, pp. 87–119.
20. The pages cited (numbers in parentheses in our text) are from the only complete English translation of Serra's book, edited by Sophus A. Reinert in 2011: Serra [1613]. This edition has parallel texts; the English text (from which we cite) is on the odd pages.
21. Cfr. Lopez, R., "Commerce in medieval Europe: The South", ch. 5 of M.M. Postan and P. Mathias (eds), *Cambridge Economic History*, vol. II, 1952, Italian trans. Turin: Einaudi, 1982, pp. 291–396, p. 307; Tabacco, G. and G.G. Merlo, *Medioevo, V–XV sec.*, Bologna: Il Mulino, 1981, pp. 306–307; Falkenhausen, V., "I ceti dirigenti prenormanni...", in G. Rossetti (ed.), *Forme di potere e struttura sociale in Italia nel Medioevo*, Bologna: Il Mulino, 1977, pp. 321–377, 321–324.
22. Pirenne, H. (1917), *Histoire de l'Europe des invasions au XVIe siècle*, Italian trans. Rome: Newton Compton, 1991, pp. 157–158.
23. See Lopez (1952), pp. 309–310; Abulafia, D., "Gli italiani fuori d'Italia", in R. Romano (ed.), *Storia dell'economia italiana*, Turin: Einaudi, 1990, vol. I, pp. 261–286; Tabacco, G., *Egemonie sociali e strutture del potere nel medioevo italiano*, Turin: Einaudi, 1979, pp. 183–188.
24. Cfr. Galasso, G., *Mezzogiorno medievale e moderno*, Turin: Einaudi, 1975, pp. 106–118. On Northern Italy, see Tabacco and Merlo, 1981, pp. 411–423, 435–446.
25. See de Santis, M.A. (1605), "Discorso intorno agli effetti che fa il cambio in Regno; and Secondo discorso Intorno...", in Colapietra, R. (ed.), *Problemi monetari negli scrittori napoletani del Seicento*, Rome: Accademia Nazionale dei Lincei, 1973, pp. 110–141.
26. Fortunato, G. (1904), "La questione meridionale e la riforma tributaria", in his *Il Mezzogiorno e lo stato italiano. Discorsi politici*, Florence: Vallecchi, 1926, vol. 2, pp. 305–375, pp. 309–318, 325–326, 335, *passim*.
27. Cfr. De Rosa, L., "Antonio Serra e i suoi critici", *Clio*, I, 1, 1965, pp. 115–136. For a detailed and updated history of Serra's fortune, see S.A. Reinert, "Introduction" in A. Serra (1613): *A Short Treatise on the Causes that can make Kingdoms abound in Gold and Silver even in the Absence of Mines*, trans. from Italian by J. Hunt, ed. by S.A. Reinert, London-New York, NY-Delhi: Anthem Press, 2011, pp. 1–85, pp. 71–85.
28. Zagari, E., "Moneta e sviluppo nel 'Breve trattato' di Antonio Serra", in Roncaglia, A. (ed.), *Alle origini del pensiero economico in Italia*, Bologna: Il Mulino, 1995, pp. 15–36, p. 26; Rosselli, A., "Antonio Serra e la teoria dei cambi", in A. Roncaglia (ed.), Bologna: Il Mulino, 1995, pp. 37–58, p. 55.
29. Cfr. Galasso, G., *Storia del regno di Napoli*, Vol. I., Turin: De Agostini, 2008, pp. 779–789.
30. Jones, P. (1980), *Economia e società nell'Italia medievale*, trans. from English, Turin: Einaudi, 1981, ch. 2; Martin, J.-M., "Città e campagna: economia

e società (sec. VII–XIII)", in Galasso, G. and R. Romeo (eds), *Storia del Mezzogiorno*, Naples: Banco di Napoli – Ed. del Sole, 1989, vol. II.2, pp. 257–382, pp. 274–276. See also Galanti (1781–1794), I, p. 59.
31. See Jones, P., "L'Italia", ch. 7.II of Postan, M.M. (ed.), *Cambridge Economic History*, vol. 1, 1966, Italian trans. Turin: Einaudi, 1976, pp. 412–526, pp. 497–498; Luzzati, M., "La dinamica secolare di un 'modello italiano'", in Romano, R. (ed.), *Storia dell'economia italiana*, Turin: Einaudi, 1990, vol. I, pp. 5–114, pp. 35–63.
32. Singer, 1950, Prebisch, 1949.
33. See e.g. Rosenstein-Rodan, P. N. (1943), "Problems of Industrialization of Eastern and South-Eastern Europe", *Economic Journal*, now in Agarwala, A.N. and S.P. Singh (eds), *The Economics of Underdevelopment*, Oxford: Oxford University Press, 1958, pp. 245–255; Kuznets, S. (1965), *Sviluppo economico e struttura*, trans. from English, Milan: Il Saggiatore, 1969, pp. 242–263; Lewis, A.W. (1954), *Economic Development with Unlimited Supply of Labour*, The Manchester School, now in Agarwala and Singh (eds) (1958), 1963, pp. 400–449, and L. (1966), *Development Planning*, Italian trans. Milan: Feltrinelli, 1968; Robinson, J., *Aspects of Development and Underdevelopment*, Cambridge: Cambridge University Press, 1979, chs 4 and 6.
34. Cfr. Perrotta, C., *Consumption as an Investment*, London-New York, NY: Routledge, 2004, ch. 10.
35. Pirenne, H. (1933), *Storia economica e sociale del medioevo*, transl. from French, Milan: Garzanti, 1967, ch. 2.1, pp. 53–58; Jones, 1966, pp. 422–428; Gerschenkron, A. (1968), *La continuità storica*, trans. from English, Turin: Einaudi, 1976, ch. 8, pp. 274–277; Cipolla, C., *Storia economica dell'Europa pre-industriale*, Bologna: Il Mulino, 1974, part 1.
36. Cfr. Tabacco and Merlo, 1981, pp. 532–533; Galasso, G. (1969), *Dal comune medievale all'unità. Linee di storia meridionale*, Bari: Laterza, 1971, pp. 64–71.
37. Cfr. Azzara, C., *Le civiltà del medioevo*, Bologna: Il Mulino, 2004, p. 202; Vitolo, G., *Città e coscienza cittadina nel Mezzogiorno medievale (secc. IX–XIII)*, Salerno: Laveglia, 1990, pp. 24–26.
38. See e.g. Genovesi (1765–1767), I, chs 8–9 and 22.
39. See Sunna, C. (a) "*La nascita della Questione meridionale*", ch. 7 of C. Perrotta and C. Sunna (eds), 2012, pp. 118–137, section 3.
40. Sunna, C. (b) "*Il meridionalismo dal primo Novecento al fascismo*", ch. 8 of Perrotta and Sunna, (eds), 2012, pp. 138–159, section 3.
41. See e.g. Abulafia, D. (1977), *Le due Italie*, trans. from English, Naples: Guida, 1991; Jones, 1980, Introduction; Martin, 1989; Azzara, 2004, pp. 223–224.
42. See Perrotta, C., "Antonio Serra's development economics: mercantilism, backwardness, dependence", *History of Economic Thought and Policy*, 2, 2013, pp. 5–19, fn. 29.
43. Cfr. Galasso, 1969, pp. 30–32, 64–65; Galasso, 1975, pp. 29, 39–40.
44. Cfr. Perrotta, C., "Medioevo. Lo sviluppo soffocato sul nascere", ch. 2 of Perrotta and Sunna (eds), 2012, pp. 25–51, sections 2 and 3.
45. Vitolo, 1990, pp. 21–29; Vitolo, "In palatio Communis", in Chittolini, G., Petti Balbi, G. Vitolo,(eds), *Città e territorio nell'Italia del medioevo*, Naples: GISEM-Liguori, 2007, pp. 243–294, pp. 250–252.
46. Cfr. Balestracci, D., *Medioevo italiano e medievistica*, Rome: Il Calamo, 1996, pp. 136–137.

47. Cfr. Jones (1980), p. 21; Sylos Labini, Paolo (1994), "Sul libro di R. D. Putnam, La tradizione civica…", in his *Scritti sul Mezzogiorno (1954–2001)*, Manduria-Bari-Rome: Lacaita, 2003, pp. 369–377.
48. Starkey, 1529–1532.
49. See Vitolo, G., *Città e contado nel Mezzogiorno tra medioevo ed età moderna*, Introduzione, Salerno: Laveglia, 2005, pp. 8–26, pp. 11–13.
50. Corrao, P., "Mercanti stranieri e regno di Sicilia", in Del Treppo, M., *Sistema di rapporti ed élites economiche in Europa (sec. XII–XVII)*, Naples: GISEM-Liguori, 1994, pp. 87–112, p. 90.
51. See e.g. Romano, A., "…stranieri e mercanti in Sicilia nei sec. XIV–XV", in Del Treppo (ed.), 1994, pp. 113–132, p. 116.
52. Cfr. Corrao, 1994, pp. 88–102; Musi, A., "Le élites internazionali a Napoli dal primo Cinquecento alla guerra dei trent'anni", in Del Treppo (ed.), 1994, pp. 133–161, p. 136; Del Treppo, M., "Stranieri nel regno di Napoli", in Rossetti, G. (ed.), *Dentro la città: stranieri e realtà urbane nell'Europa dei sec. XII–XVI*, (1st ed. 1989), Naples: GISEM-Liguori, 2004, pp. 179–233, p. 211; Del Treppo, M. and A. Leone, *Amalfi medievale*, Naples: Giannini, 1977, pp. 207–218. Yver, G., *Le commerce et les marchands dans l'Italie méridionale au XIIIe et au XIVe siècle*, Paris: Fontemoing, 1903, in the second part, gives a detailed map of the presence of foreign merchants in Southern Italian cities.
53. Galasso, G., *Storia del regno di Napoli*, Vol. VI, Turin: De Agostini, 2011, pp. 374–377.
54. See Perrotta, 2013, pp. 2–3, 9–10.
55. Myrdal, 1957, ch. 7, pp. 89, 96–99.
56. Genovesi, 1765–1767, see e.g. I.22, sections 8–24, pp. 247–256.

11
"To Console and Alleviate the Human Mind": Ferdinando Galiani's Attempted Republication of Serra in the 1750s

Koen Stapelbroek

1 Intieri and the reform of 18th-century Naples

It is very well known that Antonio Serra's *Breve trattato delle cause che possono far abbondare li regni d'oro e d'argento dove non sono miniere*, of 1613, was first "discovered" by the Tuscan born mathematician-agronomist Bartoleomo Intieri, who developed a strong interest in political economy just after Naples became an independent state in 1734.[1] Together with Celestino Galiani, Intieri had ridden out in 1734 to be the first to welcome Charles of Bourbon to his new Kingdom.[2] In the following years, the two men discussed the future of the Neapolitan state, its economic development, and financial disorders, the record of which is preserved in a series of letters by Intieri to Celestino Galiani of the late 1730s.[3]

In these letters, Intieri developed a political economic vision for the preservation of Neapolitan independence, based to a large extent on his studies of Jean-François Melon's *Essai politique sur le commerce*, the first edition of which appeared in the year that Charles of Bourbon acceded the Neapolitan throne. To respond to the complex history of the south of Italy and the difficult circumstances under which the new dynastic state was attempting to put itself on the European map, an integral political and economic vision of the future of European politics was required. Here, Intieri was quick to recognize that the principles of political economy of Melon's book could provide a realistic programme for national state development. Intieri used Melon's *Essai politique* as his guide not only in developing his ideas on the "science of commerce" [*la scienza del commercio*], but thereby also in devising an effective way to simultaneously (1) confront the threats to the fragile new Neapolitan state in the European arena of military and commercial competition between states and (2) destroy the remnants of the abusive political strategies of the Spanish viceroy and the Southern Italian aristocracy. To these ends, reforms were necessary, Intieri agreed with his contemporaries, but he worried that the difficulties of precisely reforming those things needing reforming and leaving the rest untouched might be too great, which could result in destroying the state itself.[4]

Following Melon's lead, Intieri came to view the government of the agricultural sector as crucial for the survival of Naples as an independent state. Agricultural modernization, he believed, was the key to undoing the set of perversions in Neapolitan history that had led to backwardness and that complicated feudal relationships in the country and enormous urban problems in the capital. Intieri argued that if the grain trade "were to be freed from the many obstacles that it has" and "the prince facilitated transportation to the sea by building safe and comfortable roads", then Naples would not only stop importing grain from Poland and England but be able to supply the whole of Italy.[5] Intieri identified the antiquated grain tax system as the main disorder that prevented the modernization of Neapolitan agriculture.[6] This was a worthy object of reform. In what was as much a political, moral, legal, and social argument as it was an economic one, Intieri also came to agree with Melon in arguing for the liberalization of the grain trade. Abundance of grain that could not be sold abroad led to lower domestic prices and to negligence of its production, so that in a bad year the country was prone to famines. For Intieri, this argument was the touchstone of Melon's genius: "Mr. Melon wisely writes that... abundance is more frightening than famine".[7]

Although Intieri saw the government of the country's agricultural sector as a necessary step for setting up a modern economy, Melon's *Essai politique* provided Intieri with a more complete framework for identifying what would really create long-term commercial development. Intieri paid close attention to the mechanisms governing a state's commercial system and investigated how foreign trade was generated. He used Melon's insights into the relation between technological innovation and the development of prices of manufactured, luxury, and agricultural goods, and he concluded that there were specific circumstances under which an underdeveloped country's agricultural development would take off and generate new industries. When this started to happen in a country the allocation of labour would shift from basic to more advanced forms of industry. This growth process would be unlimited and economic underdevelopment and institutional abuses would disappear automatically as a result of the changes in society. Because such a truly modern economy was a system in which the dynamic of agricultural productivity was linked to the state of its manufacturing industry, luxury played an integral role. Intieri was genuinely excited about the power of Melon's argument about luxury and economic growth. He sent a set of transcriptions from Melon's chapter on luxury in the *Essai politique* to Celestino with one of his letters.[8] When Intieri read Voltaire's famous letter to Thieriot about Law, Melon, and Dutot (immediately after its first publication), he judged that even Voltaire had failed to recognize Melon's merits.[9]

Convinced by Melon's views and the use of the *Essai politique* as a guide for the reform of Naples into a commercial monarchy, Intieri also made a clear choice about how the Neapolitan economic potential, which he believed was huge,[10] could be realized. Where others favoured isolation and the extensive protection of Neapolitan trade, Intieri held that it was necessary and decisive in the modern age to encourage industry and foreign trade and that "one could not live comfortably ... without mixing with the other nations".[11] On that principle, Celestino and Intieri understood, Naples had to try to consolidate its political independence in the modern world. Intieri hoped to persuade the government of Naples to adopt his views and rejected development projects initiated by the state that were aimed at the protection of the domestic economy. He could certainly understand that "the world desired novelties [*novità*]" (after independence the people wanted changes) and that the state council, inspired by the initiatives of the Marquis of Montealegre, who was loved by everyone, satisfied this desire with its reform programmes.[12] Indeed, it was soon to be generally recognized that the projects carried out at the time, between 1738 and 1746, did not have any real or lasting effects.[13] While this did not surprise Intieri, who did not believe in large-scale reforms without clearly set-out objectives, he was disappointed in those whom he felt were responsible for directing the state's commercial politics. Intieri complained that Neapolitan government advisers ignored the French debate on commercial politics set in motion by Melon and that members of the *Giunta del Commercio* were incompetent in economic affairs.[14]

Inspired by the ideas put forward in works on political economy that appeared throughout Europe at the time, Intieri himself started to work actively on getting a good overview of the Neapolitan situation and its real conditions from the perspective of the rapidly developing science of commerce. Applying the techniques and statistical tools that he found in English and French works of the time to Naples, Intieri put together a number of technical accounts of the state of the Neapolitan economy and sent them to Celestino Galiani. Intieri analysed fluctuations of the exchange rate and the balance of trade,[15] made observations on the apparent scarcity of money in the country,[16] and started to list demographic figures to calculate the development of the population in relation to the economic productivity of the capital and the country.[17] Intieri also wrote to Celestino about the subject of devaluation [*alzamento*], which Melon had discussed in the most controversial parts of his *Essai politique*. Intieri used Melon's ideas to justify the Neapolitan *alzamento* that had been carried out in 1691 by the Spanish viceroy Francesco Benavides, count of Santo Stefano, a measure that had been rejected, unrightfully according to Intieri, by his predecessor the marquis del Carpio.[18]

2 The discovery of Serra in 18th-century Naples

In the mid 1740s, Bartolomeo Intieri, together with his fellow Tuscan, Alessandro Rinuccini, began teaching a number of promising youngsters, among whom were Ferdinando Galiani and Antonio Genovesi, in the field of political economy.[19] In the accounts of the genealogy of the Neapolitan Enlightenment, this is seen as a decisive moment leading up to the creation of (arguably) the first-ever chair of political economy, which was personally financed by Intieri and instituted at the University of Naples in 1754.[20] Presumably, it was also in the mid 1740s that Intieri stumbled upon Antonio Serra's *Breve trattato*: a work from a different time, in which virtually no books were written on economic subjects, by a home-grown author whose ideas Intieri recognized as familiar to his own views. It is easy to see how Intieri would immediately have been attracted to this work.

Serra had presented his argument with great self-confidence as an inquiry into the origins of wealth as a consequence of "effective government" (the term that Serra uses repeatedly[21]). Serra's *Breve trattato* was written like a sober mirror for princes that did not have power but rather had money and wealth as his key subject. Any political complications in the treatment of this subject that involved the relative or weak power of the state and of international political rivalry did not enter into the picture, or had been pushed into the background. Thus, when Serra's *Breve trattato* was "discovered", the text was ideally suited to serve as a teaching source for how to understand relations between productivity in different economic sectors and international monetary flows. Next to that, Serra's book served the right rhetorical purposes: it proved that Naples had had available for a long time the answers to its economic problems. These were provided by a Southern Italian thinker. To revive these answers and a solid understanding of the real problems, Naples now needed not only to look abroad to start cultivating its knowledge of the mechanisms of wealth generation, but also to reconsider its own history and see the true nature of the errors that it had made as well as the culture that made these errors almost inevitable. If Intieri felt that his calls for more precisely aimed reforms fell on deaf ears, Serra's fate in a dark age of commerce had been far more tragic. To rehabilitate Serra and develop the kind of ideas that he had put forward meant to demonstrate that Naples had learnt its lesson from the past and had managed to gain control over the history of humankind. The combined patriotic and personal political symbolisms made Serra's *Breve trattato* a convenient text for Intieri to put up as a key document in the presentation of his own political economic reform project. Thus, Serra's *Breve trattato* also became a cult classic in Intieri's political-economy study group.

Intieri's perspective on Serra's *Breve trattato* is echoed in the famous endnote XXIX (the longest of all the notes) of the second edition of Ferdinando Galiani's *Della moneta*, of 1780.[22] Looking back on the text of his 1751 juvenile masterpiece and its gestation, here Galiani seems to convey many of the same ideas that Intieri had held some forty years earlier when he used the work in educating an entire generation of Neapolitan political economists. In the middle of a short discussion of the state of monetary debate in Naples at the beginning of the 17th century, Galiani pauses to introduce the most important thinker of this period:

> This was Doctor Antonio Serra, of Cosenza, who, in 1613, had published by Lazzaro Scorrigio a *Breve trattato delle cause che possono far abbondare li regni d'oro e d'argento dove non sono miniere, coll'applicazione al Regno di Napoli, diviso in tre parti*. Whoever reads this treatise will certainly be left surprised and filled with admiration, on seeing – in a century of total ignorance of economic science – what clear and just ideas its author held on the matters about which he wrote, and how sanely he considered the causes of our ills and of their only effective remedies. Nothing else does he retain of the unhappiness of his century, but the sterile, dry and obscure style, entirely similar to that of the scholastics, of counsellors and of repetitive lawyers, using

> many divisions and subdivisions, distinctions, articles, paragraphs, that now and then tediously prolong the argument. Despite this defect, I would not hesitate to place him in the ranks of the first and oldest writers of the politico-economic science and would concede to Calabria even the, until now, unknown honour of having been its birthplace. But such is our fate that we cannot remember this glory without meeting with some reason to recant it in part. This man, who I dare to compare to Melon, of France, and, on these matters, to Locke, of the English, but who surpasses both of them for having lived so long before them, as well as in a century of darkness and of errors in the science of economics. This man, of such a shrewd intellect, of such wholesome judgement, was scorned while he lived and was, together with his book, forgotten about after his death. No one has ever cited him.[23] And, perhaps, only the copy of the book which Bartolommeo Intieri possessed and which he gave to me, has saved it from oblivion.[24] But there is worse. Serra dedicated his treatise to the Count of Lemos, and wrote it, "from the jail at Vicaria." What marvel that monetary matters went into a precipice, as one Antonio Serra languished in prison and one Marcantonio de Santis was loaded with riches and was the oracle of the Collaterale? What then became of Serra is unknown to me. Certain it is that none of his advice was heeded, which verifies the truth of an elegant proverb, and one considerate of our common people, which says that there are three things which are not esteemed in this world; and these are: the power of a coarse man, the beauty of a prostitute, and the counsel of an ignoble man.[25]

These sentences would prove to form a canonical statement in determining Serra's legacy. However, the influence that Serra actually had on Intieri and on Galiani has never been researched in depth and with reference to actual writings and historical contextual analysis.[26] What follows are a number of tentative arguments that assess how Ferdinando Galiani perceived Serra's *Breve trattato*.

3 Serra's *Breve trattato* as a model for Galiani's *Della moneta*

Throughout his oeuvre, Ferdinando Galiani adopted different writing styles that he exploited for the optimal presentation of his political and economic views. In fact, Galiani's stylistic choices tended to be part of his argument: such as in the *Dialogues sur le commerce des bleds* of 1770, which, Galiani suggested himself, had no general message apart from that the fierce debate it sparked by itself would eventually show his French audience to what extent their serious discussions about political economic reform were driven by ideological caricatures, misguided moralizing and faction politics.[27] As a result of Galiani's treatment of genre specific literary style, interpreting Galiani's work has become a matter of reconstructing and attributing meaning to his original texts, in a way that differs from making sense of works by most other 18th-century political writers. Yet, although Galiani constructed his writings in rather indirect ways, I do not believe that he thereby distanced himself from any of their political meanings and thereby became less of a serious reform minded thinker than his contemporaries.[28] Instead, it may be useful to understand Galiani's writing habits in the light of his juvenile formation as a classicist and his own admiration of Horace, whose poetry he remained obsessed with during his entire life.[29] Galiani, it seems, viewed Horace's free treatment of poetic genre rules and techniques of connotative meaning creation as constituting an ideal and a model for the most accurate presentation of his own political ideas. For Galiani, the degree of perfection that societies reached in the art of government and in linguistic expression were also directly related.[30] And as studying Horace's poetry always formed a source of inspiration for Galiani to better understand the history of Rome and humankind alike, so he experimented with choice of style and rhetorical techniques to convey to his audience a sense of how he understood his own political economic reasoning to relate to the history of commerce. This is the way in which the otherwise excessive use of epigraphs in *Dei doveri dei principi neutrali*, Galiani's last work of 1782, is to be understood: not as bad taste in showing off superior knowledge of classical authors but as providing a separate story, about trade in antiquity and modern times, parallel to the formal-theoretical line of criticism of natural-law thinkers who had discussed the rights and duties of neutral states.[31]

Galiani's free use of style in the construction of his arguments was already present in his juvenile lectures on love, Platonic love, superstition, and the Anti-Christ and in his first published work, the satirical *Componimenti varii per la morte di Domenico Jannacone* (1748).[32] In a somewhat similar manner, one can recognize that the structure and argumentative positioning by Galiani in *Della moneta* has been taken from Antonio Serra's *Breve trattato*. The young Galiani was not a political economist but a classicist, a moral philosopher, and literary figure. From this background, he considered the situation of Naples and developed a moral philosophy and a historical perspective that explained how this situation had come about. Galiani's wider moral philosophy was designed to explain the history of the institutions created by humankind.[33] Galiani's main project in the late 1740s (which he abandoned when he realized that his ambitions had been too large) was to write a work entitled "The Art of Government" that fully integrated these two approaches into one narrative.[34] The project *Dell'arte del governo* was itself a spinoff of an intended work by Galiani on the ancient history of trade in the Mediterranean. In 1788 Galiani's first biographer, Luigi Diodati,[35] referred to this lost manuscript, entitled *Sull'antichissima storia delle navigazioni nel Mediterraneo*, and *Della moneta* contains references to it.[36] In *Della moneta*, Galiani transformed the moral-historical understanding of the development of human societies of his *Arte del Governo* into a political economic vision for the future of Naples in the international system. That was why the first chapter recounted the history of the commerce of humankind from Rome, via the Renaissance to the modern manifestations of commercial-political rivalry between European nation-states. Yet, when Galiani started to write *Della moneta*, he seems to have looked for a main structure for the presentation of his views in the form of a political economic argument, and he found it in Serra's *Breve trattato*.

In the opening paragraphs of the *Breve trattato*, Serra argues that ignorance may produce wonder and subsequently a desire to reflect on that which is not understood. This, he suggests, may be a natural explanation for his curiosity to know the causes of and remedies for the shortage of money in the Kingdom of Naples.[37] Addressing the Neapolitan viceroy, Serra writes that "in the present crisis you have striven, by forming councils and creating tribunals, to relieve the Kingdom from the crushing burden that prevents it from enjoying the fruits that nature has given it".[38] Thus, between the lines, Serra takes a highly critical position: the viceroy responded to the problems of the Kingdom with the creation of reformist institutions, yet Serra's wonder led him to explore the real causes of the problem more profoundly. The critical tone of the dedication is continued in the preface, where Serra launches an outright attack on Marc'Antonio de Santis, whose views had influenced Neapolitan financial politics. In the first sentences, Serra reasons that "it is widely believed that the art of governing...is common property, within anybody's grasp", and "we should not be surprised" to find a "highly experienced merchant" like de Santis forming ideas about it. However, "the science of government" is "as difficult and uncertain as the art of medicine".[39] To distinguish "right from wrong", in particular, is a highly uncertain affair. According to Aristotle, this was because "justice existed by position and not by nature".[40] Therefore, before narrowing down the topic of his text to money, Serra teaches that confronted with political and moral issues, "the intellect can sometimes be deceived".[41] The best attitude to the challenges of the art of government and the science of justice, exemplified by Solomon and Justinian, was to cultivate true wisdom and realize that although humankind in the course of its history might create ever-changing ideas of justice, "human knowledge could not have achieved as much without Divine assistance".[42] Because within the art of government "not a single word has been written by any of the ancient or modern writers on good government" on the subject of money, Serra set out to develop knowledge of the "causes that can make a kingdom abound in money".[43]

The opening moves of the anonymously published *Della moneta* almost run parallel to Serra's argument. After addressing King Charles of Bourbon, Galiani explains that the art of government has until then been dominated by writers who advised the prince on how to increase his power and territory, instead of on the happiness of the people and what really made nations rich and brought them happiness. For this reason, it was important to understand the nature of money and the consequences of this for politics.[44] The human record of the art of government, until then, had been "an uninterrupted history of errors, by and [self-inflicted] punishments of, the human race".[45] Yet, nonetheless, people had advanced beyond the state of simple primitive life. In this, money was crucial and it was a human creation. The value of gold and silver arose by some process of imposition, though not by convention as many had misunderstood Aristotle, and was the result of human ideas and feelings.[46] Yet, this did not at all mean that it could be dictated or altered at will through the exercise of political power. Galiani argues that money probably was created when people were filled with feelings of wonder and curiosity about the beauty of gold and silver and when it became used for religious and primitive purposes. When these metals became valuable in exchange between tribes and subsequently in the commerce between nations, this sparked an enormously rapid development of societies and contact between them. The result was a sudden increase of human happiness. Galiani stresses that people never deliberately created money. Yet, after it emerged, they imagined that they had invented it themselves:

> I believe strongly that none of the remarkable and most useful institutions of civil life are due simply to human wisdom. Instead, they are all absolute pure gifts of an amiable and beneficent Providence ... They

> are sustained by nature itself in order to give them an orderly movement. Man can neither perceive an institution at its start, nor arrest its growth. Neither can he undo it once it is established...True, as men see the good ordering of things accomplished, they credit themselves with having wished to institute such things and, so to speak, to perfect them.[47]

Galiani's idea had important consequences. Political interventions based on the wrong views violated providence and were therefore necessarily self-defeating:

> Since we have been able to advance, without suffering, by means of these otherwise useless bodies, from a primitive life in which we literally devoured each other to a civilised state in which we live peacefully, and trade with each other, we need not return, in the name of wisdom, to the barbarism from which, we have, by the grace of God, been happily delivered. The community of man can only improve its ideas within certain limits. Attempts made to exceed these limits will destroy and corrupt the order of things.[48]

Thus, it was crucial that the hitherto neglected and underestimated "Art of government" would be cultivated with regard to money. Here Galiani said that he wanted to go back to the first principles and deduce his entire perspective and detailed political economic reasoning from a few simple rules about how people formed value judgements and how these governed the life of modern commercial societies. We find a similar positioning in the *Breve trattato*, where Serra explains that there are four "primary causes" that "make kingdoms abound in gold and silver" and "that there are no other causes than these".[49] And where Galiani suggests that Serra's style was "sterile, dry and obscure" and that he used "many divisions and subdivisions, distinctions, articles, [and] paragraphs", the same might be said about large parts of *Della moneta*, even if that mechanical style was perhaps adopted only to enhance the impression that the work was systematically constructed.

Galiani's presentational style in setting up his specific arguments also resembles Serra's. Like Serra, Galiani often mentions that things at first glance may appear to be a certain way but that upon closer inspection and after applying the basic principles of the value of things, they function differently. Where Serra uses this technique quite dryly, Galiani often uses paradoxes more rhetorically. Both Serra and Galiani present themselves as not only content to simply logically refute opponents but also keen to explain precisely where the errors come from and how the matter at hand should have been approached. If these similarities by themselves are not very meaningful, since these uses of style to position oneself are to be found in many early works on political economy, the parallels are actually more significant because of their critical force. Serra insists on the fact that because "contracts are all free at first" and the rate of "exchange is a contract, it follows that, just like other contracts, it is at first free".[50] Tempted by the "superficial attractiveness" of de Santis's argument, the count of Olivares tried to "pass a decree lowering the exchange rate", but this was impossible and exactly the wrong way to go about solving what was a serious problem.[51] Galiani emphasizes time and again in *Della moneta* that attempts to tamper with the value of money were violations of the providentially orchestrated laws of commerce and were automatically punished. In this way, both Neapolitan writers directed their criticisms at those authors and government advisers who offered easy and superficial legal solutions where the real problem of economic development for Naples was of a completely different nature. These kinds of measures were incredibly harmful to the country, and not only through direct economic effects. The main aim of Galiani's *Della moneta* was to get rid of confusions that disturbed the political life of the newly independent Kingdom of Naples and made escaping from underdevelopment and backwardness virtually impossible. Galiani argued that misjudgements of the signs of the economic growth that was in fact taking place inspired well-meant reform proposals that threatened economic and political stability. Thus, Galiani felt that he had to explain in *Della moneta* that rising prices, contrary to popular belief, were a sign of increasing wealth, not of imminent famine, and that luxury was an effect of good government, not of moral decay.

In 1747, just before Galiani started writing *Della moneta*, confusion had broken out when it was discovered that the silver coins that were issued in 1735 and 1739 were underweight according to the official standard of 1689. Although the money in circulation functioned perfectly well, the Royal Mint as well as the *Deputazione delle monete* decided that a general recoinage back to the old standard was desirable, claiming that otherwise subjects would be harmed and an injustice in the tax system would arise. Four days after the report by the *Deputazione,* the king replied, ignoring the advice and ordering more money of the same quality and weight as that in circulation to be coined, thereby making the accidental devaluation [*alzamento*] of the

1730s official.[52] The protest by the *Deputazione* was supported by a pamphlet, dressed up as a scholarly treatise, written by Trojano Spinelli, entitled *Riflessioni politiche sopra alcuni punti della scienza della moneta* (n.d., probably 1748). Spinelli declared himself dogmatically in opposition to any changes of the official standard.[53] In contrast to Spinelli and the position of the *Deputazione delle monete*, Galiani thought that the government's decision to change the standard was not a devaluation policy but simply a wise judgement of economic efficacy. The 1730s coins functioned well, prices had long been modified in accordance with the tacit devaluation, and as the price of silver rose steadily, the stability of the monetary system had not been, and would not be, threatened by illegal money makers.[54]

From Galiani's point of view, the greatest obstacle for Naples was not the difficulty of the situation that the vulnerable new state found itself in but getting the right perception of it. The biggest threat to Neapolitan commercial development was the people's erroneous ideas about which general economic and monetary policies in fact facilitated economic growth and led to foreign trade. Thus, he declared towards the end of his life that his first major work, *Della moneta*, was written to be a decisive intervention in a hopelessly entangled Neapolitan debate on commercial reforms:

> The fortune [of the kingdom of Naples] had changed in 1734 with the acquisition of independent government. The long wars that were fought in Italy had not caused any significant damage to its kingdoms and had brought money from Spain, France and Germany and almost everywhere into the [Neapolitan] kingdom. The good initiatives by its government, which encouraged the arts and commerce, had completely altered the economy of the state when European peace was recovered in 1749. Hence, the new situation ensued from a fresh impulse of energy and was healthier than before, but its first appearances were trouble, complaints, dissatisfaction, ailment. There seemed to be a lack of money, the rates of exchange had altered, the prices of all goods had increased, the quick gains of whole-sale buyers and non-manufacturers were diminished. On the whole the ancient orders and the 'mainsprings' [*le molle*] of the state had been destroyed or upset. There were some who took luxury [*il lusso*], weakening of devotion or governmental negligence to be the cause. Some prescribed one thing, while others advised another. One simply could not blame the prince for new pressures and taxes, because his wisdom and moderation had been visible and clear, but for the rest every single

> thing was suggested to be the case. There were those who advised to make laws on rates of exchange, who wanted to change the type of money, who wanted to change the proportion between gold and silver or at least between silver and bronze. They believed that coined silver was liquefied by luxury. All talked about defects that did not really exist, as if they existed. And all proposed venoms [*veleni*] as the remedy. In sum, the danger was evident. The nation was deceived by the false appearance of symptoms and signs and started to scare and disturb the spirit of the prince by proposing measures that impeded the strengthening and the new salubrity of the Kingdom, up to the point that the whole state was almost threatened by some internal weakness.[55]

Against calls for further measures, Galiani took the side of the government and defended its sober attitude towards reform. In general, his judgement was that many of the problems that Naples seemed to be facing were mere teething troubles; there was no reason to panic – to which he added, after giving his account of the restless political situation around 1750, that "this was the main if not the only reason that prompted Galiani to write the present work".[56]

Thus, when Galiani structured his argument, Serra's *Breve trattato* was his model for arguing like a proper political economist – not like a classicist, a political writer, or moral philosopher. Galiani adopted Serra's style and argumentation to eliminate (also like Serra) a number of misunderstandings about monetary politics that not only led to bad politics but that also affected Neapolitan chances to ever escape from underdevelopment. Yet, in the process, Serra's rather strictly formal argument came to look baroque when Galiani added to it a number of elements that belonged to 18th-century political discourse. Galiani discussed John Law's Mississippi Scheme, public debts, self-interest, the progress of commerce in the history of humankind, the problems of reform of the French monarchy, Montesquieu, and luxury and treated the decline of Europe's dominant states throughout time by means of a notion of providence. In other words, Galiani dealt with Naples in the context of an analysis of the international realm of political and commercial competition and of the early Enlightenment debates about reform. Like Serra did with the *Breve trattato*, Galiani wrote *Della moneta* to show how Naples might develop into a flourishing country. The difference was that in Serra's time Naples was part of the Spanish Empire, while Galiani could look back on the demise of Spain as proof of his own historical and political economic vision.

4 Naples and the self-defeating mechanisms of the Spanish Empire according to Galiani

To Galiani's mind, it would have made perfect sense to use Serra at one level directly as a model for his political economic argument and at another level absorb Serra into his own moral philosophical perspective of the history of commerce. Within his political thought that underpinned his take on reforms, Galiani put history first and moral philosophy second. He favoured a moral philosophical perspective that corresponded to his historical outlook on the progress of commerce and the institutions of humankind over a general (more historically independent) moral, legal, and political analysis of human nature and its development. Likewise, understanding the Neapolitan challenge proper required careful investigation of the forces and mechanisms that produced the circumstances that determined its place in history.

This kind of historical perspective may have played a role in Intieri's appreciation of Serra's work, but for Galiani it was, as we will see, more prominent as well as of a more analytical importance. At the beginning of endnote XXIX of the second edition of *Della moneta* of 1780,[57] Ferdinando Galiani mentioned:

> Towards the beginning of the seventeenth century, when the social evils of the kingdom of Naples, which began a century earlier and slowly continued to grow, began to grow worse, general confusion along with monetary and exchange disorders became great. The latter, which had to be watched solely as an effect of the evils, because of which all of our money was flowing to other nations, was instead regarded by those ignorant of political and economic science (an ignorance in which even the most serious and celebrated men of the time lived) as their cause, which they attempted to beat with a hosts of regulations and completely erroneous laws, which instead of redressing the evils, increased them. This was a work worthy of a person fond of returning to such noble studies, to publish them anew with illuminations and notes, works already compiled on such materials the memory of which is today completely lost. I have many times considered doing this very thing myself, if only I had time enough to indulge such indolence;[58] I would, indeed, have undertaken it willingly, for nothing is more likely to console the human mind as much as the memory of past calamities. Discerning from these writings the hard and miserable state of the kingdom at that time, would increase

the comfort and jubilation of the present state. But the space of a note will not permit me to discuss this matter at great length.[59]

In the remainder of the endnote, Galiani briefly discussed the writers whose works he would have liked to republish with notes. From Giovanni Donato Turbolo (the master of the mint, who had understood but also "sought to hide [many verities] from the eyes of the multitude"), via de Santis and Serra to Don Luis Enriques de Fonseca (the treasurer of the royal income at Malaga, whose ideas – according to Galiani – were plagiarized by his own contemporary, Carlantonio Broggia),[60] there was a lively debate about the state of the Neapolitan monetary system and its disorders.[61] However, Galiani's purpose for his envisaged republication was not directly to bring to light what this debate itself was about, or to learn about monetary politics, as was the purpose of other contemporary collections of monetary texts, like the ones by Filippo Argelati and Girolamo Costantini.[62] Galiani's projected edition of rare 17th-century texts on money, as he himself wrote in his endnote in the second edition of *Della moneta*, was to discern "from these writings the hard and miserable state of the kingdom at that time" to thereby "increase the comfort and jubilation of the present state".[63]

Interestingly, the library of the *Società Napoletana di Storia Patria* preserves a short autograph manuscript text by Galiani that seems to be an attempt to write an introduction for the republication of early 17th-century texts.[64] As is clear from the textual similarities, Galiani used this text when he wrote endnote XXIX of the second edition of *Della moneta*. Concerning the dating of this text, my guess is that it is from the early to mid 1750s, when it had become known that Galiani was the author of the anonymously published *Della moneta*, and he may have wanted to publish another work, not just to capitalize on the reception of *Della moneta*, but also to hammer in the points that he made in that book.

The perspective that Galiani develops in this introductory text to Serra's *Breve trattato* and a number of other early 17th-century treatises works towards a comparison of that period with the present state of Naples. Galiani's concise narrative focuses on the train of events after the collapse of the Roman Empire and leads to a depiction of 17th-century Naples as a victim of historical processes driven by the primitive human abuse of power. Despite Galiani's eye for detail within this history, the object of the text is not to better understand the past itself as a background to the present. Rather, Galiani set out to demonstrate the difference between, on one hand, when the Neapolitan situation was really dire and there were no opportunities for Naples to reclaim its own sovereignty,[65] and, on the other, the present, which is when the main challenge was how to escape from incorrect ways of thinking about commercial politics. Galiani's brief historical sketch was a way to engage with established Neapolitan ways of looking at its own past (e.g. by Giannone[66]) as well as with dominant political currents that advocated different strategies for protecting the newly established independence in the interstate sphere.[67] He used the case of explaining the character of 17th-century writings about money to further develop his own historical-political "Art of Government". The element that he dealt with most directly was empire and how the Spanish Empire existed in relation to the laws of commerce that he had put as central to his own history of humankind. In *Della moneta*, Galiani had advanced the political side of that issue. In the introduction of the projected text edition, he returned to the analytical problem of the historian in confronting empire and commerce with each other. Yet, that did not mean that his contemporaries were not to understand this (never published) text as a statement on the reform of Naples.

The first sentence of the manuscript states that "nothing works better to console and alleviate the human mind than the memory of calamities past".[68] For that reason, "the present republication of several very rare books that appeared at the beginning of the past century would be very dear for all Italians and in particular for the subjects of the King of Naples". Galiani then explains that there are in fact two reasons for republishing these early 17th-century texts on monetary disorders and political economy: "In the first place, because after seeing to what miserable state of poverty and depopulation and hard condition a very noble and by nature very opulent part of Italy full of subtle minds and valorous people was reduced it will be a consolation to see with how much luck and marvellous fortune it has perfectly recovered from so many and such long lasting evils".[69] In other words, Galiani emphasized not the existing problems but the fact that the south of Italy had come a long way already. "In the second place it will be useful for the wise men to see how much ignorance and misunderstanding of the art of government there was in that time also in the most reputed men, from which clearly emerges how much the light of the true sciences propagated with the most useful invention of the book press has served mankind which then understood little or nothing of commerce and national economics".[70] While men in the past had buried "the freedom of human industriousness...with so many errors in false regulations...these damaged and hurt it"; in the meantime, "we have moved from the ferocious and suspicious police [*polizia*] to the human and benign art of governing [*commandare*]".[71] Galiani concludes the first paragraph of the text by declaring that "both these reasons by themselves are worthy of any honest men and of every true Italian", thus addressing himself to those contemporaries who had in mind the same patriotic objective as Galiani to let the south and indeed the whole of Italy flourish again, but whose political economic views still needed updating.

The rest of the text is a concise historical description of the history of the south of Italy from the loss of its own king in the late 14th century until the period of Spanish viceregal rule: "To give the readers more of a taste of the texts that are here republished it is useful to briefly narrate what was the internal disposition of the Kingdom of Naples, what the evils were that affected it and where they came from".[72] Moving back from the problems of independent Naples in the modern world to the state of the region in the course of the Angevin succession wars of the 15th century, Galiani describes how Naples passed through different hands while late medieval dynasties competed for territorial aggrandizement.[73] Eventually, it found itself absorbed as a "small and remote province" into the "dispersed configuration of states that made up the monarchy of Charles V".[74]

> From then on almost without any interruption for years its coasts were cruelly sacked by Turks and by Barbary corsairs and not only the small villages and the beaches and the hamlets, but also its major maritime cities Pozzuoli, Sorrento, Reggio Calabria and ultimately Manfredonia were laid in ashes and destroyed. The grave contributions exacted by the government of Philip II and the commissions to the destructive War of the Dutch Revolt [*alla distruggitrice Guerra delle Fiandre*] and against the Turk were all concurrent causes in its impoverishment. And because the Spanish nation in its valour and in its art of conquest emulated the Romans, they also imitated them in their disregard and negligence of those industries and arts of the economy and of the rules by which a people can peacefully enrich itself.[75]

In the 17th century, Naples was still sucked into the backfiring mechanisms of Spanish Empire, and a whole set of structures had developed that fed on its abuses and thereby sustained them, creating a sharp opposition between the glamorous images of empire and the bleak reality in most of the Spanish territory. Even in his own time, Galiani mentions, the years of Spanish policy in Italy were looked back upon as heroic – as heroic as fighting a self-destructive war against the Dutch.[76] Yet, in truth the contrast between the idea that the court of Spain, "which was obeyed by both the Indies" was "swimming in wealth" and the occurrences of famines was shocking. Only certain industrious people, "Genovese, Florentines and Flemings" managed to enrich themselves "and those riches for the greatest part were invested in the Kingdom of Naples", where once taxes could no longer be increased, the "perpetual fruit" of the population's productivity was now "sold to the rich at the then current rate of interest. This way, almost all of the revenues and taxes had passed into the hands of foreigners, many also to feudal rulers or were given to the *Grandi* [the aristocracy] of Spain, or were acquired by rich foreign merchants. This is what caused the great extraction of money".[77]

Thus, Naples was made to pay the price for the Spanish abuses. Yet, because of additional problems, the viceroy also did not have any room for manoeuvres to prevent the export of money: "Since the court of Rome liberally granted anyone ecclesiastical revenues also for this reason a lot of money was sent out of the country".[78] However, not only did the Church not care, but the Neapolitan aristocracy did not either:

> There was none among the great Barons who did not send one of his sons to Spain and another to Rome and from their fortune and from relations and friendships among such illustrious families was born the most significant of the non minor causes of the misfortune of the Kingdom. The power of the Barons was formidable to that of the Viceroys and able to ruin their private fortune and they were not spurned by those same kings who always doubted that the Barons (as they tried several times) might turn to the Pope, or to the King of France, or finally to the Turk.[79]

Caught between the viceroy's financial demands, the barons' abusive relations with Spanish and Papal powers,[80] and the lack of economic opportunity because of foreign ownership of capital and tax revenues, the population of the south of Italy had no other way to sustain itself than to turn to small crime. To this, the authorities stupidly responded by maintaining a rigorous observation of the law. As a consequence, "the Kingdom filled up with violent people, who because of the useless sentences against them were called Bandits".[81] Soon the local powers felt they could not control this development anymore, and so clashes between them and the bandits became increasingly violent and destructive, which led to the sacking of the town of Lucera. When "a Viceroy of greater than usual courage" managed to conquer back these places from the bandits, "a worse evil sprang up". Chased into the mountains and reduced to a wild life, "they did not find another remedy to survive than by clipping coins and so after spreading these among the farmers who could not refuse them the flood of bad money reached the capital".[82]

In this way, Galiani systematically linked the monetary abuses and disorders to the mechanisms of the Spanish Empire. Its militaristic style of exercising legal control and its total disregard for measures that stimulate industriousness and trade lay at the basis of the final perversion of the country's finances and could not be ascribed to a depravity of the people themselves, who acted out of sheer necessity. Galiani's conclusion sketched the situation of the Naples in Serra's time as a theatre of political abuse:

> In this unhappy state then was the kingdom of Naples at the beginning of the seventeenth century: neglected by its king and its faraway court, mismanaged by barons, internally destroyed by bandits and desolated and its coasts made unsafe by powerful squadrons of Turks; all its commerce interrupted, on land and at sea, almost all the funds of the crown alienated; and burdened by ever increasing taxes sold to strangers, who administrated them with no less avarice than cruelty, [the kingdom] was always forced to send people and money; and without caring at all for its manufactures and cultivation, the only things the viceroys sought for were maximum *donativi*.[83]

However insecure and fragile Neapolitan independence was, Galiani's upbeat message was that independence created opportunities that before did not exist. Independence itself was liberating as a requirement for progress, whereas being part of an empire destroyed all hope of the increase of prosperity and security. In the shift from the 17th-century situation to the 18th-century situation, Galiani's perspective is dominated by a confidence in understanding the causes of economic development as the key to protecting Neapolitan sovereignty. Galiani realized all too well that in Serra's *Breve trattato* the main argument was set up as a restricted issue of "effective government': Serra criticized the errors of de Santis implicitly as a manifestation of the abuses of empire, but Serra presented his own argument without much reference to actual policies or to the external political world. Indeed, Serra himself, at the end of his work, pointedly refused to go into how the structural underdevelopment of Naples might be counteracted by means of concrete reforms, which would have forced him to preach revolution. Thanks to its newly acquired independence and to its being supported by the idea that in the modern world trade, not conquest, was ultimately the decisive factor that determines the rise and decline of states, Galiani insisted that 18th-century Naples could plan its long-term commercial development based on its own natural resources and comparative advantages in the international market. To believe that Neapolitan markets needed extra protection from external forces was to revert to the same kind of errors that Serra criticized in de Santis, whose analysis of monetary flows by habit confused economic reasoning and the implementation of political objectives.

The weight-bearing element of Galiani's positive message was his systematic outlook on the cultural, political, and social causes of the decline of dominant states and empires. The history of humankind and its failures to set up solid, long-term, viable political societies was the counterpoint of his own theory of political economy, and the study of this history would keep Galiani busy until his death. In his later years, Galiani's work on the interpretation of Horace's poetry had become the main carrier of his juvenile work on the *Art of government*. Galiani had admired Horace all his life, but in his French years and particularly after his return to Naples in 1769, his manuscripts on Horace's poetry filled up with references to the Spanish Empire, sharp criticisms of the role of aristocracy in the modern world, and original observations on those cultural and political developments in Rome, the Middle Ages, and the Renaissance that stimulated the growth and spread of Christianity. In other words, Galiani contextualized the poetry of Horace in such a way that it brought out his own political theory. More explicitly than anywhere else in his oeuvre, Galiani expressed in his commentaries on Horace that any regime based on conquest and subsequently the institution of both privileges and inequality already sowed the seeds for its destruction in the long run. Aristocracy itself, in antiquity as well as in 18th-century Europe, was seen by Galiani as the epitome of this inferior form of state construction and the difficulties that territorial monarchies experienced in adapting themselves to the rules of the modern world, and the reality of commercial competition between states was very much a direct consequence.[81] On the European continent, where most states were monarchies and where human history after the fall of Rome had led to the creation of global empires based on radical inequality and total disregard for the laws of commerce, the model for Naples was not to be found among Europe's dominant states, what with their trade companies and protectionist policies. Instead, as Galiani argued in *Della moneta*, and as he reiterated by stressing the significance of independence in the introduction to 17th-century monetary writings, it was crucial to understand and prevent the violations to the laws of commerce of the past, of empires, and of aristocracies in order to emerge as a healthily reformed commercial society.

5 Conclusion: consolation, not defeatism, to escape underdevelopment

There were many ways to look at the challenge that Italy's old states faced in the 18th century. How this challenge in the 18th century should be dealt with was a very different question than it was in 17th century, and ideas about facing it had changed a lot around Italy. Throughout the *Breve trattato*, Serra still held Venice and to some extent Florence and Genoa as models for the success of "effective government". Yet, after a period of steady economic decline in the 17th century, Venice, by Galiani's time, was already a weak and vulnerable republic rather than an economic powerhouse. Besides, the fact that the new industries and agricultural enterprises on the Terraferma were owned by the important families from the city made it unsuitable, if not politically rejectable, as a model.[85] Genoa had been reduced to a small banking city; Florence was already a rich art centre, struggling to revive its agriculture and industry and not knowing, amidst all the moral views that crept into its native political economic discourse, where to start. One response to the issues of the decline of Italian industry and underdevelopment was to deny that there was a real problem. Thus a text from 1783, published in Venice, argues in a light-hearted tone, referring to Algarotti, that:

> The Italians have conquered the world with arms, they have enlightened it with sciences, made it beautiful with arts and they have governed it with ingenuity. At this moment, it is true, they do not cut such a fine figure. But it is quite natural that he needs to rest a bit who has worked hard and that he who has gotten up before the others in the early morning sleeps a bit during the day.[86]

This was the true opposite of the manner in which Galiani intended his republication of 17th-century texts to offer consolation to its readers. Instead of preaching defeatism or a darkly ironic relativism, Galiani devised his message as a sober hope and belief in the future, discouraging any pipedreams of glory and *grandezza*. From Galiani's point of view, the Italian wealth of the Renaissance was a by-product of a clash that emerged from the paradoxes that were inherent to European history after the fall of Rome. These paradoxes had manifested themselves in the crusades, colonialism, and conquest. If these anti-commercial crazes of European rulers had sparked trade by accident, the Italians had simply been lucky to profit from its development.

From this perspective, Naples had nothing to lose (though it was the third largest city of Europe, so it was rich in population), apart from its opportunities to escape underdevelopment. According to Galiani, these opportunities did exist: the modern world had been constructed with a number of mistakes in its political architecture. Galiani's views on the history of humankind, the decline of empires, and the laws of commerce served to identify the space left by the self-defeating political culture of Europe's dominant states for small underdeveloped states to catch up and break the deadlock of economic non-convergence without protectionist measures. This outlook defined Galiani's place in the Neapolitan reform debate[87] and lay behind his reasons for republishing 17th-century Neapolitan texts on monetary issues. Yet, even though this republication never took place, in *Della moneta* a great deal of Serra's reasoning was creatively recycled and thereby carried into the 18th century.

Notes

1. Intieri had initially trained as a mathematician, and he used his skills to design agricultural machines. See Galiani, F. [Bartolomeo Intieri on titlepage] *Della perfetta conservazione del grano, discorso di Bartolomeo Intieri*, Naples: presso Guiseppe Raimondi, 1754, a work that, scholars agree, was written by Galiani, in which the working of a storage device and its effects on agricultural productivity were explained. This source reveals Intieri's activities and commercial and political views in the mid 1730s during his employment in Naples by various Tuscan noble families is Cantù, C., "Notizie su Napoli dall'archivio di Firenze", *Archivio Storico Italiano*, 10/ I, 1869, pp. 27–39. A forthcoming special issue of the journal *Frontiera d'Europa* dedicated to Bartolomeo Intieri's work and ideas will fill the lacuna that still exists with regard to the understanding of his role in the 1740s Neapolitan reform debate.
2. Venturi, F., "La Napoli di Antonio Genovesi", in his *Settecento riformatore, Da Muratori a Beccaria*, vol. I, Turin: Einaudi, 1969, p. 556.
3. These letters are preserved in the library of the *Società Napoletana di Storia Patria* (henceforth BSNSP), with class mark indication xxx.a.7, ff. 1r-43r. The letters were transcribed and are prepared for publication in the journal *Frontiera d'Europa* by Ajello, R. and L. Palmese. Some twenty years earlier, the same letters were also transcribed by Ferrone, E., yet they remained unpublished, as a part of his research project that culminated in the publication of *Scienza, natura, religione: mondo newtoniano e cultura italiana nel primo Settecento*, Naples: Jovene, 1982 (which was translated into English and published as *The intellectual roots of the Italian Enlightenment* (Atlantic Highlands, N.J.: Humanities Press, 1995). According to R. Ajello, Celestino Galiani – whose Newtonian natural philosophy and ideas about the origins of morality have been central

to accounts of his career so far – was probably more influential and had more of a political programme, or agenda, than has been suspected until now.

4. Ajello, R., "La vita politica napoletana sotto Carlo di Borbone", in *Storia di Napoli*, vol. VII, Naples: Società Editrice Storia di Napoli, 1972, p. 489.
5. Letter to Celestino Galiani, 31 January 1739, BSNSP, xxxi.a.7, f. 30v.
6. Letter to Celestino Galiani, 31 January 1739, BSNSP, xxxi.a.7, f. 30v.
7. Letter to Celestino Galiani, 25 January 1739, BSNSP, xxxi.a.7, f. 27v.
8. Letter to Celestino Galiani, 30 December 1738, BSNSP, xxxi.a.7, ff. 23r-24v.
9. Letter to Celestino Galiani, 11 November 1738, BSNSP, xxxi.a.7, f. 12. Intieri himself was convinced that there was a wide gap between the quality of Dutot's works and Melon's works on money because Melon was simply the "man of more profound wisdom" [*l'uomo di piú profondo sapere*], as he wrote to Celestino, 30 December 1738, BSNSP, xxxi.a.7, f. 23r.
10. Intieri was "fully convinced of the happy wealth of the Kingdom" and believed its inhabitants were "capable of everything and extremely talented", letter to Celestino Galiani, 11 October 1738, BSNSP, xxxi.a.7, f. 5r. According to Intieri it had been observed by political thinkers from other countries too that the "regno diprezzato", once its economic potential was developed, could make a "bella figura" in Europe. Letter to Celestino Galiani, 13 January 1739, BSNSP, xxxi.a.7, f. 25r. This argument, an age-old one among Southern Italians, would become a commonplace in 18th-century European political thought. It would be copied by Hume, Montesquieu, and many others to pose the question of why states with natural resources and optimal conditions for trade like Naples became backward societies.
11. As he wrote to Antonio Cocchi, as late as 1752, see Venturi, F., "Alle origini dell'illuminismo napoletano, dal carteggio di Bartolomeo Intieri", *Rivista Storica Italiana*, 71[2], 1959, pp. 433–434.
12. Letter to Celestino Galiani, 27 December 1738, BSNSP, xxxi.a.7, f. 21r.
13. For the development of this line of reform strategy, see Ajello, R., "Gli 'afrancesados' a Napoli nella prima meta del settecento. Idee e progetti di sviluppo", in Di Pinto, M. (ed.), *Borbone di Napoli, Borbone di Spagna*, Naples: Guida, 1985, pp. 115–192.
14. Letter to Celestino Galiani, 13 January 1739, BSNSP, xxxi.a.7, f. 25r.
15. Letter to Celestino Galiani, 17 June 1741, BSNSP, xxxi.a.7, f. 40r.
16. Letter to Celestino Galiani, 16 December 1739, BSNSP, xxxi.a.7, f. 19v.
17. Letter to Celestino Galiani, 14 April 1739, BSNSP, xxxi.a.7, f. 39rv.
18. Letter to Celestino Galiani, 29 November 1738, BSNSP, xxxi.a.7, f.15r.
19. See Nicolini, F., "La puerizia e l'adolescenza dell'abate Galiani 1735–1745, Notizie, lettere, versi, documenti", *Archivio storico per le province napoletane*, 43, 4, 1918, pp. 105–132. Intieri set out to teach a generation of Neapolitan scholars the art of political economy, in order to catch up with the dominant states who had cultivated this knowledge in an earlier stage. This he argued in a letter to Celestino Galiani of 30 December 1738, BSNSP, ms. xxxi.a.7, f. 23r. The other dominant figure in the education of Neapolitan political economists was the Tuscan nobleman Alessandro Rinuccini, whose views are discussed by Iovine, R., "Il trattato *Della moneta* di Ferdinando Galiani: la dialettica politica a favore e contro la pubblicazione", *Frontiera d'Europa* (1999), pp. 204–210.
20. The first professor was Antonio Genovesi, see Jossa, B., R. Patalano, and E. Zagari (eds), *Genovesi Economista: nel 250° anniversario dell'istituzione della*

cattedra di commercio e meccanica, Naples: Istituto Italiano per gli Studi Filosofici, 2007. For the Enlightenment in Naples in English, see Imbruglia, G., "Enlightenment in eighteenth-century Naples", in id. (ed.), *Naples in the eighteenth century: the birth and death of a nation-state*, Cambridge: Cambridge University Press, 2000, pp. 70–94 and Robertson, J., *The Case for the Enlightenment: Scotland and Naples 1680–1760*, Cambridge: Cambridge University Press, Ideas in Context, 2005.

21. For the first time on p. 7 of *A short treatise on the causes that make kingdoms abound in gold and silver even in the absence of mines, with particular reference to the Kingdom of Naples* in this volume and particularly in chapter VI: "On the common accident of effective government".
22. Galiani, F., *Della moneta e scritti inediti*, Caracciolo, A. & A. Merola (eds), Milan: Feltrinelli, 1963 [1751]. Translations of quotations are based on Galiani, F., *On money: A Translation of Della Moneta by Ferdinando Galiani* by Toscano, P.R., Ann Arbor, MI: University Microfilms International, 1977, but often with considerable modifications to improve the readability and to correct errors. Italian original terms are occasionally added in brackets. For the discussions surrounding the publication of *Della moneta* and the crucial support for the book by N. Fraggianni, see Iovine, R., 1999 (*Frontiera d'Europa*), pp. 173–236. A previous manuscript of the work has been transcribed recently by Patalano, R., "Il manoscritto di *Della moneta*", *Il Pensiero Economico Italiano* 13, 2, 2005, pp. 115–145. While it has been supposed that manuscripts of *Della moneta* no longer exist (for example, by Diaz and Guerci in their introduction to *Opere*, Diaz, F. and L. Guerci (eds), Illuministi Italiani, vol. VI, Milan-Naples: Ricciardi, 1975, p. 3, the whole text in an earlier version, supplemented with the notes for the second edition of 1780 is among Galiani's papers in BSNSP, ms. xxix.e.13, and it remains to be studied by scholars, particularly because of the way in which its pages are mixed with the manuscript of Galiani's last work *Dei doveri dei principi neutrali*, of 1782.
23. But see S. Reinert's mentioning of Paolo Mattia Doria's manuscript "Relazione dello stato politico, economico, e civile del Regno di Napoli…", *Manoscritti napoletani di Paolo Mattia Doria*, vol. 1, Lecce: 1979, where Doria cites Serra on pp. 119, 146, in his introduction to Serra, *A Short Treatise on the Wealth and Poverty of Nations (1613)*, trans. Jonathan Hunt, London: Anthem, 2011, p. 6f15.
24. The same copy is now part of the collection of the Fondazione Einaudi in Turin; see Reinert, E.S. and S.A. Reinert, "An Early National Innovation System: The Case of Antonio Serra's *Breve trattato*", *Instituzioni e sviluppo economico*, 3, 2003, pp. 87–119.
25. Galiani, 1780, pp. 339–340.
26. For a recent article dealing with Serra from the point of view of the history of economic thought, see Rosselli, A., "Early Views on Monetary Policy: The Neapolitan Debate on the Theory of Exchange", *History of Political Economy*, 32, 1, 2000, pp. 61–82.
27. See the letters that Galiani wrote after his departure from Paris to his friends Mme. d'Épinay, Grimm, and others, in Galiani, F., *Correspondence avec Mme d'Epinay, Mme Necker, Mme Geoffrin, &c. Diderot, Grimm, d'Alembert, De Sartine, d'Holbach, &c.*, II vols, Perey, L. and G. Maugras (eds), Paris: Levy,1881.

28. On this aspect of Galiani's oeuvre, as a classical, see also (in particular the last pages of) Stapelbroek, K., "Galiani's concept of commerce in *On money* and the eighteenth-century Neapolitan languages of commerce and liberty", *History of Economic Ideas*, 2001, pp. 137–170.
29. See the admirable and extremely useful reconstruction of Galiani's Horace studies by Nicolini, F., *L'Orazio dell'abate Galiani*, Atti dell'Accademia Nazionale dei Lincei, Memorie Scienze Morali, Serie VIII, vol. xxii, fascicolo 2, 1978, which I will very briefly discuss below and refer to in some footnotes in the rest of this chapter.
30. See Nicolini, 1978, pp. 150–152, in which Galiani describes the decline of poetry after the time of Horace, the "corruption of taste" of the "ancient scholastics" of poetry and the relationships between the development of Latin, the rise of Christianity, and the plunge of human civilization into the dark Middle Ages. These passages resemble the account of the rise and decline of Rome and modern societies in the history of humankind that Galiani sketches in the first chapter of *Della moneta*.
31. Koen Stapelbroek, "The progress of humankind in Galiani's Dei Doveri dei Principi Neutrali: Natural law, Neapolitan trade and Catherine the Great", in id. (ed.), *Trade and War: The Neutrality of Commerce in the Inter-State System, special issue of COLLeGIUM: Studies Across Disciplines in the Humanities and Social Sciences published by the Helsinki Collegium for Advanced studies*, 2011, pp. 161–183.
32. Galiani himself declared (apparently referring to his own experience) that "i giovani hanno la rabbia d'imitazione e mostrare d'aver letto", Nicolini, 1978, p. 228. See also endnote XVI of the second edition of *Della moneta* for Galiani's statement about his project *Dell'arte del governo* (Galiani, 1780, p. 326; see also p. 109).
33. See Stapelbroek, K., *Love, Self-deceit and Money: Commerce and Morality in the Early Neapolitan Enlightenment*, Toronto, ON: University of Toronto Press, 2008, ch. 4.
34. See Galiani, F., *Scritti di politica economica,* (ed.) Cesarano, F., Lanciano: Rocco Carabba, 1999, pp. 1–3. The manuscript is preserved at the BSNSP ms. xxxi.c.8, ff. 1r-16v. The text that is seen as the actual remaining part of *Dell'arte del governo* is interrupted by empty pages on ff. 3–7 and 12–14r, and ff. 8–11 contain several notes on antiquarian subjects. The same manuscript volume has a few pages with lists drawn up by Galiani of subjects on which he planned to write in those years (BSNSP xxxi.c.8. ff. 121v-122r). Here, Galiani's projected writings are divided neatly into categories, like "materi d'antiquità", "teologiche", and "fisiche, e di storia naturale", which unfortunately does not represent the typological structure that Galiani put into his description of the history of humankind.
35. Luigi Diodati (1763–1832) was a close friend, and presumably a pupil in some way, of Ferdinando Galiani. He became the head of the Neapolitan mint and published a work, namely *Dello stato presente delle monete nel Regno di Napoli e della necessità di un alzamento,* in 1790 and *Risposta ad alcune critiche fatte nell'opera intitolata: Dello stato presente delle monete nel regno di Napoli e della necessità di un alzamento* in 1794. According to Venturi, F., "Una discussione tra Gianrinaldo Carli e G. Palmieri", *Rivista Storica Italiana*, 1962, p. 154, Diodati's work had a direct impact on the financial politics of Genoa and was the inspiration of a law

proclaimed on 24 April 1790. Diodati also published a biography of his brother Domenico, a prominent scholar of ancient Greek language, in 1815.

36. Diodati, L., *Vita dell'abate Ferdinando Galiani*, Naples: presso Vincenzo Orsini, 1788, p. 6; Galiani, 1780, pp. 20–29, 308–309 (endnote IV of the second edition in which Galiani explained the nature of his project on trade in antiquity).
37. Serra, 1613, p. 1.
38. *Ibid.*, p. 105.
39. *Ibid.*, p. 111.
40. *Ibid.*, p. 111.. Serra writes "position" [*posizione*], translated in this volume as "convention". The meaning is that justice is best understood as something created by humankind itself; David Hume would later call that "artificial justice".
41. *Ibid.*, p. 113..
42. *Ibid.*, p. 114.
43. *Ibid.*, p. 115. This statement is not to be taken as expressing an intention to develop the science of economics apart from politics but as a sharp critique of the approach of "good government". It would be more relevant and efficient and in the interest of societies if writers started to understand how money works (thereby furthering "effective government') than continue to operate within a tradition of discussing "good government".
44. Galiani, 1780, pp. 12–13.
45. *Ibid.*, p.12.
46. In the core chapter (book I, chapter 2) of *Della moneta*, Galiani explained that the value of money at any point in time ultimately derived from principles that were part of human nature itself; money was certainly not a human invention by which people deliberately changed the societies they lived in. It emerged naturally out of the gradual modification of people's loves into social ideas of value that inspired commercial interaction. Money did not emerge by agreement, and its existence was not reliant on promises, trust, or any additional moral capacity of self-restraint. If this had been different, commerce could never have become central to modern societies.
47. Galiani, 1780, p. 66.
48. *Ibid.*, p. 46.
49. See the titles of chapters I until VII.
50. Serra, 1613, in this volume, p. 201.
51. *Ibid.*, p. 215.
52. See Galiani, 1780, pp. 126, 324–325 (endnote XIV of the second edition of 1780). Bianchini, L., *Della storia delle finanze del regno di Napoli*, Naples: Stamperia Reale, 1859 [1835]); Venturi, F., "Il dibattito sulle monete", in *Settecento riformatore, Da Muratori a Beccaria*, vol. I, Turin: Einaudi, 1969, pp. 487–490.
53. Hardly any research exists on Spinelli. Some interesting biographical information is contained in Venturi, F., "Tre note su Carlantonio Broggia", *Rivista Storica Italiana*, 80, 4, 1986, pp. 830–853. On his monetary theory and the work on money he published, probably in 1748, see Patalano, R., "La scienza della moneta more geometrico demostrata: le Riflessioni politiche di Troiano Spinelli", *Il Pensiero Economicio Italiano*, 10, 2, 2002, pp. 7–42. See also the entry for Spinelli in Costabile, L. and R. Patalano (eds), *Repertorio Bio-bibliografico*

degli scrittori di economia in Campania. Parte Prima (1594–1861), Naples: La città del sole, 2000. Another work by Spinelli, entitled *Degli affetti umani*, Naples: Nella Stamperia Muziana, 1741, is a highly accomplished moral philosophical work, in the form of dialogues set in a Neapolitan garden looking out over the Vesuvius, and it responds to the most advanced French and English scholarship of the time. I believe that his *Degli affetti umani* was an important source for Galiani's idea of love and thereby of his entire political thought. To my knowledge, there is a conspicuous lack of any studies on Spinelli's moral philosophy as well as his other political works (on the aristocracy and on legal history).

54. Galiani, 1780, pp. 324–325 (endnote XIV of the second edition of 1780).
55. Galiani, 1780, pp. 8–9.
56. *Ibid.*, p. 10.
57. Galiani, 1780, pp. 409–410.
58. Galiani was famous for presenting plans and drawing up schemes for works that he would never write but leave at the stage of a quick chapter sketch. See for example Nicolini, 1978, p. 113, who refers to Galiani's "indolenza e pigrizia". For a fascinating account by Ludwig Heinrich von Nicolay, of the way in which Galiani worked on his books, see Heier, E., *L.H. Nicolay (1737–1820) and his contemporaries*, The Hague: Martinus Nijhoff, 1965, p. 104. However, the interconnections of Galiani's themes have been left ignored. I hope to bring to light some of these in an edited bilingual volume of some of Galiani's juvenile works, which will be published by the *Centro di studi sull'Illuminismo Giovanni Stiffoni*, Venice.
59. Galiani, 1780, pp. 337–338.
60. *Ibid.*, pp. 338–341. For more on Broggia, see chapter 5 of Stapelbroek, 2008.
61. The texts that Galiani intended to publish were collected and also supplemented with additional works by Campanella, Biblia di Catanzaro, Braccini, Lunetti, La Sena and Gascon, by Colapietra, R. (ed.), *Problemi monetari negli scrittori napoletani del seicento*, Rome, Accademia nazionale dei Lincei, 1973, yet, as noted by Rosselli, 2000, p. 63 (footnote 7), a lot of errors were made in the transcriptions.
62. Argelati, F. and C. Casanova, *De monetis Italiae variorum illustrium virorum, dissertationes quarum pars nunc primum in lucem prodit*, vols I–VI, Milan: 1750–1759, and Costantini, G., *Delle monete, controversia agitata tra due celebri scrittori altremontani*, Venice: Antonio Zatta, 1754.
63. Galiani, 1780, p. 338.
64. The class mark of the text is xxxi.c.8. fasc. 18, ff. 129r-36v. The piece has a second page numbering system, going from I to VIII. It was bound in the manuscript volume upside down so that the main pagination runs against the order of the text. For this reason, I will refer to both paginations). From Ir to IVr (so from 136v back to 133v). the text is an introduction to the republication of the old works by sketching the history of Naples until that time and a brief account of the political abuses from which Naples suffered under the Spanish viceregency. Then empty pages, then VIIv (130r) on Turbolo. Galiani left his manuscripts to his nephew Francesco Paolo Azzariti, who sold them to Niccola Nicolini, the great-grandfather of Fausto Nicoli, who then donated them to the BSNSP, where they remain (Nicolini, 1978, pp. 113–114). For an overview of Galiani's manuscripts, see Nicolini, F., "I manoscritti di

Ferdinando Galiani", *Archivio storico per le province napoletane*, 33, 1908, pp. 171–197, Galasso, G., "I manoscritti napoletani dell'abate Galiani", in *La filosofia in soccorso de' governi: la cultura napoletana del Settecento*, Naples: Guida, 1989, pp. 353–368 and the website of *L'Archivio Storico degli Economisti* on http://ase.signum.sns.it/. Only the latter mentions Galiani's manuscript on 17th-century monetary works. In this database, it is entitled "Proemio alla ristampa di libri che trattano dei disordini della moneta al tempo dei Viceré e cagioni delle misere condizioni del Regno" and described as a "Documento di Ferdinando Galiani in cui si ricostruisce la situazione politica partendo dal XVI secolo. Galiani critica il sistema fiscale adottato nel Regno di Napoli, la vendita dei dazi e delle rendite ai forestieri, i privilegi dei grandi Baroni". To my knowledge, this text has never been discussed anywhere in the secondary literature.

65. For the economic effects of the Spanish quest for Empire on the Neapolitan economy, see Calabria, A., *The Cost of Empire: The Finances of the Kingdom of Naples in the Time of Spanish Rule*, Cambridge: Cambridge University Press, 1991. For the economic and financial situation of Naples in the early 17th century, see (besides other works by the same author) De Rosa, L., *Il Mezzogiorno spagnolo tra crescita e decadenza*, Milan: Il Saggiatore, 1987 as well as Coniglio, G., *Il viceregno di Napoli nel secolo XVII. Nuove notizie sulla vita commerciale e finanziaria tratte dagli archivi napoletani*, Rome: Edizioni di storia e letteratura, 1955; Galasso, G., *Contributo alla storia delle finanze del Regno di Napoli nella prima meta del Seicento, estratto da Annuario dell'Istituto storico italiano per l'eta moderna e contemporanea, vol. 11, 1959*, Rome: s.n., 1961.
66. Giannone, P., *Istoria civile del regno di Napoli*, Naples: Niccolò Naso, 1723 famously described Neapolitan history as consisting of layers of foreign juridical principles and institutions, and Papal oppression smothering all attempts to escape the country's social and economic backwardness. This image of the history of Naples became (and remains until this day) a commonplace. For an account in English of Giannone's historical narrative, see Pocock, J.G.A., *Barbarism and Religion (Vol.2): Narratives of Civil Government*, Cambridge: Cambridge University Press, 1999.
67. See Stapelbroek, 2008, chapters 1 and 5.
68. BSNSP xxxi.c.8, f. 136v/ Ir. The central topos in the first sentence is about (im) perfection and the human condition, one that frequently recurs in Galiani's early manuscripts – as well as in *Della moneta*, which suggests that this text would stem from the same period.
69. BSNSP xxxi.c.8, f. 136v-136r/ Ir-Iv. The last part of the sentence replaces the earlier version: "the Neapolitans should console themselves with the memory of how painful and tough the past was".
70. BSNSP xxxi.c.8, f. 136r/ Iv.
71. *Ibid.*
72. BSNSP xxxi.c.8, f. 136r/ Iv.
73. *Ibid.*
74. BSNSP xxxi.c.8, f. 135v/ IIr.
75. BSNSP xxxi.c.8, f. 135v/ IIr. In the manuscript the text is interrupted frequently by deleted words, indicating that Galiani here was searching for the right words while writing these sentences. The references to the various places that Galiani mentions (particularly Manfredonia and Pozzuoli) are

interesting in the light of later detailed historical studies that Galiani carried out of the region of the old harbour of Baia and off the coast of Puglia, particularly around Mat(t)inata – the old post-Roman town that is now believed to have been destroyed by a tsunami. See, for some of Galiani's ideas, Nicolini, 1978, pp. 178–182, 256–257, 263, 272.

76. BSNSP xxxi.c.8, f. 135v/ IIr.
77. BSNSP xxxi.c.8, f. 135vr/ IIrv.
78. BSNSP xxxi.c.8, f. 135r/ IIv.
79. BSNSP xxxi.c.8, f. 134v/ IIIr.
80. BSNSP xxxi.c.8, f. 134v/IIIr. For the connections among Spain, the Italian aristocracy, and the Papal court, see Dandelet, T.J. and J.A. Marino (eds), *Spain in Italy, Politics, Society, and Religion 1500–1700*, Leiden: Brill, 2006.
81. BSNSP xxxi.c.8, f. 134vr/ IIIrv.
82. BSNSP xxxi.c.8, f. 134r/ IIIv.
83. BSNSP xxxi.c.8, f. 133v/ IVr.
84. Nicolini, 1978, pp. 156–157. The whole text is full with negative references to oligarchies and any form of government in which the aristocracy plays a role and is, I believe, the last carrier of Galiani's lifelong project to develop a history of humankind, modern government, and commercial society, which simultaneously was a critical engagement with Montesquieu's theory of modern monarchy.
85. This poses the question if there can be said to have been active any true sectoral interdependence and mechanisms of cumulative causation in the Venetian economy.
86. Quoted from Francesco Algarotti by Piazza, A., *Discorso all'orecchio di monsieur Louis [Ange] Goudar*, London [Venice]: 1776, p. 52.
87. For my ideas on Galiani's reformist views compared with Genovesi, see Stapelbroek, K. "Preserving the Neapolitan state: Antonio Genovesi and Ferdinando Galiani on commercial society and planning economic growth", *History of European Ideas* 32, 4, 2006, pp. 406–429 and chapter 5 of Stapelbroek, 2008.

12

Francesco Saverio Salfi and the Eulogy for Antonio Serra: Politics, Freemasonry, and the Consumption of Culture in the Early 19th Century

Antonio Trampus

1 Francesco Saverio Salfi: his life between Naples and Milan

Francesco Saverio Salfi published his eulogy on Antonio Serra in 1802 in Milan.[1] Although this might seem like the customary formal tribute, the text is actually full of far greater significance, of relevance to the political climate and the Italian and French freemasonry of the beginning of the 19th century, as well as the Neapolitan culture of Antonio Genovesi and Gaetano Filangieri. The aim of the present work is to illustrate the social and Masonic context in which the eulogy on Serra was written and the role and character of Francesco Saverio Salfi.

Who was Francesco Salfi? He was born in Cosenza – the same Southern Italian city where Antonio Serra was born – on 1 January 1759 – and he died in Paris on 3 September 1832. His family lived in quite humble conditions, and he was placed under a widow's charge before starting an ecclesiastical career. During the seminary period, he came across texts by Helvéticus, d'Alembert, and Rousseau, and the doctrines of the Southern adherents of the Enlightenment. He was consecrated in 1781, but differences with the curia led him to move to Naples in 1785. He then met some local exponents of the Enlightenment, in particular Francesco Mario Pagano and Gaetano Filangieri, and in 1787 published the *Saggio sui fenomeni antropologici relativi al tremuoto* (*Essay on the anthropological phenomena related to the earthquake*), an earthquake which devastated various areas of Calabria in 1783). Meanwhile, in Naples, he joined a group of friends and co-operators who had connections with the first minister, J. Fr. Acton, through the Vicar General of the Kingdom, Don Francesco Pignatelli of the Princes of Strongoli. From then on, Salfi became very active in promoting the interests of the king against the curia, and he also wrote *Allocuzione del Cardinale N. N. al papa* (*Formal address of the Cardinal N.N. to the Pope*) and *Riflessioni sulla corte romana* (*Reflection on the Roman Court*), both published in 1788.[2]

Like Francesco Mario Pagano, Salfi became popular as a playwright, especially for his works with jurisdictional themes (*Corradino, Giovanna Regina di Napoli*, c. 1789–1790). For this reason, he came under the control of the political authorities.[3] As in the case of many other Neapolitan exponents of the Enlightenment, the behaviour of the government towards him changed considerably upon exacerbation of the control that Ferdinand IV wielded over Neapolitan cultural life from autumn 1789 onwards. Thanks to the help of Acton in 1793, Salfi continued to receive the benefits of the abbey of San Nicola from Majoli, in Maida (Catanzaro), and also continued writing for the king's theatre until 1794.[4] Nevertheless, since he had joined many patriotic associations and had become a suspicious figure, he was obliged to flee Naples in 1795 to avoid arrest.[5] He went into hiding in Capri, where he left the priesthood, then in Genoa and Pavia, where he founded the "Società popolare" (People's Society). In the spring of 1796 he moved to Milan, immediately after the town had been occupied by the Napoleonic troops. He was appointed department head of the ministry of foreign affairs, started working as a journalist, and became one of the main columnists for the newspaper *Termometro politico della Lombardia*. Moreover, he also dedicated himself to the creation of a patriotic theatre repertoire with a marked pedagogic and propaganda bent. After a short period in Brescia (summer–autumn 1797), probably due to expulsion, Salfi went back to Milan, and at the beginning of 1798, he became department head of the education ministry.[6]

The year after, specifically 1799, he was called back to Naples as secretary general of the temporary government of the Neapolitan Republic. This proved to be another fundamental experience for Salfi in that he was able to take part in the discussions on and birth of the first Italian democratic constitution, the famous Constitutional Project for the Neapolitan Republic by Francesco Mario Pagano.

2 Constitutionalism and good government

The history of the Italian constitutions of the democratic triennium seems to be strictly related to the series of political events which accompanied the changes that Italy had to undergo after the French invasion. Government of the new-born republics was almost everywhere assigned to the moderates, and discussion on the constitutional projects tended to end up with imitations of the French constitution of the year III. Even the most creative adaptations – for example, in the case of religious policy – appeared to be extremely moderate. In some cases, the constitutions were simply imposed by the French (as in Rome); in some others, local legislative committees were asked to produce one (as in Naples). In the case of the Ligurian Republic, the preparatory works show that the most radical parts of the original project were emendated by the moderates.

According to some interpretations, the constitutional process was slowed down and made difficult almost everywhere by the problem of the abolition of feudalism – very often implemented with a series of compromises, bringing in laws guaranteeing the old feudal vassals their allodial property. But even where feudalism was completely abolished – as in Naples, for example – the problems of actually putting the laws into force dramatically reduced their application in practice.

Salfi was present in Naples while discussion of two main subjects was carried out: first of all, the matter of the economic and political reforms dependent on the abolition of feudalism; second, the creation of a constitutional project which had necessarily to be far from the French constitutions, because it had to be adapted to the specific conditions of the Neapolitan area and, furthermore, because it had to embody the great legacy of the Southern Enlightenment doctrines, from Serra to Vico, from Genovesi to Filangieri.

Actually, one of the main factors behind the genesis and the events related to the *Progetto di costituzione per la repubblica napoletana* lay in the possibility of studying its significance by taking a comparative approach, as many contemporaries were suggesting. The press and public opinion not only gave the measure of actual tensions but also highlighted the difficulties entailed with the democratic debate, which were also registered by Giuseppe Abamonti in his *Saggio sulle leggi fondamentali dell'Italia libera* (*Essay on the fundamental laws of free Italy*) written in Oneglia, the town where democratic debate leading to the Ligurian constitutional project was underway. The large quantity of Ligurian newspapers and constitutional clubs represent evidence of the debate that accompanied the constitutionalization process, and on 16th February 1799 the "Gazzetta nazionale della Liguria" published an article entitled *Genova e Napoli* (*Genoa and Naples*), in which the author compared the two Republics, underlining the role of the feudal yoke in slowing down the peoples' regeneration process. These difficulties were all the greater in Naples, where the population was also more indolent.

The situation in Naples was in a way mirror-like. The first discussions on the possibility of introducing a constitution for the Republic were doubtless carried out while closely following the events unfolding throughout Italy, even though there are no written records left to prove this. Nevertheless, the hypothesis is prompted by the intense printing activity of the two brothers Vincenzo and Gennaro De Simone, who also probably published the work by Pagano. At the beginning of 1799 – for some months – they printed a series of treatises that contained the texts of what were clearly considered the most important European constitutions – namely the constitutions of France (year III), the Cisalpine Republic, and the Roman Republic, as well as the constitutional project of the Ligurian Republic. Thanks to this project, the printing house (also known as the Simoniana Printing House) was simply carrying on with the traditional civil commitment dating back to the mid 18th century and revived in 1766 by the brothers Paolo and Nicola de Simone ,who, thanks to their cooperation with Domenico Terres, edited the works of Antonio Genovesi. This commitment was then continued by Gennaro and Vincenzo de Simone, up until the inauguration of the Republic.

During that same period, Francesco Mario Pagano, called back to Naples after his exile by the Republic's ministry of internal affairs, embarked upon intense publicistic activity, in October publishing his *Discorso sulla relazione dell'agricoltura, delle arti e del commercio allo spirito pubblico* (*Speech on the relation between agriculture, arts and trade with public spirit*), held a few weeks before at the Agriculture, Arts and Trade Society. It is worth remembering that the speech was also published by Vincenzo Poggioli, the republican editor from Rome who had also probably printed the text of the Roman constitution and who was, in those days, re-printing the *Scienza della legislazione* (*Legislation Science*) by Filangieri.[7]

As we know, the Neapolitan Republic ended in a blood bath, the majority of the protagonists being sentenced to death by hanging; Francesco Salfi managed to escape, hiding first in Marseille and then in Lyon. In June 1800 he went back to Milan with the Napoleonic troops and was appointed as a logic and metaphysics teacher at the Brera gymnasium. Moreover, he was also appointed as an inspector of theatrical works and the president of the Patriotic Theatre Society. From 1803 he was employed in the Milan Royal Special Schools, where he taught history and diplomacy and then public and commercial law.[8] Having decided to distance himself from the official political scenario, Salfi oriented his patriotic activity towards democratic partisanship and Carbonarism, although he had an important role in the new-born, pro-government Grande Oriente d'Italia.

It was during this period that he wrote and published the eulogy on Antonio Serra, which has been attributed with importance not only from the point of view of the history of economics but also in political and cultural terms. We can better understand the interest that Salfi showed in Serra if we take into account the fact that in those years he was working on a re-edition of the *Scienza della legislazione* by Filangieri. Salfi was well aware of the new and astonishing success that the *Scienza della legislazione* had had after the Restoration – all the more striking if we take into account the fact that in 1812, during the preparatory activities for the new constitutions, the Cortes of Cadiz improved on the Spanish translation of the *Scienza*, thus producing the first complete text after the abridgements imposed by censorship thirty years before.

In 1814, when the Italian Kingdom fell, Salfi moved to Naples, and thanks to the help of Murat, one of his old sponsors at the time of the Cisalpine Republic, he obtained the teaching post for history and chronology at the University and a Knighthood in the Royal Order of the Two Sicilies. He remained loyal to Murat up to the defeat of Tolentino, and then he took refuge in Paris at the beginning of summer 1815. During his exile, he continued with his patriotic activities and founded, together with some friends, the "Società dell'emancipazione nazionale" ("National Emancipation Society") while also keeping on good terms with Filippo Buonarroti.

The relations between constitutionalism, economy, and freemasonry emerged again a few years later in 1821, when the French editor Dufart re-published in Paris the *Scienza della legislazione*, introducing – in debate with Benjamin Constant – an important new element, namely the *Éloge de Filangieri*, written by Francesco Saverio Salfi and patterned on the same model as the eulogy on Serra.

In Salfi's pages, the biographical elements of Filangieri's life were transposed into the myth of the young jurist who died prematurely having anticipated the French Revolution and whose membership of Masonic Lodge was proudly vindicated:

> It was there that, coming to a yet fuller knowledge of the rights of man, and at the same time contemplating the fate of the just and the innocent, he felt the need and determined from then on to serve no other cause but that of humanity.

But Salfi went even farther in this direction: to him Filangieri was the guardian of republicanism, the enemy of absolutism, the sponsor of the "governments the nation participates in".[9]

He was also directly addressing an issue which could no longer be ignored, especially after the constitutional uprisings of the 1820s, namely Filangeri's apparent silence about modern forms of constitutionalism. Salfi underlined the importance of the context in which the work had been written and the importance of the fact that "Filangieri's silence on the constitution" was indeed no more than apparent because there were many references to the constitutional experiences of the American rebels. The conclusion was therefore clear.

It is hardly surprising that Filangieri did not trace out a political constitution in the vast plan of his work. Evidently, he had taught a constitutional policy method without defining a type of constitutional document to change the global balance of his work, whose aim was mainly criticism of the old regime. Salfi adds that, for Filangieri,

> it sufficed him to offer a glimpse of his principles and intentions; and his disciples, as well as his fellow citizens, made it quite clear for their part that not only had they inherited them, but also studied how to bring them ever closer to implementation.

For this reason,

> One cannot follow his entire system without feeling throughout the need for a constitution to guarantee its implementation. This is the one great goal upon which the most enlightened Neapolitans have concentrated their attention and interest. Since the dire times of 1799 the plan and hope had grown to endow themselves with a constitution; and Filangieri's greatest friend, of the ill-fated Mario Pagano, had taken it upon himself to present a project. This monument of

> patriotic aspirations survived him and served to fuel his colleagues' motivations.[10]

In those years, Salfi also attended Madame Condorcet's salon, where he met F. Guizot, J.-C. Simonde de Sismondi and P.-L. Ginguené, whose *Histoire littéraire d'Italie* was continued after the author's death by Salfi himself. He contributed to the *Biographie Universelle* by Michaud; to the "Revue Encyclopédique", for which he wrote about 300 entries (1819–1829); and to the "Antologia" by G. P. Vieusseux.[11] Moreover, he edited the *Corréspondance* of the abbot Ferdinando Galiani (1818). He died after a prolonged illness in September 1832 and was buried in the cemetery of Père Lachaise. In 2005 his body was transferred to the cemetery of Cosenza by the municipality and the local lodge named after *Francesco Saverio Salfi*.

3 The Eulogy for Antonio Serra in its Masonic Context

To better understand the cultural context in which Salfi wrote the eulogy on Serra, we must briefly consider the world of freemasonry as it was at the time. At present we have no documents to help us ascertain the date and the occasion of Salfi's initiation in freemasonry, although it might have occurred relatively early, probably during the period of his residence in Cosenza, as suggested by the fact that Calabria was one of the provinces of the Kingdom of Naples with the highest penetration of freemasonry. Traditionally, we tend to consider his initiator as being the lawyer Domenico Bisceglia, who had a very important role during Salfi's youth and also during the years he spent in the seminary, on account of the clandestine texts of the Enlightenment that he managed to read thanks to Bisceglia's help. When Salfi moved to Naples in 1785, thanks to the *Saggio di fenomeni antropologici*, he was literally thrown into the midst of the city's intellectual world, and immediately proved to be one of the leading figures of Southern Enlightenment Hermetism. All the contacts he made in the city had Masonic origins and the sensational success of the *Saggio* was amplified through the inquisition-like process brought against him by the bishop of Cosenza and through the staunch defence that the Neapolitan court offered the priest against his superior.

In the essay *Saggio di fenomeni antropologici relativi al tremuoto*, we find the cyclic vision of the cosmos which was at the basis of the philosophy of history present in the *Saggi politici* (*Political essays*) by F. M. Pagano and which was a common element of the typical "thought style" of late Neapolitan Enlightenment culture, diffused through the Masonic network. According to Salfi, faced with the "spectacle of the most extraordinary revolutions" of nature which "seems to live but to destroy itself" in a never-ending loop, the philosophical mind should have seen nothing more than an "ordinary phenomenon, similar to the cyclic setting of the sun". His cultural references were the Stoa, with the "circular-infinite-progress", Plato and the "sacred traditions of the Egyptian priests", and the myth of the phoenix. Some of his dramatic works of this period are characterized by certain elements typical of Masonic theatre. For example, the tragedy *Corradino* (1790),[12] considers the origins of the foundation of the Neapolitan regalism (in 1789 F.M. Pagano also wrote one) and in II act tells of the generous competition between the two cousins Corradino and Federico, each ready to be immolated to save the other. This type of scene is very frequent in Masonic theatre through the mythic characters of Pylades and Orestes. Also, some aspects of the contemporary unpublished tragedy *Lo spettro di Tecmessa* (*Tecmessa's ghost*) could have connections with a symbolic path derived from the ceremony of the Scottish Rite, transplanted from Marseille to the Calabrian Lodges. The subject of the play is based on a parable of civilization coming to the cessation of all human sacrifices, an prophecy pronounced by a snake, and a final scene of a blind sacrifice in a dark cavern: these are all elements which could clearly refer back to the rites of the "revenge grades", as they are called.

Salfi's Masonic experience changed greatly when the activities of the most radical part of the Neapolitan Masonic world gradually faded into Jacobin conspiratorial sectarianism. A large number of these clandestine patriotic meetings – generally held in a network of private houses – started to lose their Masonic characteristics in favour of real political conspiracy. Some of them were also held at Salfi's Neapolitan house and an increasing number of participants were attracted, including doctors and lawyers, university teachers and students, some priests, and some members of the high Neapolitan aristocracy. Some of the aristocrats included the Serra of Cassano, the Duke of Civitella, and Duke of Andria and Count of Ruvo Ettore Carafa, the lattermost of whom was then a martyr of the Bourbon reaction of 1799.

The year 1794, when the intrigue was discovered, saw the first imprisonments, (January–March) trials and convictions (October). Salfi had never aroused the suspicions of the Bourbon inquisitors, because in September 1792 he could still count on the favour of the Court for the many favours that he had offered.[13]

Up to mid 1794 Salfi continued writing librettos – under police control, like many city institutions; he was undoubtedly watched over, but not entirely compromised. Nevertheless, at the beginning of autumn, he decided to disappear while waiting to emigrate clandestinely. He was hidden for three months in the library of the house of a Masonic friend (the botanist Nicola Pacifico, a victim of the repression of 1799); he changed refuge now and then, up to his adventurous flight from Naples at the beginning of 1795. When Salfi published his eulogy for Serra, Italy was occupied by the revolutionary army, and Milan was under the Jacobin Triennium. He thus joined the "noisy, pugnacious and pushy" group of the southern exiles and refugees who were the spinal cord of the new democratic press, men who were not suffered gladly, sometimes even hated by the moderate conservative party under the French Directory. They were a small minority, but they were also the "most active and decided, politically engaged men and therefore the most dangerous ones amid the general apathy of public opinion". There are no records of Salfi's Masonic activities during the Jacobin Triennium, even though with the arrival of the Napoleonic troops in Italy, the temples could be reopened. Moreover, in many cases the officers of the revolutionary army themselves created lodges under the control of the Paris Great Orient, from which they spread the watchword of revolutionary propaganda, almost completely subject to French expansionistic policy and to the ambitious aims of the Directory and Bonaparte.

Probably the idea of the eulogy for Serra was conceived within the "Società dei Raggi", in which Salfi took part together with a large number of Southern refugees in Milan during the period of the Cisalpine Republic. This society had para-Masonic characteristics much like the clubs that he used to frequent before 1792.[14] We also have certain knowledge that Salfi founded a lodge in Milan, together with the exiles Vincenzo Cuoco, Francesco Lomonaco, Francesco Massa, and Giuseppe Abamonte; the name of the lodge is unknown, but we do know that it was abolished in 1802. The "Fondo Salfi" of the Biblioteca Nazionale di Napoli contains a letter from Francesco Saverio Salfi to Count Giuseppe Prina, minister of finance in the Cisalpine Republic, offering the eulogy for Antonio Serra: "I would not presume to submit to you the eulogy on Antonio Serra, the first writer on civil economy, which I composed, and which has already been printed and published if, being a name that touches on the honour of Italy, it could not interest persons like you who support and promote such honour".[15]

After the creation of the Grande Oriente d'Italia (1805), Salfi became increasingly involved in Masonic activities, and he also had very important roles within the Order: in 1811 he was grand master of the Milanese Lodge named after Viceroy Eugenio's mother, the *Reale Gioseffina* (*Royal Josephine*). It is worth remembering that the philosopher Gian Domenico Romagnosi was also master of this lodge. From 1807 onwards Salfi is recorded with the 32nd degree of the Rito Scozzese Antico e Accettato (Accepted Ancient Scottish Rite) (as "Sublime Principe del Real Segreto" – "Sublime Prince of the Royal Secret", a degree he still held in 1811); as emissary of the Grande Oriente he probably organized and led the obsequies for A.-C. Saliceti in Rome. In any case, during the period of the Kingdom of Italy, Salfi worked as a teacher at Brera and as theatre censor, and he "only published works on the masonry", apart from a few short essays and a few plays.[16]

In those years, Salfi produced a great many architectural designs (largely lost) and occasional Masonic verses, from the short poem *Iramo* (1807) to the *Tavole massoniche* (*Masonic Paltes*, published in 1810). He also wrote a Masonic song to celebrate the birth of the king of Rome (1811), which was then set to music by Ferdinando Orlandi. As he had done in the Neapolitan years, he wrote a number of librettos and some prose related to the world of freemasonry: 1801 is the date of the libretto of the opera *Clitennestra*,[17] which was performed at the Scala during the Carnival season of that same year, with music by Nicola Zingarelli; 1805 is the year of the translation of the tragedy *I templari* by Raynouard, performed in Milan by the Bianchi theatre company and printed – again in Milan – the same year. Salfi also translated the *Carlo IX* by Chénier, which has remained unpublished. In 1809 Salfi also did his utmost to promote the new issue of the *Lira focese* by Jerocades; this idea was also sponsored by Romagnosi, who suggested the Grande Oriente could take upon itself the distribution of the volume. V. Lancetti was asked by the officials to check the doctrinaire compliance of the work. At the end of his research, Lancetti discouraged them from sponsoring the printing "because in some parts one could detect mysteries above the third degree" and because "moral freedom was too often confused with policy, and the democratic vehemence, which had already puzzled so many men, was too intense". Printing was carried out in 1809 with tacit agreement, with a brief composition appended, *La morte di Giacobbe, Epistola, all'amico F. Salfi*, (*Jacob's death, Epistle to the friend F. Salfi*), some unrhymed verses "from the author to the friend, then young, on the occasion the composition of the *Saulle*, musical oratorio for the Naples Royal Theatre", in 1794.

His main Masonic work is the speech *Della utilità della F∴Massoneria sotto il rapporto filantropico e morale* (On the usefulness of F∴freemasonry from the moral and philanthropic point of view),[18] which won a competition organized by Lodge Napoleone of Livorno in 1811. This short but intense speech is one of the major apologies for freemasonry produced between the 18th and 19th centuries, probably the most important ever in the Napoleonic period, mainly because the theme of the relation between freemasonry and the state is explicitly addressed. In this text, Salfi shows that he can gather the whole legacy that derives from the southern Enlightenment freemasonry, with clear connections to Vico, Genovesi, Filangieri, and Pagano, but also to Masonic works by I. Bianchi and French Enlightenment culture (mainly Raynal and Condorcet).

He evaluates – from the Masonic point of view – the universal educational pursuit of the philosophes in the previous century, openly criticizing the habit of calling on public opinion, not always considered able to understand the truths of philosophy correctly. In this text, this habit is judged to be harmful if not positively disastrous. From an occultist and factional position, Salfi states that during the Enlightenment, "they had wanted to tear the veil of the sanctuary of philosophy, and philosophy had immediately been shown to be light, scorned, fossilised". With this strategy of diffusion of truth, according to Salfi, the philosophes simply wasted their knowledge since they were not able to use the right degree of moderation and graduality of revelation which were the main and distinctive characteristics of Masonic proselytism. Indeed, with its gradual and selective revelations, freemasonry aimed at "improvement of the moral and philanthropic nature of men", choosing its initiates within a selected spiritual elite – that is to say, "the best, so that the effect, which cannot be expected from everybody, would be safer and faster" – all chosen among people of impeccable morality and faith and having all the civil rights since "the atheist, the wicked and the slave deserve not to be improved, but punished". By following a cyclical regeneration model that is common to man and nature (as stated in the works of Pagano and in some early works by Salfi himself) through a series of initiation ceremonies, the initiate, by the "show of physical death", would be prepared for the "moral death, which is the beginning of a much safer and better life" in accordance with a palingenetic scheme which aimed at "the destruction the old man to build a new one".[19]

As far as the ultimate aims of freemasonry were concerned, even if "no other human institution but freemasonry celebrated equality among men", Salfi said that its main objective was to promote "sociability" through philanthropy, a secular principle as opposed to Christian piety, looking primarily to the afterlife "instead of a corrected and improved society". For this reason, "Christian charity was dissolved in a sort of spiritual bliss to be enjoyed in Heaven; the Masonic one to be enjoyed in the world". To this Christian charity which is "closed to the common man for the sake of the Christians only, who do not tolerate any other sect" (*ibid.*, 46), Salfi opposed a Masonic philanthropy, which did not admit "any difference in nationality, language and faith". In the period of the Napoleonic Caesarism, Salfi revived the traditional Masonic cosmopolitism which underwent a crisis at the end of the 18th century and which considered "the same nature, the same man, the citizen of the world, under the different costumes and uses of mankind", contrasting "the brotherhood feeling" with the "jealousy, mistrust, hostility and mutual hatred of the nations".

The "Great Masonic union" was an effective and occult instrument for progress through the communication of knowledge, and for Salfi it had the effect of uniting – for the sake of all humanity – the best representatives of enemy peoples, even those divided by perpetual wars, so that "the secrets, the discoveries and every type of knowledge that the Englishman, as a patriot would deny or sell at a high price to foreigners, would not deny or sell them as a Mason to his brothers, no matter what country they might happen to be in nor state they might belong to". For this reason this secret network of enlightened men ("union of the chosen strengths of the nations") would create "the most rapid means of communication to widely spread the important results achieved and make them universal". Salfi inserted all these considerations into a vast historical scheme that united all who had had an active role in the process for the improvement of society or simply, "had taught humanity to their families or tribes... after some great natural catastrophe".

The connection with Boulanger's catastrophism is very strong, as is the link with Pagano, who shared Salfi's opinion on the fact that the Masons were acting "as guardians of the morality of humankind, which they inherited from their ancestors to transfer it – once improved – to posterity".[20] This was a long theory of prophets and fathers of humanity that linked Osiris to Prometheus and Orpheus, Zoroaster to Moses, Pythagoras and the Eleusinian Mysteries to the Essene and John the Apostle to the Rosicrucians and the "Nuova Atlantide by Verulamio", Paracelsus and Agrippa to Boyle, to the Royal Society of London and then on to William Penn, Franklin, and Filangieri.

Surveying the new reality of the Napoleonic era, Salfi could clearly present the relations between this "union of the chosen strengths of nations" and the state, and as Filangieri had done before him, he was able to propose the creation of a pact between the two. Of course, as I. Bianchi had already pointed out in his *Dell'instituto dei veri liberi muratori* (1786), the freemasonry would need to give the state moral help in creating good citizens, "to promote the exercise of the duties and make" the people governed "progressively more docile to the laws of order". Furthermore, according to Salfi, it has a much more specific function: "it helps the projects of the government, it eliminates the obstacles, [and] it enhances the hopes and prepares that same civil raw material to receive the other changes it might be able to endure". Therefore Salfi wished to see the creation of a gentle plot in which state authority and Masonic lodges would be united as "two hidden sources of light, whose sun, remaining invisible to the populace, could rend obscurity without damaging the eyes of those who are to benefit from it". As an "example of the many services that the freemasonry could offer", Salfi considered the possibility of charging "the most intelligent Masons" with the task of accompanying the diffusion of every new law or decree produced by the state, "to underline its importance and promote its implementation". Considering that "the State cannot choose the members of the society it has to govern",[21] the freemasonry should become, according to Salfi, the core of a selective and programmed action on public opinion, aiming at creating strong consensus on the initiatives of a state which was greatly lacking in real political representation and was therefore acting only from above, along administrative channels. This proposal of intellectual cooperation was to be implemented in a subordinate condition; in fact, it is reminiscent of the experience that Salfi had in Naples: adhesion of the enlightened despots to reformism in a context in which a secret pact could also entail declared idealistic battle, free from any kind of strategies and ulterior motives, to be waged with an open call on public opinion.

Nevertheless, his activity is to some extent contradictory. It is difficult to understand how and why Salfi, while having important functions within the Grande Oriente d'Italia, continued to write plays full of anti Napoleonic contentions; Salfi was "a Masonic big fish", so powerful as to reduce to the most "mean, abject dedication" an aggressive man of letters like Vincenzo Monti, imposing "his authority on the guilty 'brother'", and yet so suspicious to the eyes of the authorities as to be jailed preventively on the eve of Napoleon's coronation as the king of Italy. Salfi then gives contradictory judgements, one shortly after the other, on the Masonic world he had known for so long. First came a peremptory judgement on what it had "become since" the golden age of Naples with Filangieri and Pagano: "a puerile exercise in insignificant formalities and, even worse, an instrument favoured by despots which it should above all abhor"; then, in another work of the previous year, total acquittal of the Italian freemasonry of the Napoleonic Age, which, as he says, although apparently favoured by the government, had always retained a "spirit of opposition".

In the same text, Salfi also states that it was actually within the lodges that "day by day desire and hope were nourished for unification of the states at Italy, and a constitution fitting its needs and spirit. Quite unlike the others, the Masons of Italy took advantage of the favour apparently accorded to them by the government to give better circulation to the doctrines which then came to light with the effect that they seemed to cosset their protector".[22]

The autobiography of the Carbonaro from Trento Gioacchino Prati will help us to see what this contradiction meant. Prati was a student of the Milan Special Royal Schools, and in the period 1810–1811, Salfi and Romagnosi were among his teachers. He reports that the two were "the heads of a political secret society teaching the passionate young sons of Italy" to "shake off the yoke of the tyrants and transform Italy into a united and independent nation". In other words, they were the brains of a patriotic conspiracy organized in the Masonic way, probably chosen for its flexibility as an "instrument to spread political doctrines all over the country". The two divergent judgements that Salfi pronounced so shortly one after the other probably referred to two different spheres: the first to the official and governmental freemasonry (in which he had an important role – aiming at exploitation of the networks), the second to the *arrière-loge* that he had created together with Romagnosi, tailoring it on their patriotic ideals: "a masonry within the masonry, unknown to many Grand Masters".

4 From Salfi's eulogy to the "Raccolta Custodi"

As we know, Salfi had obtained from Giuseppe Palmieri (1721–1793) – a leading light of Neapolitan Enlightenment – the copy of Serra's *Breve trattato*, to which he would refer to compose his eulogy.[23] It is, however, clear in the light of the scenario that we have reconstructed that Salfi's interest in Serra was not prompted solely by sheer – albeit erudite – curiosity or an appreciation of the "first writer on civil economy".[24] The reasons that drove him to take an interest in the *Breve trattato* become comprehensible precisely in the context of a form of "cultural consumption" and the interpretations that could be made of it between the 18th and 19th centuries in the light of a series of circumstances that came to coincide: the intellectual tradition of the Neapolitan Enlightenment, which, through Antonio Genovesi and Gaetano Filangieri, had stressed the connection between the need for good laws and political economy;[25] the need to revive and keep alive the lessons of the Enlightenment in the Jacobin age, when the traditions seemed to be crumbling under the tragic effects of the Revolution;[26] and – finally –the possibility to see in Serra – an author who was persecuted, imprisoned, and long forgotten – a precursor of the Neapolitan Revolution and the exiles dispersed throughout Europe.[27] In this sense, we can also understand the myth – to some extent invented by Salfi himself – of Antonio Serra as a Southern Italian follower of Giordano Bruno and Tommaso Campanella,[28] although in reality Salfi's sole aim was to revitalize an idea of republicanism of practical utility in the new climate that was emerging in 19th-century Italy.[29]

It was in fact Salfi who prompted Pietro Custodi (1771–1842) to republish the *Breve trattato* in the collection of classical writers on economics, and indeed Serra's text was printed in the first volume (1803), immediately after the publication of the eulogy.[30] Custodi himself explained in the introduction: "The copy I used for this reprint belonged to Bartolomeo Intieri; he gave it to the abbot Ferdinando Galiani, who treasured it as something practically unique; when Galiani died, it was bought by the Marquis Giuseppe Palmieri, who passed it on to the citizen Salfi, who kindly made it available to me". Thus, the "Custodi Collection" consolidated the essential core that was running through the Neapolitan Enlightenment, from Bartolomeo Intieri (the patron who had contributed to the founding of Genovesi's chair in civil economy) to the late 18th-century revolutionaries. Custodi, who started as an Illuminist to become a Jacobin, was one of the many Italian intellectuals who had changed their position with the Napoleonic regime, convinced that the revolutionary experience was over and that a new era of political realism and commitment was to begin, gradually working towards the cultural and civil formation of Italian society.[31] At the same time, his project also completed the programme of the *Breve trattato* in modern Italian culture: in fact, just as the freemasonry had abandoned its universalistic ideals to endow the budding ideals of the Risorgimento with vitality, so Serra's work – in the general framework presented by Custodi[32] – was transformed into one of the fundamental components constituting the ideal conception of history behind Italian identity.

Notes

1. Salfi, F.S., *Elogio di Antonio Serra primo scrittore di economia civile*, Milan: Nobile e Tosi, 1802. On this text, see also Addante, L., *Patriottismo e libertà. L'Elogio di Antonio Serra di Francesco Salfi*, Cosenza: Pellegrini, 2009 and, on Salfi's biography, see Tocchini, G., "Salfi, Francesco Saverio (1750–1832)", in Porset, C. And M.-C. Révauger (eds), *Le monde maçonnique des Lumières (Europe-Amérique et colonies). Dictionnaire prosopographique*, vol. 3, Paris: Honoré Champion, 2014, p. 2462–2471.
2. Ferrone, V., *I profeti dell'Illuminismo. Le metamorfosi della ragione nel tardo Settecento italiano*, Roma-Bari: Laterza, 20002, pp. 275–276, 345.
3. Giglio, R., "La poesia autobiografica di F.S. Salfi", in de Lisio, P.A. (ed.), *Francesco Saverio Salfi: un calabrese per l'Europa*, Naples: Società Editrice Napoletana, 1981.
4. Biblioteca Nazionale di Napoli, Fondo Salfi, ms. XX 65.1, "Lettere Familiari".
5. Renzi, A.M., *Vie politique et littérarie de F. Salfi, ancien Professeur dans les Universités de Bréra, de Milan, de Naples, etc. auteur-continuateur de l'Histoire Littéraire d'Italie, par feu Ginguené, de l'Institut*, Paris: Fayolle, 1834, p. 134; Mafrici, M., "Note alla biografia salfiana di A. M. Renzi", in *Francesco Saverio Salfi: un calabrese per l'Europa* (Atti del Convegno di Cosenza, 23–24 febbraio 1980), Naples: SEN, 1981, p. 85; Alfonzetti, B., *Teatro e tremuoto. Gli anni napoletani di Francesco Saverio Salfi, 1787–1794*, Milan: Franco Angeli, 1994, p. 184. Le lettere di Salfi di quegli anni sono conservate nella Biblioteca Nazionale di Napoli, Fondo Salfi, Lettere familiari, ms. XX 65.1.
6. Zaghi, C., *Il Direttorio francese e la Repubblica Cisalpina*, Rome: Istituto storico per l'età moderna e contemporanea, 1992, pp. 475, 495.
7. Trampus, A. "Un modèle pour le constitutionnalisme des Lumières : la culture napolitaine et les droits de l'homme", in *NUEVO MUNDO-MUNDOS NUEVOS*, vol. 7, 2007, pp. 1–11 ; Morelli, F. and A. Trampus (ed.), *Progetto di costituzione per la repubblica napoletana (1799)*, Venice: Edizioni della Laguna-Centro di Studi sull'illuminismo europeo, 2008.
8. Biblioteca Nazionale di Napoli, Fondo Salfi, Ms. XX 41.1, "Lezioni di diritto pubblico e commerciale delle Genti". The manuscript is not complete but includes *Lezione XXII. Del Commercio in generale* (cc. 110v.-112v.) addresses issues having to do with money, letters of exchange, intrinsic and extrinsic price of money, alteration and counterfeiting of coin, and the inequity of monopolies; *Lezione XXIII. Del Commercio in particolare* (cc. 113r.-116v.) deals with freedom of trade, fair trade, assets and liabilities, wealth of nations, the need to modify trade, home and foreign trade, the just value of money and the balance of trade; *Lezione XXIX. De' Trattati commerciali* (cc. 116v.-121) concerns commercial conventions, the differences between public and private conventions, the characteristics distinguishing contracts, agreements and treaties, the object of commercial treaties, their real and hypothetical need, and the invalidity of treaties contrary to the rights of a third party. These are important documents to form an idea of the intellectual context within which Salfi made his interpretation of Serra.
9. Trampus, A., Filangieri et Constant: constitutionnalisme des Lumières et constitutionnalisme libéral, "*Annales Benjamin Constant*" 30 (2006), pp. 51–70.

10. Salfi, F.S., "Éloge de Filangieri", in Filangieri, G. *Œuvres*, I, Paris: Dufart, 1822, pp. xx, cxxvii, xcii.
11. Galizia, N., *F. S. Salfi e la cultura europea. Inediti (1815–1832)*, Cosenza: Ed. Periferia, 1990; Froio R. (ed.), *Salfi tra Napoli e Parigi. Carteggio 1792–1832*, Naples: Macchiaroli, 1998.
12. Galizia, N. (ed.), *Il Corradino di Francesco Saverio Salfi*. S. l., s. n., 1987.
13. Salfi's original interest in Serra dates back to this period, according to the following autobiographical verses: "Despite the chains constraining me/ In the blind error author clearly present, again/I saw the light, and dared demonstrate it/To the oppressed city of Naples, which all/Suffering the ills of foreign yoke/Seek in vain the supreme causes/Of the extreme indigence under which it groans./Of public wealth I discovered/The perennial sources, and expounded the art,/To trade with foreign peoples,/Art, praise of which was thereafter obliterated,/After a century and more, industrious Franco./ And what good came of it? It ended thus,/I mourned my neglected – nay, damned – papers;/And in prison dead, I see none of my own/Who, from the unjust oblivion that enfolds me/Might save the valid work and name of Serra./Life I promise one, solace to the others/I tender", cfr. Giglio, *La poesia autobiografica*, cit., p. 120.
14. Sòriga, R., "La ristampa milanese della 'Lira Focese' di Antonio Jeròcades", in *"Rassegna Storica del Risorgimento"*, V (1918), p. 730; Nardi, C., *La vita e le opere di Francesco Saverio Salfi (1759–1832)*, Genoa: Libreria editrice moderna, 1925, p. 67; Zucco, A., *1799. La Repubblica Napoletana e la massoneria*, Cosenza: Edizioni Brenner, 1999.
15. Biblioteca Nazionale di Napoli, Fondo Salfi, ms. XX 53.1 "Minuta di lettera di Salfi", c. 76. See, moreover, Froio (ed.), *Salfi tra Napoli e Parigi*, cit., pp. 119–120.
16. Luzio, A., "La Massoneria sotto il Regno Italico e la restaurazione austriaca", in *Archivio Storico Lombardo*, XLIV (1918), pp. 241–352; Della Peruta, F., "Francesco Saverio Salfi e un progetto di riforma della Massoneria italiana nei primi anni Restaurazione", in *Storia della massoneria. Studi e testi*, n. 2, Turin: s.d. [1983], pp. 63–73.
17. *Clitennestra, melodramma in tre atti del cittadino Franco Salfi. Da rappresentarsi nel Teatro alla Scala il carnevale dell'anno 1801 v.s. anno 9. repubblicano, la musica è del celebre maestro di cappella Nicola Zingarelli*, Milan: dalla Tipografia Pirola, 1801; Tocchini, G., "Dall'Antico Regime alla Cisalpina. Morale e politica nel teatro per musica di Francesco Saverio Salfi, in *Salfi librettista*, a cura di F. P. Russo, Vibo Valentia: Ed. Monteleone, 2001, pp. 75–76.
18. *Della utilità della Franca Massoneria sotto il rapporto filantropico e morale. Discorso di F. Salfi coronato dalla R.L. Napoleone all'O. di Livorno*. Florence: Dai tipi del Grand'Oriente d'Italia, 1811. New edition Cosenza: Edizioni Brenner, 1986.
19. Salfi, (1811), 1986, pp. 15–20; see moreover Tocchini, G., "Salfi Francesco Saverio", in Porset, C. And M.C. Révauger, *Le Monde maçonnique des Lumières (Europe-Amériques). Dictionnaire prosopographique*, Paris: Honoré Champion, 2008 (in print).
20. Salfi, (1811), 1986, pp. 47–60.
21. Salfi (1811), 1986, pp. 71–75.

22. Salfi, F.S., *L'Italie au dix-neuvième siècle, ou de la nécessité d'accorder, en Italie, le pouvoir avec la liberté*, Paris: Dufart, 1821, p. 21.
23. De Rosa, L., "Antonio Serra e i suoi critici", in *Atti del III congresso storico calabrese*, Naples: F. Fiorentino, 1964, p. 117. On Palmieri also Ferrone, V., *La società giusta ed equa. Repubblicanesimo e diritti dell'uomo in Gaetano Filangieri*, Rome-Bari: Laterza, 2003, p. 193.
24. Thus evoked with Salfi's *Elogio di Antonio Serra*, 1802.
25. The bibliography on the subject has grown with a number of contributions over the last few years; for a general survey, see now Silvestrini, M.T., "Free trade, feudal remnants and international equilibrium in Gaetano Filangieri's Science of Legislation", in Stapelbroek, K. (ed.), *Commerce and morality in Eighteenth-Century Italy, "History of European Ideas"*, 32, 4 (2006), pp. 502–524.
26. Ferrone, V., "L'Illuminismo italiano e la Rivoluzione napoletana del 1799", in id., *I profeti dell'Illuminismo*, 2002.
27. Rao, A.M., *Esuli. L'emigrazione politica italiana in Francia (1792–1802)*, Naples: Guida editori, 1992.
28. Salfi (1811), 1986.
29. Little study has so far been dedicated to the topic, which would merit far more; for an initial approach, cfr. Di Napoli, M., "La "fortuna" di Tommaso Campanella in Mazzini e nei repubblicani dell'Ottocento", in *"Bollettino della Domus Mazziniana"*, 1985, 31, n. 2, pp. 199–216; Giovannozzi, D., *Libero ma cattolico pensatore. Tommaso Campanella nei manuali italiani di storia della filosofia del XIX secolo, Bruniana & Campanelliana*, II, 1996, pp. 295–307.
30. Custodi, P. (ed.), *Scrittori classici italiani di economia politica*, Milan: Destefanis, 1803.
31. Criscuolo, V., *Il giacobino Pietro Custodi. Con un'appendice di documenti inediti*, Rome: Istituto storico italiano per l'età moderna e contemporanea, 1987, p. 345. Cfr. anche Capra, C., "Alle origini del moderatismo e del giacobinismo in Lombardia: Pietro Verri e Pietro Custodi", *Studi storici*, 4 (1989), pp. 825–872.
32. On the *"Raccolta Custodi"*, see also Macchioro, A., "La Raccolta Custodi 'Scrittori classici italiani di economia' fra la statistica. e l'economia politica", in Rota, D. (ed.), *Pietro Custodi tra Rivoluzione e Restaurazione*, (Atti del primo convegno nazionale Milano-Lecco-Galbiate 2–3 ott. 1987), Lecco: Banca Popolare di Lecco, 1989; Augello, M.M. and M.E.L. Guidi, "Gli economisti e le iniziative enciclopediche nell'Italia liberale. Ricognizione e analisi storica", *Storia del pensiero economico*, 41, 2001, pp. 131–163.

13
Serra's Discovery and Ill Fate in the Liberal 19th Century

Francesco Di Battista

In the early 19th century, the discovery of Antonio Serra as an economist marked the turning point in the entire history of economic ideas in Italy with highly significant implications from our historiographical point of view. The aim of this paper is to examine the sequence of different evaluations of Serra in 19th-century Italian economic thought as it changed from the legacy of the late mercantilistic tradition of Genovesi to the new liberal economic science.

The paper consists of three parts. The first part introduces Serra as "primo scrittore di economia civile" (first writer on civil economy):[1] here is the discovery of Serra, hitherto largely unknown, except to Doria, Galiani (whose copy of the *Breve trattato* would be passed on to Salfi, who advised Custodi to open his publishing enterprise *Scrittori classici italiani di economia politica* with this work in 1803) and Diodati. But Salfi's reading was Genovesian: Serra would inquire into the causes of "ricchezza civile" (indeed Serra wrote: of the "abbondanza" of money). In general, Salfi's thesis of an Italian primacy in the early days of economic science was largely due to the emphasis on the past glories of the Italians, a sentiment typical of the period (from Cuoco to Sismondi). The thesis holds,[2] but it would later develop into the affirmation of a better, more social Italian school of Political economy.[3]

In the second part of the paper, we see the thesis of primacy, and also this evaluation of Serra, being superseded. By the mid century, the victory of the new European economic science over the Italian tradition was indisputable. Serra, and with him all the 18th-century Italian economists, came in for negative reappraisal, above all by Francesco Ferrara in 1852 but also by many others before and after. The liberal reappraisal makes the survival of the Serra myth paradoxical, but pathetic.[4] Much more interesting, in fact, was the debate between Ferrara and another brilliant Neapolitan liberal economist, who would become a famous jurist, namely Pasquale Stanislao Mancini, on the Italian contribution to the emergence of economic science, retrenched by Ferrara and claimed by Mancini.

The third part of the paper shows the end of the Serra story in the 19th century. His fall from grace was destined to continue from the Risorgimento liberal economists to the liberal marginalists. Significantly, we find more favourable evaluations only by some economists[5] in part out of the mainstream of marginalist liberalism. In the case of one of our best marginalists,[6] the evaluation remained hardly negative: the significance of Serra must be restricted because he had no modern (i.e. of the 19th century) theory of comparative costs, De Viti asserted, nor a value of money theory.

This evaluation was clearly based on a theoretical, and not a historical, point of view. Unfortunately, to some extent, this seems to have persisted to the present day, when economists look to Serra with particular regard to his monetarism. Similarly, reappraisal of Serra as precursor of modern "meridionalismo"[7] is somewhat lacking in historiographically rigorous evidence.

1 Serra, a late discovery of the great Genovesian tradition

The name of Antonio Serra found a place in the history of economic ideas only in the times of the economist Antonio Genovesi. The oblivion that had enwrapped it until 1780, naturally often noted by historians and non-historians alike, has itself constituted a historiographical problem upon which the following pages may cast some light.

Before his rediscovery, mention of the "text by a certain citizen of Cosenza, of the Serra family" by a leading figure of early 18th-century Neapolitan culture, Paolo Mattia Doria, a neo-Platonic philosopher and conservative economist, remained merely tangential to calculation of Naples' trade surplus. Yet we find the mention repeated: first in the manuscript *Report* of 1709 (or, some argue, 1711 or 1713)[8] and again much later in the manuscript work of 1740 *Del commercio del Regno di Napoli*[9] (On the trade of the Kingdom of Naples). This second, again bare, mention does, however, add a particularly interesting detail: Doria lamented that Serra's treatise had to his "immense sorrow [...] been stolen" from him. Actually, recalling how Galiani, a leading figure who was emerging from the circle of Intieri and Genovesi, was to explain in the second edition of 1780 of *Della moneta* how he came by his copy of the treatise (having failed to do so in the first edition of 1751), we cannot help thinking that it must have been the very same that was stolen from Doria: Serra "once dead, remained forgotten with his book. No one ever mentioned it, and quite possibly only the copy that was in the possession of Bartolommeo Intieri, and given to me, was saved from oblivion".[10]

Thus began the legend of the only copy of the *Breve trattato*. Salfi would take it up in 1802 to bring home his fundamental vindication of Serra, who "would be totally unknown had not a copy [...] happily been saved by a series of events. It was rediscovered and appreciated for its true worth by the celebrated Bartolommeo Intieri, who in turn gave it to Galiani, who first made brief public mention of it: after his death, having been acquired by Giuseppe Palmieri, it was passed on to me to redeem it from the ill fate it had long suffered and save it from the unjust oblivion into which, to the shame of Italian letters, it was about to fall: [...] possibly the only copy, now in my possession".[11] Custodi, too, prompted by Salfi,[12] would make use of it to inaugurate his equally fundamental publishing venture with the *Scrittori classici italiani di economia politica*, which, regardless of chronology, highly significantly opens with the treatise by Serra, whom Custodi follows Galiani and Salfi in regarding as the "first writer of Political Economy". "The copy which I used for the present reprint previously belonged to Bartolommeo Intieri, founder of the chair in Political Economy in Naples; he gave it to the abate Ferdinando Galiani, who treasured it as something practically unique; when Galiani died it was bought by the Marquis Giuseppe Palmieri, [...] who passed it on to the citizen Salfi, who in turn kindly passed it on to me. Subsequently, however, I received another copy thanks to the kind services of a friend who had taken the trouble to track it down in his family's private library".[13]

Actually, the legend of the only copy of the treatise, which Croce had to no avail corrected as "the only at that time known copy",[14] had already been rebutted by informed contemporaries like Andrea Lombardi, who commented handwritten in the margin of his copy of the *Elogio* by Salfi on the latter's assertion about the "only copy": "There are many copies in Naples: two in the Royal Library, which I have seen, one in the possession of the Judge of Appeal Giuseppe Castaldi, and yet others have copies of the original edition Lombardi".[15] In a later text,[16] Lombardi returned to Galiani and Salfi's illusion of being the only possessors "of such a treasure: but they were both misled": not only had Custodi's second copy come to light, but "in the Royal Library of Naples two copies exist, [...] which I have seen on various occasions and consulted. The celebrated Greek scholar Domenico Diodati still had a copy, and another is in the possession of the illustrious judge Giuseppe Castaldi. And who knows how many others lie gathering dust in the Libraries of the Kingdom and Italy!"

The story of the copies of Serra's treatise is not merely of bibliographical, nor indeed bibliophilic, interest. It is not only a matter of verifying whether the copy now in the Biblioteca Einaudi is in fact the one that had been in the hands of Intieri, and then Galiani, Palmieri, and Salfi, given that we read "on a typewritten card pasted to the back of the front cover: [...] This is the copy possessed by Bartolomeo Intieri and given by him to Ferdinando Galiani, who refers to the gift in his *Della moneta*. Probably it was one of the few books that, escaping the fate of Galiani's library, now dispersed, were included among the manuscripts of Galiani entailed to Francesco Paolo Azzariti (1787) and sold by the latter to the jurisconsult Nicola Nicolini (about 1808)". From the Nicolini family, it would be passed on to Croce, who gave it to Luigi Einaudi[17] in 1931, after the latter had paid a visit to him in Naples in a moment of personal and political difficulty. The fact remains that the account leading to Einaudi clashes with the version favoured by Salfi, who was bent on stressing the relationship with Galiani and Palmieri in the broader context of revival of a tradition of economic thought – the tradition of Genovesi's *civil* economy – which he traced back to Serra.

In the famous Note XXIX in the second edition of *Della moneta*, we find the first, enthusiastic appraisal of Serra: Galiani has no doubt about "attributing him with the position of the first and earliest writer on the science of political economy", much as Melon was for France and Locke (regarding money) for England – indeed, excelling them "as he had lived so long before, and in a century of darkness and error in economic science". Moreover, he had written in the tragic conditions not only of a prisoner but of a "wretched man" whose wise counsels remained unheeded by a pusillanimous government.[18] Galiani's extremely positive evaluation is all the more important for having been advanced when Genovesi reigned supreme. Indeed, although Genovesi had devoured a great deal of 16th-century and 17th-century economic literature in his transition from "metaphysician" to "merchant",[19] had belonged to the circle of Intieri and Galiani, and was familiar with the writings of Doria,[20] Genovesi's writings contain no explicit reference to Serra's treatise. Nevertheless, Galiani's discovery was clearly made in the context of Genovesi's school and heritage, which became a great Italian tradition in economic thought in the decades following the death of the master. Indeed, the names that most directly concern us here are those of Galiani, Diodati, Palmieri, and Salfi.

Significantly, the first biographer of Galiani (in 1788), Luigi Diodati, a man of the Bourbon administration, brother to the erudite antiquarian and numismatist Domenico, with whom he shared a rich library, had fine words of praise for the treatise in 1790. Diodati was involved in the debate on the Kingdom's nth monetary crisis, and his proposals were not endorsed by all the reformers. But the point here is that, as far as Serra is concerned, he clearly followed along the same line as Galiani. Reading the treatise, "anyone would be surprised and impressed to see that, in a time of total ignorance of economic science, the author had clear, correct ideas about the subject, upon which he wrote; and to see how soundly judged he causes of our ills, and the only effective remedies; indeed, it will be seen that much of the thought and schemes regarding exchange and money published by Locke in England were taken from this text, which he did not cite".[21]

However, the true author[22] of the rediscovery of and brief success enjoyed by Serra's treatise in the early years of the 19th century was Francesco Saverio Salfi, who as a Jacobin exile in Milan published with Nobile and Tosi his important *Elogio di Antonio Serra primo scrittore di Economia civile* in 1802.[23] The significant dedication "To the shade of Giuseppe Palmieri" was justified thus: "ever fearing that the copy would be lost as soon as Galiani died in 1787, arranged for the illustrious Giuseppe Palmieri, who bestowed his friendship on me and knew my intentions, to acquire it; and most readily he gave it to me to make such use of it as would redound to the glory of the Author and his country [...]. And we may well compare this with the opinion that Galiani had of Antonio Serra and his work long before [...]. I have merely confirmed it".[24] Actually, Salfi took this even further, to the extent of tracing out a continuity in the developments of economic science that were hard to demonstrate. In his opinion, in the last two centuries this science, "civil economy, I say, has remained among those that have seen most delay in becoming known and developed". Serra was "the first among those, from the very beginning of the 17th century, who knew and expounded the true theories of civil economy; moreover, he was also "the first founder of that science, which a century and a half later slowly began to revive and advance".[25]

Salfi's emphatic tones reflected a particular cultural background in the early years of the 19th century, when great claims were being made for "Italian primacy", most notably by Cuoco[26] from an anti-imperialist, anti-despotic stance,[27] followed by various other pre-Risorgimento claims like Sismondi's call for Italy's old, medieval "freedoms". In the case of Salfi, however, everything revolved around the identification of economic science with the *civil* Economy of Genovesi, debatable as it was, and as was seen immediately after. On the one hand, Genovesi's did not reflect Serra's 17th-century mercantilism, while at the same time it could hardly be seen to share much with the liberal economic science that was by then looming high on the horizon.

Obviously, Francesco Salfi had been too young at the time to follow Genovesi's lessons, but his background was nevertheless distinctly Genovesian, from his native town of Cosenza[28] and then to Naples, as was already evidenced by his *Saggio di fenomeni antropologici relativi al tremuoto del 1787*. His friendly relations with the, possibly, most representative Genovesian, Palmieri, of particular importance in our context, also showed just how much contamination their Civil economy was able to absorb. Symptomatic is the story of the translations of a spurious physiocratic work, the *Principes de la législation universelle* by Schmid d'Avenstein with the Neapolitan translation of 1791 sponsored by Palmieri, which was not the first in Italy, and the subsequent, very interesting Milanese version of 1805–1807 edited by Salfi himself and printed by the same Nobile who brought out the *Elogio*. In the latter work, Salfi, albeit not in personal terms, found it necessary to assert his identification with the "school of Genovesi" – which he effectively outlined[29] – in defence against the Milanese gossipmongers who were casting doubt on his academic qualifications.

The fact that the "school of Genovesi" lay behind his reading of Serra's text is of considerable historical importance, both for the virtual lack of any previous citations and for the role that Salfi would play in Paris, in contact with the new economic culture that was turning its back on Serra, Genovesi, and the whole of late mercantilism. He focused attention on the first part of the treatise, which goes well beyond the controversy with de Santis and the possible rules governing the rate of exchange to trace "the first outline, known to us" of economic science.[30] In this first part, Salfi argued that Serra's interest extended beyond the "use of money and exchange [...] to the true, effective and direct sources of national wealth, [...,] determining the pure causes of civil wealth".[31] These are natural, like mines, or accidental, "like all those men can more or less make use of, and which are *particular* to certain countries, or *common* to all". Lacking mines, the Kingdom of Naples "has, however, or can have *accidental* causes, whether *particular* or *common*. The particular are the surplus of commodities[32] which the state of Naples enjoys above all the others of Italy; and the position, considered to favour great traffic, in which Venice among others takes the lead. [...] The author reduces all the common accidents to the quantity of manufacturing activities, the qualities of the inhabitants, great traffic and the method of those who govern". In Naples "he saw very few and very imperfect skills, a slack population little given to industry, internal and external traffic hampered or ignored, and the art of government extremely difficult in terms of acting upon the will of the inhabitants: being free by nature, they are more attracted to comfort and may be led by indirect means rather than direct obligation". Only the government, "as acting cause, had to enliven the others, and gently lead them on, to reproduce and increase progressively the wealth and prosperity of the nation".[33] In any case, even granting government intervention, it was the real rather than the monetary economy that took pride of place: "the exchange rate is considered by the economists as the pulse of the body politic in which only the least misleading symptoms of health are to be sought".[34] From this point of view, the only positive prospect lay in industry. In fact, the shortage of money "depended absolutely on the negative balance of trade, which in turn depended upon the lack and imperfection of skills, industry and traffic".[35] The introduction of manufacturing activities would help to reduce the hold that the foreigners had over the Kingdom's economy: after all, in their "dire influence [...] lay the real and powerful cause of the poverty of the State; maintained and increased by the revenues they had there, and by the industries and trade they exercised to the almost total exclusion of the inhabitants"[36]

Comparisons between the texts by Salfi and Serra,[37] which we here briefly give examples of, however, reveal a central point: Salfi worked along a Serra–Genovesi axis, in other words mercantilist tradition-Civil economy[38], and it was along this axis that the 17th-century monetarists and mercantilists, Galiani and the Italian reformers of the latter part of the 17th century, found themselves positioned. The Serra–Genovesi connection caught the attention of Schumpeter,[39] who, moreover, in his major work, played down the insight into the particular connection between monetarism and mercantilism in Serra, "first author of a scientific treatise, albeit not systematic, on principles and economic policy" for the sake of the subsequent emphasis on automatic monetary mechanisms.[40] What, however, actually eludes Schumpeter, who pays no attention to Salfi, is the great historical significance of Salfi's work, lying in the fact that in it the groundbreaking nature of Italian economic thought was combined with affirmation of a late mercantilist tradition of a Genovesian stamp and could well stand up to comparison with the physiocrats and Smith.

Unfortunately, Salfi's contribution did not appear in the right form (it was after all a pamphlet written in haste without great care) or, even worse, at the right time. In fact, in the following year, specifically 1803, publication of the *Traité* by the great figurehead of French classical Political economy, Jean-Baptiste Say, was to upset the apple cart. The Italians were conceded a generic intellectual primacy, looking back to the Renaissance, and it was granted that Serra had "pointed out the productive power of industry; but his title alone serves to reveal his errors".[41] Say always held to this position, continuing in one way or another to defend a generic Italian primacy against MacCulloch, who claimed primacy for the British, but severely contesting the contents. "Italy, which, in the times when Europe began thinking once again, was the most erudite country in Europe, seems to have produced the first works in which the economy of the nations is seen as a system; and it was this system that was subsequently denoted with the terms of mercantile system, balance of trade system, exclusive system".[42] Serra was now condemned out of hand as being among "the true authors of the balance of trade system", unlike other Italians of the 18th century such as Verri, Beccaria, Filangieri (*not* Genovesi!), perceived to be on the same wavelength as the French and British with their major innovations in the science.[43]

At this point, the relationship between Salfi and Say takes on particular interest. Suffice it to recall that, once Salfi had settled in Paris for good – again a political exile, who published *L'Italie au dix-neuvième siècle, ou de la nécessité d'accorder, en Italie, le pouvoir avec la liberté* in Paris in 1821 – the two worked together in editing the "Revue Encyclopédique". The correspondence that they exchanged in those years[44] reveals in all its momentousness the turning point that economic science was arriving at, discussion on the primacy being a significant sign of it. The position adopted by Jean-Baptiste Say, his liberal version of Smith, was gaining increasing consensus not only in France[45] but throughout Europe. The traditional economic culture of 18th-century stamp was losing ground, and neither the counter-attack launched by Custodi (1826) and above all Gioia (1827) in the "Annali Universali di Statistica" and the "Biblioteca Italiana" (1826 and 1827),[46] nor Mugnai's,[47] strong in words but weak in content, nor indeed the far more moderate counter-attacks by Bosellini as early as 1824[48] and Romagnosi in 1828[49] could do anything to stop it. This trend inevitably also bore away the Serra that was rediscovered by Salfi. This emerges clearly from a long ignored text by an early, obscure biographer of Serra, which nevertheless showed awareness of the recent reappraisal by Galiani and Salfi: "under his pen the principles of this new science found a certain order and system, but very far from the perfection they would reach a century and a half after him".[50] The words of another, far better informed scholar involved in the short-lived fortune of his compatriot in the early 19th century, Andrea Lombardi, also show a certain bitterness over the rapid but decided defeat of the line ventured upon by Salfi. In fact, he could go no further than to define Antonio Serra as "the true founder of Political Economy [...,] who could always claim the merit of having laid the first and most solid foundations of the science".[51]

Defeat of the tradition and the first victory of economic liberalism were acknowledged in the first history of economic ideas in Italy, written by a man who had gone through and was still experiencing the cultural and political changes at this stage of transition towards the Risorgimento: Giuseppe Pecchio. He also had first-hand knowledge of the state of affairs in Great Britain. With him the idea of Italian primacy in the foundation of the science was now beginning to give way to a far more moderate and ambiguous conception of the science of the Italian economists, more "comprehensive" than the bare framework of the British science of wealth, more sensitive to moral values, "more social". Serra could remain the founder,[52] and Italy the cradle (whatever MacCulloch might think), but it was advisable to read him only for the historical interest. By now Smith was "the first of all",[53] but in a 19th-century context where "the science itself is ultimately and essentially a part of that freedom that goes under various names. Its theorems which lead to wealth are the very paths that lead to freedom".[54] Significantly, perhaps, Salfi's review of Pecchio's *Storia* betrays a sort of bitter rage: on the one hand, he seems quite happy to find errors in Pecchio's account of Serra (albeit conceding that they were only "petites taches"), while on the other hand, he seems by now to have accepted his appraisal that "Serra's book no longer merits being consulted except by those who wish to learn about the origin of the science".[55] It took only a few more years for the very name of Serra to have actually disappeared from the populari-zation produced by the deceased Salfi's nephew of his work *Genio degl' italiani e stato attuale della loro letteratura*.[56]

2 The liberalism of the Risorgimento: Serra's reappraisal and travesty

Around the mid 19th century, the rise of liberalism – both economic and political – among the Italian economists, almost all of whom were followers of Say, led to radical change in the background: the idea of Italian primacy as conceived at the time when Salfi and Custodi were discovering Serra became untenable. The majority of liberal Italian economists fell in with the position that had emerged most positively with Antonio Scialoja, the Neapolitan economist who was then to enjoy academic and political triumphs in the Turin of Cavour, the city that looked to and identified with the unity of Italy. In the fine textbook brought out early in his career, the connection between Serra and Genovesi had already become weak, and the "incident truths" of these Italian economists of the past seemed to him to have been "forced out, perhaps, by the sheer power of their genius rather than deduced from their principles".[57] When it came to the later text of his maturity, the old approach of asserting primacy appears to have been modified in the direction indicated by Pecchio, affirming the superiority of an "Italian school [...] more dialectical, wider reaching, more social, as it were, than the other schools and in particular the British School".[58] Poor Serra had only voiced "the first utterances of the newborn Science".[59]

In practice, all this amounted to a modernization of Italian economic thought which was probably inevitable, but which took place in the context of 19th-century liberalism, which meant a sharp and decisive break with the Italian and Genovesian late mercantilist tradition. One of the attempts to combine modernization with the tradition which he traced back to Serra had been made by our Salfi, a man of the 18th century who had become a friend of Say, but the attempt proved all too weak, ending up in indifference if not ambiguity in France and elsewhere.

Another of the Neapolitan liberal economists, Vincenzo Moreno, was perfectly aware of the need for a break with the mercantilist tradition, and he therefore sought to separate Serra from it: one could not "reasonably see in the *mercantile system* a prelude to the new science since the foundations cannot be seen to have been laid in what was truly the first economic doctrine, the treatise by Serra".[60] It was Moreno who, in 1834, ventured upon a publishing enterprise that was meant to take the place of Custodi's old series and that was to start life with a new translation of Say's *Cours*. Say was the great champion of the new science, the "true science", he stressed, which was at last sailing out beyond the "pillars of Hercules held to be impassable by the tradition".[61] The fact is, however, that Moreno's "pillars of Hercules" were not being passed in triumph, but were collapsing in ruins, burying poor Serra under the rubble, too.

A reappraisal of the Italian tradition destined to cause no little stir was, in fact, being formulated with Francesco Ferrara's *Biblioteca dell'Economista*. Ferrara, a Sicilian who was also in exile in Turin, was the major theoretician of Risorgimento economic liberalism, albeit often in solitude. The lively discussion he entered into with another illustrious exile, Pasquale Stanislao Mancini, was in fact over the Italian contribution to economic science. Mancini, who was close to Scialoja and who had pursued the same Neapolitan private law studies with him, contested Ferrara's support of the position taken by the French,[62] "who hailed their physiocrats as the *creators of economic science*", with no more thought for the "earlier work of the Calabrian economist: who certainly earned the sympathy of posterity for ten years passed in the horror of no fewer than fifty prisons, suffering sevenfold torture...for having taken part in Campanella's plot, but it would be far from committing an act of excessive national pride if it is proclaimed aloud that his works give him some right to the gratitude of the scholars of the economic sciences".[63]

Ferrara's reply, set out in a section reserved for the purpose in the new preface to the volume of the *Biblioteca* dedicated to the *Trattati italiani del secolo XVIII*,[64] was uncompromisingly severe. In his opinion, differing from the opinions that so many insisted upon, the title of Serra's treatise corresponded exactly to its contents, which therefore could not offer "the least phrase that might be seen as development, demonstration, nay a primordial gleam of economic science...I ask Prof. Mancini to demonstrate how on earth having proclaimed such a false idea, at the same time so fondly believed by the common people to be true, and so old in the belief of men can, because it was conceived in Italy, or because it was formed by a hapless martyr for freedom, become the *foundation* of economic science".[65] It was "probable that Galiani, exaggerating the merit of the economist, meant to refer to the politician; and yet it seems to me inexcusable that in our own times his historian and compatriot should spend so many words setting that wretched economic prattle almost above the *Wealth of Nations*".[66]

We should not overestimate the differences dividing the Italian liberal economists because they converged in a generally negative reappraisal of Serra as an economist, the emphasis shifting to the legend of the martyr with recognition of his "unvanquished civil courage". The way was thus opened to Croce's final interpretation – serving, on the one hand, for his appraisal of the Spanish viceregal government, and, on the other hand, for his focus on the problems of southern Italy. However, this interpretation – destined to last to the present day – explicitly acknowledged that Serra's treatise may have no great importance in the history of economic ideas: "whatever place it may have merited in the history of economic theories, his is an essentially political text, a political critique of the conditions prevailing in the Kingdom of Naples. This he observed in its stark reality, and perceived, recognised, and clearly stated that it was not a rich country, but poor".[67]

The reappraisal of Serra was a sign of the times, accomplished not only with the rise of a certain type of economic liberalism but after the failure of the line pursued by Salfi with the aim of placing the *Breve trattato* at the root of the sturdy tree of industrialist economic ideas that had found in Genovesi's Civil economy a branch that could bear fruitful developments in modern times. It was indeed significant that the ever rarer positive appraisals of Serra at the time included one by Friedrich List.[68] The perspective that he took was a long way from the view taken by Mancini and the majority of liberals in their work, delineating a more *social* Italian school which left no real room for the Serra–Genovesi connection but painted a hazy picture of Serra as precursor of liberalism itself. Mancini was the man who had triumphantly welcomed Cobden to Naples with lavish Italian and Neapolitan display dedicated to "this magic word of *freedom of trade*": here he also reserved a place for "that austere Calabrian mind of Serra, who in the depths of prison wrote the first scientific treatise of public economy [...]. It was thus rightful that you, Richard Cobden, proclaimer of the same doctrines in the 19th century, should find the warmest appreciation among us".[69]

These were no longer the times of Salfi, who had gone through and paid the price of the clash between Say and Gioia. Now, after the victory of liberalism, even the French were ready to tone down Say's harsh observations, seeing that "the father of modern political economy, Adam Smith, proceeds along the path opened by Serra in viewing the liberal institutions as indispensable for the material prosperity of nations".[70] Now it was the turn of a certain Francesco Cerillo, another minor figure in Scialoja's circle who was devising a "science of political economy in relation to ethics". He, too, had acclaimed Cobden,[71] and his reaction to the ostracism of Italian economists shown by Daire in his *Collection des principaux économistes*, published by Guillaumin, was very different from that which was aroused in 1803 by the opening of Say's *Traité*. It was unjust to exclude Serra since in reality his treatise had been the "source of the true school of economics", including even its "last stage", which he saw as being represented by Dunoyer. The Calabrian was to be hailed as "the true precursor of the school of industrial economics, rather than [...] founder of the barbarous mercantile school".[72]

Such travesty of Serra served basically for a token cause of Risorgimento liberalism, which actually became pathetic with Francesco Trinchera. Another anti-Bourbon exile, author of a fairly decent *Corso di Economia politica*,[73] was now brazenly pursuing Cerillo's line,[74] serving up in liberal sauce regurgitations of the old story of Italian primacy.

3 Marginalist liberalism: Serra moved up to the attic

The demolition of Serra as theoretical economist, started by Ferrara with a decidedly radical turn in the period of the Risorgimento, was to be completed with more refined approaches by a new generation of Italian liberal economists formed in the closing years of the 19th century, taking the new marginalist viewpoint. One of the best of them, Antonio De Viti De Marco, took it upon himself to establish in a comprehensive study that was almost entirely devoid of extra scientific considerations the definitive picture of Serra as economist. An important point is that he saw Serra as a "solitary thinker",[75] without placing him historically within a broad tradition of economic thought. What really mattered to him was demonstrating the theoretical limits of the analysis. The treatment of the causes ("accidents") of wealth (but for De Viti only the abundance of money), so central to Serra's industrialist perspective, was rejected simply because it was extraneous to the current (19th-century) theories of international trade and the territorial division of labour and industries.[76] His rejection of limitations to exchange negotiation, as called for by de Santis, was commendable, but having no modern theory of value, Serra could not come up with "economic demonstration of the harm done in all cases to private interests, taken individually, when their freedom of negotiation is limited, nor of the advantage they enjoy when it is granted".[77] The value of money was seen solely in terms of the quantity of fine metal; there was nothing that might be seen as anticipating modern quantity theory, which Serra "did not know".[78] He saw the free export of money "solely as the legally necessary effect of debts contracted, not a comparatively useful effect of foreign trade. Missing from his book is the supreme economic reason for the phenomenon; and this is the point that determines the limits to and the real nature of Serra's economic doctrine".[79] The conclusion was that his interventionist, protectionist economic policy resulting from this absence of theory was to be condemned.[80]

De Viti's approach was naturally destined to prevail. Before, economists of various schools, not marginalists like Fornari[81] and, to a lesser extent, Gobbi,[82] had sought to save something of Serra's economic ideas, but now all bowed to the judgement dictated by De Viti. So it was for Ugo Rabbeno[83]; and Benini himself, much as he was inclined to justify the "Calabrian protectionist"[84], actually followed the same marginalist method as De Viti, judging Serra on the basis of an implausible comparison with modern theories and so determining to what extent he might be considered precursor. This was the line subsequently taken by Augusto

Graziani, another victim of the marginalist obsession with precursors,[85] in his modest (apparently influenced by Nicolini, a Crocian) edition of the *Breve trattato* for the Laterza publishing house.

Dismissed as an economist, isolated from the great Genovesian tradition that had discovered him, still lacking any critical edition of his work, with no reliable biography ever dedicated to him, Antonio Serra has become easy prey to the untender attention (not always rising to the level of interpretation) of all sorts, generally tainted with the precursor fixation,[86] and he still awaits rigorous historiographic evaluation that is able to appreciate him for what he represented in the history of 17th-century and 18th-century economic ideas.

Notes

1. Salfi, F.S., *Elogio di Antonio Serra primo scrittore di Economia civile*, Milan: Nobile e Tosi, 1802.
2. Lombardi, A. [1818], "Sull'origine, progressi e stato attuale dell'economia politica nel Regnó di Napoli", in *Discorsi accademici*, Potenza: Santanello, 1828, pp. 145–189.
3. Pecchio, G., *Storia della Economia pubblica in Italia*, Lugano: Ruggia, 1829, and others until Scialoja, A., *I principî della Economia sociale esposti in ordine ideologico*, Naples: Palma, 1840.
4. Cerillo, F., *Intorno alla raccolta dei principali economisti pubblicata in Francia*, Naples: Androsio, 1848; Trinchera, F., *Di Antonio Serra e del suo libro*, Naples: n. p., 1865.
5. Fornari, T., *Studi sopra Antonio Serra e Marc'Antonio de Santis*, Pavia: Fusi, 1879; Benini, R., "Sulle dottrine economiche di Antonio Serra", in *Giornale degli economisti*, s.II a.III, vol. V, 1892, pp. 222–248.
6. De Viti De Marco, A. [1890], "Le teorie economiche di Antonio Serra", in *Saggi di economia e finanza*, Rome: Lapi, 1898, pp. 3–58.
7. De Rosa, L., "Fortuna e sfortuna di Antonio Serra", in *Economisti meridionali*, Naples: Istituto italiano per gli studi filosofici, 1995; and others.
8. Doria, P.M., *Massime generali e particolari colle quali di tempo in tempo hanno gli Spagnoli governato il Regno di Napoli*, Naples: Guida, 1973, pp. 140–141.
9. Doria, P.M., *Manoscritti napoletani*, vol. 1, Galatina: Congedo, 1979, p.146. The text had already been published, but possibly in a less rigorous form, by Vidal, E., *Il pensiero civile di Paolo Mattia Doria negli scritti inediti*, Milan: Giuffrè, 1953, p.166.
10. Galiani, F., *Opere*, Diaz, F., and L. Guerci, (eds), Milan: Ricciardi, 1975, p. 309.
11. Salfi, 1802, pp. 7–8. Subsequently, in one of his notes to the *Correspondance inédite de l'abbé Ferdinand Galiani*, Paris: Treuttel et Würtz, 1818, I, p. LXV, he mentioned that Galiani "considered it the one copy that had escaped the Spanish Inquisition".
12. *Ibid.*, p. 83.
13. [P. Custodi], *Notizie intorno agli autori contenuti nel presente volume*, in Serra, A., "Breve trattato delle cause che possono far abbondare li Regni d'oro e

d'argento dove non sono miniere", *Scrittori classisi italiani di economia politica*, parte antica, vol.1, Milan: Destefanis, 1803, pp. XXVII–XXVIII. It is most likely this second copy that ended up in the Biblioteca Ambrosiana, and not Salfi's copy, as stated by Fornari, 1879, p. 44.

14. Croce, B., *Storia del Regno di Napoli*, Bari: Laterza, 1925, p. 160. However, Croce was mistaken, too: we know that one copy, for example, was then conserved in the library of the Diodati brothers: Diodati, L., *Dello stato presente della moneta nel Regno di Napoli e della necessità di un alzamento*, Naples: Migliaccio, 1790, p. XI.
15. Salfi, 1802, p. 8 in the Lombardi copy, now in my library.
16. Lombardi, 1828, pp. 150–151. Other copies are also listed by Fornari, 1879, *loc.cit.*
17. *Catalogo della Biblioteca di Luigi Einaudi*, Franceschi Spinazzola, D. (ed.), Turin: Fondazione Luigi Einaudi, 1981, p. 782.
18. Galiani, 1975, *loc. cit.*
19. Cfr. Di Battista, F., "L'economia civile genovesiana e la moderna economia politica", in Jossa, B., R. Patalano and E. Zagari (eds), *Genovesi economista*, Naples: Arte tipografica, 2007, pp. 292 ff.
20. Genovesi, A., *Delle lezioni di commercio o sia di economia civile con elementi del commercio*, Perna, M.L. (ed.), Naples: Istituto italiano per gli studi filosofici, 2005, p. 729.
21. Diodati, 1790, p. XI.
22. Roncaglia, A., *La ricchezza delle idee*, Rome: Laterza, 2001, uses the same term, "artefice", pp. 55–56, with reference to Custodi, behind whom, in fact – with regard to Serra's treatise, his rare copy and his position of openness towards the entire series – was Salfi himself, author of the *Elogio* the year before. Salfi's text also fails to find mention in Faucci R., *L'Economia politica in Italia..Dal Cinquecento ai nostri giorni*, Turin: UTET, 2000, pp. 32–35.
23. On this, from a different, more political perspective, cfr. Addante, L., *Patriottismo e libertà. L'"Elogio" di Antonio Serra di Francesco Salfi*, Cosenza: Pellegrini, 2009.
24. Salfi, 1802, p. 74.
25. *Ibid.*, pp. 46, 69, 52.
26. "Mio amico", said Salfi, *ibid.*, p. 79.
27. Cfr. Salfi's denunciation of Spanish misgovernment, *ibid.*, pp. 18–19.
28. Cfr. Nardi, C., *La vita e le opere di Francesco Saverio Salfi (1759–1832)*, Genova: Libreria Editrice Moderna, Rome: Pinnarò, 1925, pp. 2 ff.
29. Salfi, 1802, pp. 78–81.
30. *Ibid.*, p. 82.
31. *Ibid.*, pp. 26–28, 33, italics in the original text. Actually, for Serra, 1613, p. 6, "the causes that can make a Kingdom abound in money".
32. Genovesian term. For Serra, 1613, p. 9 and *passim: La superabondantia delle robbe* (The superabundance of goods).
33. This, too, was quite clearly a 17th-century Genovesian formulation. Serra, A., *Breve trattato delle cause che possono far abbondare li regni d'oro e d'argento dove non sono miniere, con applicatione al Regno di Napoli*, Naples: Lazzaro Scorriggio, 1613, pp. 19 ff.; Salfi's "art of governing" had been in Serra "when effective government [...:] as accident is perfectly operative in a certain Kingdom, there is no doubt that it will be the most powerful of all in making it abound

in gold and silver since, as efficient cause, it can be said to be an agent more efficient than all the other accidents".

34. Salfi, 1802, p. 35. The "body politic" was a fundamental category in Genovesian Civil economy. Serra, 1613, p. 25 *passim*: the level of the exchange rate, and in general monetary factors, "cannot be said to be causes, nor subsidiary, but opportunity, for they do not necessarily produce the effect".
35. Salfi, 1802, pp. 32–33; Serra, 1613, p. 18: "the great traffic and the advantage of the position grow with the quantity of manufacturing activities, and the quantity of manufacturing activities grows thanks to the great traffic, which through this combination increases".
36. Salfi, 1802, pp. 37–38; Serra, 1613, p. 110: "The real reason why money does not enter the Kingdom in exchange for exported goods is the income that foreigners have from their investments in the Kingdom and their earnings from the businesses that they own there.Therefore, the more opportunities one gives them to trade with advantage and profit and to buy shares and assets, the less money will enter the country in exchange for the exported goods".
37. Challenging, often confused, and far from accurate. This hampers, above all, an understanding and a historical interpretation of Serra's text: it is a great shame that economists and economic historians, ever ready to bring out new editions and reprints of the treatise, have not got down to hard work on a critical edition, as Perna did for Genovesi.
38. On Civil economy, today distorted and violated by undiscerning historiography, I can refer readers only to Di Battista, 2007. In the past, Salfi's position could obviously not be understood by the sorts of scholars who even deformed the title of the *Elogio*, putting "first writer on Political economy" and not *civil* Economy: Nuccio, O., *Investigazioni nella storia del pensiero economico*, Rome: Edizioni dell'Ateneo & Bizzarri, 1980, p. 43. It was no misprint: the same wrong title also appeared in the appendix (p. LXXVI) of the 1965 reprint in the Custodi series.
39. *Epoche di storia delle dottrine e dei metodi. Dieci grandi economisti* [1951], Italian Translation, Torino: UTET, 1956, p. 32.
40. Schumpeter, J.A. [1954], *Storia dell'analisi economica*, Turin: Boringhieri, 1959, pp. 236–237, 446.
41. Say, J.-B. [1803, 1841], *Traité d'Economie politique*, Paris: Economica, 2006, I, p. 25.
42. Say, J.-B., *Cours complet d'Economie politique pratique*, vol. VI, Paris: Rapilly, 1829, p. 366.
43. Say, J.-B., *Economie politique*, in Guizot, F. (ed.), *Encyclopédie progressive*, vol. I. Paris: Bureau de l'Encyclopédie progressive, 1826, pp. 260, 270.
44. Which I used in Di Battista, F., *L'emergenza ottocentesca dell'Economia politica a Napoli*, Bari: Facoltà di economia e commercio, 1983.
45. Charles Ganilh, whose work the Italian Francesco Fuoco was, significantly, to draw upon, was among the few who tried to stop it: according to Ganilh, C., *Des systèmes d'Economie politique*, 2nd ed., Paris: Treuttel et Würtz, I, p. 65, Italy had, up to the time of Smith, held the primacy, "Italy was infinitely superior to the rest of Europe in the science of political economy".
46. It would be particularly interesting to follow the criticisms of Say made by Gioia with regard to his erroneous assessment of the Italian economists of the past: the debate that it led to in the "Revue Encyclopédique", in 1827,

gave rise to significant friction and divergence within the editorial board between Salfi and the French, leading to the publication of an editorial note pointing out that these economists had simply grasped intuitively certain points of economic science without developing them.

47. Mugnai, A., *In dimostrazione che gl'italiani sono stati i primi cultori, ed i promotori insieme della moderna scienza di pubblica economia* (no place, no publisher), 1825: the viewpoint was far more limited, practically revealing a local preference by emphasizing the role of the Tuscan Bandini in contrast to the interesting operation of Salfi; on Serra, in fact, he confined his remarks to citing Galiani.
48. Bosellini, C., "Progressi delle scienze economiche sino al terminare del secolo passato", in *Giornale Arcadico di Scienze Lettere ed Arti*, XXV, 1825, pp. 280–305; XXVI, 1825, pp. 5–52, e.g. pp. 11, 46: "To tell the truth, one cannot see created" by the writers collected by Custodi, but if anything they "were the first to restore economic science".
49. Romagnosi, G.D. [1828], "Sull'anteriorità degl'italiani nella scienza della politica economia", in *Collezione degli articoli di economia politica e statistica*, Prato: Guasti, 1836, I, p. 636.
50. Boccanera, G., in Martuscelli, D., *Biografia degli uomini illustri del Regno di Napoli*, Naples: Gervasi, 1816, III *ad vocem*.
51. Lombardi, 1828, pp. 148–149.
52. His message was, however, totally travestied. See Pecchio, 1829, pp. 60–61, 64.
53. *Ibid.*, pp. 64, 72: "neither can the Italians claim any more, nor can the foreigners take exception to an incidental precedence, which does not deprive their authors of the merit of their discoveries. For while the Italian authors were indisputably the forerunners, it is nevertheless beyond all doubt that the foreigners were in no way guided by them in their discoveries".
54. *Ibid.*, p. 21.
55. "Revue Encyclopédique", a, XI, t.XLII, 1829, pp. 443–444.
56. Cosenza: Migliaccio, 1836.
57. Scialoja, 1840, pp. 12, 15, 19.
58. Scialoja, A., *Trattato elementare di economia sociale*, Turin: Pomba, 1848 (but 1849), p. 196.
59. So he put it in a then unpublished lecture given in Turin in 1846, now published in *Opere*, Milan: Angeli, 2006, III, p. 71.
60. Moreno, V., *Lezioni di Publica [sic] economia*, Naples: Virgilio, 1845–1848, p. 32.
61. Moreno, V., *Proemio* a Say, J.-B., *Corso compiuto di Economia politica pratica*, Naples: Tramater, 1834, pp. XIX–XX.
62. Expressed in the preface to the book dedicated to them with which he opened the *Biblioteca dell'Economista* in 1850, now in Ferrara, F., *Opere complete*, vol. II *Prefazioni alla Biblioteca dell'economista*, P.I, Rome: Istituto Grafico Tiberino, 1955, pp. 1–105.
63. Mancini, P.S., *Intorno alle dottrine dei fisiocrati e ad un giudizio del professore Ferrara sulle medesime*, no place (but Turin): no printer, 1851, pp. 24–25 of the rare extract bringing together the writings that appeared in issues 151–152 and 154–155 of that year's *"Gazzetta Piemontese"*.
64. *Digressione sulla priorità degli economisti italiani; Bandini, Serra. Risposta al prof. Mancini*, now in Ferrara, 1955, pp. 167–251.

65. *Ibid.*, p. 230.
66. *Ibid.*, p. 234. Here Ferrara is referring to the claims made for Serra as "father of the science" by Bianchini, L., *Della scienza del ben vivere sociale e della economia pubblicae degli stati: parte storica e di preliminari dottrine [1845]*, Naples: Stamperia Reale, 1857, p. 156.
67. Croce, 1925, pp. 149–150.
68. List, F. [1844, 1931], *Il sistema nazionale di economia politica*, trad. it., Milan: ISEDI, 1972, pp. 320–322.
69. Mancini, P.S., *Parole dette nella R. Accademia delle Scienze di Napoli dal socio Pasquale Stanislao Mancini nella seduta del dì 16 marzo 1847 in occasione della presentazione del Cobden all'Accademia stessa*, no place (but Naples): n.p., 1847, pp. 7–8. The farcical show organized at the Accademia Pontaniana found its culmination in Cobden's reply which, according to the reports, observed "modestly that he and his friends in England had merely disseminated those very same economic truths to the discovery of which he was glad to acknowledge how much the generous efforts of the Italians, and particularly of the Neapolitans, had contributed"! *Ibid.*, p. 11.
70. Wolowski, L., *Introduction* to L.Cibrario, *Economie politique du Moyen Age*, Paris: Guillaumin, 1859, pp. XIX–XX.
71. Cerillo, 1848, p. 4.
72. *Ibid.*, pp. 1, 21, 29, 35–36.
73. Turin: Pons, 1854. In the *Prologo*, p. 4, he movingly recalled the four years spent "in that same sombre, dismal Vicaria prison in Naples, where, outstandingly, the brave Calabrian Antonio Serra announced to Italy and the world the principles of economic science".
74. Trinchera, 1865. Cited on p. 43.
75. De Viti De Marco, 1898, p. 58.
76. *Ibid.*, pp. 27–28. "This supreme economic reason Serra failed to understand".
77. *Ibid.*, p. 39.
78. *Ibid.*, pp. 44, 48.
79. *Ibid.*, p. 49: "the principle of comparative cost [...] eluded him", p. 48.
80. *Ibid.*, p. 54.
81. Fornari, 1879, in particular pp. 40, 71–72, 105. But De Viti De Marco, 1898, p. 4, criticized him for his illusion that he could find in Serra the modern theory of foreign exchange expounded by Goschen.
82. Gobbi, U., *La concorrenza estera e gli antichi economisti italiani*, Milan: Hoepli, 1884, pp. 53–60, tried to save his "theory of international payments", but of course "it would now be quite useless even to raise the question as to whether Serra might be considered the founder of Political economy".
83. In his entry in R.H.I. Palgrave (ed.), *Dictionary of Political Economy* [1894], London: Macmillan, 1913, III, p. 381.
84. Benini, 1892, p. 248.
85. A.Graziani (ed.), *Economisti del Cinque e Seicento*, Bari: Laterza, 1913, pp. 388–389.
86. Particularly abused now is the superficial approach along the lines of "first, perspicacious analysis in terms of the Meridionalismo" (De Rosa, 1995, p. 30).

14
The Heritage of Antonio Serra

Alessandro Roncaglia[1]

1 Introduction

My aim in this chapter is to summarize the salient points in Antonio Serra's contribution to economic culture, starting from some reflections on the fortunes, or perhaps, rather, misfortunes that it subsequently met with.

Here we can distinguish various phases, which we will take in chronological sequence only in part. First was the long silence, lasting nearly two hundred years, after which came the rediscovery of Serra in the guise of patriot. Later came Serra the expert on the problems of Southern Italy, but between these phases, at the height of the fascist period, the stress fell on his voluntarism. Finally, rather more complex and less readily exploitable politically, came the more balanced evaluation by historians of economics.

Like all reconstructions, what we present here is in fact a simplification of a far more variegated process, as the literature on Serra extends far beyond the scope of this chapter.

2 From oblivion to a medal for patriotism

A short treatise on the causes that can make kingdoms abound in gold and silver even in the absence of mines (*Breve trattato delle cause che possono fare abbondare li regni d'oro e d'argento dove non sono miniere con applicazione al Regno di Napoli*) came out in 1613; the dedication to the viceroy of the Kingdom of Naples was signed by Antonio Serra, a native of Cosenza, in the Neapolitan prison of Vicaria on 10 July 1613. From then on, for nearly two centuries, a long silence fell over Serra's work. Later on, when the *Short Treatise* began to receive mention and praise, it was no easy task to reconstruct a few reliable facts about the author.

We may add that until relatively recent times virtually all the literature on Serra was Italian. Before the few pages published by Monroe in 1924 in English translation, the language barrier had proved practically insurmountable, due also to Serra's archaic style. It was only in 2011 that the complete text of the *Short Treatise* came out in English, edited by Sophus A. Reinert.

The *Short Treatise* was first cited by Ferdinando Galiani in note XXIX of the notes added to the second edition, published in 1780, of his celebrated *Della Moneta* (*On Money*). The mention is marginal but decidedly appreciative because Serra is pointed out as the "first and earliest writer on political-economic science".[2] However, this brief note has precious little to add: just over three pages in length, having dealt with the monetary disorders of the Kingdom of Naples between the late 16th century and early 17th century and drawn attention to some points in the work of Giovanni Donato Turbolo, he comes to Serra to remark that he had found some reference to the monetary theses of Marc'Antonio de Santis (1605) in the *Short Treatise*; only at this point does Galiani come to his few words of praise, without, however, referring to any specific merits of Serra's work, and indeed adding some remarks that are hardly likely to entice a hesitant reader: "Of his unhappy century he retains nothing else, apart from his dry, arid and obscure style, much like that of the exponents of scholasticism, legal counsellors or teachers, using many divisions and subdivisions, distinctions, articles and clauses, at times stretching out the discourse tediously". The context of the words of praise suggests that Galiani was referring mainly, if not solely, to Serra's theses on money and exchange, also for the sake of a comparison as rhetorical as it is unsubstantiated, with those of de Santis, which he was acquainted with only via Serra's criticisms. In any case, Galiani states that he is in possession of a copy of the *Short Treatise* given to him by Bartolomeo Intieri (1678–1757, the Tuscan administrator of the Neapolitan estates of the Corsini family, and then of the Medicis, celebrated for financing the first chair in political economy in the world, bestowed according to his wishes on Antonio Genovesi).

Galiani's account of Serra as founder of the science of political economy was taken up by "citizen Salfi" (Francesco, or Franco, Salfi, 1759–1832: a priest, mason and patriot originally from Cosenza but Neapolitan by adoption before exile in Genoa, Milan, and Paris – having served as counsellor to Gioacchino Murat), in a text of 1802 entitled *Elogio di Antonio Serra primo scrittore di economia civile (In praise of Antonio*

Serra the first writer on civil economy).[3] To Salfi we owe the account – fascinating but probably no more than a legend – of Serra as a patriot and companion of Tommaso Campanella not only in internment in the prison of Vicaria but also as sharing in a scheme for the secession of the southern provinces of Italy from the Spanish Empire.[4]

There are no documents to bear out this thesis, but it seems quite plausible, although the documentation cannot be considered conclusive, that Serra was imprisoned, rightly or wrongly, on the accusation of forging money.[5] Moreover, the crime of forgery also included what is now called market rigging: spreading false information. At the time, this could even extend to an evaluation of the situation, including measures suggested to deal with it, deemed erroneous by the political authorities, even if well founded.[6] Be that as it may, the account of Serra as patriot was again taken up by Baron Pietro Custodi in the preface to the first volume of the series of Classical Italian Writers on political economy, published in fifty volumes between 1803 and 1816. We may reasonably suppose that it was mainly for this reason that Serra's work was given its place of honour at the beginning of the first volume.

3 Serra according to Pietro Custodi

Custodi (1771–1842) was indeed a patriot who held a number of political-administration posts of a certain importance, including that of general secretary of the ministry of finance during the Napoleonic occupation. In the dedication that introduced the first volume of the series, Custodi spelt out the goal he had set for himself:

> I address this Collection to those Italians who still respond to the spur of honour and ardent desire to be of use to their common homeland. Without the support of their concurrent, concordant and constant efforts, Italy could have no hope of rising once again from her ruins.

Custodi's aim was thus to present anew the Italian contributions to a discipline, political economy, which plays an important role in guiding not only material but also civil development. At the same time, he wished to demonstrate the existence of a rich and important culture in the common language of the country, which had yet to become united, rekindling the pride of the Italians and showing foreigners how false their idea was that Italy "is not fit for self-government, and should therefore bow under its deserved abasement" (pp. xii–xiii). "If only all the generous Italians, despite the state-lines chance has traced which seem to divide their country, could grow accustomed to seeing themselves as offspring of a common homeland; and…for at least fifty years the practice introduced of serious and thorough study of political economy, under the protection of enlightened governments, all rivalry silenced, Italy would soon arise flourishing and happy" (p. xviii). Clearly, Custodi attributes importance to the study of economics for guidance in wise choices for policies that favour economic and civil development.

These goals account for some of Custodi's choices. Here we will dwell on two of them. First, there is the effort to make texts comprehensible to the readers of his time: "As for the earlier writers, I have taken on the discretion and labour to adapt the style to current usage without, however, in any way departing in the least part from faithfulness to the text" (p. xiv). This was no easy task, which Custodi himself pointed out: "just how difficult it has been for me anyone can see who has the opportunity to leaf through the poorly produced and roughly assembled original editions of the works themselves" (p. xxiv). Moreover, it contrasted with the philological rigour that Custodi claimed to pursue (indeed, a century later this choice was to come under the scathing criticism of Graziani).[7] Nevertheless, it was an important choice to guarantee circulation and readership for the series, which in fact met with great public favour (and is still used by those who study the history of Italian economic thought).

Second, there was the decision to open the series with Antonio Serra's book, published, as we have seen, in 1613, and thus some three decades after the brief texts by Bernardo Davanzati and Gaspare Scaruffi[8] were included in volume II. Serra's work was virtually unknown: Custodi knew of only two copies,[9] one of which belonged to Galiani. From then on, however, thanks precisely to his inclusion in a publishing venture finding wide circulation, as indeed did Custodi's, Serra's work became a fundamental reference point for Italian economic culture. Not even Custodi, however, dwelt on making clear the scientific merits of Serra's work: he recalls Galiani's praise, recalls "citizen Salfi's conjecture" (p. xxxi), and dedicates some space to Campanella's revolutionary project. As for Serra, the only reference that Custodi effectively makes to his economic thought in his introduction – following Galiani in this respect – concerns his criticisms of de Santis on devaluation as the only remedy to the problems of the Kingdom.

In this period, then, Serra comes back into vogue as a patriot and monetary economist, without bringing the focus to bear on his "real" theory. Exemplary of this state of affairs, basically, is the position taken by Francesco Ferrara, who justifies non-inclusion of the *Brief Treatise* in his *Biblioteca dell'economista*, expressing sympathy for the figure of the patriot but belittling his economic contribution. In fact, Ferrara follows Galiani and Custodi in concentrating his attention on Serra's contribution to monetary theory, but even here he looks little further than the title, deducing from it that "gold and silver were for him the greatest possible wealth".[10] Hence the a priori antipathy of Ferrara, an extremist in economic liberalism (in the second volume of his *Biblioteca*, he went as far as prefacing Smith's *The Wealth of Nations* with a text by Garnier, 1851, critical of the Scottish economist's scant liberalism), to Serra, the mercantilist-bullionist, quoting and commenting negatively on some passages removed from their context, and in conclusion speaking of "abject economic blathering".[11]

Ferrara's misunderstandings – shared by many others – of the identification that Serra was supposed to make between precious metals and the wealth of the country derived from the total lack at that time of statistics on what we would today call national income; thus, many economists of the period took the abundance or scarcity of gold and silver in a country as indicators of the wealth that it enjoyed (understood, moreover, as income and not as wealth).[12]

4 The effective contribution of Serra[13]

Was Ferrara right, apart from the misunderstanding mentioned above, in deeming that Serra's contribution was of no real importance? To answer this question, we need to spend a few words on it.

We will begin by looking into the structure and content of the book. After the dedication and the introduction, the *Short Treatise* is divided into three parts. The first, and for us today probably the most interesting, looks into "the causes which make kingdoms abound in gold and silver", as the title of chapter I reads,[14] in practice the causes – albeit not the nature – of the economic prosperity of nations in the broad sense, also going on to a comparison between the conditions of the Kingdom of Naples and those in other parts of Italy, and in particular Venice. The second part is dedicated essentially to confuting some proposals advanced a few years before by Marc'Antonio de Santis (1605) – and taken up in a "prammatica" (government decree) of June 1607 but rapidly abandoned[15] – aiming to lower the exchange rate in order to attract money into the Kingdom from abroad. The third section discusses systematically, but always with critical reference to de Santis's theses, the various interventions in monetary policy tried out or proposed "for making the Kingdom abound in money".[16]

The economic prosperity of a country, Serra explains, depends on "proper accidents" ("accidenti propri") – that is, the original specific characteristics of each country – and on "common accidents" ("accidenti comuni"), which are the more or less favourable circumstances that can be brought about anywhere. Of the former, Serra mentions "a domestic agricultural surplus" ("la superabondanzia delle robbe") – that is, the endowment of natural wealth – and in particular the fertility of the soil (Serra generally uses the term "robbe" to refer to agricultural produce), and the "geographical position" ("il sito"), or in other words the location "with respect to other kingdoms and parts of the world". Coming to the "common accidents", he mentions four: "a multiplicity of manufacturing activities, an enterprising population, extensive trade and effective government" ("quantità d'artifici, qualità de genti, trafico grande de negozi e provisione di quel che governa")[17] – in other words, artisanal production, moral qualities and professional skills of the population, extension of trade (especially international transit trade), and political-institutional arrangements. The latter is the most important element, "for it may be described as the efficient cause and superior agent of all the other accidents".[18]

Having analysed these elements in the first seven chapters of the first part, Serra observes that in terms of "proper accidents", the Kingdom of Naples enjoys a certain advantage (apart from the location), in particular over Venice: if Naples is so much poorer than Venice, it can only be put down to "common accidents". In showing how this comes about, and the reasons for the outflow of gold and silver from the Kingdom of Naples, Serra shrewdly reconstructs the situation of the country's balance of payments, albeit without providing systematic analysis of the concept.

The second part of the *Short Treatise* is the longest and most convoluted of the three. Half of it (the first five chapters) is dedicated to confuting de Santis's thesis that "the high exchange rate on the Naples market as against the other markets of Italy is the sole cause of the shortage of money in the Kingdom", because the consequence is that payments from abroad are made with bills of exchange while foreign payments are made in cash.[19] Serra, however, argues that the imbalance cannot derive from the bill of exchange mechanism; the scarcity of money in the Kingdom depends upon the underlying imbalance in what we would now call the balance of payments. In fact, if we translate into our terminology Serra's argument as set out in chapter X, the inflow of currency that corresponds to exports of agricultural produce is more than counterbalanced by the remittances for interest on the public debt bonds and profits on business conducted by citizens from elsewhere, and above all Genoese and Florentine merchants-bankers. The remaining chapters of the second part of the *Short Treatise*, from the sixth to the twelfth, form a critique of the *prammatica* (government decree) proposed by de Santis (and, in chapter VIII, of the similar proposal previously adopted by the count of Olivares) with the aim of fixing a lower exchange rate between Naples and the other financial markets.

Finally, the third part discusses economic policies of use in improving the situation of the Kingdom, developing the analysis performed in the previous two parts. In the first four chapters, Serra reviews the various administrative interventions on the financial and currency markets, some already tried out (a ban on the export of coins and precious metals, reduction of the exchange rate, utilization of foreign currency as means of domestic payment, overvaluation of foreign currencies, and/or obligation to deliver to the national mint) and others – our author prudently points out – that were only proposed (an increase in the face value of national currencies and a reduction of their gold or silver content). The fifth chapter offers a brief discussion of "the correct ratio of gold to silver in ancient and modern times".[20] While not in principle objecting to administrative measures, Serra advances some more or less drastic critiques of such interventions: when they are not actually counter-productive, they nevertheless prove ineffective in that – as we have seen – the real problem lies in the imbalance in the balance of payments.

Finally, in the closing chapters, Serra points out how difficult it is to address these basic problems, indicating as a main objective the development of the Kingdom's productive activity, while leaving specification of a detailed programme of interventions for the direct audience with the political authorities which he hoped to have. In fact, we must not forget that Serra's aim in writing the *Short Treatise* was not to provide an exhaustive treatment of the subject chosen – as an economist would attempt to do nowadays – or provide a detailed account of measures in economic policy, but rather to draw attention to his abilities with the hope of being freed from prison and called upon by the government authorities for direct collaboration.

5 Money and exchange rates

As we have seen, Serra's immediate concern in his *Short Treatise* is critiquing a specific proposal for currency policy advanced by Marc'Antonio de Santis (1605): de Santis called for the authorities to fix a price lower than the current standard market price for foreign currency acquired with bills of exchange (or, as it was more succinctly put, a lower exchange rate). In fact, de Santis argued a cause-and-effect connection between the high exchange rate and the scarcity of money afflicting the Kingdom of Naples.

Effectively, with the price for currency acquired with bills of exchange well above the ratio between the metal content of foreign and national currency, it would certainly have been in the interests of the agents who had to make foreign payments to send the silver coin of the Kingdom of Naples abroad to be converted into foreign currency in the mint of the country of destination. Conversely, it would be to the advantage of agents who wish to move money from abroad to the Kingdom of Naples to acquire bills of exchange, given the greater quantity of Neapolitan currency that could be obtained in this way, rather than importing metal currency into the Kingdom.[21]

Thus, according to de Santis (1605), there was an outflow from the Kingdom of coin and precious metals (gold and silver) that corresponded to the liabilities in the balance of payments, while the inflow that corresponded to assets came not in coin and metals but in bills of exchange. If, however, a government decree officially fixed a price for foreign currency acquired through bills of exchange lower than their respective content of gold and metal, de Santis argued, the reverse situation would come about: money and metals would flow into the Kingdom, while only bills of exchange would flow out for foreign payments.[22]

As we have seen, Serra, by contrast, maintained that it was not the high price of foreign currency acquired through bills of exchange that caused the imbalance on the currency markets but instead persisting liabilities in what we would now call the balance of payments, including the so-called invisibles. This state of affairs, in turn, is ascribed to the weakness of the productive structure and the feeble spirit of enterprise shown by the citizens of the Kingdom of Naples: it is with this issue in mind that Serra embarks upon his *Short Treatise*. Thus, de Santis's proposal is rejected: as ineffective since it would not remove the real causes of the situation; as wishful thinking since the agents on the foreign currency markets could easily get round it; and as counter-productive since it would throw further obstacles in the way of trade.

Objections along the same lines as Serra's regarding the impossibility of officially fixing maximum prices for bills of exchange had already been advanced by an anonymous gentleman, possibly a Genoese merchant, and quoted by de Santis himself, who refutes them.[23] Moreover, this anonymous critic argues, like Serra later on, that "the first and principal causes" of the high exchange rate are the remittances abroad of the income received on capital invested in the Kingdom of Naples by Genoese and Florentine merchants. Here the anonymous critic of de Santis attributes the deterioration observed in the state of affairs to growing misgivings about the economic prospects of the Kingdom of Naples, due to the insolvency of some debtors (private and "università", i.e. municipalities) and worsening quality of the public debt itself, leading foreign merchants to avoid reinvesting their revenues in the Kingdom and rather to send them abroad.[24]

Serra, too, attributes decisive importance to the balance of payments invisibles. Indeed, while recognizing (in chapter XI of the first part, in contrast with de Santis's assessments) the importance of manufactured article imports, he maintains that essentially they lead to equilibrium or possibly a slight surplus, even though they are of appreciably less value than are the exports. In comparison with the anonymous critic of de Santis, however, Serra appears to attribute less importance to confidence in the Kingdom's financial activities and greater importance to the real long-term factors – that is, the prospects for productive activity, and in particular foreign direct investments. However, this is a matter of nuances in an essentially analogous assessment that ascribes the shortage of money in the Kingdom to the balance of payments deficit that is the result of mainly, if not solely, remittances of revenues from foreign capital invested in the Kingdom.[25]

6 Cattaneo: "Del pensiero come principio d'economia pubblica"

One author who cites Serra is Carlo Cattaneo, having had the opportunity to read the text in Custodi's edition. And at last we have an author who mentions him neither for his patriotism nor for his monetary ideas, but for his contribution – together with others – to the birth of economics, albeit pointing out the limitations: "The early efforts by Serra, Mun, Child, Locke and Bandini could not create the science all at once".[26] He cites Serra in passing, then, and it is hard to say whether the *Short Treatise* had any influence or what influence the *Short Treatise* may have had on Cattaneo's thought. However, we can point out certain affinities.

In one of his best-known writings, *Del pensiero come principio d'economia pubblica* (*On thought as a principle of political economy*, originally published on the *Politecnico* in 1861),[27] Cattaneo dwells on the role of intelligence as "source of production", and it is in fact precisely for this reason that his text receives frequent mention. The mind turns to Serra's "qualità de' genti". It seems to boil down to the same thing, namely the importance of what is now reductively called "human capital", although Cattaneo takes it significantly further, placing the qualities of the good citizen at the basis of a healthy and prosperous economy, and, albeit in the context of his thought, his is a position that fits in with the broader strategy of constructing the Italian nation "bottom up" on the basis of a recognized common culture.

Like Serra, Cattaneo did not come up against that one-dimensional conception of *homo oeconomicus* that would come to the fore as the "marginalist revolution" got under way. To Cattaneo, as indeed to Serra, it came quite naturally to associate political ("effective government"), social ("enterprising population"), and economic ("multiplicity of manufacturing activities" and "extensive trade") aspects in accounting for what Adam Smith calls the wealth of nations.

However, when pursuing this line, we must be careful not to confuse it with the "voluntarism" that permeated culture in the fascist period, which, for example, Tagliacozzo[28] appears to do when he stresses in Serra a mentality that was "activistic, voluntaristic, idealistic, in contrast with the fatalistic, mechanistic, materialistic attitude of the classical economists" (just as we must take care not to confuse the one-dimensional nature of the marginalist *homo oeconomicus* with the far more open-minded notion of "personal interest" – self-interest, not selfishness – to be found in Smith, for example, or John Stuart Mill).

7 Serra and the problems of Southern Italy

Over the course of the 20th century, many authors have seen in Serra a precursor in accounting for the lag shown by Southern Italy, trailing behind the regions of the north. In fact, there is an extensive literature ranging – to name but a few – from Arias to Nigro and De Rosa, among whom we may also include Benedetto Croce.[29]

To some extent, this literature bears out the picture of Serra the patriot, but the literature attributes a different significance to it, in the sense that this native of Cosenza took to heart the conditions of the country's southern regions, to which he owed his origins, and his ideas were intended as a contribution towards solving the problem of Southern Italy's backwardness.

However, we must not lose sight of the fact that Serra's primary aim was to shake off the fetters of imprisonment and that his suggestions for economic policy, essentially regarding the management of exchange, disregard the underdeveloped conditions in southern regions, except for their effects on the balance of payments. Moreover, the problem of Southern Italy is not simply one of underdevelopment: rather, it is a problem of economic dualism,[30] and is to be approached as such.[31] When countries at different levels of development find themselves side by side, the problem lies in understanding what the different degree of development depends upon in order to favour those factors that can help the country that is lagging behind to catch up. In the case of economic dualism, instead, we have two areas that show different levels of development but that belong to the same country, the development of one and the underdevelopment of the other being connected – the result of the same set of circumstances. The problem addressed by Serra was the former, not the latter. In the first part of his work, he indicates the factors that account for the different rates of economic development of diverse states – that account for the wealth of nations, as Smith would put it – as the basis to address the issues of international finance and currency in the second and third parts of the *Short Treatise*, and by so doing – here lies the aspect that makes it so important for the history of economic thought – he provides a major contribution, albeit unacknowledged, to the birth of political economy.[32]

It is these latter points that loom large in more recent researches in the history of economic thought, focusing on Serra's contribution and seeking to shed clearer light on the connection between his thought and the culture of his time.[33] Of course, the monetary and currency issues have also received due attention. Thanks, then, to the intellectual forcefulness of his work, Serra has survived not only two centuries of silence but also the misunderstandings of authors who have in the course of time portrayed him as bullionist, patriot, or proto-meridionalist.

Over the ages, unprejudiced readers (who can cast their eyes beyond their ideological position, unlike some exponents of extreme economic liberalism, such as Ferrara) have sensed something quite special in Serra, even when they have been unable to define exactly what. This is a characteristic of the great works of all ages, and the *Short Treatise* can claim a rightful place among them. Nevertheless, philological reconstruction still has an essential role to play in determining the nature of and limitations to his effective contribution to the foundations of economic science.

Notes

1. Sapienza University of Rome, Department of Statistical Sciences. In part, I draw here on a previous study on Serra: Roncaglia, A., "Antonio Serra", *Rivista italiana degli economisti*, 4, 1999, pp. 421–438, and on the typescript of a lecture given at the Accademia dei Lincei on "The civil commitment of the economists", 15.12.2011.
2. Galiani, F., *Della moneta*, Naples: Giuseppe Raimondi, 1751; second edition, Naples: Stamperia Simoniana, 1780; reprinted Milan: Feltrinelli, 1963, p. 340.
3. Salfi's text has recently been reprinted with an interesting and extensive introduction in Addante, L., *Patriottismo e libertà. L'Elogio di Antonio Serra di Francesco Salfi*, Cosenza: Luigi Pellegrini, 2009. (Salfi, F., *Elogio di Antonio Serra*, Milan: Nobile e Tosi, 1802; reprinted in Addante, L., 2009.)
4. This account was again taken up a few years ago by Argemì, L., *Liberalismo mercantilista. Un cuasi sistema*, Madrid: Editorial Sintesis, 2004, pp. 38–39, but only in the context of a brief reference to Serra's mercantilism.
5. Cfr. Amabile, L., *Fra Tommaso Campanella, la sua congiura, i suoi processi e la sua pazzia*, Naples: Morano, 1882, vol. 3, pp. 646–648.
6. For this point I am grateful to Gaetano Sabatini.
7. "Custodi, for all his good intentions, did not confine himself to faithfully reproducing the texts but, as was the custom then, sought to patch them together, here modernising or standardising antiquated or dialect expressions, there pulling shaky sentences into shape, omitting sentences and sometimes even whole passages that did not chime too well with the a-religious language of the years leading up to the Revolution; at times falling (as tends to happen to those who take such perilous paths) into actual errors of interpretation, in other words lapsing in faithfulness not only to the form but even to the thought of the individual authors" (Graziani, A. (ed.), *Economisti del Cinque e Seicento*. Bari: Laterza, 1913, p. 383). Any such errors are avoided in the recent, accurate English translation of the writings of Serra by Sophus A. Reinert (Reinert, S.A., "Introduction", in A. Serra, *A short treatise on the wealth and poverty of nations (1613)*, ed. by S.A. Reinert, London: Anthem Press, 2011, pp. 1–93), drawn upon in these pages. However, even the use of modern terms, inevitable as it is, can lead inexpert readers into misunderstandings (for example, in 17th-century Southern Italy "manufacturing production" refers to craft activities mostly on a small scale, while "agricultural surplus" does not refer to surplus in the specific sense that it would take on with the classical economists, as a difference between output and physical production costs; obviously, in the generic sense of "extra", the concept of surplus goes back to ancient times, as for example in the Bible).
8. Davanzati, B. (1582), *Notizia dei cambi*; reprinted in *Scrittori classici italiani di economia politica*, parte antica, vol. 2, Milan: Destefanis, 1804, pp. 51–69; Scaruffi, G., *Alitinonfo*, Reggio: per Hercoliano Bartoli, 1582; reprinted as *Discorso sopra le monete*, in *Scrittori classici italiani di economia politica*, parte antica, vol. 2, ed. by P. Custodi, Milan: Destefanis, 1804.
9. Cfr. Custodi, P., "Notizie degli autori contenuti nel presente volume", in *Scrittori classici italiani di economia politica*, parte antica, vol. 1, Milan: Destefanis, 1803, p. xxviii, note. The copies known to us as extant today number about thirty.

10. Ferrara, F., "Prefazione" to *"Trattati italiani del secolo XVIII"*, in *Biblioteca dell'economista*, Prima serie, vol. 3, Turin: Pomba, 1852, pp. v–lxx, p. xlix. Preceding Ferrara on similar lines of interpretation were authors such as Say (Say, J.-B., *A treatise on political economy*, Philadelphia, PA: Lippincott, Brambo & Co, 1803, p. 15) and McCulloch, (McCulloch, J.R., *The literature of political economy*. London: Longman, 1845, p. 189). A contrasting opinion was advanced by List (List, F., *Das nationale System der politischen Ökonomie*, Stuttgart: J.G. Cotta, 1841; Italian translation *Il sistema nazionale di economia politica*, Milan: Isedi, 1972, pp. 320–322, 326), who saw in Serra the first signs of a new science precisely on account of the references to the real economy and the role of industry, in the original sense as active spirit of initiative. Similar interpretations were subsequently proposed by Einaudi (Einaudi, L., "Una disputa a torto dimenticata fra autarcisti e liberisti", *Rivista di storia economica*, 3, 1938, pp. 132–133; reprinted in L. Einaudi, *Saggi bibliografici e storici intorno alle dottrine economiche*, Rome: Edizioni di storia e letteratura, 1953, pp. 117–151) and Schumpeter (Schumpeter, J., *History of economic analysis*, ed. by E. B. Schumpeter, New York, NY: Oxford University Press, 1954; reprinted, New York, NY: Oxford University Press, 1994, pp. 353–355).
11. *Ibid.*, p. lvi, cfr. Garnier, G., "Metodo di Germano Garnier per facilitare lo studio dell'opera di Smith", in F. Ferrara (ed.), 1851, pp. lxxiii–lxxx.
12. Towards the end of the 19th century, two of the leading Italian economists of the time, Benini (Benini, R., "Sulle dottrine economiche di Antonio Serra: appunti critici", *Giornale degli economisti*, 3, 1892, pp. 222–248) and De Viti De Marco (De Viti De Marco, A., "Le teorie economiche di Antonio Serra", in A. De Viti De Marco, *Saggi di economia e finanza*, Rome: Giornale degli economisti, 1889, pp. 3–58) dealt with Serra in extensive studies.
13. This section and the following two are drawn with some modifications from Roncaglia, 1999.
14. Serra, A., *Breve trattato delle cause che possono far abbondare li regni d'oro e d'argento dove non sono miniere con applicazione al Regno di Napoli*, Naples: L. Scorriggio, 1613; reprinted in P. Custodi (ed.), *Scrittori classici italiani di economia politica*, parte antica, vol.1, Milan: Destefanis, 1803, pp. 1–179 (anastatic reprint, ed. by Nuccio, 1965); Graziani, 1913, pp. 141–235; Colapietra, 1973, pp. 163–228; Trasselli (Trasselli, C., "Introduzione" to A. Serra, *Breve trattato*, Reggio Calabria: Editori Meridionali Riuniti, 1974), Rotelli (Rotelli, E., "Introduzione" to A. Serra, *Breve trattato*, Cosenza: Mediocredito regionale della Calabria, 1985), Ricossa (Ricossa, S., "Introduzione" to A. Serra, *Breve trattato*, facsimile reprint of the first edition, Naples: Generoso Procaccini Editore, 1986), Schefold (Schefold, B. (ed.), *Antonio Serra und sein Breve Trattato*, Dusseldorf: Verlag Wirtschaft und Finanzen Gmb, 1994, and Schefold, B., "Antonio Serra: der Stifter der Wirtschaftslehre?", in B. Schefold (ed.), 1994, pp. 5–38), Landolfi, A. and D. Luciano (eds), A. Serra, *Breve trattato*, Vibo Valentia: Sistema bibliotecario territoriale vibonese, 1999); the selected pages in Grilli (Grilli, E., *Serra visto da Enzo Grilli*, Rome: Luiss University Press, 2007) and, in English translation, in Monroe (Monroe, A. E. (ed.), *Early economic thought. Selections from economic literature prior to Adam Smith*, Cambridge, MA: Harvard University Press, 1924), up to the complete English translation, together with the Italian text, A. Serra, *A short treatise on*

the wealth and poverty of nations (1613), ed. by S.A. Reinert, London: Anthem Press, 2011.

15. Cfr. Colapietra (Colapietra, R. (ed.), *Problemi monetari negli scrittori napoletani del Seicento*, Rome: Accademia Nazionale dei Lincei, 1973, pp. 24–28) for illustration of the main decrees adopted in the monetary field between 1605 – the date of publication of de Santis's text – and 1613, when Serra's *A Short Treatise* went to press.
16. Serra, 1613, p. 209.
17. Serra, 1613, p. 119.
18. Serra, 1613, p. 129.
19. Serra, 1613, pp. 157, 159.
20. Serra, 1613, p. 233.
21. The classical theory of exchange, based on a rate of exchange between currencies corresponding to the ratio between the respective gold contents plus or minus a margin of fluctuation limited within the transport and insurance costs, cannot, however, be applied directly to the case in question due to certain complications. To begin with, bills of exchange also include an element of interest (although it is possible to take it into account: cfr. Marcuzzo, C. and A. Rosselli, *Ricardo and the Gold Standard*, London: Macmillan, 1991, chap.6) and an insolvency risk premium, associated with the nature of the credit instrument. Moreover, reference would often be made to an accounting currency (the scudo of Piacenza) that did not exist in concrete terms. Finally, the Neapolitan currency, the carlino, was of silver, while foreign coins were generally of gold. (Cfr. De Rosa, L., *I cambi esteri del Regno di Napoli dal 1591 al 1707*, Naples: Biblioteca del Bollettino dell'Archivio storico del Banco di Napoli, 1955, and De Rosa, L. (ed.), *Il Mezzogiorno agli inizi del '600*, Rome-Bari: Laterza, 1994, for a description of the exchange markets in the Kingdom of Naples at the time). Consequently, the rate of exchange depended not only on the supply of and demand for foreign currency resulting from the balance of payments (the element which, in traditional theory, made the exchange rate fluctuate around gold parity) but also on the rate of interest and on the relative prices of the two precious metals, gold and silver (an aspect upon which Serra himself dwells in Chapter IV of the second part and Chapter V of the third part of *A Short Treatise*); moreover, the exchange rate with respect to the accounting currency being given, the rate for foreign currencies was not univocally determined, since they could continue to fluctuate with respect to the accounting currency. Many apparently obscure points in the works of de Santis and Serra are due to these complicating factors. (For fuller treatment of these issues, see Rosselli, A., "Antonio Serra e la teoria dei cambi", in Roncaglia, A. (ed.), *Alle origini del pensiero economico in Italia. 1. Moneta e sviluppo negli economisti napoletani dei secoli XVII–XVIII*, Bologna: Mulino, 1995, pp. 37–58.)
22. The writings of de Santis are provided in Colapietra (1973), respectively pp. 111–141 and 143–162, and De Rosa (1994), pp. 3–45 and 47–74. (de Santis, M.A., *Discorso di Marc'Antonio de Santis intorno a gli effetti, che fa il cambio in Regno*, Naples: Costantino Vitale, 1605, and de Santis, M.A., *Secondo discorso di Marc'Antonio de Santis intorno a gli effetti, che fa il cambio in Regno. Sopra una risposta, che è stata fatta adverso del primo*, Naples: Costantino Vitale, 1605).

23. The *Risposta sopra il discorso fatto per Marc'Antonio de Santis intorno a gli effetti, che fa il cambio in Regno*, by an anonymous author, is quoted by de Santis at the beginning of his *Secondo discorso*. Cfr. Colapietra (1973), pp. 145–149, and De Rosa (1994), pp. 51–56. (Anonimo, *Risposta sopra il discorso fatto per Marc'Antonio de Santis intorno a gli effetti, che fa il cambio in Regno*, in de Santis, M.A., *Secondo discorso di Marc'Antonio de Santis intorno a gli effetti, che fa il cambio in Regno. Sopra una risposta, che è stata fatta adverso del primo*, Naples: Costantino Vitale, 1605; reprinted in Colapietra, 1973, pp. 143–162, and in De Rosa, 1994, pp. 47–74.
24. "In the past it was the usual practice to re-employ in other loans to municipalities, individuals or the Sovereign the income stemming from their share of the rents, but in the last few years municipalities and individuals have often gone bankrupt and the Sovereign does no longer issue good bonds, so that nobody reinvests here and as a consequence all the money goes to the Piacenza market". (In Colapietra 1973, pp. 146–147.)
25. It is worth noting in this connection that both de Santis and his anonymous critic of 1605, as well as Serra, showed rather more perspicacity with regard to the importance of the invisibles in the balance of payments and more in general of the financial movements in the actual operations of the currency markets than did many later authors. Even some interpreters of Serra, while endorsing his position vis-à-vis de Santis on the role of exchange, confine their attention to the balance of trade alone. We can find examples from Fornari (Fornari, T., *Studi sopra Antonio Serra e Marc'Antonio Dd Santis*, Pavia: Fratelli Fusi, 1879, p. 45) up to Landolfi (Landolfi, A., "Attualità di Antonio Serra economista cosentino", *Sviluppo*, 24, 1980, pp. 54–58, pp. 54 and 57), Toscano (Toscano, T., "Il Breve trattato di Antonio Serra e la disputa sui cambi esteri del Regno di Napoli", *Rivista di politica economica*, 75, 1985, pp. 205–217, pp. 209–210), and Spiegel (Spiegel, H.W., *The growth of economic thought*, Englewood Cliffs, NJ: Prentice-Hall, 1971; 3rd edition, Durham, NC: Duke University Press, 1991, p.713). However, we must add that Fornari (1879, p. 6), probably responding to the anticlerical climate of the time, observed that "towards the end of the 16th century the Church possessed two thirds of the Kingdom's private property…Nor did all the rents from this property remain in the Kingdom, a good part being sent to Rome"
26. Cattaneo, C., "Ricerche economiche sulle interdizioni imposte dalla legge civile agli Israeliti", *Annali di giurisprudenza pratica*, vol. 23, 1836, Milan; reprinted with the title "Interdizioni israelitiche" in C. Cattaneo, *Memorie di economia pubblica dal 1833 al 1860*, Milan: Sanvito, 1860, pp. 1–143; excerpts in C. Cattaneo, *Opere*, Rome: Istituto della Enciclopedia Italiana, 2006, pp. 71–108, p. 73.
27. Cattaneo, C., "Del pensiero come principio d'economia pubblica", *Politecnico*, 10 (58), 1861, pp. 402–528.
28. Tagliacozzo, G. (ed.), *Economisti napoletani dei sec. xvii e xviii*, Bologna: Cappelli, 1937, p. xxxiv.
29. Arias, G., "Il pensiero economico di Antonio Serra", *Politica*, 16, 1923, pp. 129–146; Nigro, M., "Antonio Serra", *Almanacco calabrese*, 1953, pp. 79–88; De Rosa, L., "Antonio Serra e i suoi critici", *Clio*, 1 (1), 1965, pp. 115–137; De Rosa, L., 1994; Croce, B., *Storia del Regno di Napoli*, Bari: Laterza, 1925.

30. Cfr. Spaventa, L., "Dualism in economic growth", *BNL Quarterly Review*, 12 (51), 1959, pp. 386–434; reprinted in *PSL Quarterly Review*, 66 (266), pp. 201–253 (available at www.pslquarterlyreview.info).
31. This is also attested by the numerous reprints of the text: after the reprint by Custodi (1803) mentioned above, we may also recall those edited by Graziani (1913), Colapietra (1973), Trasselli (1974), Rotelli (1985), Ricossa (1986), Schefold (1994), Landolfi and Luciano (1999), the selected pages in Grilli (2007), and, in English translation, in Monroe (1924), up to the complete English translation edited by S. Reinert (2011).
32. Despite the lack of documentary evidence, it is worth recalling the hypothesis of an influence of Serra on Mun (Mun, T., *A discourse of trade from England unto the East-Indies*, London: John Piper, 1621) and thus on the British economic literature of the 17th century. The language barrier was certainly less of an obstacle than it was later to become; in more recent times, references to Serra in the Anglo-Saxon literature have gone no further than the occasional mention, apparently indirect in a number of cases, all based on the evidence of the few pages translated in Monroe (1924). Cfr. e.g. Schumpeter 1954, pp. 353–355; Hutchison (Hutchison, T., *Before Adam Smith. The Emergence of Political Economy 1662–1776*, Oxford: Basil Blackwell, 1988, pp. 19–29); Spiegel, 1991, pp. 713–714. Finally, we have two examples of more extensive treatment: the entry "Serra" in the New Palgrave Dictionary edited by Groenewegen (Groenewegen, P., "Serra, Antonio", in *The New Palgrave. A Dictionary of Economics*, ed. by J. Eatwell, M. Milgate, P. Newman, London: Macmillan, 1987, vol. 4, pp. 313–314) and S. Reinert (2011) .
33. Cfr. e.g. Poni, C. and B. Ragosta Portioli, "Serras Text und sein historischer Hintergrund", in B. Schefold (ed.), 1994, pp. 67–107; Schefold 1994; Vaggi, G., Teorie della ricchezza dal mercantilismo a Smith", in G. Lunghini (ed.), *Valori e prezzi*, Turin: Boringhieri, 1993, pp. 21–62; S. Reinert (2011).

15

Serra's *Breve trattato* and the Theory of Economic Development

Jan Kregel

1 Serra in the 21st century

What can we take away from reading an obscure treatise, written some four hundred years ago? One might expect that it would allow us to measure the progress that has been made in economics since that time. However, what it does is make very evident how much economics has changed from a practical subject that deals with economic policy to improve living conditions, to a theoretical subject carried on primarily for the amusement of its practitioners.

One of the most striking aspects of Serra's *Breve trattato* is the way in which it brings into focus the difference between what used to be called "Political Economy" and modern day theoretical economics. Instead of starting from a mass of identical economic agents in a closed economy without a government that has real endowments of undifferentiated resources, Serra starts with an economy in which international trade is an integral part and the government is responsible for the operation of the economy. He also stresses the importance of skill and quality differences in the labour force and the different performance of different economic activities, in particular between agriculture and manufacturing. Furthermore, he gives a prominent role to uncertainty in assessing the contribution of different types of economic activity. Finally, Serra is clear on the importance of monetary analysis, declaring early in his *Breve trattato* that anyone who does not recognize the benefits of the economy of abundant supplies of gold and silver should be considered for an extended stay in a lunatic asylum. It is particularly touching that being in prison at the time, he points out that one of the benefits of abundant supplies of money is a reduction in the crime rate. We don't know why he was in prison, but we might accept arguments suggesting he was a counterfeiter or even assume that it was for lack of sufficient funds to meet a contractual commitment.

From this starting point, it is not surprising that Serra provides what is the first modern account of a country's balance of payments, including the importance of international capital flows, as well as the importance of domestic and external indebtedness. It is this aspect which provides a special view on the real views of the mercantilists. These economists came under heavy criticism from both the physiocrats and classical economists for a supposed failure to distinguish between gold and what could be bought with it. The former pointed out that only the natural productivity of land provided for increasing wealth, while we are still living with the mistaken extension of Hume's argument that the value of gold depended on the amount of goods it could buy in the form of the quantity theory of money. Locke was much more sensible in arguing that it depended on the labour available to be put to work.

But Serra clearly cannot be convicted of this kind of error, because he argues against policies of prohibition of the export of gold normally associated with the mercantilists. Instead, he sees the world more from the point of view of Marx and Keynes (a well-known defender of the mercantilists), arguing that you have to spend money to get money. M-C-M'. If you don't use the money to buy inputs or imports, you cannot get more of it by selling at a profit. Further, he argues that you can profit more by engaging in particular kinds of economic activities such as entrepôt trade and manufacturing.

In addition, Serra provides a theory of economic development that previews the theories that became popular in the wake of World War II, associated with the works of Raul Prebisch, Ragnar Nurkse, Gunner Myrdal, and other pioneers of development – in particular, the impact of external capital flows and the importance of the development of domestic industry to a successful development strategy. In this respect, Serra becomes not only a precursor of Adam Smith in analysing the causes of the wealth of nations but also a pre-pioneer development economist.

2 Serra's main message

Unfortunately, much of Serra's main message is hidden in a dispute with de Santis. The point at issue is how the deficiency of money in Naples can be remedied, but this really means how the poverty of the Kingdom of Naples can be overcome and how the growth of per capita Neapolitan domestic incomes can increase. The position of de Santis was that the lack of money in the Kingdom was due to the excessively high level of the exchange rate, leading to the use of bills of exchange instead of monetary metals. Thus, bills were substituting for metallic currency. On the basis of his theory, several measures had been introduced to manage the rate of exchange and to limit the export of metallic money, without producing any positive impact on the situation.

Serra, on the other hand, starts by noting that there are countries with no natural supplies of metals from domestic mines but that nevertheless manage to have an abundance of money. He thus seeks to develop a general theory of how countries without natural supplies of precious metals manage to accumulate them, then to apply this theory of the conditions present in Naples, and then to use it to assess the impact of the exchange rate.

Rather than deal with the technicalities of foreign exchange markets and financial derivatives[1], his approach is straight forward – look at the factors that create an abundance of metals in those countries that do not possess the natural advantage of having domestic mines of gold or silver. He notes that these countries can be divided into two groups: those that have other inherent domestic or natural advantages other than domestic gold mines, such as exceptionally productive land or climate or a peculiar geographical position; and those that allow them to act as an entrepôt for trade. For these countries that are subject to conditions that are more or less equivalent to the accident of discovering a gold mine, there can be no general explanation or policy, since the conditions cannot be replicated by policy and as such Serra excludes them as possible remedies for the problems confronting the Kingdom of Naples.

Thus, Serra concludes that the answer has to be sought elsewhere, in conditions that could be applied in any country, what he calls common causes or common "accidents"; in the sense that they can potentially be introduced by any country, they are not particular or peculiar to its position. Of these "accidents", he identifies four that are associated with the existence of an abundance of metals – extensive manufacturing, integration into the international trading system, a skilled and enterprising labour force, and good government.

3 The four common factors

Here Serra is clear of the standard criticism of mercantilism because there is no mistaking gold for what it can buy. Instead, Serra starts by looking at the real conditions of production – you can acquire gold only if you have something to exchange for it. He notes that Naples does have a natural predisposition to produce more than it needs for its subsistence, which means that a simple excess of production cannot be a sufficient explanation for the lack of metals, since Naples has excess production that it exports and still has a deficiency of domestic circulation.

This brings him to the nature of production, and here he departs from the physiocrats by noting that manufacturing, as well as agriculture, allows for surplus production. In particular, he notes that manufactures will differ from agriculture because of the existence of increasing returns that will ensure an abundance of goods available for trade. But it is not only this technical condition of production that he considered important. Serra notes that since agricultural production will be subject to the vagaries of the weather, it would be ill-suited to the needs of trade. It will also be subject to the vagaries of fluctuations in demand since commodities are in general perishable. Manufactures, on the other hand, can always be stored and sold abroad in the event of fluctuations in domestic demand. He thus concludes that returns to manufacturing should be higher due to the lower uncertainty of earnings.

In addition, a multiplicity of manufactures will be beneficial to providing more stable external markets since it provides for diversification across different sources of external demand. Serra thus concludes that the existence of a multiplicity of manufactured goods will be more important than the natural excess capacity in the production of commodities.

But, Serra goes on to note that even a multiplicity of manufactures may not be enough to produce an abundance of money if the domestic population is not sufficiently skilled and industrious to engage in manufactures and creative in seeking markets in which to trade them. Indeed, this second common cause that is the result of an enterprising population becomes a major factor in his explanation of the absence of money in Naples since it provides an opening for foreign investors to dominate the local market.

Serra suggests that the domestic Neapolitan population is indolent, which means that it is little involved in manufacturing or creative innovation and seeks little in trade opportunities outside the Kingdom of Naples. As a result, what domestic manufacturing exists is in the hands of foreigners, who also are in control of the export trades and of import and the domestic sale of manufactured goods. This, in the end, becomes the key to Serra's explanation of the problems facing Naples.

Further, Serra notes the interactive and cumulative effect of manufactures and extensive trade: the larger the range of manufactures, the larger the possibilities for trade; and the larger the possibilities for trade, the more manufacturing businesses that can be supported. It is important to note that for Serra, the idea of extensive trade is different than that of the export of surplus goods that results from the natural advantage of an excess of domestic production over domestic use. Rather, it relates to the kind of entrepôt trade that results from a natural geographical location but that can be the result of an industrious population even in the absence of the locational advantage. But, as Serra notes, Naples has neither the appropriate population, nor the correct geopolitical location to take advantage of this accident.

Finally, having outlined the three main common factors or accidents that could be introduced in order to produce an abundance of money, Serra notes that they will exist only if the government is sufficiently knowledgeable and has the capacity to introduce them and make them effective. This, then should become the necessary condition to ensure the introduction of measures that create the other common accidents and ensure the inflow of precious metals. However, Serra does not follow this logic, instead falling back on the importance of uncertainty in economic analysis. In ranking the potential impact of the common causes, he notes that that of the multiplicity of manufactures is more certain in its impact than any of the others, including good government, which depends on the volition of an individual leader. Serra thus concludes that since Naples has no natural accidents or advantages and that since its government, no matter how effective, has not been able to ensure an active manufacturing sector or extensive trade – because of the unskilled and unmotivated population – it should not be a surprise that Naples lacks wealth and money.

However Serra's adversary – de Santis – had already argued and convinced the rulers of Naples that although the Kingdom had plenty of gold at one time, an inappropriate high exchange rate had caused it to be sent abroad. The problem was thus not in the existence or absence of common accidents, as Serra proposed, but rather in the setting the appropriate exchange rate.

4 Confuting de Santis

Since the exchange rate does not enter as one of Serra's common causes, it is necessary for him to counter de Santis's argument. Serra does this by arguing on both the theoretical level and the empirical level. His clearest area of dispute with de Santis concerns the quantitative facts of the case in dispute. Both agree that Naples satisfies Serra's natural advantage of being able to produce more than it consumes, and thus, it should be able to export the difference, receiving large inflows of precious metals in return. Thus, the question at issue is then why these massive exports do not generate earnings and provide for an abundance of money. But here the agreement between the two writers ends. For de Santis, Neapolitan exports are around five million ducats per annum; Serra, on the other hand, credits Neapolitan exports with earnings of more than six million ducats. Given this large export base, the question that is in dispute is why it does not produce a greater flow of precious metals. Here, both agree that the important point to debate is what prevents gold from flowing into the country of an amount equal to the Kingdom's exports.

But here the agreement stops: although both agree that the important figure is not gross exports but instead net exports, there is no agreement on whether net exports are positive or negative and why. For de Santis, Naples has annual imports around 600,000 ducats and has a foreign resident population that expatriates their investment earnings in a roughly equal amount, leaving a net external surplus position of 3 million less 1.3 million ducats, which leaves 3.8 million ducats (or 4.8 on Serra's estimate of gross exports). Given a metallic standard for the currency, this should produce an inflow of gold or silver of a similar amount. The explanation given by de Santis for why this does not happen is that the high exchange rate induces foreigners to use bills of exchange to pay for the goods that they export from Naples, rather than using money. But, as Serra counters in an argument that becomes repetitious, if bills are used to buy Neapolitan exports rather than money, then some money to meet the bills must have been brought into the country previously, in which case Naples would not lack metals.

Serra's more direct argument disputes the calculation of imports, noting that the lack of manufacturing capacity makes it necessary to import textiles of an amount that could be as high as three million, spices of an equivalent amount, as well as drugs, books, processed metals, and on occasion even wheat, producing as estimate of imports that is in the range of the entire value of exports. But that is not all. Serra notes that foreigners account for the major part of domestic investment and thus have investment earnings, that they are the major exporters and manufacturers and thus earn large domestic profits, and finally that they are responsible for the import and sale of manufactures, which also earns income for them.

What Serra has done is introduce the concept of the factor services balance and the capital account into the argument. He thus offers a counterargument to de Santis, noting that even if there is a small surplus in the commercial balance, the prior capital inflow has been sufficient to offset any possible export surplus, so that when the factor services balance is taken into account, the current account is most certainly in deficit. This leads to the conclusion that the mystery is really not at all about what happened to the missing 4.8 million ducats but the explanation of why there is any money left in the Kingdom at all! Indeed, Serra argues that it is only because foreigners do not repatriate their earnings that there is any gold left in the country. If this were not enough to make the argument, it ignores the fact that Naples was required to make tax payments to Spain as a colony. All of these factors, taken together, suggest that foreign claims more than exhaust the demand for domestic claims due to exports.

Thus, the argument about the facts seems to provide full support for Serra's theoretical position. While Naples has large exports, those exports are of primary commodities, not manufactures. Nor does Naples engage in extensive or entrepôt trade, and both of these factors can be attributed to the indolence of the domestic population. Thus, there is no reason to expect that there should be a current account balance that leads to an inflow of money.

5 Reading the balance of payments through the common factors

We can thus link each of Serra's proper and common causes or accidents to his interpretation of the sign of the entries in the Neapolitan balance of payments accounts. The large export credits in the goods balance are explained by the proper accident of an abundant natural production of commodities that exceed domestic needs. However, this is more than offset by the size of manufactured imports, due to the absence of the common accident of a diverse manufacturing sector and the absence of the common accident number two of an energetic and skilled population that together lead to the absence of extensive trade in manufactures. The negative factor services balance is also explained by the lack of common accident number two because the lack of initiative in the domestic population allows foreign owners to dominate external trade and domestic investment and production. The deficit is further aggravated by the lack of common accident number four, effective government, which leads to charges payable to the Spanish government (although both seem to argue that there is an inflow of funds on this account that are wholly spent within the country). Finally, the capital account balance is determined by the dominance of foreign investment, again due to the lack of domestic initiative and the colonial status of the Kingdom.

This is the positive part of Serra's argument. However, most of the book is dedicated to disputing de Santis's claims by showing that the lack of the common factors is more important than the impact of the exchange rate. Thus, he argues that even if it were true that de Santis's argument were correct, that thus the exchange rate influenced the use of bills of exchange (which, as noted, Serra did not accept), a change in the exchange rate could not benefit Naples, because it would not induce any of the common factors required to produce an inflow of money.[2]

6 The real problem – foreign investment

Despite his emphasis on the common accidents, Serra's final judgement is that the problems facing Naples are caused by the negative capital services account because "the income that foreigners receive from their businesses, combined with their income from imported goods far exceeds any income that could be made from the export of goods".[3] He again repeats the point when discussing the embargo on exports of money introduced on the basis of de Santis's arguments and a standard mercantilist position, noting that "the reason why the exportation of money causes such harm in our Kingdom is the disorder which has been allowed to develop of foreigners receiving too much income from investments and controlling all the businesses of the kingdom; for, this being the case, since the exportation of money is permitted, there is no need for the money that leaves the Kingdom ever to return".[4] Indeed, he argues that the only benefit of a ban on currency exports would be preventing foreigners from expatriating their profits.

Serra thus continually repeats that the "real reason" why money does not come into the Kingdom in exchange for exported goods is the income that foreigners have from their investments in the Kingdom and their profits from the businesses that they own there. Therefore, the more opportunities that one gives them to trade with advantage and profit and to buy shares and assets, the less money will enter the country in exchange for the exported goods. And those goods are the Kingdom's only resource".[5] Again, "where the export of money is positively harmful is when the money derives from the income from investment and profits from businesses that foreigners receive in the Kingdom. In such cases, as

I have explained a ban on the exportation of money is advisable in the Kingdom, even though it would not be elsewhere".[6]

7 What is to be done?

Thus, when Serra considers the conclusions of his analysis, he is hesitant to give any particular proposals, but rather, he relies on very general proposals based on his basic approach: first, remove the cause that prevents money from entering the Kingdom – basically, the factor services deficits caused by foreign investment; second, introduce those common accidents that will increase the inflow of money; and finally, ensure that the first two measures succeed.

Thus, the first order of business is to eliminate "[t]he causes that prevent money from entering the Kingdom even though about six million ducats' worth of goods are exported every year", they "are three in number: first, the income that foreigners receive from their investments in the Kingdom;... second, their profits from the businesses that they own here; third, their profits from the importation of essential goods into the Kingdom. The total value of these causes is far higher than that of the exported goods, even if the level of exportation were increased, and this is why money does not enter the Kingdom in exchange for exports" (p. 52).

The natural remedy would be to limit foreigners' income, but Serra notes that there is no money to give back to them, and he is not willing to consider limiting their capital exports or expropriation, although he does suggest that such limiting is a possibility in the name of the public good, but that it is not consistent with the normal definition of justice, and that, in any case, it might cause more harm than good. The same arguments apply for the business interests of foreigners, as well as their financing of the imports trade.

This creates a policy conundrum for Serra since it appears that nothing can be done to remove the causes that impede the inflow of money since it is difficult if not impossible to limit the negative impact of foreign direct investment. But here Serra's general theory comes to his aid in that he notes that the second cause of the lack of money flowing into the country is directly linked to the absence of the most important of the common accidents. Thus, he suggests that it is better for the government to try to create the appropriate common accidents – that is, to build a domestic industrial sector and to build a domestic entrepreneurial class and a skilled labour force – than to try to remove the impact of foreign direct investment. And the introduction of the domestic manufacturing industry will automatically solve the problem of the profits made by foreigners from manufactured imports.

This, of course, sounds very much like the much maligned policies of import substitution industrialization much criticized in Latin America following World War II However, it is much closer to the more refined policies of the early pioneers of development, who argued that developing countries could overcome their external, balance of payments constraint only by building up a source of domestic exports capable of generating foreign exchange. While Serra does not invoke the traditional argument of the trend deterioration in the terms of trade, he does recognize an even more important constraint: the difficulty of meeting external claims that result from foreign investment. He recognized this some four hundred years before the difficulties that resulted from the same problems and produced the lost decade of the 1980s. Serra provides not only evidence of the importance of political economy but also an answer to the problems of developing countries in the 1980s. Had Serra lived in the current century, he certainly would have provided cogent arguments against the early liberalization of capital accounts for countries undergoing development.

Notes

1. Without direct knowledge of the conditions of foreign exchange markets in 17th-century Italy, this discussion is virtually impossible to understand. Rosselli, A., "Early Views on Monetary Policy: The Neapolitan Debate on the Theory of Exchange" *History of Political Economy* Vol. 32 No. 1, 2000, provides a useful guide to conditions prevailing at the time, but even this does not provide a clear guide to understanding de Santis's argument on the issue.
2. Here the argument follows Roncaglia, A. (*The Wealth of Ideas: A History of Economic Thought*, Cambridge, Cambridge University Press, 2005, p. 50) who notes that "Serra considered the unbalance in the currency market to stem from a negative balance of payments, inclusive of so-called invisible items. In turn, this situation was seen to derive from a feeble productive structure and the scant entrepreneurial spirit of the subjects of the Kingdom of Naples: the theme that Serra chose to open his *Breve trattato*. There was, then, a decisive connection between scarcity of money in the Kingdom and its feeble productive structure".
3. Serra, A., *A Short Treatise on the Wealth and Poverty of Nations*, ed. S. A. Reinert, trans. Jonatan Hunt, London: Dehli: Anthem, 2011, p. 195.
4. *Ibid.*, p. 215.
5. *Ibid.*, p. 219.
6. *Ibid.*, p. 231.

16
Antonio Serra and the Problems of Today

Erik S. Reinert

These are times of crisis. Almost daily, newspapers inform us of human misery and human migrations caused not only by wars and terrorism, but also by sheer economic necessity. Why do around 1 billion people – as the United Nations has calculated – experience hunger in a world of plenty? Why do so many people every day risk their lives fleeing Africa attempting to reach the shores of the European Union? Why do people who cannot find employment in Eritrea – a country with just over 40 inhabitants per square kilometre – have few problems finding a job when they arrive in Holland, where the population density is more than 400 per square kilometre? Why has more than 20% of the Latvian population left the country during a period of a few years? Why do Ukrainian economists estimate that ten million people will leave the country if it is subjected to a free-trade shock with the European Union? Why do EU researchers – contrary to expectations – find that EU incomes are not converging as expected, but rather follow the path that is establishing two convergence groups, one of wealthy countries and one of considerably poorer ones?[1]

A second crisis is formed around the concerns over the future of the planet. Many are calling for an end to economic growth, in the name of respecting ecological limits and finite planetary resources[2] and even calling for de growth.[3] When growth is based on assumptions that it necessarily means increasing resource throughput, it is clear that it must one day come to a halt and be succeeded by a stationary state – if human beings and life in general are to survive.

A third crisis is the financial crisis started in 2007 and the subsequent Great Recession. This crisis has been counteracted mainly with palliative measures that have "solved" the financial crisis by creating huge amounts of liquidity without significant impact on the problems of the real economy. Joseph Schumpeter famously told his students that crises were like "a cold *douche*" for capitalism.[4] Are the present policies only saving the financial economy and consequently preventing a necessary "cold shower"?

Can Antonio Serra – an obscure economist who wrote a thesis in a Neapolitan jail in 1613 – really assist us today by shedding new light on the important issues mentioned above? My answer in what follows is a resounding yes, and to this end, I will explore some of Serra's key theoretical insights, their origins, why they were largely discarded by professional economists, and their continuing relevance for some of the most pressing problems of today. The rediscovery of Serra is not merely an erudite conceit. Schumpeter gave Serra the honour of having been "the first to compose a scientific treatise…on Economic Principles and Policy".[5] Schumpeter's succinct description of Serra's work confirms the author's anti-bullionist bias, the normal criticism against mercantilists:

> Its chief merit does not consist in his having explained the outflow of gold and silver from the Neapolitan Kingdom by the state of the balance of payments but in the fact that he did not stop there but went on to explain the latter by a general analysis of the conditions that determine the state of an economic organism. Essentially, the treatise is about the factors on which depend the abundance not of money but of *commodities* – natural resources, quality of the people, the development of industry and trade, the efficiency of government – the implication being that if the economic process as a whole functions properly, the monetary element will take care of itself and not require any specific therapy.[6]

Giovanni Botero[7] – the economist on whom Serra built and to whom he added an important theoretical dimension – represented the start of an economic tradition that became a key building block for the type of economic theory which built the Europe that would soon take over world economic leadership from China.[8] The modern world as we know it, in short, emerged from the sort of economic ideas and policies that Serra represented.

Regardless of whether this long theoretical tradition which dominated Europe until the late 18th century be labelled mercantilist, Colbertist, or cameralist, Botero's narratives and Serra's theories in a sense laid the foundations for both schools by establishing two crucial dichotomies in economics. In this chapter, I will argue that the taxonomy that Serra established with these two dichotomies is important for understanding the wealth and poverty of nations and indeed continues to provide a key to what his contemporaries called *buon governo*, or "good government".

Serra's two dichotomies were in the recent past still part and parcel of all three dominant ideologies and their economic policies in the 1930s,[9] but they were subsequently lost with the formalization of modern neo-classical economics and are conspicuously absent in the rather superficial discussion of *good governance* presented by Washington institutions today.

1 A dichotomy separating economic activities subject to increasing from those subject to diminishing returns

Putting "manufacturing" in another category than "raw materials" from the point of view of policymaking had already been the core element of the English Tudor Strategy from 1485, promoting woollen manufactures at the expense of the export of raw wool.[10] There had been scattered references to the wisdom of such practices, but what Giovanni Botero did in his slim volume was elaborate the vision of the role of manufacturing, the insight that civilization was based on adding knowledge and value to nature's raw material, into a full-fledged theory of economic development.[11]

In Botero's volume, the degree of economic and societal development manifested itself as the ability of a city to hold the maximum number of inhabitants in satisfactory conditions. This again was the result of the number of different professions that were exercised in the city: in other words, *the degree of division of labour* would determine the wealth of a city. Botero explained the mechanisms, but Serra's big contribution to this was to explain *why*. He did so by highlighting the key difference between the production of raw materials and manufactured goods – that is, what happens to the development of costs as production is increased. In manufacturing, there were increasing returns, and the synergies of the multitude of artisanal and manufacturing activities, each of them subject to increasing returns, produced the linkages and cumulative causations that Botero and Serra saw as being the main factors which attracted so many people to the city-states that had specialized in manufacturing.

In the first edition of his *Principles of Economics*, Alfred Marshall, the founder of neo-classical economics, emphasizes the crucial importance of diminishing returns: "The tendency to a Diminishing Return was the cause of Abraham's parting from Lot,[12] and of most of the migrations of which history tells".[13] Today, the migration experienced in Europe is from nations dominated by diminishing returns activities (Eritrea) to nations where increasing returns activities dominate (Holland).

2 A dichotomy separating the financial sector from the real economy

This dichotomy is of course much older than Serra's work. The problems which may arise when the financial and monetary spheres decouple hail back at least to Nicolaus Oresme (c. 1320–1382).[14] This dichotomy is not present in Botero's *Greatness of Cities* – which concentrates on the real economy – but it is very much present in Antonio Serra's discussion with his contemporary Marc'Antonio de Santis on how to deal with the outflow of money from the Kingdom.[15] De Santis was of the opinion that the lack of money in the Kingdom was due to the excessively high level of the exchange rate. On the basis of his theory, several measures had been introduced to manage the rate of exchange and limit the export of metallic money, without positive results. Serra, on the other hand, starts by noting that there are countries with no natural supplies of metals from domestic mines that nevertheless manage to have an abundance of money.[16] In other words, Serra asks, why on earth do the gold and silver which flow into Spain from the New World end up accumulating in places like Venice which have no mines or raw materials at all?

Serra's reply was based on Botero's analysis of what attracted people and resources to some cities and not to others, above all the abundance of different manufacturing industries. In other words, the solution to the problems posed by dichotomy 2 – the conflict between the financial and the real economy – lies in observing the insights emanating from dichotomy 1: money will leave the cities and countries with no increasing returns activities, being attracted to cities with manufacturing and increasing returns. In Schumpeter's quote above, he emphasizes Serra's putting the real economy at centre stage: "if the economic process as a whole functions properly, the monetary element will take care of itself and not require any specific therapy".[17]

In fact, digging deeper into Serra's arguments, we can argue with him that de Santis's fiddling with monetary variables, as long as these monetary variables did not positively affect the health of the real economy – was not only completely in vain but also potentially destructive to the real economy. The present tragedy of Greece inside the European Union carries with it the same type of discussion as that between Messrs de Santis and Serra more than 400 years ago.

The jury is still out on whether the policies that were carried out from the start of the financial crisis until the present (2015) by the Federal Reserve – and even more so those of Mario Draghi and the European Central Bank – again will justify Antonio Serra's warning: fiddling around with financial variables, which in reality does not improve conditions in the real economy, will not help but will probably worsen the situation. Schumpeter was in favour of "cold showers" because unproductive capital lost its value and the system was reset with a clean slate. From that point of view, we can ask if Draghi – by providing more liquidity and more debt – presently prevents Europe from taking the necessary "shower" to cleanse itself from a huge debt overhang and revitalize the real economy. Increasing debt and demand contraction in vicious circles – as a result of policies of austerity – seems to prevent the virtuous circles that originate in Serra's increasing returns to scale (i.e. falling unit costs as the volume of production increases).

Serra's distinction between increasing and diminishing returns is crucial in our understanding of technology optimism and technology pessimism, in discussing the situation where "limits to growth" may be converted to "green sustainability". Based on Serra's insights about increasing returns, it is perfectly possible to have intensive growth – that is, growth in incomes without a corresponding growth in resource throughput. This is what is meant, in fact, by increasing returns: getting more out of what is put in. So capturing increasing returns means, essentially, embarking on a process of intensive growth, which if based on renewable energies and resource recirculation, can be accurately called "green growth". Using Serra's terminology, green growth in the energy sector would mean transitioning away from a system of *extracting* fossil fuel to instead *harvesting* renewable energy.

3 Serra's background: Giovanni Botero's 1588 "On the Greatness of Cities"

It is probably fair to say that early economic theory – mercantilism and cameralism – grew out of two much older and overlapping traditions:

(1) The tradition of Xenophon's *Poroi*, a literary tradition later generally labelled *Hausväterliteratur* (it tends to be discussed in the German language), gives advice on how to run estates, small and large.[18] The *Fürstenspiegel* ("Kings' Mirror") literature, bringing advice to the rulers on how to govern, can be seen as part of this broader tradition. The *Sachsenspiegel*, from German Saxony, from about 1230, is

the best known, but even in peripheral Norway, this tradition goes back to a text from around 1250: *Konungs skuggsjá* (Old Norse for "King's mirror").

(2) The tradition of accurate country surveys and descriptions dates back to *De magnalibus urbis mediolani* of Bonvesin de la Riva (1288) and later works also on the Florentine state. Such descriptive surveys were the purpose of costly and extensive *visitas* in the Spanish provinces of the New World, some of which have been republished.[19]

It now seems that the apparently different theories – mercantilism and cameralism – did not grow independently out of the two traditions mentioned above and that many authors both cameralist and mercantilist used the extremely widely diffused works of Giovanni Botero (c. 1544–1617) as a common platform and point of reference. Botero's *Ragion di Stato* (1589) satisfied the *Fürstenspiegel* tradition, while his *Relazioni Universali* (1591) satisfied the need for surveys and the fact-finding missions' quest for geographical, cultural, and anthropological knowledge. All in all, at the time when the knowledge of the whole world and its cultures became codifiable, Giovanno Botero provided an unusually complete range of social sciences. It is worth noting that in contrast to the many utopias of the period, Botero's reasoning was based on the observation of history and of facts.[20]

Apparently few things unite Sir Walter Raleigh (1554–1618), Tommaso Campanella (1568–1639), English economist Edward Misselden (1608–1654), and Swedish technologist and economist Christopher Polhem (1661–1751). But one thing does: they all convey key insights found originally in Giovanni Botero, and they do not quote him or anyone else as to the origins of these insights.

Botero studied and practised to become a Jesuit, but at the age of thirty-five – after many years as a postulant – he was not admitted to the Society of Jesus. Botero's open-minded attitudes to the world and its many cultures were, however, consistent with the Jesuit tradition. From the very start, the Jesuits were focused on non-European cultures. From the point of view of now long-standing Western Eurocentrism, the ability of the Jesuits also to engage in two-way cultural communication reminds us that Eurocentrism is not necessarily a "natural" state of affairs. Later, as a member of the committee in Rome that decided what books should be put on the index of prohibited books, Botero would gain unusual insights into the debates of the day, as well as those which were never published.

The Jesuit Matteo Ricci (1552–1610) – a contemporary of Botero – ventured with a small group to China, where he translated not only Christian and Western scientific texts into Chinese but also Chinese texts into Latin.[21] The Jesuits in China "went native" to the extent that they started dressing like Chinese literati. By entering inside foreign cultures – from the Chinese to the Guaraní in South America – Jesuit travellers also played the role of anthropologists. Botero's own *Relazioni Universali*[22] is organized by geography and ethnicity more than by nation-states proper. As one observer says, Botero "brought together an immense mass of geographical and anthropological information, which he tried to organize according to broad methodological categories (like 'resources', 'government', and 'religion')".[23] Following the first 1591 edition, Botero's *Relazioni Universali* was published in an incredible eighty-four editions – in Italian, German, Latin, English, and Spanish[24] – over the next 200 years.[25] The cosmopolitan life of Botero is reflected by the fact that his first five publications appeared, respectively, in Krakow, Würzburg, Nürnberg, Frankfurt, and Milan.[26]

I am involved in a project to produce a volume on the bestselling economics books before 1850, and it has become clear that Giovanni Botero's small book (3 + 79 pages) *The Cause of the Greatnesse of Cities/Sulla Grandezza delle Città* (first edition 1588) is the first economic bestseller, reaching a record forty editions before 1850, thirty-eight of them between 1588 and 1671. Only one year later, this volume was included in a much larger work, namely *Ragion di Stato* (8 + 368 pages), which in English came to be called *Reason of State* and in German *Staatsräson*. In his 1925 work on *Staatsräson*, Meinecke mentions Botero's many followers and the "true catacombs of forgotten literature",[27] which follow in Botero's path (for details of the publication record, see Appendix I).[28]

As was the habit with translations at the time,[29] sources were frequently not acknowledged. In early economic thought, very assertive statements are sometimes made as if everyone should know where they came from. In various forms, the statement that manufacturing was the real gold mine, much more valuable than gold mines themselves, is found all over Europe from the late 1500s through the 1700s. It now appears that this statement and this understanding originate with Giovanni Botero's 1588 work. We find them from Tommaso Campanella (1602) and Antonio Genovesi (in the 1770s), both in Italy, to Sir Walter Raleigh[30] in England, Gerónimo Uztáriz in Spain, and Anders Berch, the first economics professor outside Germany, in Uppsala in Sweden in the 1740s.[31]

These people shared a basic understanding that only in barren areas that lack natural resources and with few possibilities for food production – such as in Venice and in the Dutch Republic – economic development would tend to come "naturally". In other areas, the transition from diminishing returns activities (agriculture) to increasing returns activities (manufacturing) – as they were identified by Serra (1613) – from "natural activities" to "artificial activities" – using the usual terminology which may have originated with Botero – required heavy-handed government policies.[32] What Venice and the Dutch Republic had achieved – rather than the policies of Venice and of the Dutch Republic – was the object of attention of foreign economists and foreign rulers alike.

The theoretical conflict between the forefathers of today's mainstream canon and the Renaissance canon has existed at least since the 1622–1623 "English" debate between Gerard de Malynes[33] and Edward Misselden,[34] where Malynes represented a static theory rooted in *barter* and Misselden represented a theory centred on *learning* and *production*. In the history of economic thought, their debate is interpreted as being about exchange controls and the balance of trade.[35] The controversy between the two was an "acrimonious, even abusive" one, in which "ink was shed like water".[36]

However, by going back to the sources, one finds that the main line of attack by Misselden against Malynes is his "mechanical" view of humankind – Malynes has left out humankind's "art" and "soul". Misselden quotes at length a paragraph from Malynes, where Malynes reduces trade to three elements, "namely, Commodities, Money, and Exchange".[37] Objecting to this definition, Misselden says: "It is against Art to dispute with a man that denyeth the *Principles* of Art". Misselden scorns Malynes for not seeing the difference between a heap of stones and logs, on one hand, and a house, on the other – because humankind's productive powers and its soul, which produce the house, have been left out. Typically, the wealth of a nation was seen as lying in its capacity to produce, its "productive powers", as Friedrich List later would put it.[38]

The importance of the difference between heaps of stones and logs, on one hand, and a house, on the other, rings a bell when reading Botero, the first English translation of which appeared in 1605:

> some will aske me; whether Fertilitie of Land, or Industrie of Man, importeth more to make a place Great, or populous? Industrie, assuredly. First because Manufactures framed by the skilfull hand of Man, are more in number,[39] and price,[40] than things produced by Nature: For Nature giveth matter, and subject: but the Curiositie and Art of Man addeth unspeakable varietie of formes. Wool, from Nature, is

> a rude and simple Commoditie: What fair things, how various, and infinite, doth Art make out of it?[41]
>
> Compare the Marbles, with the Statues, Colossuses, Columns, Borders, and infinite other Labours, taken. Compare the Timber, with the Galleys, Galleons, Vessels of many sorts, both of Warre, Burthen, and Pleasure: Compare also the Timber, with the Statues, the Furnitures for Building, and other things innumerable, which are built with the Plane, Chesill, and Turners-Wheele. Compare the Colours with the Pictures ... (etc.).[42]

Botero's distinction between raw materials and the finished goods which are created by the arts recalls Thorstein Veblen's later insistence on the *instinct of workmanship* – rather than Adam Smith's *barter instinct* – as the origin of economic growth.[43] Misselden represents the acute Renaissance awareness of the vast territory to be covered between humankind's present poverty and ignorance, on the one hand, and its enormous potentials, on the other. This released enthusiasm and energy, and many Renaissance philosophers/economists were actively searching for the formula needed to liberate society from its obviously suboptimal position at the time. It is an attitude very different from humankind as the passive victim of "two sovereign masters, pain and pleasure",[44] which soon would become the philosophical foundation of English classical and modern neo-classical economics.

4 Serra's key dichotomy: increasing versus diminishing returns and its crucial importance as the determining factor of wealth and poverty

As Sophus A. Reinert has argued, Antonio Serra's treatise could be read as an extended meditation on one of Giovanni Botero's most crucial passages. In his *Ragion di stato*, Botero wrote:

> such is the power of industry that no mine of silver or gold in New Spain or Peru can compare with it, and the duties from the merchan dise of Milan are worth more to the Catholic King than the mines of Potosí and Jalisco. Italy is a country in which ... there is no important gold or silver mine, and so is France: yet both countries are rich in money and treasure thanks to industry.[45]

Throughout his work, Botero argues for the superiority of industry in terms of what we would call synergies from a diversity of economic activities, in terms of the greater possibility of innovation in city activities and in terms of these activities' ability to yield a larger profit than would countryside activities. His observations were certainly shared by any experienced traveller in Europe, but Botero fails to provide a convincing theoretical argument for *why this is so*. What are the qualitative differences between city activities and countryside activities? Explaining this is Antonio Serra's greatest contribution to economics and one of the reasons that Joseph Schumpeter argued that Serra's work amounted to the earliest scientific treatise on economic principles and policy.[46]

Serra wrote in Naples: a poor city with lack of food and occasional food riots; a particularly violent one had taken place in 1585.[47] He followed Botero's lead in differentiating work in the agricultural and manufacturing sectors, but he qualified the distinction further by grounding it in the theories of increasing and diminishing returns to scale – whether unit production costs would rise or fall if a nation chose to specialize in any particular activity – to produce the first coherent statement of this important economic law.[48] Manufactures, Serra argued, are unique because the costs of labour proportionally go down with increasing volumes of production:

> There can be multiplications in manufactures which lead to a multiplication of profits, something which does not happen in agriculture as one cannot multiply it. Nobody, for example, having a territory upon which only a hundred *tomola* of wheat can be sown, will be able to have a hundred and fifty sown; but among the manufactures, it is just the other way, since they may be multiplied not only two-fold but two hundred-fold, and with proportionately less expense.[49]

Increasing and diminishing returns – more often separately than together – have played an important role in the history of economic thought. The first to describe these mechanisms was no doubt Antonio Serra, who in this way added the theoretical mechanisms behind Botero's astute observations and explanations. Examining Serra's argument more closely, it is essentially one which explains the difference in *purchasing power* in manufacturing in competition with other nations, as well as one about how manufacturing and increasing returns create *barriers to entry* and *imperfect competition* on a company level. Today, increasing returns are important in industrial economics as a main source of *barriers to entry*.[50] In Joe Bain's classical work on the subject, he defined as a barrier to entry *anything that allows incumbent firms to earn supernormal profits without threat of entry*.[51]

If we ask ourselves why Bill Gates makes more money than a Seattle housepainter, the differences in scale effects, and consequently in barriers to entry, is an important part of the explanation. The house painter in practice operates under constant returns to scale: after having painted one house, the time and material employed to paint a second, identical house will be the same as it was with the first house. In Bill Gates' Microsoft, it may take an investment of 500 million dollars to develop a new generation of programs – in other words, unit number one produced costs 500 million dollars – but subsequent units produced will cost only fractions of a dollar to distribute electronically. In this way, Gates' profits, as opposed to that of the house painter, are protected by the high fixed costs of producing unit number one. The lowering of the cost of producing additional units, extreme in the case of Gates, is what is found at differing degrees in manufacturing, but – as Serra concluded above – this is not found in agriculture, because in agriculture (and mining), one factor of production (land and ore) comes in different qualities and is limited by an act of nature. Serra was the first to describe increasing and diminishing returns, the virtuous circles of cumulative causations where – protected from tiny margins of perfect competition – the dynamic increasing returns of manufacturing allow profits, wages, and tax income to create economic development.[52]

5 Antonio Serra and the Marshall Plan

If necessity is the mother of inventions, then US Secretary of State George Marshall, facing a burgeoning post-WWII depression in Europe, reinvented a theoretical principle which flows in face of mainstream economic theory from Adam Smith onwards. Marshall reinvented an economic principle first established by Italian social scientist Giovanni Botero in his 1588 work "On the Greatnesse of Cities": a nation's carrying capacity in terms of population density depends on its economic structure – which is explained in theory by Antonio Serra.

Secretary of State Marshall used an unusually broad historical canvas when he presented the visions behind what was to be called the Marshall Plan at Harvard University:

> There is a phase of this matter which is both interesting and serious. The farmer has always produced the foodstuffs to exchange with the city dweller for the other necessities of life. *This division of labor is the basis of modern civilization* (my italics).[53]

The importance of this speech – delivered at the commencement ceremony at Harvard University on June 5, 1947 – was not immediately recognized, but fifty years later it was celebrated as "the most important Commencement address ever given at Harvard" [54]. Six years later, George Marshall – the first ever five-star general in the US Army – received the Nobel Peace Prize.

The analysis which went into Marshall's Harvard speech appears largely to have been a product of the fact-finding mission of former President Herbert Hoover,[55] who, in January 1947, was asked by President Truman "to go to Germany and Austria to address the food and economic problems in the British and American occupation zones".[56] The subjugated Germany of World War II was, according to the Morgenthau Plan, to be de-industrialized and made into an agricultural and pastoral nation. By January 1947, the huge unforeseen consequences of the Morgenthau Plan were becoming evident.[57]

In March 1947 Herbert Hoover reported back to President Truman: "There is the illusion that the New Germany left after the annexations can be reduced to a 'pastoral state'. It cannot be done unless we exterminate or move 25,000,000 out of it". Hoover arrives at this number, 25,000,000 people, by assuming that the population density of a de-industrialized Germany will have to be reduced approximately to that of France. [58]

Herbert Hoover determined a nation's ability to sustain a large population by studying its economic structure. Hoover was a collector of old books, especially on mining, and with his wife he made a scholarly translation of Agricola's 1556 *De Re Metallica* from Latin into English. It is not clear if Hoover ever came across Botero or where he got his methodology[59] – linking a nation's carrying capacity in terms of population to its economic structure – but his approach very clearly recalls the theories of Giovanni Botero in his 1588 *On the Greatnesse of Cities*, which explained the mechanisms by which adding value to a large diversity of manufacturing activities made it possible for a city and nation to hold a large population. But it was Antonio Serra who in 1613 added the theory which explains the difference between city activities and countryside activities: increasing and diminishing returns, respectively.

6 "That wretched division of labour and increasing returns"

Peter Groenewegen, the celebrated historian of economic thought, titled a book chapter: "That wretched division of labour and increasing returns", explaining that the reason economists see "increasing returns and the division of labour as wretched (is) because they play havoc with conventional notions of competition and equilibrium".[60] Kenneth Arrow recognized in his introduction to W. Brian Arthur's book on *Increasing Returns and Path Dependency in the Economy* that

> The concept of increasing returns has had a long but uneasy presence in economic analysis. The opening chapters of Adam Smith's *Wealth of Nations* put great emphasis on increasing returns to explain both specialization and economic growth. Yet the object of study moves quickly to a competitive system and a cost-of-production theory of value, which cannot be made rigorous except by assuming constant returns. The English school (David Ricardo, John Stuart Mill) followed the competitive assumptions and quietly dropped Smith's boldly-stated proposition that, "the division of labor is limited by the extent of the market," division of labor having been shown to lead to increased productivity.[61]

The increasing returns which were first described as an economic phenomenon by Antonio Serra have led a perilous and marginal existence in economics because it is essentially incompatible with perfect competition and with equilibrium. Those who have tried to deal with the problem, like French mathematician and economist Cournot (1838), develop theories of monopoly and oligopoly. Formalizing Serra's model numerically is not a problem. This was done convincingly in 1923 by the Princeton economist Frank Graham (Appendix II).[62] The problem is that this key factor of determining the wealth and poverty of nations is not compatible with what has been selected as the key metaphor in economics: equilibrium.

In the 20th century, increasing returns were also discussed by Allyn Young in 1928,[63] Edward Chamberlin and Joan Robinson in the 1930s, and then again by Nicholas Kaldor in the 1950s. But, as Kenneth Arrow puts it, "this tradition acts like an underground river, springing to the surface only every few decades".[64]

7 Renewables, path dependence, and technoeconomic paradigm shifts

For the 400 years since Serra wrote his treatise in Naples, the history of industrialization has been one of poor countries becoming rich by focusing policy on building and protecting a manufacturing base. This was the policy of the Italian city-states; it was also the policy of European nation-states from England, starting in 1485 through the post-WWII Marshall Plan, which had as its main purpose to resurrect the European manufacturing (i.e. increasing returns) sector, not to mention the recent Asian Tigers and contemporary China.

The key is to reap the advantages of market expansion, specialization, and increasing returns that unfold in the processes of circular and cumulative causation – or the "chain reaction" that expands wealth. This has been the key in previous dominant and general-purpose technologies – steam engines, railroads, power stations, automobiles, electrical goods, and most recently electronics and IT. Each of these could be viewed as carriers of new waves of technoeconomic development, driving a new surge of investment and propagating its effects through competitive emulation and productivity enhancement across the entire economy.

The central idea in the depiction of these successive waves of industrial transformation, or creative destruction, is that they are driven by a new "lead" technology that is widely available and applicable across all sectors; that is subject to dramatically falling costs; and that is cheaper than its competitors. As argued by John Mathews,[65] these three conditions are all satisfied (or in the case of the third, on the verge of being satisfied) by renewables. This carries the implication that renewables are on the cusp of a vast investment surge, one that will carry within it some speculative activity but where, according to the framework introduced by Carlota Perez,[66] real investment in new infrastructure will rapidly take over.

China already demonstrates these characteristics of a "sixth TEP" vanguard country, where investment in renewable energy systems vastly outranks that of any other country – even of industrial giants like the US and Germany. Chinese investment in new renewables installations each year is far ahead of industrial rivals. In 2010 China invested $54.4 billion in clean energy systems, of which $47 billion was invested in hard asset installations such as wind farms and solar arrays. By contrast, the US private investment in clean energy totalled $34 billion, of which only $21 billion went into hard assets. In 2012 China's investments in renewable energy systems rose to $65.1 billion – while that of the US and Germany plummeted. Of the leading powers, only Japan also raised its investment levels to $16.3 billion, a 75% increase.[67] China's investments are channelled towards clean energy in terms laid down by the 12th Five Year Plan, covering the years 2011 to 2015. This envisages a total of $760 billion being invested over ten years in seven strategic industries, dominated by clean energy and clean technology. It is these strong investments that underwrite the global success of China's renewable energy industries and exports, not low labour costs; if anything, it is low capital costs, with low-interest loans from state-owned banks and local administrations that are driving China's energy trajectories.[68]

The emphasis in authors who have recently "rediscovered" increasing returns – such as Arthur (1996) in the context of technological change and path dependence or Krugman (1991) in the context of geographical clustering and interregional trade – is that increasing returns are generated by positive feedback loops that magnify small initial conditions and thereby generate path dependence, whether of a technology or a geographical location. We do not deny the importance of these arguments, but we wish to point out that they do not depend fundamentally on the distinction between industries generating increasing returns and those condemned to diminishing returns. It is this distinction between increasing and diminishing returns that is the more fundamental and that will play an important role now in energy debates. But path dependence will of course play its role here too as a new energy-based technoeconomic paradigm gets under way based on renewables.

8 Paul Krugman's brief flirtation with Serra's dichotomy

"About a year ago I more or less suddenly realized that I have spent my whole professional life as an international economist thinking and writing about economic geography, without being aware of it" said Paul Krugman in a 1990 lecture which was later published as *Geography and Trade*.[69] In this volume, Krugman essentially explained why the theoretical approaches of Giovanni Botero and Antonio Serra, whose main goal was to explain why wealth was geographically so unevenly spread, were not compatible with standard economic theory:

> The neglect of spatial issues in economics arises for the most part from one simple problem: how to think about market structure. Essentially, to say anything useful or interesting about the location of economic activity in space, it is necessary to get away from the constant-returns, perfect-competition approach that still dominates most economic analysis. As long as economists lacked the analytical tools to think rigorously about increasing returns and imperfect competition, the study of economic geography was condemned to lie outside the mainstream of the profession. Indeed, as standards of rigor in economics have risen over time, the study of location has been pushed further and further into the intellectual periphery.[70]

Krugman correctly claimed that the reason that scale effects were excluded was that the profession was unable to express these mathematically. Starting in 1979, Krugman published a series of articles that introduced increasing returns in international trade theory. His 1979 and 1980 articles, reproduced in the volume cited, model a world where an initial discrepancy in the capital-labour ratio exists between two countries or groups of countries. A period of increasing international trade follows, where only the industrial sector works under increasing returns to scale. The result of this is a world divided into two groups: a rich industrialized centre and a poor underdeveloped periphery. In these papers, Krugman referred approvingly to Myrdal, Frank, Baran, Wallerstein, and even Lenin.

This breakthrough in international trade theory was the result of using models that originated in the study of imperfectly competitive markets in the field of industrial economics. Krugman inadvertently opened a Pandora's Box, where international markets are no longer fully competitive but systematically asymmetrical (increasing vs diminishing returns) and where countries therefore may grow poorer in the presence of free trade than under autarky. Paradoxically, the wave of Reaganomics' free-market policies, which hit the developing countries in the early 1980s, coincided with the first proof of neo-classical trade theorists that government intervention really could improve the free-trade situation of a poor country.[71] Krugman's conclusions are no more precise than were Alfred Marshall's in 1890: a country can be better off subsidizing its increasing returns activities and taxing those under diminishing returns. However, Krugman does not refer to Alfred Marshall. Krugman's history of increasing returns starts with Graham's 1923 article, and he makes no mention of the long history of increasing returns – going back to Serra in 1613 – as a cause of imperfect competition and consequently as a factor determining economic policy, especially the support and protection of national industry.

Krugman's imaginative models have extended to "a clever paper on interstellar trade, where goods are transported from one stellar system to another at speeds close to that of light; the resulting relativistic correction to time entails different interest rates in different frames of reference".[72] The problem in today's economic theory is that writing a model of a phenomenon proves next to nothing. Any good graduate student in economics can write a model that shows his or her pet theory. The problem lies in verifying the models and deciding which ones contain elements which point at important relationships in the real world. After siding with the dependency school, and with Lenin, in his 1979 and 1980 articles, Krugman had been sitting on the lid of the Pandora's Box that he opened. By the 1990s, the asymmetrical aspects (Serra's increasing vs diminishing returns) of Krugman's work were again reduced to a Ricardian model with increasing (but *not* diminishing) returns added. The new insights based on Serra's dichotomy of increasing vs diminishing returns were – inexplicably in our opinion – lost.

The 1979 and 1980 articles, which provided very important insights into the structure of north-south trade, were relegated to the same level as the interstellar paper: clever uses of mathematics with no practical consequences. Krugman's emphasis later has been able to use the existence of increasing returns as an argument for more free trade, which is the case with "symmetrical" relationships. The fact that neither Krugman nor his colleagues tend to use actual economic data either from industrial countries or from the Third World to verify their models effectively blocks his important insights from being used in economic policy. So not only has geography been pushed further and further into the periphery, but also any qualitative differences between economic activities and between economic actors have effectively disappeared from the economics profession. As Nobel laureate James Buchanan puts it:

> Any generalized prediction in social science implies at its basis a theoretical model that embodies elements of an *equality assumption*. If individuals differ, one from the other, in all attributes, social science becomes impossible.[73]

9 Serra and the technology optimism/technology pessimism debate

The 1972 book *Limits to Growth*[74] marked a turning point in our understanding of the relationship between planet earth and its people. What is not so well known is that the year after, a group of researchers – most of whom based at the University of Sussex – produced a volume in response: *Models of Doom. A Critique of the Limits to Growth.*[75] The Sussex group's response to the MIT model used in *Limits to Growth* was essentially "Malthus in, Malthus out": any models based on diminishing returns – as that of Malthus – would produce very pessimistic results. *Limits to Growth* had underestimated the potential for technological change and increasing returns.

Since 1972 two camps seem to have formed, one of notorious technology pessimists and the other of notorious technology optimists. Mainstream economics, with its insistence on constant returns to scale, has not enlightened the debate between the two opposing camps. In a 2014 article in *Futures*,[76] John Mathews and I argued that the insights of Antonio Serra should be used in deciding when technology optimism and when technology pessimism are respectively appropriate. The article also describes some of the industrial dynamics which result from a world dominated by increasing and diminishing returns and technological learning.

The paper uses the energy sector as an example, arguing for renewable energy based on the difference between *extracting* and *harvesting* energy. *Extraction* of fossil fuel takes place under diminishing returns, in a situation where technological change fights to counteract the fact that resources are increasingly costly to reach. *Harvesting* nature's renewable energy, on the other hand, is subject to no such limits. Costs per unit of extracted energy are bound to increase after a certain point, and this point has been reached long ago. Renewables, on the other hand, are harvested and manufactured – as are all manufactures – under conditions of increasing returns: costs tend to decrease with increased volume of production.

Increasing returns are found also when technology is held constant – that is, as production moves along the cost curve into higher volumes. But this phenomenon of falling costs is particularly important because cost curves tend to shift with new technologies. Plotting the actual cost of production over time gives us the learning curve. This curve describes how every time the quantity of units manufactured doubles, the number of direct labour hours tends to decrease at a uniform rate.[77] A related phenomenon, the experience curve, is found when total costs rather than only labour costs are imputed.[78]

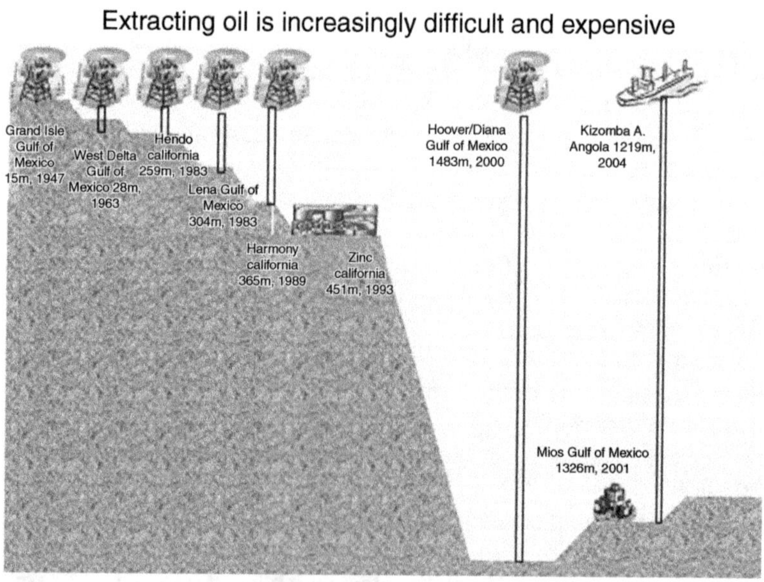

Figure 16.1 Extracting energy: the fight between diminishing returns and technological change in the oil industry

Extracting oil from tar sands or gas from coal seams is what Klare[79] calls "extreme resources" – in the sense that they are extremely difficult to extract, extremely dangerous, and extremely dirty. Oil from tar sands pollutes not just the land where it is extracted but everything downstream as well – including, it would seem, the media.

The world of energy is only now discovering the key differences between manufacturing as a source of wealth (utilizing manufactured renewables) and resource extraction, which is subject to diminishing returns. The importance of diminishing returns was clearly recognized by 19th century English pre-industrial economists – including Malthus, Ricardo, and Mill, and extending to Marshall. Indeed diminishing returns were central to Malthus's (1798) arguments that agricultural (and extractive) productivity could not keep pace with population growth. Diminishing returns were central to Ricardo's doctrine of rent, whereby he argued that landlords were a parasitic class helping themselves to the surplus created by farmers as they extracted returns from soils of ever declining levels of fertility, subject to perfect competition. The same argument carried over to miners and resource extraction, and it could today be applied to the superior profits in the oilfields that operate under the lowest cost.

Learning curves therefore tend to be very steep – indicating very fast learning – when industries and technologies are relatively new. This gives cost advantages to producers who enter the game early, but – as a corollary to this – the competitive race down learning curves tends to create overproduction and apparently destructive industry shake-outs.[80] At one point in the 1920s, there were more than 250 car manufacturers in the United States. Fifty years later, there were only four of them left. This shake-out phenomenon will also take place in the field of renewable energy. Which country will win the war on low cost based on volume will to a large extent be influenced by government policies.[81]

Over time – let's say in Henry Ford's car factories – it is impossible to attribute what part of the observed productivity increase is the result of pure scale effects and what is a result of technological change, simply because the new technology never existed in a plant on the old and smaller scale. Faced with this dilemma of not being able to distinguish the effects of scale from the effects of technological change, Joseph Schumpeter coined the term "historical increasing returns", which includes both factors, theoretically separable but in practice inseparable. Renewables may in this sense be viewed as a developmental strategic choice – and the effects on climate-change mitigation, energy security, and environmental cleanliness are useful and desirable adjuncts. Because they are produced by manufacturing activities, which can be conducted virtually anywhere, rather than on arbitrary geographic allocations of fossil fuels, they offer real long-term energy security.

Choosing manufacturing (increasing returns) over extraction (diminishing returns) has a long history in economic theory, hailing back to Antonio Serra's 1613 book on why cities with no mines or agriculture (both subject to diminishing returns) – like Venice or Amsterdam – were the only wealthy places in Europe, while countries abounding in agricultural or mining wealth – even gold, like in Spain – were poor. As we know, Serra explained why by contrasting the impoverishing effects of diminishing returns with the cumulative causation – they would later be called virtuous circles – emanating from increasing returns.

Later – in 1798 – diminishing returns were at the core of Malthus's pessimistic treatise, gaining economics the label of "the dismal science". Also, the 19th-century classical economists – like John Stuart Mill – were aware of the importance of diminishing returns.

> I apprehend (the elimination of Diminishing Returns) to be not only an error, but the most serious one, to be found in the whole field of political economy. The question is more important and fundamental than any other; it involves the whole subject of the causes of poverty; ... and unless this matter be thoroughly understood, it is to no purpose proceeding any further in our inquiry. [82]

I argue that while diminishing returns indeed give reason for pessimism, increasing returns make it possible to take a more optimistic view. US economist Erasmus Peshine Smith (1814–1882) was in a sense a visionary of renewable energy when he argued: "The entire universe then *is* motion, and the only point is how much of the universal and ceaseless motion we shall utilize, and how much we shall permit to be working against us"[83]

I argue that these choices in favour of manufacturing and the capture of increasing returns actually have a long history. They have always been the choices in practice of city-states and then nations that were able and willing to drive themselves up the ladder of development. We argue that it is long overdue to translate these arguments into the realm of energy policy. Renewables are the option of choice for all countries because of their capacity to generate synergies, learning curve effects, and increasing returns. Moreover, they are the option of choice when contrasted with nuclear, which is based on complex reactors that have to be built one by one, with few economies of scale or learning curve effects and large risks and where toxic fuel and waste represent a risk and a cost which more than counteract any learning that may take place in the production process.

There is a continuity between arguments mounted over past centuries in favour of manufacturing and increasing returns and today's arguments over energy choices. In particular, we make the case that choices made by countries in favour of "green growth" (e.g. by China or Korea) are part of a long developmental tradition that is now about to be given a new lease on life by the renewable energies question. As neo-classical economics developed, however, the dichotomy between increasing and diminishing returns tended to disappear. The decreasing role of increasing and diminishing returns can actually be traced over the eight editions of Alfred Marshall's *Principles of Economics*. This development was driven by the economics profession's choice of tools, comparative statics based on 19th-century physics, which meant that all factors that were not compatible with equilibrium – such as the dichotomy of increasing and diminishing returns – had to be left out of the theory. As Paul Krugman later succinctly put it, "[e]conomic theory came to follow the path of least mathematical resistance".[84] We find that the energy debate is an excellent occasion for bringing back increasing and diminishing returns to the core of economic theory.

10 How the manufacturing of renewables generates increasing returns

At the core of manufacturing lies its capacity to generate increasing returns, where for every unit of input there is a greater than proportional increase in output. Such a state of affairs is – after a certain point – impossible in agriculture or in extractive industries, where by contrast diminishing returns prevail. But in manufacturing, whether carried out in a single establishment (Adam Smith's famous pin factory) or more significantly across a cluster of associated activities, systemic interactions can occur (termed synergies) that make the whole output greater than the sum of its individual parts. Systemic interactions lie at the core of increasing returns – which are found in manufacturing industries but not in extractive and agricultural activities. This is why the cities that grew to prominence in the early modern era were all based on manufacturing and why manufacturing remained the option of choice for all countries that industrialized and thus grew wealthy.

Firms that earn increasing returns are attracted to each other, forming value chains of manufacturing activities where the whole chain earns returns greater than those available to individual members of the chain.

This again is a systemic effect – and is captured in phrases such as synergies, linkages (Albert Hirschman), "external economies" (Alfred Marshall), cumulative causations (Gunnar Myrdal), positive feedback effects, or manufacturing multipliers. The reduction in costs sometimes takes place as major technological breakthroughs, but more often, it is the result of thousands of small increments and innovations introduced by firms at different points along the value chain, each one building on those that came before and paving the way for subsequent improvements. The costs reduction is a systemic end result – a measure of the dynamism of the economic system, in much the same way that temperature is a physical measure of the molecular movement of a gas or liquid.

When mass production is added to this economic process, it brings in the role of the market as well. As the market expands (through declining costs and increasing returns), it generates opportunities for specialization – for an increased division of labour – which improve productivity – generating further increasing returns – that enable the market to expand still further, generating another round of increasing returns and so on, the process continuing without end.[85]

It was the American economist Allyn Young who best explained this process, in a remarkable paper read to the British Association in 1928.[86] Young dispensed with the usual abstractions used by economists – marginal revenues, equilibrium, and so on – and instead focused on the principal issue, which is how through specialization and division of labour markets are expanded and wealth is accumulated. Young emphasized that in the real economy, large investment decisions are needed before firms enter markets, in order to produce in quantities anticipated by market growth rather than at the current (possibly very small) market size. Thus, all the "theory" to do with marginal pricing is irrelevant to real decision-making in mass-production industries – as amply verified in the near-century of industrial experience since Young was writing. But it is only by contrasting increasing returns with diminishing returns – as Serra did in 1613 and Graham did in 1923 (Appendix II) – that the virtuous circles created by increasing returns and the vicious circles created by diminishing returns open up in all their drama.

Scholars grapple with phrases or metaphors to describe this amazing reality – as in phrases like "virtuous circles" or "circular and cumulative causation" – all of which are based on increasing returns or manufacturing multipliers. The best and most graphic phrase is that coined by Kaldor – increasing returns propagate through manufacturing value chains like a "chain reaction", where each addition of an increasing return (multiplier) is based on earlier such multipliers.[87] The greater the intensity of linkages secured, the greater the multiplier effect. This is the secret of the effectiveness of manufacturing clusters or of industrial districts – or, in the case of green production, of eco-industrial clusters or parks.

China is taking advantage of all these positive effects with its focus on building green industries such as renewable energy industries and eco-industrial parks. These are usually viewed through climate-change mitigation lenses or energy security lenses – but they can also be viewed, we argue, as green developmental strategies where increasing returns underpin the whole process. China has created the world's largest solar PV industry and the largest wind power industry, and it promises to build imminently the world's largest concentrated solar power (mirrors and lenses) industry – all through a clear understanding and focus on manufacturing and the generation of increasing returns – just like previous rising powers. The US by contrast, with its current mantra of "energy security" achieved through domestic promotion of unconventional coal seam gas and shale oil, and its continuing dependence on fossil-fuelled industry, is locking itself out of these vanguard manufacturing industries.

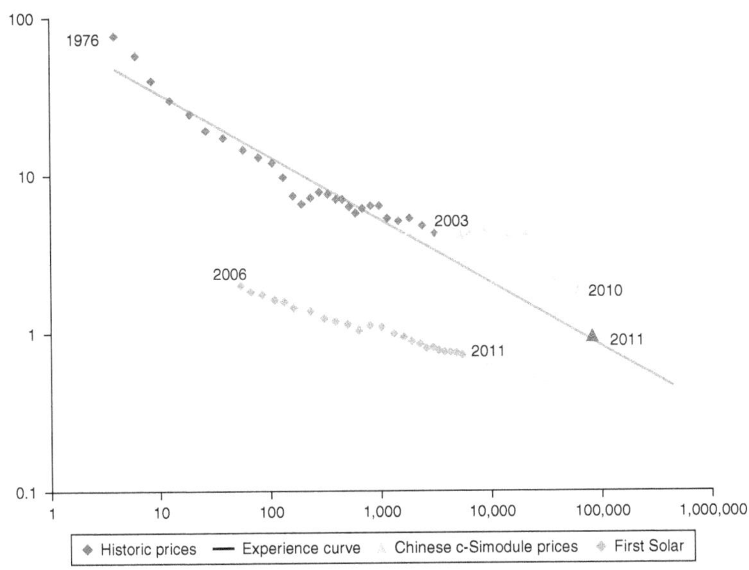

Figure 16.2 Harvesting energy: how increasing returns and technological change mutually reinforce each other; cost reductions for solar photovoltaic power, 1976–2011

Source: Bazilian et al., 2013.[88]

Mainstream economics completely obscures this process with its relentless focus on equilibrium, perfect competition, constant returns to scale, and the representative firm. All these concepts make sense only in a world of free trade abstracted from any resemblance to real business processes – which is why all the successful and wealthy countries today pursue strategies based on developmentalism and industry policy rather than purist free trade based on equilibrium reasoning.

Here is where we see a real advantage for the major industrializing powers today as they contemplate their future trajectories. The advanced and wealthy world is trapped not just in its "carbon lock-in" – meaning the preponderance of fossil-fuelled activities, technologies, and infrastructure. But at a deeper level, it is trapped in its economic reasoning, which fails to represent the reality of the processes which countries pursued in order to grow wealthy and which favours policies that take these countries away from the manufacturing benefits of opting for renewables. Insofar as these wealthy countries use their own institutions like the World Trade Organization, World Bank, and International Monetary Fund to propagate free trade and hold back the forces of development, their intellectual apparatus of mainstream economic reasoning also damages developing countries. But insofar as such countries break with this reasoning, and with the nostrums of the Washington Consensus, they are free to generate their own developmental strategies – as China has done, and as India and Brazil are now doing, in ways that are sure to be emulated by other developing countries.

Renewable energies could well prove to be the "tipping point" in this process of transformation. They may be said to be leading the world into its new Anthropocene era – when human activities shape the earth and biological world.[89]

11 Green growth vs zero growth

In response to concerns over the future of the planet, many are calling for an end to economic growth – in the name of respecting ecological limits and finite planetary resources.[90] The problem is that this concern is based on a misunderstanding of the character of economic growth. If it is extensive growth – that is, based on increasing resource throughput – then it is clear that it must one day come to a halt and be succeeded by a stationary state – if humans and life in general are to survive. But it is perfectly possible to have intensive growth – that is, growth in incomes without a corresponding growth in resource throughput. This is what is meant, in fact, by increasing returns: getting more out of what is put in. So capturing increasing returns means, essentially, embarking on a process of intensive growth – which if based on renewable energies (always available) and resource recirculation can be accurately called "green growth".

China, India, and others have embarked on a vast historic transition away from extensive growth to intensive (green) growth – because they understand that this is the only economic paradigm that will generate rising incomes without risking war over disputed fossil fuel extraction. At the same time, these countries are also ramping up their fossil fuel (black) industries and global fossil fuel extraction systems. This "race" between their green and black industrial revolutions is the key, critical feature of the global economy – and which one "wins" is of critical importance to every person and country.

It is to be expected that new "green" sectors like renewable energies and circular economy linkages (industrial symbiosis) will grow and propagate based on their capacity to generate synergies and increasing returns, in exactly the same way that Kaldor[91] foresaw that regions based on manufacturing activities would flourish at the expense of regions locked into diminishing returns activities.

Our argument is that China's opting for green growth is likely to trump its black growth (i.e. fossil-fuelled, resource-extensive) model, for the very distinctive reason that green growth promises to propagate through increasing returns, synergies, and multipliers, in a process best described as a chain reaction. By contrast, black development is subject to diminishing returns and fails to capture economies of scale or synergistic linkages. While its scale is currently expanding, it is destined to shrink in relative terms while the green growth sector of the economy expands. This is an optimistic perspective – one that is grounded in reality. The contrast with the pessimism of conventional economics – known for good reasons as the "dismal science" – is stark indeed.

12 Conclusion

If we look at the history of economic policy – rather than the history of economic ideas – the record of the last 500 years of world economic history has been one of heavy-handed industrial policy that favoured manufacturing over the production of raw materials. One aspect of this heavy-handed policy has been the prohibition of manufacturing in Europe's colonies, an aspect which contributed to many colonial uprisings, including the independence movement of the United States.

From the point of view of economic textbooks, students of course get an entirely different picture. Free trade – "doux commerce" – is being presented as the key to economic growth and welfare. However, when we go back to the historical record, we find that only industrialized countries have ever made it into the club of the rich.[92] The only exceptions here are countries living off petroleum rents, generally with a very skewed income distribution. So sweet commerce – "doux commerce" – is clearly not the key to wealth; it is rather a much less poetic "sweet increasing returns" or "doux rendements d'échelle croissants". In 1588 Giovanni Botero gave us the narrative explaining this, and in 1613 Antonio Serra added the key theoretical point: the key lies in what happens to a nation's production costs as production increases – that is, in increasing and diminishing returns to scale.

Hundreds of years of economic theory and policy under the labels "mercantilism" and "cameralism" testify to Serra's main point. While classical development economists may have argued whether to adopt a gradual and balanced development or a big push, and while they may have argued about the importance of linkages and of the terms of trade, they all agreed with Serra that industrialization was a necessity. In classical development economics increasing returns were always the key argument for industrialization, and the 1947 Havana Charter (formally the *Final Act of the United Nations Conference on Trade and Employment*) allowed for nations to protect their manufacturing industry (1) as long as their production was not at the Production Possibility Frontier (i.e. as long as there was unemployment) or (2) if the country had a plan for industrialization. With the victory of neo-classical economics other models took over and the World Bank started using models that assumed full employment even in countries – like Haiti – where a maximum of 20% of the adult population have what one could define as a job.

Going back to Serra, however, we find that the key factor is not industry or manufacturing per se; it is the virtuous cumulative causations set in motion by increasing returns which may also be found in the service sector. However, a country based on the export of raw materials is unlikely to develop large demand for advanced service products, so the industrial sector is still needed.

As Groenewegen noted, the increasing returns that Serra first described are "wretched" because this very real fact of everyday life is fundamentally incompatible with the main metaphor on which the economics profession has chosen to construct its edifice – equilibrium – and the standard assumption of constant returns to scale. In an economy where all production takes place with constant returns to scale over all ranges of output for all goods, there would be no trade at all (except presumably in raw materials). Each person would become "a microcosm of the whole society", as James Buchanan puts it.[93] And a new "anti-textbook" of economics hammers in that "all factors can earn their marginal product only if there are constant returns to scale".[94]

We are faced with the fundamental paradox that under the standard assumptions underlying Paul Samuelson's proof that free trade will tend to lead to the equalization of world wages – perfect information and constant returns to scale – all trade would cease to exist. Every individual on earth would be completely self-sufficient in everything but raw materials. In order to explain why trade exists at all, we have to introduce factors that violate the assumptions which prove that we shall all be equally rich if we only let free trade be the governing principle of the world economic order. The very factors which cause international trade are the very same reasons that we live in a world where economic development is uneven. Two fundamental factors at work here are the dynamic and cumulative effects of Serra's innovations: diminishing and increasing returns to scale, respectively leading to imperfect and perfect competition.

Almost six decades ago, development economist and Nobel laureate Gunnar Myrdal foresaw "that within the next ten or twenty years the now fashionable highly abstract analysis of conventional economists will lose out. Though its logical base is weak – it is founded on utterly unrealistic, poorly scrutinized, and rarely even explicitly stated assumptions – its decline will mainly be an outcome of the tremendous changes which, with crushing weight, are falling upon us". It is indeed likely that Myrdal was wrong only about the timing. Just as physiocratic theory – in all practical matters – lost its lustre after the famines caused by speculations and excessively "free markets" leading up to the French Revolution[95] and as David Ricardo lost out the theoretical battle after 1848, today's abstract theory is likely to lose ground. However, the moves to build alternative theories based on the cumulative causations set in motion by increasing and diminishing returns are not widespread.[96]

Regardless of what happens to economic theory, increasing and diminishing returns are in real life going to play key roles in determining the wealth and poverty of nations. In which technological and economic contexts these two factors are going to develop is an open question. On the one hand, we find a tendency towards extreme cases of increasing returns where information technology has opened up for production and distribution at marginal costs, which are close to zero. This may result in the extreme concentration of wealth and power – economically and politically – especially as the climate for establishing a global antitrust organization is extremely weak.[97]

On the other hand, 3D printing might become part of a process of "distributed manufacturing" which counteracts the traditional industrial paradigm based on economies of scale and cheap transport. Another term – coined by Harvard Law School Professor Yochai Benkler – is "commons-based peer production", also called "social production". These terms describe a new model of socioeconomic production in which the creative energy of large numbers of people is coordinated (usually with the aid of the Internet) into large projects without traditional hierarchical organization. Wikipedia, Facebook, and YouTube are examples of such peer production, creating economies of scope (in a shared infrastructure) rather than economies of scale. So – in a somewhat paradoxical way – the hugely increasing returns to scale in IT infrastructure seem to lead to huge potentials for decentralization and less reliance on increasing returns in the final stages of production.

In whatever way the future balance of increasing and diminishing returns may play out, it is increasingly obvious that the continuing marginalization – even disregard – of Antonio Serra's great contribution to the science of economics is very costly both in terms of scientific relevance and in terms of eradicating world poverty.

* * *

To this volume's celebrating the pathbreaking work of Antonio Serra – carried out under conditions that must have been exasperating – I would like to add a small epilogue: I think Antonio Serra thoroughly deserves this very belated recognition – in fact for almost forty years, I have felt that I personally owed it to him – and I am therefore extremely grateful to the editors and authors who carried this project through.

My first meeting with Antonio Serra's work took place in January 1977, at the start of my PhD studies in economic development, in the open stack library system – that perhaps greatest of US inventions before Google – of Cornell University. My background was in practical development economics and business. I had a BA in economics from St. Gallen in Switzerland, earned an MBA from Harvard, and had run my own manufacturing company for five years, partly on the side. At the time, I set out in order to understand why economic development – contrary to the predictions of neo-classical theory – was such an obviously uneven process across the planet.

I found the discrepancies between economics and the world of business bewildering to say the least, and I decided to explore whether economics had always been like it was at the time. My approach consisted in starting with the oldest economics text in the library, which happened to be Serra's *Breve trattato*. To my surprise, in him I found an understanding which spoke to me both as a businessperson and an aspiring development economist. My thesis, *International Trade and the Economic Mechanisms of Underdevelopment*, set out to check whether Serra's assertion that manufacturing and raw materials obeyed different laws – increasing and diminishing returns respectively – was correct and, if so, how significant this was, and it opened with a quote from Serra.

Case studies in countries where I had already worked – Ecuador, Peru, and Bolivia – provided overwhelming evidence as to the importance of Serra's insights. My thesis was defended two days before our youngest son, Sophus, was born. It is therefore particularly satisfying that it is above all thanks to Sophus, his foreword to the first English translation of Serra's *Breve trattato*, his organization of conferences on Serra, and his being a co-editor of this volume that my strange sense of obligation to Serra has been fulfilled. The world has come around to Serra's conclusions time and again, but also lost them. The 2012 statement from World Bank chief economist Justin Yifu Lin again supports Serra's assertion that the increasing returns found in manufacturing are essential for development: "Except for a few oil-exporting countries, no countries have ever gotten rich without industrialization first". [98]

Appendix I

GIOVANNI BOTERO: *Cause della Grandezza delle Cittá/Della Ragion di Stato*/also listing *Relazioni Universali* when *Grandezza* is included in that publication. Editions before 1850.

1.	Rome	1588 (only *Grandezza*)
2.	Rome	1588 (only *Grandezza* + historical piece on Rome)
3.	Venice	1589 (1st edition of *Ragion di Stato*, also including *Grandezza*)
4.	Ferrara	1589 (from here on, clean entries indicate both works in one)
5.	Ferrara	1590 (only *Grandezza*)
6.	Ferrara	1590
7.	Roma	1590
8.	Madrid	1593 (Spanish)
9.	Milan	1596 (only *Grandezza*, publisher Pacifico Ponzio)
10.	Milan	1596 (only *Grandezza*, publisher S. Barberino)
11.	Turin	1596
12.	Milan	1596
13.	Milan	1597/98 (*Ragione* 1597, *Cause* 1598)

14.	Venice	1598
15.	Pavia	1598 (without *Cause*)
16.	Venice	1598 (without *Cause*)
17.	Paris	1599 (French, without *Cause*)
18.	Barcelona	1599 (Spanish, without *Cause*)
19.	Venice	1601
20.	Ursellis / Oberursel	1602 (Latin)
21.	Strasbourg	1602 (Latin)
22.	Burgos	1602 (Spanish, without *Cause*)
23.	Burgos	1603 (Spanish, without *Cause*)
24.	Barcelona	1605 (Italian + *Relazioni*)
25.	London	1606 (English, only *Grandezza*)
26.	Burgos	1606 (Spanish, without *Cause*)
27.	Turin	1606
28.	Paris	1606 (French, *Maximes d'estat militaires et politiques…)*
29.	Venice	1606
30.	Venice	1608 (+*Relazioni…*)
31.	Milan	1609
32.	Bologna	1609
33.	Turin	1610
34.	Cologne	1613 (Latin)
35.	Cologne	1615 (Latin)
36.	Venice	1619
37.	Venice	1619
38.	London	1635 (English, only *Grandezza*)
39.	Venice	1640 (+*Relazioni*)
40.	Frankfurt	1657 (German)
41.	Venice	1659 (+*Relazioni*)
42.	Venice	1659
43.	Frankfurt	1661 (1664?) (German)
44.	Helmstedt, Germany	1666 (Latin)
45.	Venice	1671 (+*Relazioni…*)
46.	Milan	1830
47.	Milan	1839

Appendix II

Frank Graham's dynamic theory of uneven development based on increasing and diminishing returns (1923)

Stage 1: World income and its distribution before trade:

Country A				Country B			
Man-days	Output per man-day		Production	Man-days	Output per man-day		Production
200	4	Wheat	800	200	4	Wheat	800
200	4	Watches	800	200	3	Watches	600

World production: 1.600 wheat + 1.400 watches. In wheat equivalents: 3.200

Country A's income in wheat equivalents: 1.714 wheat

Country B's income in wheat equivalents: 1.486 wheat

Price: 4 wheat = 3.5 watches

Stage 2: World income and its distribution after each country specializes according to its comparative advantage:

Country A				Country B			
Man-days	Output per man-day		Production	Man-days	Output per man-day		Production
100	4.5	Wheat	450	300	3.5	Wheat	1.050
300	4.5	Watches	1.350	100	2	Watches	200

World production w. trade: 1.500 wheat + 1.550 watches. In wheat equivalents: 3.271

Country A's income in wheat equivalents: 1.993 wheat

Country B's income in wheat equivalents: 1.278 wheat

Conclusion: the country which specialized in the economic activity subject to diminishing returns grew poorer than it had been before trade. The opposite happened to the country specializing in increasing returns activities.

Notes

1. See Borsi, M.T. and N. Metui, "The Evolution of Economic Convergence in the European Union", *Deutsche Bundesbank, Discussion Paper*, no. 28, 2013. http://www.bundesbank.de/Redaktion/EN/Downloads/Publications/Discussion_Paper_1/2013/2013_08_13_dkp_28.pdf?__blob=publicationFile. Accessed April 2015.
2. See for example Jackson, T. *Prosperity without Growth: Economics for a Finite Planet*, London: Earthscan, 2009.
3. D'Alisa, G., F. Demaria and G. Kallis, *DeGrowth: A vocabulary for a New Era*, London: Routledge, 2014.
4. Quoted in Heilbronner, R.L., *The Worldly Philosophers: The Lives, Times and Ideas of the Great Economic Thinkers*, 7th ed., New York, NY: Simon and Schuster, 1999, p. 291.
5. Schumpeter, J., *History of Economic Analysis*, New York, NY: Oxford University Press, 1954, p. 195.
6. Schumpeter, 1954, p. 195. Note the term *economic organism* which indicates a type of economic theory based on biological metaphors, rather than on metaphors from physics as is present-day theory.
7. For an indication of the enormous influence of Botero's work at the time, see Appendix I. For a biography and bibliography of Botero, see Firpo, L. http://www.treccani.it/enciclopedia/giovanni-botero_%28Dizionario-Biografico%29/.
8. See for data Bolt, J. and J.L.Van Zanden, "The Maddison Project: Collaborative Research on Historical National Accounts", *Economic History Review*, vol. 67, no. 3, 2014, pp. 627–651.
9. I am here referring to communism, fascism, and Roosevelt's New Deal.
10. For a thorough discussion see Reinert, E.S., *How Rich Countries Got Rich…And Why Poor Countries Stay Poor.* London: Constable, 2007.
11. Luis Ortiz's 1558 memorandum to King Philip II of Spain is a famous example.
12. This is Marshall's footnote here: "'The land was not able to bear them that they might dwell together; for their substance was great so that they could not dwell together'. Genesis xiii. 6".
13. Marshall, A., *Principles of Economics*, London: Macmillan, 1890, p. 201.
14. Nicolas Oresme, *De Moneta*, 1356. For a recent discussion see Avril, F. et al., *Nicolaus Oresmus und sein "Tractatus de origine et natura, iure and mutationibus monetarum"*, Düsseldorf: Verlag Wirtschaft und Finanzen, 1995.
15. This was a problem of the whole of Spain, not only in the Spanish viceroyalty of Naples where the discussions between Serra and de Santis took place.
16. This discussion is based on Jan Kregel's chapter in the present volume.
17. Schumpeter, 1954, p. 195.
18. On the *Hausväterliteratur* as an alternative type of economic theory, originating on the European continent, see the interesting discussion in Burkhardt, J. and B. Priddat, *Geschichte der Ökonomie*, Frankfurt: Deutsche Klassiker Verlag, 2000.
19. See e.g. Ortiz de Zúñiga, I., *Visita de la Provincia de León de Huánuco en 1562*, ed. by J.V. Murra, 2 vols, Huánuco, Perú: Universidad Nacional Hermilio Valdizán, Facultad de Letras y Educación, 1967/1972.

20. Of course Botero made mistakes, as when his sources were not correct. His descriptions of China, for example, depend too much on Marco Polo. The remarkable thing, however, is the acuteness of his policy prescriptions.
21. See Spence, J.D., *The Memory Palace of Matteo Ricci*, London: Penguin, 1983.
22. The first three parts of which were published in Rome in 1591 (presso Giorgio Ferrari).
23. Rubies, J.-P., *Travel and Ethnology in the Renaissance*, Cambridge: Cambridge University Press, 2000, p. 294.
24. Botero's biographer (see below) indicates that the lack of a French translation is the result of this work being banned there.
25. This is found in the main bibliographical source on Giovanni Botero: Note biografiche e bibliografiche di Giuseppe Assandra suo concittadino (ed. by G. Borghezio), in *Bollettino storico-bibliografico subalpino*, XXVIII, Turin, 1926, pp. 407–442 and vol. XXX, *ibid.* 1928, pp. 29–63, 307–351.
26. See Firpo, L., *Gli scritti giovanili de Giovanni Botero*, Florence: Sansoni, 1960, pp. 12–22
27. "Wahre Katakomben von vergessener Literatur", Meinecke, F., *Die Idee der Staatsräson in der neueren Geschichte*, Munich: Oldenbourg, 2nd ed., 1925, p. 83n.
28. It is not yet completely clear which editions of *Ragion di Stato* contained *The Greatnesse of Cities* and which did not.
29. On translations, see Reinert, S.A., *Translating Empire*, Cambridge, MA: Harvard University Press, 2011.
30. A discussion of Botero and Raleigh is found in Symcox, G., "Introduction" to Giovanni Botero *On the Causes of the Greatness and Magnificence of Cities*, Toronto, ON: University of Toronto Press, 2012, p. xiv.
31. Berch, A., *Inledning til Almänna Hushålningen, innefattande Grunden til Politie, Oeconomie och Cameralwetenskaperna*, Stockholm: Lars Salvius, 1747. For an account of Berch and the teaching of economics in 18th century Sweden, see Liedman, S.-E., *Den Synliga Handen* (The Visible Hand), Stockholm: Arbetarkultur, 1986.
32. This is discussed in Reinert, E.S., "The role of the state in economic growth", in *Journal of Economic Studies*, 26 (4/5), 1999, pp. 268–326.
33. Malynes, G., *The Maintenance of Free Trade, According to the three essentiall* [sic] *Parts…Commodities, Moneys and Exchange of Moneys*, London: William Sheffard, 1622, and *The Center of the Circle of Commerce, or, A Refutation of a Treatise,…lately published by E.M.*, London: Nicholas Bourne, 1623.
34. Misselden, E., *Free Trade and the Meanes* [sic] *to Make Trade Flourish*, London: Simon Waterson, 1622, and, *The Circle of Commerce or the Ballance* [sic] *of Trade*, London: Nicholas Bourne, 1623,
35. Schumpeter discusses the controversy between the two men in his *History of Economic Analysis*, New York: Oxford University Press, 1954, pp. 344–345. See also their respective entries in "The New Palgrave". In all cases, these references are purely to the mechanics of money and exchange.
36. Buck, P., *The Politics of Mercantilism*, New York: Henry Holt, 1942, p. 23.
37. Misselden, 1623, p. 8.
38. List, F., *Das nationale System der politischen Oekonomie: Der internationale Handel, die Handelspolitik und der deutsche Zollverein*, Stuttgart and Tübingen: Gottascher Verlag, 1841.

39. I.e. greater diversity of products.
40. Presumably, this indicates that these products command a higher price and therefore a higher profit to the producer. Today, we could say that manufactured goods are produced under higher barriers to entry than most raw materials and under increasing rather than diminishing returns. Both of these factors would produce a higher profit margin for manufactured goods than for raw materials.
41. The second English translation is clearer on this and is used here: *The Cause of the Greatnesse of Cities. Three Bookes, With Certaine Observations concerning the Sea. Written in Italian by John Botero...* London: Printed by E.P. for Henry Seile, 1635, pp. 85–86.
42. *Ibid.*, pp. 88–89.
43. For a discussion, see Reinert, E. and F. Viano, *Thorstein Veblen: Economist for an Age of Crises*, London: Anthem, 2012.
44. Bentham, J., *An Introduction to the Principles of Morals and Legislation* (first privately printed 1780), London: W. Pickering, 1823 (2nd ed.).
45. Botero, G., *Ragion di stato*, p. 152. Following Botero, the use of the Potosí mines to highlight the importance of manufactures becomes a leitmotif in early modern political economy across Europe. For example, we find Geronimo de Uztáriz in 1751 proclaiming this: "[Manufactures] is a mine more fruitful of gain, riches, and plenty, than those of Potosí". Uztáriz, G. de. *The Theory and Practice of Commerce and Maritime Affairs*, 2 vols. vol. 1. London: John and James Rivington, 1751, p. 9. The first professor of economics outside Germany, Anders Berch in Uppsala, compares manufacturing to "inexhaustible gold mines": Berch, A., *Inledning til Almänna Hushålningen, innefattande Grunden til Politie, Oeconomie och Cameralwetenskaperna*, Stockholm: Lars Salvius, 1747. The term used is "outlöselige Guldgrufwor", p. 216.
46. Schumpeter, 1954, pp. 194–195.
47. Selwyn, J.D., *A Paradise Inhabited by Devils. The Jesuits' Civilizing Mission in Early Modern Naples*, Aldershot: Ashgate Publishing, 2004. See page 73 for the 1585 bread riot.
48. De Luca, M., *Gli economisti napoletani del settecento e la politica dello sviluppo*, Naples: Morano Editore, 1968, p. 33.
49. Serra, A., *Breve trattato*, p. 11–12: "nell'artefici vi può essere moltiplicatione, e per quella moltiplicarsi il guadagno, lo che non può succedere nella robba, non si possendo quella multiplicare, che nissuno (per essempio) se in alcuin suo territorio non si può seminare se non cento tomola di frumento, potrà fare che se ne siminino centocinquanta, ma nell'artificii è il contrario, che si possano moltiplicare non solo al doppio, ma a cento doppi e con minor proportione di spesa".
50. Tirole, J., *The Theory of Industrial Organization*, Cambridge, MA: The MIT Press, 1982, p. 305.
51. Bain, J.S., *Barriers to New Competition Their Character and Consequences in Manufacturing Industries*, Cambridge, MA: Harvard University Press, 1956.
52. Antonio Serra's theories form the theoretical basis for Reinert, E., *International Trade and the Economic Mechanisms of Underdevelopment*, Ph. D. Thesis, Cornell University, 1980.
53. Marshall, G.C., "Foreword: The Marshall Plan Speech," in Agnew, J. and J. N. Entrikin, *The Marshall Plan Today: Model and Metaphor*, London: Routledge, 2004, xiii-xvi, p. xiv.

54. http://harvardmagazine.com/1997/05/marshall.html
55. For a German view on this issue, see Baade, F., "Gruß und Dank an Herbert Hoover", in *Weltwirtschaftliches Archiv*, vol. 74, no. 1, 1955, pp. 1–6..
56. http://www.trumanlibrary.org/hoover/documents.php?page=3
57. A book by R.F. Keeling, *Gruesome Harvest. The Costly Attempt to Exterminate the People of Germany* (Chicago, IL: Institute of American Economics, 1947) appears to try to make the parallel between the post-war plight of the Germans and the plight of many Americans during the 1930s evident.
58. Hoover to Truman, letter dated March 18, 1947, page 12.
59. But we know that Moses Abramowitz (later of Stanford University), Chief of the European Industry and Trade Section at the War Production Board and in the US Office of Strategic Services during WW II, very early had warned against the serious consequences if the Morgenthau Plan was ever to be carried out.
60. *Classics and Moderns in Economics*, volume 1, London: Routledge, 2003, page 186.
61. W.B. Arthur, *Increasing Returns and Path Dependence in the Economy*, Ann Arbor, MI: University of Michigan Press, 1994, p. ix.
62. Graham, F., "Some Aspects of Protection Further Considered", *Quarterly Journal of Economics*, vol. 37, 1923, pp. 199–227.
63. Young, A.A., "Increasing Returns and Economic Progress", *The Economic Journal*, vol. 38, 1928, pp. 527–542.
64. Arthur, 1994.
65. Mathews, J.A., "Green growth strategies: Korea's initiatives", *Futures*, 44, 2012, pp. 761–769.
66. Perez, C., *Technological Revolutions and Financial Capital: The Dynamics of Bubbles and Golden Ages*, Cheltenham: Edward Elgar, 2002; id., "Technological revolutions and techno-economic paradigms", *Cambridge Journal of Economics*, 34, 2010, pp. 185–202.
67. See the Keynote presentation by M. Liebreich, Bloomberg New Energy Finance, at the BNEF Summit in New York, 2013, available at: http://about.bnef.com/presentations/bnef-summit-2013-keynote-presentation-michael-liebreich-bnef-chief-executive/.
68. Of course, China's renewable energy industries have been buffeted by competitive forces, and some firms, like Suntech in solar PV and Huarui in wind power have crashed. While these collapses have attracted widespread adverse comment, we see them on the contrary as a healthy sign, meaning that the renewable-energy sector really is competitive – meaning that inefficient firms or over-leveraged firms are being subjected to market discipline.
69. In *Geography and Trade*, Cambridge, MA: MIT Press, 1991, p. 1.
70. *Ibid.*, p. 4.
71. A collection of papers on this subject is in Grossman, G. (ed.), *Imperfect Competition and International Trade*, Cambridge, MA: MIT Press, 1992.
72. Dixit, A., "In Honor of Paul Krugman: Winner of the John Bates Clark Medal", in *Journal of Economic Perspectives*, vol. 7, no. 2, Spring 1993, p. 173.
73. Buchanan, J., *What Should Economists Do?*, Indianapolis, IN: Liberty Press, 1979, p. 231. Italics added.
74. Meadows, D.H., D.L. Meadows, J. Randers and W.W. Behrens III, *Limits to Growth*, New York, NY: Universe Books, 1972.

75. Cole, H.S.D. et al., *Models of Doom. A Critique of the Limits to Growth*, New York, NY: Universe Books, 1973.
76. "Renewables, manufacturing and green growth: An energy strategy based on capturing increasing returns", in *Futures*, vol. 61, 2014, pp. 13–22. The rest of this section builds on this article.
77. Hirschman, W., "Profit from the Learning Curve", *Harvard Business Review*, 42, 1964, pp. 125–139 and Reinert, E.S., *International Trade and the Economic Mechanisms of Underdevelopment*, PhD thesis, Cornell University, 1980.
78. Boston Consulting Group, *Perspectives on Experience*, Boston, MA: BCG, 1972; Reinert, E.S., *International Trade and the Economic Mechanisms of Underdevelopment*, PhD thesis, Cornell University, 1980.
79. Klare, M.T., *The Race for What's Left: The Global Scramble for the World's Last Resources*, New York, NY: Metropolitan Books, 2012.
80. Klepper, S. and K. Simons, "Industry Shakeouts and Technological Change", in *International Journal of Industrial Organization*, 23 (February), 2005, pp. 22–43.
81. This issue is discussed in Reinert, E.S., 1999.
82. Mill, J.S., *Principles of Political Economy*, London: Longmans, 1848, p. 176.
83. Quoted in Hudson, M., *E. Peshine Smith: A Study in Protectionist Growth Theory and American Sectionalism*, PhD thesis, New York University, 1968, p. 104.
84. For a discussion, see Reinert, E.S., "Diminishing Returns and Economic Sustainability: The dilemma of resource-based economies under a free trade regime", in Hansen, S., J. Hesselberg, and H. Hveem (eds), *International Trade Regulation, National Development Strategies and the Environment: Towards Sustainable Development?*, Oslo: Centre for Development and the Environment, University of Oslo, 1996, pp. 119–150. Downloadable at http://www.other-canon.org/papers/.
85. The most important theorem in economics is Adam Smith's proposition that the division of labour is limited by the extent of the market – meaning that market size sets a limit on specialization, and as specialization is increased, so market size can expand. Serra already gives us the basis for this insight in 1613, when he describes how the multiplicity of manufacturing activities in Venice and the increasing number of customers attracted by this multiplicity are factors which mutually reinforce each other: "each of which lends force to the other" he says, in describing what we would call a virtuous circle. (Serra 1613/2011, p. 127.)
86. Young, A., "Increasing returns and economic progress", *The Economic Journal*, 38, (152), 1928, pp. 527–542.
87. The notion of "circular and cumulative causation" was introduced into economic reasoning by Myrdal, and it was taken up by Kaldor, N., "The case for regional policies", *Scottish Journal of Political Economy*, 17, 1970, pp. 337–348 – as explained in detail by Toner, P., *Main Currents in Cumulative Causation: The Dynamics of Growth and Development*, London: Palgrave Macmillan, 2000. Related concepts in the setting of development economics are the "big push" (Rosenstein-Rodan) and balanced vs unbalanced growth (Nurkse, Hirschman).
88. Bazilian, M., I. Onyeji, M. Liebreich, I. MacGill, J. Chase, J. Shah, D. Gielen, D. Arent, D. Landfear, and S. Zhengrong, "Re-considering the economics of photovoltaic power", *Renewable Energy*, 53, 2013, pp. 329–338.

89. The Anthropocene was a term coined by Nobel Prize–winning chemist-geologist Paul Crutzen.
90. See for example Jackson, 2009.
91. Kaldor, N., "The case for regional policies", *Scottish Journal of Political Economy*, 17, 1970, pp. 337–348.
92. P. Vries' 2013 volume "Escaping Poverty" (Vienna: University of Vienna Press) makes this same point, as does former World Bank chief economist J. Lin in his 2012 book, *New Structural Economics* (Washington: World Bank, 2012). At page 350, Lin states, "[e]xcept for a few oil-exporting countries, no countries have ever gotten rich without industrialization first". Even the World Bank chief economist admits that to Serra's point, and to the theories of classical development economics, this insight hardly influences the policies of the World Bank or the Washington institutions in general.
93. Buchanan, J., 1979, p. 236.
94. Hill, R. and T. Myatt, *The Economics Anti-Textbook. A Critical Thinker's Guide to Microeconomics*, Halifax: Firewood Publishing – London: Zed Books, 2010, p. 180.
95. Kaplan, S.L., *Bread, Politics and Political Economy in the Reign of Louis XV*, 2nd ed., London: Anthem, 2015.
96. One example is Berger, S., *The Foundations of Non-Equilibrium Economics. The Principle of Circular and Cumulative Causations*, London: Routledge, 2009.
97. An international antitrust organization was suggested by the UN Report on the Financial Crisis (the so-called "Stiglitz Report").
98. Lin, Justin Yifu, *New Structural Economics: A Framework for Rethinking Development and Policy*, Washington, DC: World Bank Publications, 2012, p. 350.

Index

GPSR Compliance
The European Union's (EU) General Product Safety Regulation (GPSR) is a set of rules that requires consumer products to be safe and our obligations to ensure this.

If you have any concerns about our products, you can contact us on

ProductSafety@springernature.com

In case Publisher is established outside the EU, the EU authorized representative is:

Springer Nature Customer Service Center GmbH
Europaplatz 3
69115 Heidelberg, Germany

www.ingramcontent.com/pod-product-compliance
Lightning Source LLC
LaVergne TN
LVHW021606180326
834233LV00004B/1226
9781137539953